# PLEDGES OF JUBILEE

# Pledges of Jubilee

*Essays on the Arts and Culture,*
*in Honor of Calvin G. Seerveld*

*edited by*

Lambert Zuidervaart
*and*
Henry Luttikhuizen

WILLIAM B. EERDMANS PUBLISHING COMPANY
GRAND RAPIDS, MICHIGAN

© 1995 Wm. B. Eerdmans Publishing Co.
255 Jefferson Ave. S.E., Grand Rapids, Michigan 49503

Printed in the United States of America

00 99 98 97 96 95    7 6 5 4 3 2 1

**Library of Congress Cataloging-in-Publication Data**

Pledges of jubilee: a festschrift for Calvin G. Seerveld /
edited by Lambert Zuidervaart and Henry Luttikhuizen.
p.    cm.
Includes bibliographical references.
ISBN  0-8028-3792-1 (alk. paper)
1. Christianity and the arts.  2. Christianity and culture.
3. Seerveld, Calvin.  I. Seerveld, Calvin.  II. Zuidervaart, Lambert.
III. Luttikhuizen, Henry, 1964–    .
BR115.A8P57    1995
261.5'7 — dc20                    95-22995
CIP

The publication of this book is supported by a grant
from the Institute for Christian Studies in Toronto.

# Contents

# CONTENTS

## Contents

# Publisher's Preface

We always liked, my Trinity car-mates and I, to wind up driving behind Cal Seerveld the last mile or two to school, as we occasionally did. There was first of all the car itself, a white Nash Rambler that in the heyday still of flamboyant tailfins and the Chrysler Imperial suggested less a vehicle designed for adventure, let alone soaring flight, than, in the words of E. B. White, a badly laid egg — stubby, ill-formed, and decidedly earthbound.

The beauty and fun were in the irony, because the lone occupant of this mundane anti-car did in fact seem to ramble dreamily along, looking to the left and to the right out the window, and sometimes — even as he drove — down at the carseat beside him, surveying, we imagined, some choice page in Dooyeweerd's *New Critique of Theoretical Thought.*

In other words, the picture fit a myth we students were happily cultivating about a man who did seem to us from the start extraordinary. The car in its resolute plainness was nothing less than a summons to rethink our cultural values, and the man — well, we knew that what *we* saw outside the window as mere random grass and trees, Seerveld was perceiving through the powerful unifying eye of a *Weltanschauung!*

Cal and we came to Trinity Christian College not only early in his teaching career but in the very first year of the college itself, and the adventure of studying with him fit wonderfully a general atmosphere of academic embarkment. The school was new, the faculty idealistic and superb, the curriculum aborning, and the student body small, only thirty or so of us at most. This frequently gave us as freshmen a gift that ordinarily comes only to juniors and seniors — small classes and the heady possibilities of the seminar and tutorial.

For many of us, an astonishing number of these classes were with Seerveld. The student body was small, but so was the faculty, which meant that Seerveld was pressed into service teaching not only all the philosophy (a core requirement for all four semesters of the then two-year college), but also history and even German. I recall that during one semester I had Cal for three out of four courses. This included my first course in German, which he began by marching into the room and, with no announcement, opening with the Lord's Prayer *auf Deutsch,* thereby inaugurating what was to all of us a stunningly novel method of teaching a language. So far as was possible, the new language was immediately to be the *lingua franca* of the room. No question could come from us in English without the prior, however wretchedly pronounced, *Darf ich etwas auf Englisch fragen?*

Seerveld's teaching more than one subject, while unusual, never seemed to us unnatural. For one thing, he was splendid at them all. But also, his approach in whatever course was always pervasively interdisciplinary. One didn't have to be in his introduction to philosophy class for more than a week before words like *Gegenstand* and *pou stou* joined *Weltanschauung* on a blackboard frenetically filling up with the multi-lingual Seerveldian vocabulary. And to take from him in the same term both ancient philosophy and ancient history, as I did, was constantly to be shown in each course the resonances between the pre-Socratics, Plato, and Aristotle on the one hand and Greek religion and the Greek arts on the other. Cal was intensely concerned with the encultured character of ideas — how the culture shaped the ideas and how the ideas shaped the culture.

The ideas of the culture were always presented to us through original sources. I can't recall any textbook for Cal's classes — only a mountain of paperbacks. Cal insisted on his own selective and rigorously perspectival approach to his subjects. A glance at the catalog descriptions for his courses in those years invariably spots the words, repeated as a *leitmotif,* "a critical exposition of selected texts." From Plato to Lucretius; from Tertullian to Aquinas; from Calvin and Luther to Giovanni Pico della Mirandola and Pietro Pomponazzi (sonorous names we loved to mouth); from Locke to Comte; from Kierkegaard to Heidegger — the exposition needed to be direct, immediate, and fair. But one never approached the texts neutrally out of mere intellectual curiosity. Ideas, no matter how attractive, were deeply rooted in presuppositions, and everywhere there lurked for the unwary Christian the dangers of accommodation. Cal was not enthusiastic, as I learned in an early paper, about trying, like the Israelites, to take the gold out of Egypt. One needed the discerning and critical eye of faith and, in particular, of deep Reformational commitment. For Cal that meant the vision of Vollenhoven and Dooyeweerd, but he allowed breathing room for students who could get no further than a more general Kuyperian outlook.

I don't suppose that Cal hated anything more than he disliked academic indifference or disinterestedness. He had no room for laziness or, heaven forbid, for the cultured dilettante. Ideas were a matter of life and death. Perhaps his greatest gift to us who were his early students, and I suspect to students throughout his career, was the overpowering sense he gave that all our work, in whatever sphere — from fishmongering in West Sayville on Long Island (where he was proud to come from) to studying philosophy — profoundly mattered in God's kingdom. Going to college wasn't a frivolous thing, and failing to do our work wasn't simple malfeasance but sacrilege. And we worked terribly hard — prodigious reading assignments, a good many papers, and exams that could take as long as four hours, if you had enough diligence (or fear) really to tackle the two or three epic questions. Even then, one didn't so much finish the test as abandon it at some point you had to live with.

Cal acted and looked the part of his intellectual passion — the edge of his lecturing hand cleaving the air before him, the sharp little intake of breath, perhaps as he moved from exposition to critique, and even, let it be affectionately said, the look of his clothes. The bow tie he often wore seemed a natty anomaly against a field of sartorial rumple, and one of his jackets — a grey corduroy, I believe — was for months torn open at the shoulder joint, with the stuffing leaking out. Clearly this was a man who wrestled with the angel to gain his wisdom, and we had better pay attention.

Cal's passion for ideas was matched by his concern for those students for whom these ideas were supposed to matter. Which was all of us. He didn't simply *present* his material, for us to follow as best we could. He meant to *communicate* it. Classes rarely ended on the hour, but only after the last student who stayed behind with questions finally drifted off. For a man pent up with all the things he wanted to get across, Cal was gratifyingly patient with queries and naive challenges that must sometimes have tried his soul.

Not all of our instruction came from Cal in the classroom. He was also generous in his counsel over coffee or in the hallway, though we always felt in his manner a slight (but not unappealing) urgency about time, as though his angel might be waiting in the wings.

And there were those marvelous chapel talks, in particular Cal's own unprettified and riveting translations of Scripture, some of which eventually made their way into books. *Take Hold of God and Pull* was one such book, and these translations did just that, pulling us along as well into a worship unlike anything we had ever encountered before. "Beauty exalts, but beauty also lulls," C. S. Lewis once cautioned about the lofty eloquence of the King James version. Seerveld's translations decidedly did not lull, in the craggy grandeur, the raw physicality, the jarring syntax, and the plain-spoken vernacular with which he struggled to produce a dynamic contemporary equivalent to the Hebrew and the Greek.

Nothing, it can be said, that Cal Seerveld ever did managed to lull, though much of it came infused with a spirit of play. I have noted his patience with querying and long-winded students. One small — but of course instructive! — exception comes to mind. "Please," Seerveld once implored at the beginning of a class, "hold your questions until I'm finished. And then make sure your questions are *pertinent.*" At the end of the lecture, silence. Finally, when even one of his more voluble nuisances sat on his hands, came the gentle, good-natured professorial voice, "And what about you, Mr. Pott? Silenced by pertinence?"

Now, some thirty years later, I raise my hand again — this time, with my colleagues at Eerdmans, to join the contributors to this volume in saluting a scholar, a teacher, a friend who mattered much to so many in our Reformed community and beyond. Cal, modest man that he is, will doubtless find reason to draw back from this gesture and challenge its pertinence. But I hope he will like the book nonetheless.

— Jon Pott

# A Letter from a Friend

Dear Cal,

It must have been in the fall of 1949 that we first met, you, a sophomore at Calvin College, I, a newly arrived freshman, you, the son of fishmonger parents in a small village on Long Island, I, the son of a cabinetmaker in a tiny farming village on the prairies of southwest Minnesota.

At Calvin College you and I and all the rest of us were inducted into a tradition — into the tradition of Reformed Christianity, especially as that had taken shape at the end of the nineteenth century in the Netherlands at the hands of Abraham Kuyper. It was magical. The tradition, for the most part, was not laid on us as burden but set before us as vision. It had its rough edges; it didn't lack for things for us to get angry about, to resist, to ridicule. Nonetheless, magisterial teachers helped us to discern, beneath the rough edges, a grand picture of how to live with joy before the face of God in the world. That picture gripped you and me then; on neither of us has its grip ever relaxed.

It wasn't an apologetic tradition. I don't remember anybody ever mounting arguments for the existence of God, for the infallibility of Scripture, or anything of the sort. What was set before us was instead the challenge of thinking and making and doing as followers of Christ, nourished on Scripture. In pretty much any area of life. In politics. In business. In the arts. In academia. There wasn't any index of forbidden books — none that I was aware of, anyway. The fallenness of our human existence was by no means taken lightly. But we were taught not to turn away from that but to struggle with it redemptively. The *civitas dei* struggling with the *civitas mundi*.

The motto was *faith seeking understanding*. We heard it over and over. I now know that the way it was interpreted for us was not what Augustine meant by it. But that's OK. Augustine meant that the calling of the Christian is to seek to *understand* those very things that he or she already *believes*. What your and my teachers meant by it is that we are called to understand all of reality in the light of faith.

As in any tradition, there were masters. At least three of our own teachers were indisputably such: Harry Jellema, Henry Zylstra, Henry Stob. They had caught the genius of the tradition and had the gift of appropriating and articulating that genius for new issues in a new day. But behind them, other masters, especially Kuyper, Calvin, and Augustine — and more recently, Dooyeweerd and Vollenhoven.

We learned about the arts, especially music and the literary arts. And we didn't just learn about them as something "out there." They became part of us, emotionally, intellectually. We came to see the world through the metaphors of the grand literary tradition. We came to experience our faith through the polyphony and monophony of the grand musical tradition. Visual art at the time didn't come to much. To this day I find that last strange. How could one be Dutch in origin and ignore the visual arts?

We were aware that our teachers felt they could not take for granted, in their students and in the supporting community, a sense of the need for art in their lives. We noticed them going out of their way to *affirm* the arts. They were hortatory, unmistakably so. They felt they had to be hortatory. They went beyond the hortatory, however, to *nourish* the artists among us — and the artistic impulses in those of us who were no more than would-be artists.

You and I carried on that part of the tradition as we received it. We too have *affirmed* the arts. We too have felt we had to do that — to Christians in general, to Reformed Christians in particular. We have felt we could not take for granted in them a sense of the need for art. And you, much more than I, have gone beyond exhortation to the nourishing of artists.

What made, and continues to make, that affirmation necessary? I'm not entirely sure. I know what makes it necessary in large swaths of evangelical Christianity. But to this day I don't feel I understand what makes it necessary in Reformed Christianity. Possibly that's because of a peculiarity of my own rearing. I indicated above that my father was by training and inclination a cabinetmaker in a place where there was no market for painstakingly crafted cabinets. I now know, after his death, that the desire of his heart was to be a visual artist. The depression made it impossible for him to satisfy that desire. But I can see him yet — after hours, doing pen and ink drawings. So in my own heart I have never felt any suspicion of the arts.

The customary thing to do, in answering the question I've posed, is to spotlight some deficiency of attitude in the community and then to chastise the community for its negative attitude toward the arts. I don't doubt the propriety of some of that. But maybe their antennae told them something. Maybe it told them that art in the modern world is often a surrogate for Christianity, and not only for Christianity, but for any community-embodied religion. That art could indeed be such a surrogate was also something we learned from our teachers. We learned from them the use of the concept of *idol* as a category of social analysis.

One more thing you and I together learned, back there in those magical student days: We learned that the work of the Christian academic can be a form of *diakonia* to the people of God, and to humanity in general; and that if we ourselves entered academia, we were called to make it such. We learned indeed the delights of such work — and the agonies! But we were taught to look beyond the delight and the agony to the human flourishing which faithful learning serves.

You will by now suspect that my aim in all this recounting is to praise with faint praise. Calvin Seerveld: good student he. He has done as he was taught.

No. The recounting was so that I could say this: In all the ways I have mentioned, you, Cal, have become one of the masters of the tradition. This book is testimony to a *magister*.

Your old friend,

Nick
(Nicholas Wolterstorff)

# INTRODUCTION

# Transforming Aesthetics: Reflections on the Work of Calvin G. Seerveld

## LAMBERT ZUIDERVAART

At a heady Reformation Day Rally during the early 1970s, John Vander Stelt introduced a nervous philosophy and music student from Dordt College to a Trinity Christian College professor known as a leader of the so-called Reformational Movement. The forty-year-old professor seemed more reserved than his colorful prose had led one to expect. Yet a breadth of knowledge and a depth of wisdom permeated his conversation. During that visit, as at so many encounters with students around the world, this man's challenging discourse planted an irresistible sense of Christian vocation.

In September 1972 the professor and student would meet again, now at the five-year-old Institute for Christian Studies (ICS), which had just moved to 229 College Street in Toronto. The professor was beginning nearly a quarter century as the first full-time Senior Member in Philosophical Aesthetics at ICS. I had the privilege of becoming one of his first graduate students.

## Polyphonic Wisdom

No one who has studied with Calvin G. Seerveld can deny the impact of his teaching. Fluent in several modern languages and well-versed in Latin,

Greek, and Hebrew, Seerveld would turn his graduate seminars into concerts of cross-cultural polyphony whose subjects came from central texts by major figures. Although Seerveld served as orchestrator and conductor, every student soon learned to play a part. One felt the push and pull of a common project whose significance far exceeded the particular task at hand.

The diversity of intellectual interests among Seerveld's students reflects his own restless curiosity in matters cultural and artistic. Writers, painters, dramatists, photographers, musicians, film makers, philosophy students, art historians, cultural critics — all came to study with him at ICS and to learn from one another.[1] Seerveld's graduate students have also come from many different religious and national backgrounds, matching the flexibility in his own embrace of the Reformed tradition. In the 1970s many were graduates of the three American colleges affiliated with the Christian Reformed Church (i.e., Calvin, Dordt, and Trinity). Soon, however, Cal was also attracting students from other church backgrounds, partly because of

1. Of the twenty or so master's theses and doctoral dissertations directed by Seerveld, about half examine important figures in the arts and cultural criticism, while the others discuss the contributions of philosophers and other cultural theorists. Master's theses directed by Seerveld, in chronological order, include Lambert Zuidervaart, *Kant's Critique of Beauty and Taste: Explorations into a Philosophical Aesthetics* (1975); Peter Enneson, *On Spectation: Mikel Dufrenne's Valuation of Aesthetic Experience* (1981); Adrienne Dengerink, *Kunst als symbol by Susanne K. Langer* (1982); Carroll Guen, *A Critical Exploration of Jane Austen's Persuasion* (1983); Michael Ophardt, *Metaphor, An Aesthetic Figure: An Analysis of Philip Wheelwright's Theory* (1983); Lloyd Davies, *Owen Barfield's Aesthetics: Worldview and Poetic Consciousness* (1986); Donald Knudsen, *A Crushing Truth for Art: Martin Heidegger's Meditation on Truth and the Work of Art in Der Ursprung des Kunstwerkes* (1987); Henry Luttikhuizen, *Not Very Modern but Very Twentieth Century: An Interpretation of José Ortega y Gasset's Categories for Art Historiography* (1989); Priscilla Reimer, *The World-and-Life-Vision Permeating Käthe Kollwitz's Graphic Art* (1989); Paul Ferdinand, *The Seduction of Jean Baudrillard: A Philosophical Critique of Fatal Theory* (1991); Barbara Douglas, *Musicology or Musikwissenschaft? A Study of the Work of Carl Dahlhaus* (1991); Fran Wong, *The Journey to Manhood: George Lucas' Saga of Sacrifice and Salvation* (1992); James Leach, *Instructive Ambiguities: Brecht and Müller's Experiments with Lehrstücke* (1992); Greg Linnell, *Prospects for a Historical Poetics of Cinema* (1993); Andrea Bush, *Tradition, Innovation, Wholeness, and the Future in the Art of Paul Klee* (1993); Brent Adkins, *Soliciting the Decisions of Philosophy: An Examination of Plato's Pharmacy by Jacques Derrida* (1994). Doctoral dissertations supervised by Seerveld include Lambert Zuidervaart, *Refractions: Truth in Adorno's Aesthetic Theory* (1981); Gudrun Kuschke, *The Christian Ethos in the Poetry of Bergengruen: An Integrated Approach* (1981); Dirk van den Berg, *'N Ondersoek na die Estetiese en Kunsthistoriese Probleme verbonde aan die sogenaamde Moderne Religieuse Skilderkuns* (1984).

2

campus ministries in western Pennsylvania carried out by Pete Steen, Perry Recker, and the Pittsburgh Coalition for Christian Outreach. Students also began to arrive from South Africa, the Netherlands, and England. To all of these students Seerveld conveyed the worth and legitimacy of ground-breaking scholarship, despite suspicion or ignorance toward the arts in many Christian traditions, and amid societal problems and personal struggles that could often seem more pressing. He always held up the vision of Christian scholarship as a "diaconal service" on behalf of the church worldwide.

\*       \*       \*

Born in 1930, Seerveld grew up during the Depression and World War II on Long Island, where his parents ran a local fish market in West Sayville, New York. He entered Calvin College in 1948 when this small Midwestern liberal arts school was experiencing an enrollment boom, thanks in part to war veterans making use of the G.I. Bill. Seerveld studied English literature with Henry Zylstra and philosophy with Henry Stob and William Harry Jellema, three professors who deeply influenced not only Seerveld's intellectual development but also the college as a whole and the Christian Reformed denomination for which the college trained pastors, teachers, and other leaders.[2]

In Seerveld's senior year (1951-52), H. Evan Runner, a dynamic younger philosopher, joined the faculty. Runner would soon provide intellectual inspiration for the Reformational Movement, an offshoot of Dutch-North American Calvinism that emphasizes the transformation of society according to norms in the fabric of creation and by way of organized Christian efforts in politics, education, labor, and the arts. Although Seerveld did not study with Runner as long and as intently as did Hendrik Hart, James Olthuis, and Bernard Zylstra (younger contemporaries who also became senior members at ICS), the direction of Seerveld's intellectual

---

2. For a historical account of the religious and ethnic subculture in which Seerveld grew up, see James D. Bratt, *Dutch Calvinism in Modern America: A History of a Conservative Subculture* (Grand Rapids, Mich.: Eerdmans, 1984). Bratt pays special attention to the struggles over Christian involvement in culture to which the Reformational Movement has made a unique contribution. See also John J. Timmerman, *Promises to Keep: A Centennial History of Calvin College* (Grand Rapids, Mich.: Calvin College and Seminary with Eerdmans, 1975).

development was set when Runner pointed him to the philosophy of Herman Dooyeweerd and D. H. Th. Vollenhoven, the Dutch followers of Abraham Kuyper with whom Runner himself had studied.[3]

After a year at the University of Michigan to get an M.A. in English literature and classics, Seerveld headed for Europe to study philosophy with Vollenhoven at the Free University of Amsterdam. During a five-year European sojourn (1953-58) he met and married Inés Cécile Naudin ten Cate, studied philosophy and theology with Karl Jaspers, Karl Barth, and Oscar Cullman in Basel, Switzerland, and did research in aesthetics with Carlo Antoni at the University of Rome. Seerveld received his doctorate in philosophy and comparative literature from the Free University in 1958 with a dissertation on the aesthetics of Italian philosopher Benedetto Croce.[4]

Seerveld's work on Croce was cut short by a job offer to teach philosophy and English literature at Belhaven College, a small school in the heart of the old South at Jackson, Mississippi. Within a year he and his Dutch bride were on the move again, this time to Palos Heights, Illinois, where Seerveld became one of the first faculty members of Trinity Christian College, the newest CRC-affiliated college (Dordt College having opened as a two-year college in 1955). As he and Inés reared a young family of three children (Anya, Gioia, and Lucas, born in 1960, 1961, and 1962, respectively), Cal nurtured an entire generation of Trinity students from 1959 until the move to Toronto in 1972.

Despite his location at small and newly founded schools in North America, Seerveld's teaching and scholarship have retained the cosmopolitan range of his own graduate studies, and he has frequently returned to Europe to do research and to speak at international congresses in aesthetics.[5] At the same time, he has played an active role in North American

---

3. For a discussion of Seerveld's aesthetics that places it in the context of Dutch Neo-Calvinism, see Jeremy Begbie, *Voicing Creation's Praise: Towards a Theology of the Arts* (Edinburgh: T & T Clark, 1991).

4. Published as *Benedetto Croce's Earlier Aesthetics Theories and Literary Criticism* (Kampen: J. H. Kok, 1958).

5. A Fulbright Travel Award allowed Seerveld to spend his sabbatical in 1966-67 doing research in biblical wisdom literature with Gerhard von Rad. He has spent subsequent sabbaticals and leaves in Munich and London (1980), Paris and London (1986-87), and Germany (1993-94), this last by virtue of a research grant from the Social Sciences and Humanities Research Council of Canada. He has also presented papers

aesthetics, frequently taking his graduate students to annual meetings of the American Society for Aesthetics, and serving from 1984 through 1987 as the co-chair of its Canadian counterpart.

It would be hard to overestimate the scope and significance of Calvin Seerveld's work. A gifted and respected philosopher, historian, teacher, and cultural critic, he is equally well known as a stimulating lecturer and an indefatigable builder of Christian organizations. Cal has given selflessly of his time and talents to Christian artists and arts organizations, most notably the Patmos Workshop and Gallery in Toronto. He has played central roles in the formation of a fledgling college (Trinity), the growth of a unique graduate school for cross-disciplinary philosophy and theology (ICS), and the founding of the bilingual Canadian Society for Aesthetics/Société canadienne d'esthétique. Trained in literature and philosophy, Seerveld has also composed songs, written psalm versifications, translated Scripture, published on art history, and become a film aficionado. The bibliography in this volume shows that he has addressed an amazing variety of audiences — high school, college, and university students and faculty; trade unionists, cosmetologists, and media executives; church groups, pastors, and mission-aries; radio audiences, television viewers, and newspaper readers; family conferences, cultural festivals, and scholarly meetings; artists, scientists, historians, philosophers, and theologians — not only across North American but also around the world.

\*     \*     \*

Given the range of Seerveld's interests and the variety of his audiences, it may be presumptuous to identify central themes in his work as a scholar. Yet I think certain motifs in his published writings and certain inflections of the Reformed tradition mark his scholarship to date. Many of the motifs and inflections can be discovered in the inaugural lecture he gave upon accepting the chair of philosophical aesthetics at ICS in 1972.[6] Let me

---

and organized sessions at the International Congresses of Aesthetics held in Darmstadt, Germany (1976), Dubrovnik, Yugoslavia (1980), Montreal (1984), and Nottingham, England (1988). For details, and for information about presentations at other international conferences and symposia, see the bibliography in this volume.

6. Published as *A Turnabout in Aesthetics to Understanding* (Toronto: Institute for Christian Studies, 1974), from which the in-text citations derive.

mention three, and then identify his main contributions to the field of aesthetics.

Like so many of Seerveld's speeches, his inaugural lecture begins with a gutsy translation of Scripture, in this case Psalm 147. Seerveld is one of the few philosophers of this century whose writings continually resonate with scriptural references. Indeed, he is one of the few to undertake fresh translations of Scripture from the original languages and to attend closely to the literary structure and aesthetic nuances of the passages he quotes. This gives many of his speeches and writings a hortatory tone, as if they are an indirect form of argument. Although other philosophers may find such features puzzling or disturbing, they jibe with Seerveld's own theories concerning literature and the arts, about which more will be said below.

Continual engagement with the original Scriptures gives a unique cast to Seerveld's pursuit of Christian scholarship. Unlike many Evangelicals who try to spell out a Christian worldview and then apply this to some topic or discipline; unlike many mainline Protestants for whom the inter-section between faith and learning arises from the scholar's own character or practices; and unlike many Catholic scholars who orient their work to church teachings and the Thomistic intellectual tradition, Seerveld's scholarship drinks deeply from the wells of scriptural translation and med-itation. He does not deny the need for an articulated worldview or for proper character and practices; nor does he run roughshod over church teachings and intellectual traditions; but he turns scriptural interpretation into the touchstone for all of these other matters. At the same time, however, he rejects any cookie-cutter hermeneutic that would turn Scripture into a collection of proof texts or a batch of hard-baked axioms. Imagination and reliance on the Spirit figure prominently in his understanding of how Scripture should be read, lived, and used in scholarship.

Seerveld's inaugural lecture moves directly from Psalm 147 to a learned discourse on the "historical predicament" facing any Christian who wishes to help transform aesthetics (pp. 6-12). The lecture examines the modern setting in which aesthetics has become a distinct field of inquiry. Seerveld relates this development to cultural struggles over the independence and legitimacy of the arts, and he shows why, despite a problematic history, aesthetics merits the attention of Christian scholars. If pursued in the proper fashion, according to Seerveld, "aesthetics can be a blessing to God's people, society at large, artists too, every other science, and even other institutions within society" (p. 11).

Such use of history to get one's bearings characterizes Seerveld's work as a scholar. Seldom does he treat a topic or issue without studying the history from which it arises. The emphasis on history sets his work apart from many of his North American contemporaries in philosophy, who often treat historical inquiry as not properly philosophical and, accordingly, address philosophical problems in abstraction from their historical contexts. Moreover, Seerveld's historical accounts have a critical edge. They attempt to discern the spirits at work in human affairs and to sift the wheat from the chaff in what other scholars have achieved. To use Seerveld's own coinage, his model of historical inquiry in philosophy is to read "anti-sympathetically."[7] He is a master of what Walter Benjamin describes as brushing history against the grain.[8]

A third characteristic of Seerveld's scholarship, in addition to its engagement with Scripture and its critical-historical bent, emerges in the section of the lecture titled "Rightful Task" (pp. 12-20). Here Seerveld notes the perpetual tension in Western culture between theory and practice, particularly in matters aesthetic and artistic. Yet he insists that the two can be mutually beneficial if their institutional contexts are transformed. This means, he says, that neither Christian theorists nor Christian artists should try to go it alone. They need each other, and they need the other members of Christ's body, especially as these achieve institutional expression by way of educational, political, ecclesiastical, and cultural organizations.

The same principle of mutual service within institutional contexts prevails in his sketch of an academic flower within the garden of various organized means of Christian endeavor. (See p. 8.) The flower's three

---

7. In the essay "Biblical Wisdom underneath Vollenhoven's Categories for Philosophical Historiography," *The Idea of a Christian Philosophy: Essays in Honour of D. H. Th. Vollenhoven* (Toronto: Wedge Publishing Foundation, 1973), pp. 127-43, Seerveld argues that Vollenhoven's problem-historical method provides the historian of philosophy with "technically precise categories which make possible a truly transcendental christian critique of other philosophies." Such transcendental critique "asks christian questions within the other thinker's assumed framework" in order to listen "intently to the (checkmated) contribution of non-christian philosophies to our (faulty) christian understanding of reality" (pp. 135-36). See also the companion piece "The Pedagogical Strength of a Christian Methodology in Philosophical Historiography," *Crosscuts and Perspectives: Philosophical Essays in Honour of J. A. L. Taljaard*, published as a special issue of *Koers* 40 (nos. 4-6, 1975), pp. 269-313.

8. Walter Benjamin, "Theses on the Philosophy of History," *Illuminations*, ed. Hannah Arendt, trans. Harry Zohn (New York: Schocken Books, 1968), p. 257.

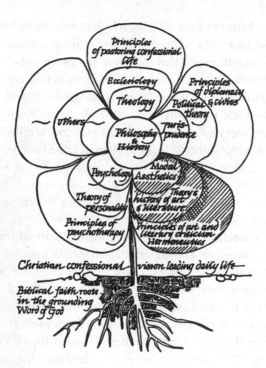

From Calvin G. Seerveld, *A Turnabout in Aesthetics to Understanding* (Toronto: Institute for Christian Studies, 1974), p. 17. Illustration by Willem Hart.

"aesthetic petals" are "modal aesthetics," as the study of the aesthetic dimension of reality; theory and historiography of the arts; and hermeneutics, as the study of the principles of arts criticism. Although aesthetic theorists have the rightful task of piecing out the structure and role of the aesthetic dimension as well as of the various arts, they must do so in collaboration with other disciplines and together with other scholars and practitioners of the arts:

> . . . the closest consultation on the definitive issues among art theorists, art historians and artists . . . — not to speak of art critics and knowledgeable art viewers . . . : such willing, communal research would be a mark of happy obedience and a step toward experiencing communion of the saints as a professional reality too, so that leadership in the area of art and literature could be a co-norming responsibility of practicing art theorists, art historiographers, critics, and actual performing and producing artists. (p. 18)

It is common, of course, for Christian scholars and schools to pay homage to the principle of mutual service. What is striking about Seerveld's bold sketch in 1972, and what distinguishes his subsequent work, is the thoroughness with which he pursues this principle in the details of his discipline. It is no accident that the contributors to this Festschrift come from so many diverse fields of study. Calvin Seerveld has always promoted collaboration within and among the fields of scholarship, even as he has single-mindedly given himself to fashioning a new approach to aesthetics.

*       *       *

Four claims constitute the core of Seerveld's contribution to his chosen field. The first is that the aesthetic dimension inheres in the fabric of created reality, and that aesthetic norms can be violated or ignored only at great cost to human culture and society. With this claim, Seerveld counters the tendency either to turn aesthetic activities and objects into poor imitations of a transcendent Beauty (e.g., Plato) or to treat aesthetic experience as a mere matter of personal preference (e.g., C. J. Ducasse). Seerveld's approach provides a basis for calling people to lives of aesthetic responsibility and service.

The second claim is that the arts, despite their tremendous variety and continual development, make up a unified family distinct from other branches of culture. The fact that the distinct lineage of the arts did not become obvious until modern times does not argue against their having a common and distinctive structure. This means that the arts can present a bona fide sphere for contemporary Christian endeavor, even though not every individual is called to be an artist.

The third claim is that the aesthetic dimension encompasses much more than the arts, just as the arts have many more dimensions than the aesthetic dimension. Hence those aestheticians who spend all their time discussing the arts (as has been common for the greater part of the twentieth century) miss much of significance in human life, just as those theorists who spend all of their energy sorting out the nature of aesthetic experience overlook much of importance about the arts.

The fourth, and perhaps the most difficult claim, is that "allusiveness" or "imaginativity" makes up the central trait of the aesthetic dimension and the defining characteristic of the arts as a unified family of cultural endeavor. By allusiveness or imaginativity, Seerveld means the nuances, indirection, metaphorical suggestion, and playfulness that seem always to accompany aesthetic activities and experience. The main point here is that such features ought neither to be denigrated nor to be blown out of proportion, but rather should be recognized and respected as ordinary constituents of human life, constituents to which the arts call special attention.

None of these claims lies beyond dispute. Indeed, several essays in this volume question or revise one or another of Seerveld's insights. In their interconnections, however, and in their detailed elaboration, the four claims indicate a substantial and provocative attempt to transform the field of aesthetics, and to do so in a way that makes it serviceable for other disciplines and for people's lives.

## New Fields and Old Friends

Fruits of Seerveld's transforming aesthetics can be found in the essays that follow. The essayists include persons who have studied with Seerveld as well as other Christians who have been in dialogue with him about issues in the arts and culture. All of the authors have taken up the challenge of nurturing a Christian approach to culture at the end of the twentieth century. And in doing so, they extend Seerveld's efforts to new areas, reexamine the tools he has devised for work in the field of aesthetics, and revisit the traditions on which his academic gardening relies for sustenance.

The two inner petals of Seerveld's flower — modal aesthetics and philosophy of the arts — are represented here by four essays in cultural theory (Part I). Each essay carries a planting from Seerveld's garden into fields of study that have opened in recent years: popular culture, performance art, computer imagery, and the "new art history."

William D. Romanowski, who teaches communications and film studies at Calvin College, explores the relevance of Seerveld's modal aesthetics for popular culture. Romanowski shows that Seerveld's philosophy transcends the opposition between high culture and low, a polarity that has plagued North American artists and theorists alike and has served as a way to denigrate popular culture in the Reformed community of which Seerveld is a lifelong member. As Romanowski puts it, quoting his subject along the way, Seerveld's " 'single, unifying vision' for aesthetic life . . . provides a useful framework not only for theoreticians and artists but also for viewers and consumers, the 'so-called pop and hot dog masses' " (p. 31 below).

Romanowski illustrates how Seerveld's emphasis on allusiveness or imaginativity can help one evaluate the aesthetic merits of the rock film *A Hard Day's Night* (1964) and compare these with the features of a knock-off such as *Hold On* (1965). The point of making such evaluations is not simply to exercise discernment in consuming popular culture, however, but also to learn how to build an alternative. For, as Romanowski says, Seerveld "envisions obedient aesthetic life and Christian cultural activity that transform both elite and popular art with a style which is decidedly Christian" (p. 36 below).

Whereas Romanowski shows the relevance of Seerveld's modal aesthetics for the study of popular culture, Jim Leach seeks to revise Seerveld's philosophy of the arts in order to accommodate "proto-arts" and "anti-arts." Leach, a playwright and a doctoral candidate at ICS, examines Seerveld's proposal for an encyclopedic theory of the arts, made during his "Unionville" lectures to Canadian university students in the early 1960s. Although Leach worries that Seerveld's emphasis on differences among various art forms might obscure their commonalities, he wants to retain the insight, derived from Kuyper and Dooyeweerd, that the arts evidence the same coherence-in-diversity characterizing the rest of God's creation.

Leach suggests two revisions to Seerveld's proposal. The first is to think of the various arts, such as music, drama, and dance, as together constituting a "constellation" rather than an "encyclopedia." The notion of a constellation suggests some of the historical permutations and social variability that characterize the arts and their interrelations, but does not discourage attempts to find order and to offer normative critique. The second revision is to distinguish the constellation of the *arts* from what Leach describes as a constellation of *aesthetic practices,* which include the "proto-arts" of popular culture and the "anti-arts" of a high culture attacking its own societal structures. Both revisions aim to emphasize the sociohistorical contexts of the arts and of their close cousins rather than to deduce their natures from a transhistorical ontology.

Art historian Mary Leigh Morbey takes a similar tack in the uncharted channels of electronic imagery. Her exploratory essay examines the adequacy of Seerveld's categories for art history in light of two simultaneous developments: the marriage of art and electronic technologies, and the rise of postmodernist critiques of modernist approaches to art criticism and art history. Morbey shows that modernist approaches such as the formalism of Clement Greenberg lead to either neglect or misunderstanding of

11

process-oriented artmaking such as the computer imagery of Harold Cohen. More appropriate categories are needed for the criticism and history of computer-related art.

In search of such categories, Morbey turns first to Walter Benjamin's famous essay on art's technical reproducibility and then to the critiques of modernism provided by Jean-François Lyotard and Charles Jencks. Appropriate categories for interpreting computer-related art will need to do three things, she says: acknowledge the dramatic impact of electronic technologies on artistic practices, question the grand narratives of certainty and progress that sustained modernist approaches, and take into account such "postmodern" features of contemporary society as cyclical time, postindustrial production, the rise of a "cognitariat," and the simultaneity of cultural genres.

Morbey does not propose specific new categories. She does suggest, however, that Seerveld's art-historical methodology, with its emphasis on cultural periods, worldview traditions, and generational contributions, seems more modernist than postmodernist. Seerveld's approach does not fully acknowledge the impact of electronic technologies, nor does it sufficiently take into account the postmodern features of today's society. At the same time, Morbey points out that the biblical narrative informing Seerveld's historiography transcends the polarities of modern versus postmodern and modernism versus postmodernism. The challenge facing Seerveld and his students is to devise categories that allow the story of creation, fall, redemption, and renewal to speak afresh to a postmodern society and within a postmodernist intellectual culture. Morbey concludes with suggestions along these lines for the understanding and evaluation of computer-related art.

Henry Luttikhuizen, a philosophically trained art historian, continues this exploration of art historiographic categories while introducing several of the themes in the next three essays. Wishing to put into practice the Seerveldian insight that living in a tradition involves "setting the table for the next generation" (p. 78 below), Luttikhuizen reviews the art historiography of Hans Rookmaaker and Calvin Seerveld, sorts out their contributions and limitations, and proposes a new goblet for drinking their vintage wisdom.

Like much of the so-called "new art history," Rookmaaker's and Seerveld's art histories reject the positivist notion that art historical interpretations should be value-free. Unlike most "new art historians," however, Rookmaaker and Seerveld include religious commitment among the "values" that necessarily and legitimately shape both art and scholarship. Whereas Rookmaaker turns this insight into an emphasis on the worldview signified by the artistic image, Seerveld provides a more complex methodology, one which distinguishes, traces, and interrelates synchronic periods, perchronic styles or traditions, and diachronic developments and contributions. Seerveld also insists on the open-ended character of historical interpretation as well as the allusive character of the artistic image.

Despite his appreciation for Seerveld's approach, Luttikhuizen worries that the proposed methodology can encourage pigeonholing, for it seems to reduce images to words and treats periods and styles as realities rather than as merely heuristic devices. His main criticism concerns the typically Neo-Calvinian emphasis on worldviews that is common to both Rookmaaker and Seerveld. Luttikhuizen connects the limitations of worldview analyses with flaws in the Renaissance theory of linear perspective. The danger is that the scholar treats his or her own stance as a timeless truth removed from its cultural and historical context, with ideological dogmatism and hypocritical slander as the all-too-common result. Like Merold Westphal in the next essay, Luttikhuizen would have us affirm the fallen and finite character of our own interpretations rather than act as if any of us has a transcendent point of view. To accomplish this, he introduces the concept of ideology, insists on the materiality of visual images, and explores their substitutive power. Christian interpreters of art must confront images humbly, he says, keeping their own religious convictions intact, but not shielding these from critical scrutiny.

\*        \*        \*

The essays of the next section, titled "Philosophical Dialogue," give testimony to the close and engaged reading of major philosophers that has always characterized Seerveld's teaching and scholarship. The philosophers discussed include the French postmodernist Jacques Derrida (b. 1930), the American pragmatist John Dewey (1859-1952), and the German "existentialist" Martin Heidegger (1889-1976).

Merold Westphal, a prominent American philosopher currently at Fordham University, takes to task those Christian scholars who seek to demonize postmodernism. Responding in particular to a book by literary theorist Roger Lundin, Westphal wittily skewers the folly and fallacies in simplistic attacks on the thought of Jacques Derrida. According to Westphal,

Derrida does not embrace relativism and nihilism, as too many Christian scholars have claimed. Instead, Derrida points out the finitude and fallibility of all human theories and practices — an inadvertently Augustinian insight which epistemic and moral absolutists would rather not apply to their own positions. Derrida will not let us forget that none of us is God.

Beyond this timely reminder, however, Derrida's deconstruction also brings to the surface three themes that Christians should appropriate into their cultural interpretations and critiques. The first, Westphal says, is the need to achieve congruence between the claim that humans are not God and the manner in which Christians maintain their own traditions and answer their critics. The second theme is the recognition that even those to whom God has spoken can formulate what they have heard only in their own human discourse. The third is that all cultural processes and artifacts are relative and finite; their being and meaning are always contextual and never final. Derrida's deconstructive theory of textuality points toward "an overcoming of nihilism that is willing to remain human," and it does so by seeking "to articulate the coexistence of relativity and critique" (p. 125 below). A Christian cultural theory has something important to learn from this.

A similar emphasis on context and process occurs in Carroll Guen Hart's pioneering comparison of Seerveld's systematic aesthetics with that of John Dewey. Guen Hart, a feminist philosopher and educator, draws upon her extensive knowledge of Dewey's work to defend him against the charge that his aesthetic theory dissolves art into undifferentiated experience. Her twofold aim is to show that Dewey shares many concerns with Seerveld and to identify the important elements Dewey's aesthetics may contribute to a contemporary Christian aesthetic theory.

According to Guen Hart, Dewey aims to counter the separation of art from ordinary life that accompanies the growth of nationalism, capitalism, and industrialization, but he does not deny the special place of art in contemporary society. His notion of "art as experience" presupposes an "ecology of experience" encompassing individuals, groups, and the natural and cultural environment. Human beings are responsible for their part in the unfolding of experience, at present and in the future. "Art" is a way of refining experience for specific purposes, and "aesthetic art" is a way of refining experience for the purpose of "delightful perception." Although works of aesthetic art do not function as straightforward instruments, they do serve "to refresh and enlarge our communal experience of the world" (p. 136 below).

Building on this account, Guen Hart shows that, despite Seerveld's criticisms of Deweyan philosophy, his own emphases are not that far removed from Dewey's. Seerveld, too, rejects elitist understandings of art and regards aesthetic life as intrinsic to ordinary human existence. Moreover, Dewey's attention to process and context provides an important correction to what Guen Hart regards as Seerveld's undue stress on meeting God-given norms. Whereas such an emphasis can stifle the experimentation needed for aesthetic education and artistic endeavor, Dewey gives us a way to nurture experimentation without becoming indiscriminate in our judgments. Both in aesthetic education and in the work of artists, the process of "poeming" is just as important as the "poetry" produced. Dewey can teach a Christian aesthetic theory to recognize "a more generous and flexible normativity." By embracing both the process and the product, such a theory can encourage Christians "to bring redeeming love into the world of contemporary art" (p. 152 below).

As Guen Hart points out early in her essay, Seerveld sometimes pits Dewey against Martin Heidegger as two extremes to be rejected in favor of a "third way." The next essay, by philosopher and community worker Donald Knudsen, addresses the second figure in this polarity. Joining the recent battle over Heidegger's cultural politics, Knudsen demonstrates a mythologizing turn in Heidegger's thought during the Nazi era. Knudsen's essay examines the language of *"Ereignis"* (roughly, "historically freighted event") in a previously hidden passage from Heidegger's 1936-37 lectures on Nietzsche. After discussing the circumstances under which Heidegger deleted this passage from the published lectures, Knudsen shows that the passage transfigures Heidegger's own appropriation of Nietzsche's anti-democratic "nihilism" into an event of worldwide significance. The passage also aligns this event with Heidegger's earlier use of Nietzsche to support Nazi cultural policies.

Knudsen carefully elaborates the twists and turns in Heidegger's complex reception of Nietzsche. He shows how a preoccupation with a mythical origin ("Being") — typical of mythologizing thinkers, according to Seerveld — goes hand in hand with Heidegger's concern for the super-human "truth" in "great" works of art. Far from abandoning the reactionary cultural politics of his year as rector at the University of Freiburg (1933-34), Heidegger "simply transmuted elements of his previous political program into the status of principle, the truth and greatness of which could be understood by the community of the great." Recognition of Heidegger's mythologizing tendency around 1936-37 lets one "follow clearly the political component of his turn *(Kehre)* to poetry, language, and the work of art" (p. 174 below).

*     *     *

The outer petal of Seerveld's flower — hermeneutics, as the study of the principles of art and literary criticism — is represented in this collection by four essays in cultural critique. Each essay combines reflection on principles for appreciating cultural practices with commentary on specific cultural products: a public monument, a film, a painted collage, and a lyric poem. Common to all four essays is their concern for justice and solidarity amid oppression and conflict.

The South African philosopher and social critic Johan Snyman asks how the political system of apartheid could be instituted by people whose ancestors had suffered similar atrocities in the concentration camps of the Anglo-Boer War. Part of the explanation lies in the kinds of memorials that Afrikaners have used to represent and express their suffering.

Snyman's eloquent essay begins by distinguishing between memorials, with which we honor the dead, and monuments, with which we honor ourselves: the Vietnam Veterans Memorial in Washington D.C. has a different social function from the Washington Monument. Genuine memorial sculpture refuses to serve as an aesthetic theodicy of war and the suffering it causes. This is particularly so of Holocaust art, such as the Dachau Memorial by Glid Nandor, which records and interprets the suffering of Jews and other victims of the Nazi concentration camps.

Unlike genuine war memorials, Snyman claims, the Women's Memorial (1913) in Bloemfontein "is not so much a memorial dedicated to the suffering of the dead, as a monument for the grief of those left behind" (p. 192 below). His thesis is borne out by a close reading of the written record surrounding the Women's Memorial sculpture, by careful attention to its placement and structure, and by historical understanding of the culture and ethos of the Afrikaner survivors. Hence it is not surprising that this so-called memorial quickly turned into a nationalist shrine celebrating "love of the fatherland, bravery, and unwavering faith" (p. 204 below).

The irony in all of this is that Emily Hobhouse, the driving force behind the Women's Memorial, was neither an Afrikaner nor a nationalist. An English feminist, she wanted the memorial to elevate the Boer woman "to the ranks of the Universal Woman's struggle for recognition" (p. 205 below). Unlike Afrikaner leaders who upheld national pride and ethnic loyalty, Hobhouse appealed to the universal moral principles of the Enlightenment. But sanitized versions of Hobhouse's dedication speech have omitted her most pungent appeals for universal liberty and equality, just as the official accounts of Afrikaner suffering have ignored the suffering of black people in English concentration camps. Against such selective and self-congratulatory memory, as embodied in cultural practices and products, Snyman posits a new moral imperative derived from the German Jewish philosopher Theodor Adorno, namely, to prevent repetitions of the deadly domination that genuine memorials protest and of the horrific suffering they express. "Memorials should not . . . invoke the discourse of greatness by elevating victims to the purported height of their . . . victimizers and thereby offering false restitution. Memorials vow silently for the sake of future victims" (p. 209 below).

Racial conflict and oppression, which form the social context for Snyman's essay, provide the main theme of Fran Wong's essay on *The Crying Game,* a film by Irish writer and director Neil Jordan. A Canadian film critic, musician, and educator, Wong brings to her analysis the concerns of a Christian feminist and the sensibilities of someone who has lived simultaneously in both majority and minority cultures. Her essay argues that the film's depiction of race relations in contemporary Britain encourages filmgoers "to examine their own racial attitudes, their interracial relationships . . . , and their society's racial interactions" (p. 211 below).

Wong concentrates on the visual aspects of *The Crying Game,* for it is in how the film is shot, more than in the dialogue or the soundtrack, that racial identities and tensions are most directly explored. At the center of this exploration lies the complex and evolving relationship between Jody, a black English soldier captured by a cell of the Irish Republican Army, and Fergus, one of Jody's Caucasian Irish captors. Over three days of captivity an uneasy friendship develops that unravels the stereotypes of both characters, as well as of the filmgoing public — stereotypes not only of political allegiance and racial identity but also of sexual orientation. What emerges, ever so slowly and ambiguously, is a universal principle of giving rather than taking, of doing as one would be done by, over against the ignorance, hatred, and violence in much of the world the film presents. Under Wong's observant eye, the issues raised by Snyman's essay return with all the expressive power of a definitive film from the early 1990s.

Peter Enneson, a graphic designer and art director in Toronto, devotes his attention to the work of Henk Krijger, the accomplished painter, sculptor, and book designer whom Seerveld helped bring to the Patmos Workshop and Gallery as its master artist in the early 1970s. Enneson's innovative piece of "artwriting" provides a suitably multifaceted meditation on Krijger's painted collage *The Survivors* of 1972. After describing Krijger's associative and constructive modus operandi, his history as a survivor from the Dutch resistance movement in World War II, and the range of works he completed in 1972, Enneson provides a nuanced account of the structure, significations, and narrative technique of this powerful work. It is at once a product of personal memory, social critique, and communal lament. Like many other of Krijger's works, writes Enneson, *The Survivors* transforms "attentiveness to the self and its ravages" into "an act of empathetic human solidarity." As a significant experimenter of Dutch Calvinist extraction, Krijger strove for "an aesthetically worthwhile, multifaceted, existentially engaged . . . and contemporary artistry" (p. 248 below). From his life and work younger artists can take both inspiration and instruction.

The concluding commentary in this part of the collection is by the South African Germanist and literary theorist Gudrun Kuschke. Like the preceding essayists, Dr. Kuschke is interested in how Christian intellectuals should conduct themselves in times of social upheaval and political struggle. For clues she turns to the life and writing of the German poet Werner Bergengruen, a member of the "inner resistance" to the Nazis from 1933 to 1945. Kuschke suggests that Christian poetry will be characterized by an ethos that flows into the poetry from the person as a poet. To detect such an ethos requires both "faith-bound sensitivity" and "an integrated structural approach" on the part of the literary critic (p. 251 below).

Kuschke shows how to detect a Christian ethos by providing a precise and illuminating interpretation of Bergengruen's poem "Nichts gib mir, Gott" ("Nothing Give Me, God"). Employing categories derived from the modal theory of Dooyeweerd and Seerveld, she distinguishes three levels of literary analysis: technical foundation, aesthetic imaginativity, and religious ethos. There follows a detailed commentary on this particular poem's stanzaic division, rhyme scheme, rhythm, climactic development, movement, composition, and technical structure, all of which belong to the poem's "technical foundation." The subsequent section on "aesthetic imaginativity" demonstrates that the poem's allusive expression is tightly bound to triadic patterns, paradoxical tensions, and various poetic devices such as metaphor and alliteration.

18

Kuschke concludes that Bergengruen's poem "does not negate the present creation, but rather it unites earth and heaven, humanity and God, through the love and sovereignty of God evidenced in the order of nature." Indeed, the poem's integral Christian ethos "emanates from the poem as a coherent whole" (p. 266 below). Through his poetry Bergengruen helps people take confidence in God's faithful care, "despite catastrophe and crisis"; the poet is able "to lead us . . . to inner confrontation, and to an understanding of reality from the ever present eschaton" (p. 268 below).

\*      \*      \*

An outstanding feature of Seerveld's life and work is his passion for the imagery, liturgy, and literature of his own religious tradition. The expression of this passion has been ecumenical in scope and innovative in effect, ranging from illustrated lectures on religious iconography to compositions of new psalm tunes and texts and fresh translations of books and passages from the Hebrew Scriptures. The essays in the final section exemplify Seerveld's concern for renewing and reclaiming the artistic heritage of Christianity, especially within the Reformed tradition.

Bert Polman, a musicologist at Redeemer College and one of Cal's collaborators in revising the Christian Reformed Church's *Psalter Hymnal,* provides a fascinating account of the image of Mary as the breastfeeding mother of God. After tracing the earliest sources for this image, Polman explores its shifting connotations of nourishment, humility, power, full humanity, spiritual sustenance, and divine grace. Many paintings of the nursing Madonna, he argues, have erotic overtones that the Catholic Reformation tried to suppress and that Christians in the West continue to find disturbing. Polman, however, thinks the image, including its eroticism, needs to be celebrated: "Patriarchal fears of powerful nursing women notwithstanding, the image of the breastfeeding Virgin Mary continues to inspire human culture as a symbol of maternal nourishment, divine grace, and erotic pleasure, if not also of a humility which is sometimes wrongly focussed only on women" (p. 284 below).

Barbara Jo Douglas, also a musicologist, writes with obvious admiration about the Genevan psalm settings that Seerveld has helped restore to their rightful place in contemporary Reformed liturgy. Douglas recounts the history of the Genevan Psalter in order to raise issues about church music today. She writes that the Reformers tried to fashion a liturgy which broke with the obscurity and elitism of the aesthetically rich but inaccessible mass in the late medieval church. It was in this context that Jean Calvin and his musical and poetic collaborators introduced congregational psalm-singing in sixteenth-century Geneva.

According to Douglas, the Genevan Psalter sprang from a "pastoral theology of music" (p. 289 below), articulated by Calvin, that considers music a pleasurable gift whose emotional power must be moderated by scriptural texts and placed in the service of fervent prayer. This theology accords with the liturgical and pedagogical uses to which the Psalter was put, as enthusiastic congregational psalm singing became a distinctive trait of Reformed churches in many lands.

Douglas also describes the stylistic features of the Genevan tunes, compares them with Lutheran church music from the same time, and, using Seerveld's notion of allusiveness, praises their rigor, variety, and expressive range. She concludes that the Genevan Psalter provides a solid and rich liturgical legacy whose combination of accessibility and quality is well worth emulating in contemporary church music. Indeed, the postmodern era may be the right time to revitalize the practice of psalm singing and to revive the entire Psalter for contemporary use.

Ray Van Leeuwen, an Old Testament scholar, pays homage to Calvin Seerveld's passion for biblical Wisdom literature. This passion has led Seerveld to a new translation and many performances of *The Greatest Song* (otherwise known as the Song of Songs), as well as numerous commentaries and sermons on passages from the books of Proverbs and Ecclesiastes. Van Leeuwen first explores the historical reasons why all manner of proverbs have fallen on hard times among modern intellectuals. Then he describes features common to all proverbs and illustrates these with biblical sayings from the book of Proverbs. To do their work, he says, proverbs must fit the situation, and the speaker must have wisdom to use a proverb fittingly.

Van Leeuwen suggests that the dominant proverbs in a society, such as "Money talks" or "Sex sells," reveal where a culture's heart lies. By contrast, what guides the wise sayings in Proverbs, and what should guide all who wish to follow Wisdom's path, is a verse that could well serve as a motto for Seerveld's own teaching: "The fear of the Lord is beginning of knowledge; fools despise wisdom and instruction" (Prov. 1:7). In this proverb of proverbs Van Leeuwen hears a fundamental challenge to the assumptions of modernity and postmodernity alike.

# Harvest Home

When Calvin Seerveld envisioned three aesthetic "petals" in 1972, he had little assurance that what he planted would not die in the greenhouse. Nor, for that matter, did he need such assurance. Seerveld's walk with God exudes a Calvinist piety that affirms, with Isaiah: "The grass withers and the flowers fall, but the word of our God stands forever" (Isaiah 40:8, NIV). Such piety is not an exhausted resignation, but rather the persistent confidence that God will bless what is planted in faithfulness and love.

During the intervening years Seerveld has been steadily at work in his garden, training apprentices, inspiring visitors, and turning his sketches into thriving plants and vibrant flower beds. At the same time, however, the terrain of intellectual culture has shifted dramatically, and neither Seerveld nor his students and younger colleagues have ignored changes in the academic landscape. Instead they have refined and reformulated, trying to design appropriate theories and methods for a new environment. The essays in this Festschrift bear witness not only to the genial expanse of Seerveld's original vision but also to its transformative potential. Indeed, the cross-fertilizing of theory, criticism, and history, along with the concern to help transform culture through scholarship, make these essays a fitting tribute to a Reformational interdisciplinarian par excellence.

What Seerveld has envisioned, and what he has labored energetically and faithfully to provide, is nothing less than a "doxological aesthetics," one which, "within . . . its rich zone of creation, engaged according to its educational formative nature, not abandoning . . . the tentative caution proper to theoretic work, not short-changing . . . its conceptual knowledge-getting, yet within all that knowledge-getting, [is] an aesthetics that gets Understanding." Such an aesthetics "builds up the praise in the world for the Lord by breaking open a consciousness of the dead ends" in aesthetic life and in the artworld. It also "invites the aesthetic lost in to serve with joy on what is fruitful aesthetically, artistically, and can be blessed."[9] This is the challenge he has presented his students. This is the task he himself has taken up.

Seerveld's call to work in anticipation of God's reign is as urgent now as it was more than twenty years ago. In the intervening years he has proved a master gardener, not only as a scholar but also as a teacher and cultural leader. There is now an international community of scholars, artists, and

---

9. *A Turnabout in Aesthetics to Understanding*, p. 20.

educators who have learned from his work and who pursue a transformational aesthetic in the Neo-Calvinian tradition. Seerveld's sixty-fifth birthday on August 18, 1995, shortly after his retirement from ICS, offers an appropriate occasion to thank and honor him for his pioneering work.

With this book, then, and with a festive banquet on the eve of his birthday, the editors and authors join hundreds of well-wishers around the world to say thank you to a tireless leader and faithful friend. May he enjoy the fruits of his labors, even as he continues to help us imagine the day when all of culture and society, yes, all of creation, will be made new, when, as in the apostle John's great vision, God's dwelling is with humanity and God tenderly wipes each tear from every eye. To that end we offer our own pledges of jubilee.

# I. CULTURAL THEORY

# The Joys Are Simply Told:
# Calvin Seerveld's Contribution
# to the Study of Popular Culture

## WILLIAM D. ROMANOWSKI

In the early 1980s, Cal Seerveld spent the night as a guest in my home. After dinner, my wife and I introduced him to MTV: Music Television. Curled up in a chair, wrapped in a red blanket, and drinking herbal tea, he sat silent for awhile, mesmerized at first by the images flashing across the screen to rock music accompaniment. Very quickly, however, he began to observe surreal and dadaist elements in contemporary music videos. It was a great night!

Seerveld has not written about popular culture specifically, at least not in the terms of contemporary cultural studies. His Reformed concept of culture effaces somewhat the categorical distinctions among elite, popular, and folk. I have learned from him that aesthetic life in all its variegated forms is to be unfolded in responsible obedience to the Lord. The effects of the antithesis are all too evident in aesthetic life *in toto;* popular art, though in different form than "high" or "elite" art, still deserves Christian analysis. But Seerveld's own ethno-religious tradition has militated against the formulation of a Christian approach to popular culture, virtually eliminating the institutions of popular art from any serious consideration or reforming activity on the part of Christians. Although the Christian Reformed Church's official condemnation of "worldly amusements" earlier this century included popular art forms, Seerveld has remained faithful to the principles of the Kuyperian tradition. He recognizes the value and meaning of popular art for the majority of people, and especially the young. Perhaps this explains in part his popularity among evangelical college students and his repeat performances at the Jubilee Conference in Pittsburgh and the Greenbelt Festival in England. Beginning with his art historiography, this essay shows how aspects of Seerveld's theorizing about art and culture can be employed in the development of a Christian approach to popular art and entertainment.

## The Emergence of High and Popular Art

The intent of Seerveld's art historiography is to show how aesthetic life has been suffocated by the disaffection of art from the affairs of everyday life and people. In so doing, it also aims to shed light on the meaning of the emergence of popular art and culture. Prior to the Renaissance, such categorical distinctions as "high" and "popular" art did not exist. What we think of as the "fine" arts existed alongside the crafts; the work of poets, painters, sculptors, and architects was not distinguished from that of silversmiths, carpenters, stone cutters, and armorers. The differentiation of the *beaux arts,* the *fine* arts, from the crafts began with the separation of artists from trade guilds in the sixteenth century. But while painting, sculpture, architecture, music, and poetry won a level of distinction from the crafts, Seerveld explains, "they were still on the leash of their royal patrons, landed gentry, wealthy businessmen, Tory and Whig politicians" until the late eighteenth century. Only then did the idea of an autonomous art emerge, and only in the nineteenth century would "aesthetes," as they were called, argue that "art was to be in bond to no man: art is not for the infallible pope and his red hat church, it is not for the kings — may they be decapitated — and keep your money! Art is for nobody! Art is good for nothing! Art is for art's sake!"[1]

In one sense, these developments were part of the gradual unfolding of the aesthetic mode of creation according to "the basic cosmogonic law of differentiating to the primary," Seerveld explains. Art was no longer qualified or defined by some other interest, social, economic, or con-

---

1. Calvin G. Seerveld, *A Turnabout in Aesthetics to Understanding* (Toronto: Wedge Publishing, 1974), pp. 9-10.

fessional, but had a distinction of its own, "fully recognized as a cultural product with its own specific character, its own particularly identifying idiom and unmistakably 'artistic' requirements." This affords the theoretician a moment in the development of art to look for its qualifying function. As Seerveld says, "art in museum and gallery today, unbeholden to anything but what is artistic, offers us a choice opportunity to probe what is characteristically art-as-such (and can condemn itself, I know, to the sterilization of an important gift God has given mankind)."[2]

The parenthetical note, however, points to the modern dilemma of art, as Seerveld sees it. Art came into its own as a distinct activity, "something deserving full-fledged attention proper to its own nature," Seerveld says. But he laments that "this proper historical differentiation of art suffered because it was secularistically spirited by a devil-may-care elitism."[3] The side effect of this differentiation was that artistic activity was gradually torn from the fabric of daily existence for the vast majority of people. High Art (with a capital "A") became the exclusive property of an educated elite, composed of *virtuosos* and *connoisseurs,* who thought they alone could understand and properly appreciate Art.

These ideas took hold and became significant for similar developments in America in the late nineteenth century. The modern period began with enormous transformations marked by rapid industrialization, urbanization, and huge population growth and fueled primarily by immigrants from southeastern Europe and Asia, and by African-Americans migrating to the North. Nineteenth-century Victorian ideals and assumptions based on individual self-sufficiency — ceaseless work, Puritan moral virtue, deferred gratification — were swallowed up in routinized work and by limitations for social mobility in the corporate system. A different culture that seriously threatened the reigning Victorian worldview was forged in the cities, and it reflected the beliefs and values of the new industrial democracy.

Matthew Arnold's hegemonic concept of culture as "the best that has been thought and said in the world" gave the wealthy and educated native Protestant elite the intellectual justification they needed to maintain the dominance of the Eurocentric cultural tradition in American institutional life. This relegated other cultures — Native American, African-American,

---

2. Calvin Seerveld, *Rainbows for the Fallen World* (Toronto: Tuppence Press, 1980), pp. 110, 113-14.
3. *Rainbows,* pp. 112-13.

Asian, and the array of immigrant cultures — to an inferior status. By the turn of the century, American life was fragmented into highbrow and lowbrow cultures with different institutions and standards. Susan Sontag has observed that this cultural distinction was based in part on "the difference between unique and mass-produced objects."[4] The "legitimate" theater, opera, symphony, museums, and galleries were funded by wealthy patrons in order to present and preserve the best of Hellenistic and western European culture. Those who did not belong to the American cultural elite still desired art that entertained as well as expressed their ideals and problems, tastes, and values. "Popular" theater, especially vaudeville, native African-American music, Tin Pan Alley, and the new silent motion pictures, competed in the commercial marketplace by expressing the dreams and realities of the middle and working classes.

Ironically, leaders in the Christian Reformed Church (CRC) gradually appropriated Arnold's humanistic concept of culture to Neo-Calvinist principles as a resolution to the Christ-and-culture issue. More specifically, it was a means to resolve tensions among the Dutch Reformed immigrants about how to be *in* the dominant American culture of twentieth-century modernism without being *of* it. Essentially, they drew the line of the spiritual antithesis between elite and traditional culture, on the one hand, and popular and contemporary culture, on the other hand.

In 1928, for example, a synodical committee ruled that the movies (and theater) "as an institution, taken in its general influence, is on the side of Satan against the Kingdom of Christ."[5] In an attack on worldliness, the church banned movie attendance as one of the "worldly amusements." This action was taken not only because attending the movie theater put Christians in the company of the ungodly, but also because movies presented "a false view of life" and "commercialize[d] and therefore lower[ed] art and literature to an alarming degree."[6] It was not until 1967, and then under tremendous pressure from the penetration of television into CRC homes, that the church reversed the 1928 decision and concluded that film and television were not merely amusements, but "legitimate cultural

---

4. Susan Sontag, *Against Interpretation and Other Essays* (New York: Farrar, Straus & Giroux, 1966), p. 297.

5. "Report of the Committee on Worldly Amusements," *Agenda: Synod of the Christian Reformed Church, 1928,* pp. 32-33.

6. Henry Beets, Editorial, *The Banner,* 12 November 1908, p. 724.

[media] to be used by the Christian in the fulfillment of the cultural mandate."[7]

Music, too, was divided into "classical" and "popular," the one sacred and the other secular. "We believe that there are two kinds of music, radically different — the one inspired by the Spirit of God, the other by demons," H. J. Kuiper wrote as editor of *The Banner* in 1944. "The former is truly melodious and harmonious, reminding one of heavenly perfection; the latter, in its crazy rhythm, its sensual swing, and hideous tunes, reflects the spirit of hell."[8] In a similar vein, after World War II, Calvin College English professor Henry Zylstra created two distinct categories for literature. Real Literature was the canon of classics from Western civilization, "the honest and soul-searching literature, the valid and undissimulating literature." Popular fiction, which included romance, science fiction, mystery novels, detective stories, and westerns, he called "mere entertainment," "canned opiate or tonic for frightened or bored people."[9]

In effect, then, these Reformed Christians decided they could be "in the world" by participating in elite art and culture, establishing standards for evaluation, making moral, aesthetic, and confessional judgments. Involvement in popular art and culture, by way of production, consumption, or even analysis, meant being "of the world." Popular culture was an inferior sort, an evil to be avoided, a moral, spiritual, intellectual, and aesthetic risk. But this establishment of a cultural hierarchy relegated much of the fabric of American culture, most notably women, youth, and minority cultures, to an inferior status as popular or folk culture. Their exclusion from academic study and the curriculum is at the center of the current debates about higher education and the battles between those who advocate a return to the classicist tradition and those who argue for a multicultural curriculum. The entanglement of Reformed principles with the humanistic ideals of the

7. *The Church and the Film Arts*, Henry C. Van Deelen, Chairman (Grand Rapids, Mich.: Christian Reformed Publishing House, 1967), p. 38. Seerveld told me that while movies were forbidden when he was growing up, the approach his parents took was "not prohibition or repression," but presenting alternatives like sports or working in the family's fish store. The first film he saw, however, "made a deep impression," he said. During his years at the Free University of Amsterdam, he was exposed to European films, and later he started a foreign film series at Trinity Christian College in Palos Heights, Illinois.

8. H. J. Kuiper, "Foolish Song," Editorial, *The Banner*, 5 May 1944, p. 412.

9. Henry Zylstra, *Testament of Vision* (Grand Rapids, Mich.: Eerdmans, 1958, 1961), pp. 5, 50-52.

Victorian era, as articulated by Matthew Arnold, has seriously handicapped the Reformed community in its efforts to develop a Christian approach to the increasing heterogeneity of American cultural life in the twentieth century.

## Modal Aesthetics and Popular Art

Seerveld knows that "you cannot stop the sound of eight million Fleetwood Mac records by raising the volume of Mozart or dancing Viennese waltzes on widescreen cinema." He rejects Arnold's humanistic idea of Culture "as the achieved state of historically developed refinement on the model of metropolitan France and England in the eighteenth century," as well as Arnold's cultural chauvinism, "making believe Asia and Africa had next to no culture and that the Americas had to import it from Europe or made do with themselves as 'noble savages.'" Instead, he works with the idea of culture "in its original sense of cultivation, cultivation of the earth . . . the whole gamut of taking care of things, one's self and others in the world," as he writes in *Rainbows for the Fallen World*. This concept of culture, "the cultivation of creation by humankind, the formative development in history of creaturely life tended by human creatures," provides a way of thinking about aesthetic life that makes a legitimate place for popular culture.[10] Seerveld's aesthetic theorizing, then, while at odds with aspects of his ethno-religious background in the Christian Reformed Church, remains faithful to the principle of the Kuyperian intellectual tradition that all the rich possibilities in God's creation are to be cultivated in responsible service to the Lord. He has established a conceptual framework that not only legitimizes the study of popular art but also encourages Christian participation in it by applying the norms for aesthetic life in the evaluation of popular culture texts.

The historical separation of high art from everyday life had two important consequences. First, the "aesthetic" dimension of human life was limited to esoteric activities involving elite art — production and performance, criticism and philosophical speculation. Restricted to disinterested contemplation, "serious" art became devoid of social functions or significance for daily life. Second, while aestheticians established standards for

10. *Rainbows*, pp. 177-79.

30

evaluation and discussion of elite art, the general public was left with a "do-it-yourself, democratic ethic: you know what you like . . . you don't need somebody to tell you what to think about a painting, poem, or the nature of music, do you?"[11] With few generally accepted criteria to evaluate popular art as art, it was abandoned to criticism based on current moral or religious values and accepted social standards. Popular art remains ever vulnerable to efforts at censorship, usually ideologically motivated, though often employing the rhetoric of protecting the impressionable young. Moreover, aesthetic values are subjugated to the gauge of box office success or unit sales.

Seerveld has developed a "single, unifying vision" for aesthetic life that provides a useful framework not only for theoreticians and artists but also for viewers and consumers, the "so-called pop and hot dog masses."[12] His modal aesthetics is an articulation of the nature of the aesthetic mode of created reality, of "aesthetic life," as he calls it, "an irreducible aspect of creaturely reality."[13] He conceives of aesthetic life as "a cosmic dimension, a certain way the Lord asks us to respond. . . ."[14] The task of the theoretician is to uncover and posit the creational norms for aesthetic life that require responsible obedience before God. Seerveld identifies "allusiveness" or "nuancefulness" as the nuclear moment of aesthetic life. It is also the primary differentiation between the artistic and other kinds of activities.[15]

While the emphasis of Seerveld's own work is largely on traditional forms of high art, the aesthetic dimension of life, as he conceives it, is all of one piece, including the art gallery and museum as well as the cinema and disc-jockeyed radio. What have become the dominant forms of popular art — radio, television, and film — are human inventions by which people continue to explore and cultivate the rich potentials in God's creation. Artists working in these media use tools different from those used by practitioners of the high arts; nevertheless, if I understand Seerveld correctly, he considers high art neither better nor more valuable than popular art, just different.

No doubt, much of what he observes coming out of Nashville and

---

11. *Turnabout,* p. 11.
12. *Turnabout,* p. 12.
13. *Rainbows,* p. 105.
14. *Turnabout,* p. 11.
15. *Rainbows,* p. 105.

Hollywood he considers "kitsch," slick and glittery, but emotionally cheap and thriving on sentimentality. "Mindless entertainment, pop star culture, and films interrupted by paid advertisements train children from youth up on TV," Seerveld has said. "Superb means of mass communication rain secular art upon the earth with an almost brainwashing effect." But the pervasiveness of mass-mediated art, its synthesis of the aesthetic with the values of production and consumption, does not mean it is somehow unclean and not worth the salt and light of Christian reflection and criticism, the course the Kuyperian Calvinists followed. Seerveld observes, for example, that Stanley Kubrick's film *A Clockwork Orange* (1972) was a "brilliant portrayal of aimless violence as a way of life and death" seen by millions of people, and that the "self-righteous pornography" of *Oh! Calcutta* ran for years in London and New York theaters.[16] In fact, the pervasiveness of popular art makes Christian analysis of it all the more important, not only for critique of secular ideas presented in entertainment, but also for a Christian evaluation of popular art works as they affirm or violate the norms for aesthetic life.

For example, The Beatles' *A Hard Day's Night* (1964), a film directed by Richard Lester, stands out from the commercial reproductions of rock groups by recording and movie companies trying to capitalize on the popularity of the British Invasion in the 1960s. Film critic Andrew Sarris has called it "the *Citizen Kane* of juke box musicals" because of its brilliant synthesis of rock music and *cinema verité*.[17] This cinematic style immerses the viewer in the pandemonium when the Beatles were mobbed by adoring fans, surrounded by reporters, or performing on stage. The black-and-white cinematography and close-range camera work enhance the visual effect of scenes shot in crowded trains and cars, underground cafes, cramped hotel accommodations, and backstage dressing rooms. Standing in contrast but for a moment are long-range shots of the four Beatles celebrating a moment of freedom in an open field. These aesthetic elements allude to the Beatles' own personal entrapment resulting from their celebrity. The inclusion of chase sequences fashioned after Mack Sennett's Keystone Kops and the sharp, witty dialogue reminiscent of the Marx Brothers give *A Hard Day's Night* an extended ambiance of social satire by placing it in this rich comedic tradition of the American cinema.

16. Calvin Seerveld, "Relating Christianity to the Arts," *Christianity Today*, 7 November 1980, p. 49.

17. Andrew Sarris, "Bravo Beatles!" *Village Voice*, 27 August 1964, p. 13.

Lester devised a bitter satire of British society, revealing class and generational conflicts, by showing the response of the British press, aristocracy, police, marketing entrepreneurs, and screaming fans to Beatlemania as a popular culture phenomenon. The film is loaded with nuance: the Beatles trapped by their own fame singing in a cage surrounded by adoring fans; the press metaphorically feeding off the Beatles as they stuff their faces with hors d'oeuvres at a press conference; the generational clash symbolized by a British gentleman on a train claiming that his rights take precedent over the young, long-haired Beatles; the intentional irony of the Beatles' escaping their status as "public property" for a moment, only to be told they cannot play in the fresh air of an open field because it is "private property." The allusiveness of *A Hard Day's Night* gave artistic insight into the turmoil of British life marked by an aristocratic sex scandal and political and economic upheaval in the early 1960s. Lester and the Beatles captured the ambience of "Swingin' London" and the flowering youth movement which challenged the tastes and values of established British aristocracy. Critical response also indicated that the film itself shook traditional distinctions between high and popular culture.

In contrast, *Hold On* (1965), starring British rock group Herman's Hermits and Shelley Fabares, contains many elements Seerveld describes as "kitsch." It features an inane plot built around a predictable teenage love story that lacks any of the social commentary and aesthetic richness of *A Hard Day's Night*. Capitalizing on the Beatles' cinematic success, *Hold On* was merely a commercialized imitation used primarily as a way to expose the Hermits' music.

The idea of allusiveness is useful for evaluating popular art and making critical distinctions within genres; however, because it is exclusively an aesthetic criterion, it does not adequately account for the wide range of dynamics involved in the production process of commercial art. Relative budgets can and do have an impact on the allusive quality of television programs as compared with the more expensive process of filmmaking, for example. Even within specific genres in music, television, or film, the quality of production can be dependent on financial resources. Likewise, marketing and demographic factors wield a strong influence over the style of communication of mass media. In order to reach a wider audience or secure a certain MPAA rating, the most nuanceful material may end up on the cutting room floor. Regarding film, perhaps the increased availability of the "director's cut" released on video will allow better assessment of a film-maker's work according to the law of allusiveness and keener insight into their vision of the world.

The assumption that art is a "symbolically significant expression" of an artist's worldview is central to Seerveld's aesthetics. "Art is worship," he says, "a consecrated offering, a disconcertingly undogmatic yet terribly moving attempt to bring honor and glory and power to something."[18] Popular art, in part because of its heavy reliance on immediate commercial success, tends to reflect the current cultural mood and trends of society, addressing the preoccupations of people at given moments. This has not escaped the attention of scholars in various fields who have identified certain works of entertainment as uncanny cultural barometers. The late H. R. Rookmaaker, Seerveld's discussion partner at the Free University of Amsterdam, did as much in his study *Modern Art and the Death of a Culture.* He began by examining works of art that belonged to "the great tradition that began in the later middle ages, and ended during the nineteenth century — the period when the new world emerged and modern art slowly took shape." At that point, he included jazz, blues, gospel, and rock music, film, and the Pop and psychedelic art of the 1960s, demonstrating the significance of popular culture for understanding "the general spirit of the age."[19]

An analysis uncovering the worldview that orders the elements of a film, television program, or popular song gives valuable insight into the beliefs, values, fears, and anxieties of those who are called to serve as ambassadors of Christ. Vaudeville theater, for example, reflected the changing values of urban working and middle classes and the rejection of the Victorian mentality. Black rhythm-and-blues fused the frustrations of African-Americans under the oppression of Jim Crow laws with the tempo and sound of the industrial city. The hero of *The Graduate* (1968) became an icon of the social and cultural alienation of the postwar baby boom generation in America; the disco music of *Saturday Night Fever* (1977) expressed the preoccupation with self during the Me Decade. More recently, Oliver Stone's *JFK* became a cinematic metaphor of the search for the truth about American government and practices during the Cold War.

18. Calvin Seerveld, *A Christian Critique of Art and Literature* (Toronto: Association for Reformed Scientific Studies, 1968), p. 28.
19. H. R. Rookmaaker, *Modern Art and the Death of a Culture* (Downers Grove, Ill.: InterVarsity Press, 1970), pp. 9 and 11.

## Christian Art and Cultural Activity

The ultimate aim of Seerveld's "doxological aesthetics" is to encourage the development of "a biblically reforming, wide-open Christian culture, a minority culture in our post-Christian age."[20] His choice of African-American culture in the first half of the twentieth century, which has largely been relegated to an inferior status as popular or folk culture, to illuminate the possibility of Christian culture as a minority culture perhaps best reveals the integrality of aesthetic life for Seerveld. "From the nineteenth-century black spirituals and hollers of the cotton fields to the New Orleans jazz which King Oliver brought North, and from sermon chants of the 1920s on to Gospel song of Ethel Davenport, Mahalia Jackson, and Black churches of the 1940s, there is a rhythmic style, tone, and beat fused with a continuing vision that give black song its own identity that one may . . . call Christian," he writes in *Rainbows*.[21] Here is a group of people who developed enough homogeneity based on racial identity to fashion a distinct cultural tradition manifested in sermons, songs, worship, work, dress, language, humor, poetry, painting, dance, and music. And they did it with extraordinary style, "the allusive, playful, imaginative fabric consistently showing up in someone's or some group's activities," as Seerveld defines it.[22] The African-American style permeates not only specific artistic activities — music, poetry, painting, for example — but can also be seen in the daily activities of life — work, play, language, dress, humor, and flirting. Here is anthropological evidence for the existence of the aesthetic dimension of reality, and further, a manifestation that shows how it is characterized by an allusiveness and style peculiar to a minority culture.

Seerveld envisions as much cultural cohesion for communities of people bonded together by religious convictions as for African-Americans who have established an identity and cultural tradition based on race.[23] The effects of secularization have fragmented our creaturely experience, however, carving it up into sacred and secular, highbrow and lowbrow, distinctions that have intensified cultural conflict and division among God's people. Seerveld claims that art and aesthetic sensibilities ought to be an important and integral aspect of daily life for everyone, and especially for

20. *Turnabout*, p. 20.
21. *Rainbows*, pp. 184-85.
22. "Seerveld's Glossary," a handout he has provided at seminar presentations.
23. See *Rainbows*, p. 186.

Christians who are trying to learn what is pleasing to God in every area of life. He envisions obedient aesthetic life and Christian cultural activity that transform both elite and popular art with a style which is decidedly Christian — as Seerveld puts it, a style "marked by compassionate judgment aware of the world under Jesus Christ's rule."[24] Fairy tales, novels, paintings, movies, music — the sorrows and joys of life are simply told.

Traditional aesthetics has probed the work of art for the personal vision of an artist and for truth and nuanceful insight into some aspect of reality, valuing the unity, harmony, and complexity of a work of art. The aesthetic qualities of popular art are entangled in the values of production and consumption, marketing demographics, the pressure for formulas that will prove successful and can be repeated at the box office, on Top Forty radio, or in a television network's fall lineup. The complexity of the institution of popular art raises many questions that need serious attention. What makes a work popular? How are we to explain the paradoxical relation between aesthetic quality and economic success? What are the determining factors in the relation of content and function to the social institutional structure of commercial art? These aspects of the social and cultural context in which popular art is created and consumed complicate the Christian response; they demand Christian analysis and transformation, and not the simpleminded condemnation religious conservatives have espoused. But relatively little attention has been given to popular culture by Reformed scholars.[25] Seerveld's work gives more than "a couple of unripe figs and fig leaves"[26] for those Christians interested in transforming popular culture, whether through analysis or through vocations in the entertainment industry.

---

24. *Rainbows,* p. 185.

25. One exception to this statement is the book produced by the Calvin Center for Christian Scholarship and titled *Dancing in the Dark: Youth, Popular Culture, and the Electronic Media,* coordinated by Quentin Schultze, edited by Roy Anker (Grand Rapids, Mich.: Eerdmans, 1991).

26. *Rainbows,* p. 105.

# Playful Constellations:
# A Gentle Critique of Calvin Seerveld's
# "Encyclopedia of the Arts"

## JIM LEACH

Nothing seems further from contemporary temper than the delineation of borders among artistic disciplines. Practices such as performance and video; artifacts such as constructions, fiber art, and graphic literature; and fields such as literary theory, cultural studies, and worldview analysis have emerged seemingly just to confound the tried and true distinctions that theorists have worked decades to hone. Are such divisions merely lines drawn in the sand of power politics between artists and theorists? Or worse, are they delusions of star-blind theorists, the retinal after-images from staring too long at the bright Platonic forms? How might a relationship with a personally loving, faithful God affect the consideration of such matters?

This paper will suggest that a theory which flexibly indicates differences among various aesthetic practices and artifacts, one that is as sure-footed and playful as a dance step, can guide and benefit contemporary aesthetic practices, artifact-making, and studies. The groundwork for such a theory, I believe, was laid by Calvin Seerveld in his comments on an "encyclopedia of the arts." Seerveld's "encyclopedia" springs from a tradition of interpreting God's commands as the norming conditions that allow blessing in creation. This tradition imparts a different spirit to theorizing from that found in the deadening pigeonholes of previous, more rationalistic schemata.

However, Seerveld's published remarks on the "encyclopedia" are frustratingly brief: only a few pages from a lecture written over thirty years ago. Since I believe his project to be good work and of strategic importance now, I offer these reflections as a development of what Seerveld called an "encyclopedia of the arts."

## Seerveld's Encyclopedia

Seerveld proposed his model of an encyclopedia of the arts in "Literature among the Arts," a talk given in the early 1960s and later published as the third chapter (pp. 61-93) of *A Christian Critique of Art and Literature*.[1] In this lecture, Seerveld sends out many tantalizing probes into various important matters relating to literature. He begins by establishing the imagination as a mode of knowledge not reducible to scientific knowing or to "naive" experience (pp. 63-72). Literature, as art in language, is also distinguished from clearer, more semantic uses of language; "symbols" are not "signs" (pp. 73-76). Seerveld also devotes a couple of pages to the foundational element of craft in artistic production (pp. 76-80), before proposing his "encyclopedia" under the subtitle "a reasoned spectrum of the arts" (pp. 80-88). He then examines the specific glories of literature, nested in this broad horizon (pp. 88-93). The encyclopedia itself is not Seerveld's focus, rather it is the most substantial of several evocative strokes made to establish the "cosmonomic theater" in which literature exists. This context should be remembered so as not to misunderstand the criticisms I will raise: I am not supplanting Seerveld's theory so much as further exploring the same terrain with the guidance of his wise comments.

Within the pages devoted specifically to the encyclopedia, Seerveld accomplishes three things: he describes the pedigree of the question, presents his own encyclopedia, and examines the examples of dance and poetry to explain what this theory means. Seerveld begins by quickly noting other solutions to the problem of a reasoned spectrum of the arts. Within a

1. Citations will be from the first printing that combined Seerveld's presentations from 1962 and 1963 under the title *A Christian Critique of Art and Literature* (Toronto: Association for Reformed Scientific Studies, 1968). Though this volume has several errors and has been out of print for some time, a fully corrected version is forthcoming.

paragraph he mentions and dismisses the contributions of Friedrich Schlegel ("architecture is frozen music"[2]), Max Schasler (*Systeme der Künste,* 1885), Thomas Munro (*The Arts and Their Interrelations,* 1949), Paul Weiss (*Nine Basic Arts,* 1961), Susanne Langer (*Feeling and Form,* 1953), and Benedetto Croce's dismissal of the whole problem (*Estetica,* 1950). This annotated roster of names suggests that a reasoned spectrum has a valid history as a problem within philosophical aesthetics while it notes no general consensus of method or conclusions. The attempts cited range from Munro's alphabetized list of the names of a hundred arts to Weiss's arrangement around his basic ontology, a triad of space, time, and energy. Having shown his audience that this question is not radically unheard of, Seerveld goes on to posit his own encyclopedia.

This prolegomenal aspect of Seerveld's project, needless to say, is underdeveloped. The overall persuasive appeal of his reasoned spectrum could be greatly bolstered by further systematic and historiographic work. For instance, since pursuit of an "encyclopedia" of knowledge is one of the continuing legacies of the eighteenth century, Seerveld might be criticized for merely adopting and fine-tuning this Enlightenment project rather than affecting a radical reformation of it. To answer this possible charge, a systematically reasoned case for an art encyclopedia could be pursued to fully explicate the distinctive grounding of Seerveld's spectrum. In addition, though I appreciate Seerveld's impulse to "crash the act rather than join it" (p. 82), some work is needed to investigate whether Seerveld's solution can successfully redeem the insights of previous attempts at similar projects.[3] In other words, further work on a reasoned spectrum must not only attempt to collate the art-theory of specific art-kinds but also critically address other attempts at systematic correlations of those theories. Finally, a more his-

2. Though Seerveld does not cite the location of this particular quotation, Schlegel (1771-1829) was probably coining a catchy maxim based on the observation of Friedrich Schelling (1775-1854) that architecture is music solidified in space (*Philosophy of Art,* 1801-1804, §107 & §116).

3. This essay, in fact, grew out of research I did into the *Laocöon* (1766) of Gotthold Ephraim Lessing (1729-1781), an Enlightenment attempt to distinguish poetry from "painting." I had originally intended to show how Seerveld's more comprehensive system can account for the features that Lessing noticed and can set them in the wider sweep of a God-led cosmos. For instance, ironically, in the completed section of the *Laocöon,* Lessing does not establish a firm home for his specific art, drama: it straddles the two realms of poetry and "painting." (Lessing's category of "painting" includes sculpture and should perhaps be understood as "visual arts" in general.)

toriographic legitimation might attempt to date more precisely when comprehensive systems of comparative art theory, even if not explicitly termed "encyclopedia," have been posited, and note what other aesthetic questions are addressed and not addressed in those epochs. In other words, work could be done to see how such theorizing might be affected by the synchronic "period-spirits" discussed by Seerveld in his cartographic methodology.[4] Seerveld's proposed encyclopedia deserves such research to knit it into the intertextual mesh of previous attempts; without such links, his hypothesis might remain unintelligible, even to other aestheticians.

Seerveld's reasoned spectrum of the arts builds on a tradition of theorizing about "modal law-spheres."[5] I find it easiest to explain modal law-spheres and Seerveld's encyclopedia with reference to the philosophy of Herman Dooyeweerd (1894-1977), which extended systematically the societal reflections of Abraham Kuyper (1837-1920). Theories of modal law-spheres try to take account of the reliably guiding presence of God, who established and sustains creation and directs creatures "according to their kind." For Kuyper, working as a political and religious leader, these "kinds" meant that various spheres of society, once differentiated in history, were properly "sovereign" and should resist any attempts to be absorbed by or de-differentiated into other spheres. Kuyper writes in his lecture "Calvinism and Art":

> Religion and Art have each a life-sphere of their own: these may be scarcely distinguishable from each other and therefore closely intertwined, but with a richer development, these two spheres necessarily separate. . . . And so, arrived at their highest development, both Religion and Art demand an independent existence, and the two stems which at first were intertwined and seemed to belong to the same plant, now appear to spring from a root of their own.[6]

4. Seerveld's initial presentation of his art-historical method appears in "Toward a Cartographic Methodology for Art Historiography," *Journal of Aesthetics and Art Criticism* 39 (1980): 143-54.

5. Seerveld writes: "I wonder: if the *theory* of modal law-spheres is not a blank check, if it has cash value, if it is indeed getting theoretically at the way our God's creation is set up; since it has afforded Christian insight, it seems to me, into the order of the sciences, shown the rightful, richly integrated, fallible, and relative human service of the various special sciences; could not an encyclopedia of the arts be attempted, openly pendent from the same fruitful principle?" p. 82.

6. Abraham Kuyper, *Lectures on Calvinism* (Grand Rapids, Mich.: Wm. B. Eerd-

Dooyeweerd's theory of irreducibly distinct "modes" developed reflection on these "kinds" into an ontology that would account for such "sphere sovereignty."

It would be incorrect to stop there, since creation is not a rag-tag assemblage of creatures of various kinds; rather creation as a whole has a coherence within itself whereby it stands in subjection to our Creator. This interrelational aspect of creation, I believe, appears in Dooyeweerd as "sphere universality," the idea that within any sovereign sphere all other spheres still appear and impinge. Accordingly, Dooyeweerd developed a theory of "modal analogies," stating that within any irreducible mode all other modes are present analogously. In these ways, the tradition of theorizing about what Seerveld calls "modal law-spheres," based on biblical insight, tries to do justice to both the overall coherence of creation and the particular integrity of various creatural kinds.

In applying this theory of modal law-spheres to the classification of the arts, Seerveld states what might be an hypothesis behind every attempt at an encyclopedia of the arts: "every art betrays a localized turn to its structure" (p. 84). The Reformational tradition has given the project a firm ontological map to "localize" the specific core moments that different arts may take as their window on reality. Seerveld compiles these suggestions into a table (Figure 1). Such a table is predicated on a feature of the modal scale, that the modes themselves can be ordered, along the axis of increasing complexity, such that later modes (those higher up) are less foundational than earlier ones (lower down.) This quality of the modal scale must be noted to forestall, if not dispel, suspicions that the chart contains an implicit hierarchy. These suspicions are well founded in other attempts at an ordering of the arts, perhaps especially in historicistic ones, where lower arts are superseded by higher ones.[7] With this arrangement, however, the danger of special pleading is avoided, since no particular honor is attached to occupying any one modal slot.[8]

---

mans), p. 148. Kuyper's use of "religion" in this quotation should not be taken to mean that religion as a world-and-life-view ("Weltanschauung") is irrelevant to art. His project in the Stone Lectures, rather, is to distinguish "religion" in the narrow sense of a societal sphere from the life-embracing perspective of historical Calvinism.

7. The swooping categories of sculpture, architecture, poetry found in the *Aesthetics* of G. W. F. Hegel (1770-1831) come to mind, where each form is transcended ("aufgehoben") by a subsequent form more perfect for the time.

8. Those who suspect that a "Christian" theory of the arts should necessarily privilege

| theology | confessional (belief) | poetry |
|---|---|---|
| ethics | ethical (troth) | song |
| jurisprudence | jural (right) | drama |
| economics | economic (thrift) | typography * |
| sociology | social (intercourse) | ——— |
| logic | analytic (distinguishment) | dialectic |
| linguistics | semantic (clarity) | rhetoric |
| aesthetics | aesthetic (suggestion) | ——— |
| technology | technical (form) | architecture |
| psychology | psychic (sensitivity) | painting |
| biology | bio-organic (life) | dance |
| physics | physical (energy) | sculpture |
| mathematics | mathematical (movement) | music |
| ——— | spatial (continuity) | ——— |
| ——— | numerical (discreteness) | drawing |
| **Corpus of human sciences** | **From a theory of the various prime ways things are** | **Proposal toward an encyclopedia of the arts** |

* Chart from Seerveld, *A Christian Critique of Art and Literature,* p. 83. Seerveld added "typography" in a handwritten note to column 3 in his own copy of the book.

FIGURE 1.   **Seerveld's Proposed Encyclopedia of the Arts**

Seerveld presents his chart with several carefully specified directions for proper use. These may be summarized in a general warning: this is *theory* — use only as directed. That is, this tidy scheme is how a theorist, operating within the analytic mode of behavior (since only within that mode does the modal scale as modal scale present itself), sees the arts: this is not necessarily how the arts experience each other. And since the modal

confessional arts should consult Seerveld's "A Tin-Can Theory of Man," where he distinguishes between an inner faith and the collective corporate confession of that faith. This inner faith bleeds out, as it were, through all the ways we are, not only and not necessarily best in the modally confessional way. See Calvin Seerveld, "A Tin-Can Theory of Man," *Journal of the American Scientific Affiliation* 33 (June 1981): 74-81.

scale that provides the principle of division is a spectrum of kinds of calls and responses, not carved niches, not entitary "modalities," these windows are not the rigid pigeonholes that Seerveld perceives in Lessing's *Laocöon*.

My slight criticism of Seerveld's reasoned spectrum as depicted here stems from a different emphasis in its grounding rationale. Seerveld indicates that his table builds primarily upon the theory of modal differences, that is, of sphere sovereignty (p. 83). The different art-kinds, for Seerveld, must exhibit a rounded-off character similar to an irreducible sphere, and hence resist any conflation with each other. (Understanding an art-kind as irreducible to another kind, however, does not necessarily imply stasis, since even sovereign spheres behave historically.) Based on this notion that artistic disciplines possess a certain degree of identifiable, necessary integrity, Seerveld's "encyclopedia" arranges a systematic correlation of these building blocks.

However, when compared with other types of artifacts and practices, products of the various art-kinds have much more in common than is appropriate for the results of irreducibly different disciplines. This relative commonality suggests to me that reference to both the theory of modal analogies as well as the theory of modal distinctions is necessary to grasp the genius of Seerveld's reasoned spectrum. Within the societal sphere of the art world (just as within the wider class of aesthetic phenomena), a variety of aesthetic behaviors appear, just as within any modality there are a plethora of modal analogies. But Seerveld instead appeals to the doctrine of modal analogies only to account for the variety of elements within a given art-kind. For instance, theater involves an orchestrated totality of character, diction, staging, etc. under the lead of a plot. I would suggest that, though the subject matter of the "encyclopedia" is based on sphere sovereignty (since only arts are considered), the doctrine of modal analogies should allow the qualities of other irreducible modes to provide insight into how the arts could be ordered within the artistic sphere.

Let me restate the relative insignificance of my disagreement. Granted, it is good work to map systematically the sovereign sphere of the arts, the societally delimited and sanctioned space where aesthetic matters are allowed to predominate. In this task, I too believe a modal arrangement is a valid way of interpreting and continuing the Reformational legacy in considering the question of a reasoned spectrum of the arts as it arises in philosophical aesthetics.[9] My only concern is that by emphasizing modal

9. Earlier in this lecture (p. 66f.), Seerveld criticizes on methodological grounds

differences as the ground of this table, which undeniably contributes a principle for explaining the variety of art-kinds, Seerveld overestimates the irreducibility of each art-kind.

Seerveld concludes his direct comments on an encyclopedia with a description of two arts to indicate some of the "analytic bite" of his theory. He examines poetry and dance as art forms.[10] Instead of examining those examples, let me propose a similar account of the modal "window" of an art with which I am more familiar, namely, drama.

In determining modal analogies, Dooyeweerd suggests that the interlocking coherence to reality is present even within the way we speak, with scientific precision, about various phenomena.[11] Various concepts that are important to understanding a given realm are phrased in analogies such as "legal fictions" or, more contemporarily, "cyberspace." According to Dooyeweerd, these phrases suggest phenomena that are analogous between the modes involved. The realm of the arts is rife with these kinds of analogical phrases, for instance, a painting's "rhythm" or the notion of "poetic justice."

Drama, by which I mean the plotted scheme that is often written down, seems to bank heavily on "poetic justice." We call something dramatic that is suspenseful, where anticipations have been piqued to expect and desire a result from some action. In a drama's plot, these dramatic moments are organized in a series so that one dramatic question is answered by another, usually by one with even more significance in the world of the drama. In this

---

another attempt at such a reasoned spectrum from within the Reformational tradition, Hans Rookmaaker's "Ontwerp ener Aesthetica," *Philosophia Reformata* 11, no. 3-4 (1946). Rookmaaker's system picks up Dooyeweerd's distinction between phenotypes and genotypes to ascertain art-kinds.

10. I question the continuing validity of Seerveld's comments concerning what he calls "social" dance "where a deep kind of erotic rhythm persists under the blunted, secularized surface of a current twist or fox trot," p. 85. (At the time these comments were made, remember, dance was still forbidden to proper Reformed persons.) Granted, popular dance may not have the societally-sanctioned status of "art," but perhaps everyday dance could be seen, in one of its moments, as an aesthetic responding-in-kind to the mathematically-proportioned rhythm of certain music.

11. Dooyeweerd writes: "It will be clear why the ambiguity in the pre-scientific use of terms does not concern us in this context. Our inquiry exclusively refers to the modal structures of meaning. Pre-theoretical experience does not explicitly distinguish the modal aspects as such; it conceives them only implicitly within the typical total structures of individuality. Therefore pre-theoretical terms are not the subject of our present inquiry." Herman Dooyeweerd, *A New Critique of Theoretical Thought*, 4 vols. (Jordan Station, Ontario: Paideia Press, 1983), vol. 2, p. 61.

way, suspense is strung along and intensified. At the climax of a play, the plot must snap shut: the dramatic question, asked at the play's attack, must be answered definitively in a way consonant with the story's development; the world order troubled at the play's beginning is re-established, though sometimes not without substantial re-alignment. Consequently, characters seem to get what is coming to them, based on their behavior in the context of the plot. If its magic involves crafting this poetic justice, then drama, the art of the playwright in Western culture,[12] may provide a jural "window" onto the aesthetic nuance of creation. Similarly, an aesthetic analogy within the jural might be "courtroom drama," where the exciting suspense implicit in applying a law to a given case unfolds inexorably toward a judgment, a suspense some trial lawyers exploit to great rhetorical effect.

There is really not much more to Seerveld's explanation than the three areas summarized above. Like a guerrilla, Seerveld makes a bold and evocative strike, then disappears to hit other targets. Seerveld's encyclopedia is one tactical challenge, I feel, that deserves reinforcement. My criticisms and revisions of Seerveld's spectrum revolve mostly around two points: that it apparently attempts to be an "encyclopedia," and that it encloses only the "arts."

## Artistic Constellation

Seerveld refers to his project as both a "reasoned spectrum of the arts" (in the heading to the section) and as an "encyclopedia of the arts" (the title on the chart). The second name mimics the encyclopedia of the special sciences, a contribution of Dooyeweerd's modal scale to interdisciplinary understanding that Seerveld applauds.[13] However, certain connotations of

12. I am not prepared to claim that drama is the most important component even in Western theater. Richard Schechner perceptively places "drama" within the context of "theater," "performance," and "script." Schechner uses these four related foci to examine both artistic and ritual events from various cultures. He notes pithily: "The drama is the domain of the author, the composer, scenarist, shaman; the script is the domain of the teacher, guru, master; the theater is the domain of the performers; the performance is the domain of the audience." "Drama, Script, Theater and Performance," in *Performance Theory* (New York and London: Routledge, 1988), p. 71.

13. Seerveld has a brief discussion of Dooyeweerd's arrangement of the special sciences in his article "Dooyeweerd's Legacy for Aesthetics," in *The Legacy of Herman Dooyeweerd: Reflections on Critical Philosophy in the Christian Tradition*, ed. C. T. McIntire (Lanham, Md.: University Press of America, 1985), pp. 41-79, esp. 44-46.

the term "encyclopedia" make me feel uneasy when it is applied to the arts. A "reasoned spectrum" seems a much better phrase for the project under consideration. In this section, I will clarify and describe my problems with an artistic "encyclopedia" and then suggest "constellation" as a better synonym for a "reasoned spectrum."

First, my problem is not that Seerveld's project is "encyclopedic": it is the limited glory of theorizing to encircle phenomena within definitions that indicate their boundaries and interrelations with the rest of creation. To mark ontic boundaries is a properly human task; to establish those boundaries is divine creation, an accomplishment that has, thankfully, already been provided for us. Humanist philosophy mistakes these tasks, confusing ontological rules given in theory with the ontic regularities given by God. Despite such confusion, I believe that reasoning, defining, and theorizing, when kept humble before the face of God, remain valid avenues for praise and service to the Creator.

Second, I am not claiming, as some do, that the arts are somehow particularly beyond the grasp of analysis. Many who argue that aesthetic products are uniquely intractable to definition attempt to compensate for the apparent ubiquity of rational order by construing art as a realm of almost chaotic inspiration beyond lawful regularity. As a critique of rationalism, such an understanding has not gone far enough; the full meaning of all non-conceptual phenomena (and even the fullest meaning of concepts) expresses the dependable providence of God, not the ordered necessity of logic. Even though aesthetic products accent connotation, playfulness, and allusion, they can serve adequately as the object of philosophical reflection if the purpose is to get a theory. The problem I am addressing in this section occurs when the fruit of such an encyclopedic inquiry into the arts becomes an encyclopedia.

Third, I am not entirely rejecting the category of encyclopedia. An encyclopedia is fully appropriate and practical for the principial sciences, that is, for fields whose subject matter is conceptually delimited, such as modal psychology or modal aesthetics. An encyclopedia of such sciences could order and correlate the various projects implied by a larger ontological basis, insuring, for instance, that no valid areas are overlooked. An encyclopedia, since it roots the daisy chain of more specific projects in the conceptual implications of an ontology, has the limited mandate of proclaiming: Let there be research in the following areas. . . .

However, not all valid sciences are called forth by such an encyclopedia;

in addition to principial sciences, another range of analytic inquiries could be called entitary sciences, or those which investigate relatively specific creatural types. Beyond modal aesthetic theory, a rich and ongoing field itself, most analyses of aesthetic matters and those of art-kinds in particular are more properly considered entitary rather than principial investigations. Entitary sciences depend for their coherence on the identifiable regularities and character of the phenomena they study; this coherence cannot be assured conceptually, as by an encyclopedia, since that would be to mistake the ordering of theory with the order of creation.

This conceptual quibble may become more tangible with an image. My experience of an encyclopedia is as a set of books, a summary of vast knowledge indexed alphabetically. The encyclopedia in the house where I grew up had been purchased at great expense by my parents. It filled an entire shelf with its thick volumes, bound in imitation leather, richly il-lustrated, reeking of erudition. I could sit, legs akimbo, in that hallway and pleasantly page through the very warp and weft of creation, it seemed. Generals, insects, countries . . . all could be researched by looking up a key word. At the end of each entry was a list of words in bold-face type which could lead to entries about other, related phenomena. To my young mind, it seemed that everything one needed to know could be found easily on these pages.

Let me relate this image to my problem with an encyclopedia of the arts. The "localized turn" of each prime art that Seerveld spoke of suggests a leather-bound casing that binds together apparently disparate pages into a coherent volume. Imagine a collection of such books, each of which comprehensively treats a "prime" art: theater, painting, sculpture, etc. An encyclopedist of the arts must edit the contents of these books and arrange the various volumes on one shelf, perhaps compiling an index of the less explicit interrelations.

However, when I pick up the volume whose spine bears the gold em-bossed letters "theater," I am struck at how the book threatens to fall apart. The pages that are bound into the spine are filled with vague comments about the barest minimum requirements of theater across its great and varied history. Reading them reveals more the rough permutations of an ontology than perceptive observations about how theater relates to the other arts. To supplement these notes, many sheets filled with examples from particular theater pieces have been inserted between the pages. The comments on these sheets are varied; the leaves that most snugly fit between the pages contain material pruned to rarefied examples which perfectly express the relevant theory; other sheets feature more vivid descriptions capturing the particularity of the artworks considered, but some of these sheets almost fall to the floor when the volume is opened. Regardless, these interpolated pages have weakened the binding, loosening even some of the original sheets. Upon further inspection, the pages of every volume in this encyclopedia threaten to come loose from their cases, both the inserted examples as well as the original comments. Viewed from their spines, this encyclopedia is an impressively ordered collection; viewed from the other side, from the pages closest to the particular arts, they spill out, leaving the casings hollow.

Let me juxtapose another image with this exploding encyclopedia. Imagine instead a very large wooden desk, the top of which is strewn with papers, in places over a dozen sheets thick, written on a variety of paper stocks. At first the pages seem too slovenly placed to be in discrete piles; some of the pages even seem to be in more than one pile! Apparently the scholar has stepped out for a moment and left the work in progress. After a moment of impatient waiting, we gain the courage to examine a pile, which happens to treat theater. On each sheet is a pithy comment, observing some aspect of theater in contemporary society. Reading down through the whole stack of pages (and skimming the sheets that lay across this pile and another), we gain an idea of what theater means in this society. The comments, none remarkable on their own, acquire a coherence by their context in the stack. Now, if we squint when we look at the table, a pattern emerges of both the interrelations between the arranged texts and the gaps where the naked table shows through. Sounds of the scholar's approach make us cease our investigations.

The messy desk I have sketched above presents another image of a "reasoned spectrum" of the arts, one that could hardly be called an "encyclopedia" yet which might better be termed a "constellation."[14] I will note

14. "Constellation," as I use it in this paper, should significantly recall the "constellations" of Walter Benjamin (1892-1940) and Theodor Adorno (1903-1969). I borrow their word to evoke systematic thinking that is intrinsically respectful of the nontheoretical nature of its objects. On this point, Benjamin notes: "Ideas are to objects as constellations are to stars." *The Origin of German Tragic Drama,* trans. John Osborne (London: London, 1977), p. 34. Adorno also writes: "The constellation illuminates the specific side of the object, the side which to a classifying procedure is either a matter of indifference or a burden." *Negative Dialectics,* trans. E. B. Ashton (New York: Continuum, 1973), p. 162.

three aspects of this constellation: as research it is ordered, critical, and ongoing.

The constellation spread out across the table is ordered in three dimensions. First, only arts, the products of a particular societal sphere, are examined. Second, the various arts are separated, to the degree that they possess an identifiable difference. Third, within each art, the comments are arranged according to a modal ontology. Since art-kinds are general but not conceptual, their modal qualities can at best only suggest their distinctive character; they do not possess an historically immutable "essence" to slip peacefully within a definition. Nor is an art-kind's character grasped by a description only of its societal role. A constellation must describe the character of individual art-kinds by relating them to the character of the sphere of the arts in general, in addition to arranging notable observations of their modal behavior.

In contrast to an encyclopedia, a constellation must treat aspects of the arts that are not purely aesthetic, since the distinctive character of an art-kind often importantly involves extra-aesthetic facets. For instance, Abraham Kuyper, in the lecture cited earlier, comments about theater, explaining why it ranks among the sins proscribed by Calvinism. Kuyper is careful not to rule out fictive depictions; he approves of Milton's work, and Milton must have been familiar with Shakespeare's work. Kuyper's critique centers on the immorality historically associated with the theater, though he notes that theater might have had a different character in ancient times when women were not allowed on stage. One could transcribe the content of Kuyper's comments scholastically, flogging the largely dead horse of live theater and declaring "Christian theater" a demonic oxymoron. One could also reduce Kuyper's proscription to its context, branding it the outmoded prudishness of an earlier, less enlightened generation, caution that we have outgrown. However, the character of theater, even today, contains a continuing deposit from such moral evaluations.[15] Where a definitionally based encyclopedia might ignore such non-aesthetic phenomena, the perceived immorality of theater practitioners would be intrinsically important to a constellation, not taking a back seat to formal analysis.

An artistic constellation also has a critical focus. The observations noted

---

15. Though a critique of theater based on the participation of women might sound alien to our ears today, a continuing suspicion of theater, also based on supposedly moral grounds, notes the apparently high proportion of homosexuals involved in theater.

in a constellation are arranged modally. Modal analysis, applied in this manner, implicitly values practices and artifacts that are diversely enriched to the fullest extent allowed by their qualifying identity. The modal arrangement of observations in a constellation implies criticism both through explicit comments and their significant omission. Art-kinds can deviate from their richest normative glory both when particular aspects are underdeveloped as well as when they are cluttered with exaggerated elements. An overdeveloped aspect suggests that the art-kind is overcompensating for a relative thinness in another art-kind or elsewhere in society. The constellation of art-kinds, used in this manner, can be a diagnostic and prescriptive tool for cultural as well as artistic criticism.

Oscar Kristeller's 1951 article "A Modern System of the Arts" provides a foil to this critical function of a constellation. Both Kristeller's system and my proposed constellation are historically sensitive. Kristeller shows how the modern (i.e., eighteenth-century) understanding of the five prime arts ("painting, sculpture, architecture, music, and poetry . . . the irreducible nucleus of the modern system of the arts, on which all writers and thinkers seem to agree") has jelled relatively recently. Kristeller, though, attempts to be as innocently descriptive as a lexicon, basing his descriptions on history rather than ontology. An ontologically directed, historically-sensitive correlation, a constellation, would always have another layer to it: not only saying "this is how it is" but also "this and that is how it should be."[16]

Finally, a constellation is an ongoing project that never has the finality of an encyclopedia. An art-kind's character (and hence the overall character of the interrelating sphere of the arts) does not have the necessary, logical quality of concepts derived purely from an ontology. This lack of finality does not, however, mean that the results of a constellation are never definite. Rather, the character of the artworld, for instance, will be changed (one hopes, improved) with every constellation published. Results of constellation research are constantly reportable, and their definitive effects continually affect rearrangement of the arts: there is no reason for shame that such work is never finished.

16. This critical facet, I believe, will appear even when a constellation sketches non-contemporary society, for much of an art-kind's contemporary cultural meaning includes residue from its past meaning. A constellation even retains its critical edge when it depicts a radically alien culture, since much of the concrete future of cultural practices, like art-kinds, depends upon practices that can be tangibly imagined.

## Genres, Proto-Arts, and Anti-Arts

If one range of problems surrounds the fact that a reasoned spectrum seemed to be an encyclopedia, another kind of objection involves its treatment of the arts. Three relatively distinct problems arise from the spectrum's subject matter, involving specifically what can be included or excluded from consideration. The first concern questions the relation of genre to prime art; the second prompts consideration of aesthetic practices that are not societally sanctioned as arts (what could be called "proto-arts"); and the third involves artistic practices directed at modifying the societal niche of the arts (what could be termed, broadly speaking, "anti-arts").

The relation of prime art to the genres possible and present within that art troubles a constellation more than an encyclopedia. More accurately, it is not a concern for Seerveld, who explicitly excludes all genre-talk from his encyclopedia:

> Nota bene: I am not talking about genres. . . . I am inclined to view the sonnet, waltz, farce and sonata as professionally adopted manners adopted and finally accepted by society with no ontical significance or inviolate aesthetical laws to them, recognizing that genres typify the *Zeitgeist* of their originating age and carry along loosely its confining traditions. But I am after something more fundamental yet restricted than genre catalogization here in hope of ordering without organizing and illuminating without distorting prime modes of imaginative symbolical objectification. (p. 82)

This exclusion is problematic because the meaning of an art depends on the genres practiced within it at a given time. "Theater" means something different in, say, eighteenth-century Paris, where mainly tragedies were performed, than in late twentieth-century New York, where live theater often means large-scale musicals. No reasoned spectrum of the *arts* can afford to ignore such basic differences.

However, Seerveld's last sentence shows a way out of this conundrum. He is after the "prime modes of imaginative symbolical objectification." The criticism mentioned above only holds if Seerveld is arranging the various arts. Here, Seerveld suggests a much different project than a reasoned spectrum of the arts. A catalogue of prime imaginative modes is indeed also good work, work which could be fittingly placed in an encyclopedia. It is a proper task of modal aesthetic theory. (Since constellations are modally arranged, such a handbook would be a great tool in the task of constructing constellations.) However, it is illegitimate, I believe, to conflate an ordered list of these prime imaginative modes with the historically varied practices of the arts. Faced with what I see as mutually enriching interplay among the arts, I am compelled to disagree with Seerveld: no art perfectly captures a single prime mode; there are no "prime" arts. To suggest that there are confuses the norming conditions that provide coherence and blessing to various creatural kinds with the logical sequence of ontological thought. Seerveld, it seems, must decide whether he is describing an encyclopedia of analogies within the aesthetic mode, or a reasoned spectrum of the arts. From my perspective, his project is the former.

Even if a constellation refuses to divide ephemeral and essential aspects in the arts, another perhaps more serious objection arises from the relative specificity of its resulting subject matter. Both Seerveld and I would treat the arts, but I base my study more on the societal sphere of the arts, rather than on a purely ontological grounding. Consequently, a constellation seems only capable of dealing with societies in which the arts have achieved the status of a relatively sovereign sphere. In other words, constellations could only be properly construed, apparently, for European-influenced societies after, say, the eighteenth century. Before that time, it could be argued, no artistic realm existed with a sovereign character.

The cultural specificity of an artistic constellation, I admit, is a serious, though not ultimately disabling objection. Granted: the term "art" has acquired a different meaning since the cultural practices of the arts came into their own: one might even say that in pre-"modern" societies, there was no "art" in exactly the sense we understand it now as an autonomously aesthetic phenomenon. This distinction has great bearing on questions like whether statues from a Greek temple "belong" in a museum or whether the semi-liturgical tropes of early medieval drama can now be performed as theater. But despite the lack of a consolidated realm for aesthetic behavior, non-"modern" societies had elements that were playful, allusive, etc. In other words, creative aesthetic phenomena are not the exclusive invention of the "modern" era. Even now, the realm of the arts does not exhaust aesthetic practice.[17] If the constellation of the arts described earlier is a messy desk, much valid aesthetic activity occurs, as it were, under the table.

---

17. Seerveld has long been a defender of the aesthetic aspects of everyday life. See "Obedient Aesthetic Life," in *Rainbows for the Fallen World* (Toronto: Tuppence Press, 1980), pp. 42-76.

Much of what is termed "popular culture," for instance, occurs under the table of accepted artistic practice and might be addressed as proto-art.[18] I freely admit that these "proto-arts" might only be related with difficulty to a constellation of the arts, since the character of "arts" and "proto-arts" would tend to be radically different, at least concerning societal autonomy.

Another "constellation" could be constructed, for a given period, not of the arts but of less autonomous aesthetic practices. With Seerveld's encyclopedia of prime aesthetic windows as a guidebook, a search could be made throughout a culture to discern phenomena behaving according to the various aesthetic windows. Having identified which modal foci each activity participates in, these practices could be arranged in a constellation as well. An aesthetic constellation, admittedly, might not have the same coherence as an artistic constellation, due to the widely scattered origin of its subjects as compared to the cohesion of art products.

Though difficult, relations can be sketched between the practices of the aesthetic constellation and those of the artistic constellation. I take as a premise that a healthy society must function aesthetically in all prime aesthetic moments, whether that functioning occurs via a consolidated, distinctly aesthetic sphere, such as the arts, or through a dispersed variety of activities with enhanced aesthetic aspects. I suggested as much when I noted that over- or underdeveloped aspects in the arts might indicate compensatory behavior for other parts of society. In order that our aesthetic life not be famished or cancerous, particularly in "modern" societies, it is important to examine this delicate interplay of aesthetic and artistic practices.

In the present century, at least, another class of aesthetic practices has risen to importance, practices that cannot easily be called arts. In fact, these practices direct themselves to challenging, if not dismantling, the societal structures of high art, and have often been dubbed "anti-art." Though genuinely art historical analysis can and should be directed to such anti-art,

---

18. Defined modally, much popular culture is merchandise: that is, economically qualified objects, manipulated within the sphere of the marketplace, intended for private consumption. As such, popular culture lacks the public quality of access implied by a societally autonomous art. For example, comic books are only rarely available in libraries, hence to be read they first must be bought. Their nature as scarce commodity often militates against their consideration as literature; the X-men are more likely to be collected than read. However, for good or ill, much of how we "play" in the twentieth century is mediated through merchandise and, though such play is related to consumption, aesthetic interaction per se ultimately cannot be reduced to economic trade. An adequate analysis of popular culture, though, must address at least both these facets.

the products of such anti-generic impulses offer a particular conundrum to theorists, especially those concerned about a reasoned spectrum of the arts. What makes these provocative guerrilla pieces so intractable to traditional analysis is that they often employ the trappings and authority of high art to show how the pronouncements of high art are not to be trusted.

An example of such uneasy artistry is the theater work of Heiner Müller (b. 1929). Müller was, at least before reunification, the most widely produced living German playwright and a citizen of East Germany. In his works, Müller often borrows and reworks images and characters from German stage history. Hence Müller's plays are not fully intelligible to those unfamiliar with this legacy. But rather than continuing this rich tradition, Müller's project is to end it: he calls himself "the last German playwright."[19] This apocalyptic project does not mean that he writes badly; he writes with great skill and poetry, but in a way that deeply disrupts the institution of theater.[20] For Müller, dismantling theater has a strongly ethical drive, to destroy these enchanted spots called the arts where special privileges are extended beyond the reach of other, more mundane workers.[21]

Anti-arts present a challenge to the project of a reasoned spectrum of the arts, a challenge I believe a constellation can meet. Though examples of "anti-arts" can probably be found that employ any given art-kind as a means, it is a mistake to identify an "anti-art" as existing "within" an art-kind. With our metaphor of the constellation as a cluttered table, "anti-artworks" seem to focus on discerning the shape of the table, sometimes with the intention of sawing off portions. If a constellation of non-artistic aesthetic practices was needed to better understand "proto-arts," perhaps "anti-arts" are better understood when the arts are seen in the full context of other spheres which provide societal sanction for the autonomy of the arts. The full societal matrix for the arts at any point in a society is necessary to determine the authenticity of an anti-artist's critique. Though "anti-art"

19. In an interview after re-unification published as "Winds," Müller laughed nervously when asked: "Do you think you might be, after all, not the last German writer, as you claimed, but the last East German writer?" Heiner Müller, *Germania* (New York: Semiotext[e], 1990), p. 96.

20. "The first preoccupation I have when I write is to destroy things. For thirty years Hamlet was a real obsession for me, so I tried to destroy him by writing a short text, *Hamletmachine*." Müller, *Germania*, pp. 55-56.

21. In an earlier interview in the volume cited above, Müller laconically notes: "Talent is the first privilege and the next privilege is to use it." Müller, *Germania*, p. 29.

offers, at least potentially, a deeply prophetic critique of the self-legitimating artworld, in the hands of false prophets it becomes coy self-referentiality, a dandy parodic decadence squandering its critique on mere effect.

It would appear, then, that to discern the difference between authentic anti-art and its decadent simulation, a complete set of societal constellations would be necessary which map the entire range of cultural practices in a given society. If a constellation required explicit definition, this perception would be correct; only when all societal relations had been explicitly articulated could critique begin. However, since concrete realities like arts and "anti-arts" are not themselves identical with their conceptual descriptions, their character must be defined so as to retain their non-identical particularity. By presenting this definition in a constellation, as I understand it, one can describe the character of a practice as much by suggestive omission as by direct utterance. The flexible pattern of speech and silence in a constellation allows it, I believe, to address adequately the societal impact of anti-arts, even without reference to a comprehensive map of a society. The character inferred from a constellational definition might in that way be holographic, in the sense that even a fragment of a holograph contains a picture of the whole.

From *Ubu Roi* (1896) of Alfred Jarry (1873-1907) to *HamletMachine* (1977) by Heiner Müller, much intriguing work produced this century has been openly and explicitly "anti-art." In large part the impact of anti-art banks on transgressing the societal role of art. A constellation offers a way to pursue the insights of anti-art, I argue, since it assays the character of an anti-art, both its structure as well as its stance.

With his suggestion of a modally arranged "encyclopedia of the arts," Seerveld has firmly laid a stone, not the cornerstone of an edifice, but a paving stone to give sure footing down a long and evocative trail. In this essay I have tried to lay another block along that path by developing Seerveld's remarks into a project that can address contemporary emphases on interdisciplinary studies and practices. I began by suggesting that two facets of Seerveld's original meditation are inadequate to the contemporary challenge: the final a-historicity of an "encyclopedia," and the narrowed scope of addressing only "arts." But Seerveld's modally arranged art spectrum overcomes these problems if interpreted along slightly different lines. My reflections have been guided, as I believe Seerveld's own project was, by a deep realization that only through meditating upon and following God's ordinances can true, fruitful shalom be achieved in our aesthetic life as in our entire walk with the Creator.

55

# Sorties into Cyberspace:
# Art and Electronic Technologies

## MARY LEIGH MORBEY

In *A Turnabout in Aesthetics to Understanding* Calvin Seerveld challenges Christians to be forthright, scandalous, humble, and open in their aesthetics.[1] His call suggests the need for Christian leadership and scholarship in the development of aesthetics, art history, and art criticism, not only in the traditional arts but also in the contemporary interdisciplinary marriage of art and electronic technologies, and specifically in the area of computer-related art. This essay will point out difficulties with art critical analysis and art historical categorization of computer-related art. The work of artist Harold Cohen will be used as a case study to illustrate the difficulties. Further, I will show how Seerveld's cartographic methodology for art historiography fails to address the Cohen problem, and I will begin to map out an alternative approach for understanding art making that employs electronic, computer-based technologies.[2] My concluding comments will identify new challenges in the contemporary milieu for Christian scholars engaged in art criticism and art history.

---

1. Calvin Seerveld, *A Turnabout in Aesthetics to Understanding* (Toronto: Institute for Christian Studies, 1974), p. 21.
2. During the last few years Calvin Seerveld and I have had an ongoing discussion concerning how his present cartographic methodology might give a place to contemporary electronically-based visual arts. Section five of this essay, "Seerveld's Cartography in a Postmodern Shift," is a continuation of that exchange.

# The Problem

The contemporary interactions of art, science, and technology, and in particular recent developments in computer-related arts occur outside the parameters of the canon of Western art history and its aesthetic concerns. Current discourse that is pushing to expand the established boundaries of art history, for example in the areas of multiculturalism, the environment, and race, class, and gender concerns, also has not warmly embraced computer-based visual arts that employ electronic technologies.

This cool response is understandable because computer graphics developed in the mid 1960s for scientific purposes. The first graphic accomplishments were produced by scientists, mathematicians, and engineers who had access to powerful mainframe computers and the expert knowledge necessary to use them to produce visual imagery.[3] Ben F. Laposky's "oscillions" or "electronic abstractions," created in 1950, are considered the first graphic imagery generated by an electronic machine.[4] The technology that brought about computer graphics was originally produced for aerospace research, and was further developed by the military for surveillance and by industry for the design and manufacture of airplanes and automobiles. Later the textile and printing industries used computer graphic techniques for specific artistic applications, and now these tools, along with advances in telecommunications, have become available on a broader scale to the artist.[5] Thus, the interactivity of art making and the computer originated from scientific research and found its early manifestation in computer science computer graphics, rather than within the traditions of the visual arts.

Much computer-based imagery has come from computer scientists who understand the technology and not the art making. This has resulted in a low quality of art production and a negative reputation for computer-related art.[6] In contrast to the body of weak computer-related art produced

---

3. Cynthia Goodman, *Digital Visions: Computers and Art* (New York: Abrams, 1987), p. 18.

4. Douglas Davis, *Art and the Future* (New York: Praeger, 1973), p. 98.

5. Darcy Gerbarg, a traditionally trained artist who uses the computer for art making, discusses the recent historical development of such use in Sue Dunlap, *The Computer as an Artistic Tool* (Greenwich, Conn.: The Friends of the Greenwich Library, 1986), p. 1.

6. The descriptive terms "computer-related art" and "computer-based arts" differ

by computer scientists and programmers, a small group of traditionally trained fine artists, having already made a reputation for excellent work in more traditional media, have succeeded in generating strong computer imagery. Three notable examples are American Charles Csuri (b. 1922), Englishman Harold Cohen (b. 1928), and Dutchman Peter Struycken (b. 1939). These early pioneers hold in common nuanced knowledge and expertise in both art making and computer science. In addition to these artists, well-trained younger artists continue to experiment with contemporary computer technology. A few of these, experimenting with computer-based "virtual reality," have made headway in the arena of cyberspace, the name given to the vast network of computers and communication lines.[7]

Cyberspace, a world foreign to many contemporary art makers, is a space native to electronic technologies and telecommunications. The word cyber, from the Greek word *kybernan,* meaning to steer, guide, or govern, suggests a space steered by electronic technologies. Computer-based cyberspace does not parallel sea space nor air space, for it moves beyond the tangible world that we know; it is a new phenomenon. The ancient concept of a transmission of common beliefs and practices that unite people who are physically separated[8] is manifested again in our late twentieth century culture through any computer linked to transcontinental telecommunications systems. For example, through electronic mail linked into the international Internet system, an academic located at a university in Toronto

---

from the category of "computer art," which historically has become the label for most art made on the computer and carries a negative connotation. The phrases "computer-related art" and "computer-based arts" refer specifically to the art production of trained fine artists who employ the computer for art making. Historically, most art made on the computer has come to receive negative criticism, for it falls under one rubric. A distinction in terminology delineates the categories and thereby makes possible a careful critique of work produced by trained fine artists who employ electronic technologies, and specifically the computer, for their art making.

7. For a more thorough introduction to the concept of cyberspace see Michael Benedikt, Introduction, *Cyberspace: First Steps* (Cambridge, Mass.: MIT Press, 1992), pp. 1-25. The Internet telecommunications system for academics and Compuserve system for international business persons enable continual, cross-continental discussion in cyberspace. For example, for those working in the area of computers and the fine arts, there is a series of networks carrying interactive deliberations on developing concepts and contemporary concerns that one can join at any time.

8. Allucquere Rosanne Stone, "Will the Real Body Please Stand Up?: Boundary Stories about Virtual Cultures," in Michael Benedikt, ed., *Cyberspace: First Steps* (Cambridge, Mass.: MIT Press, 1992), p. 85.

can talk through electronically-based communication lines to an academic situated at a university in Moscow. Their conversation takes place in cyberspace. More specific to the world of art making, Charles Csuri, working in his computer laboratory-studio at Ohio State University's Advanced Computing Center for the Arts and Design, can transmit his current image through cyberspace to a colleague working in The Netherlands. The image can be received, critiqued, and even altered in cyberspace. Research and development in both industry and the academy daily expand the possibilities of this electronically-based space.

Although a few visual artists have been working with electronic technologies for more than two decades, the problem of validity continues to plague the making and reception of electronically-based, computer-related art. David Carrier, in a 1988 *Leonardo* editorial, notes that neither art historical nor commercial journals have provided any model for studying the interaction of art, science, and technology.[9] There are no adequate theoretical bases in art criticism or art history for criticizing computer-based visual arts.

## A Case Study: Harold Cohen

A case study of the art making of Englishman Harold Cohen will help illustrate the difficulties computer-related art poses for the practice of art criticism and art history. Harold Cohen is renowned for the abstract expressionist paintings he rendered from 1960 through 1968. His works *Tribune* of 1962 and *Before the Event* (Figure 1) of 1963 were purchased by the Tate Gallery, London. *Before the Event* hangs in a prominent gallery focusing on modern British art of the 1960s. In 1965 Cohen's work was included in Documenta III, held in Kassel, Germany, and in 1966, along with four other visual artists, he was chosen to represent Great Britain at the XXIII Venice Biennale, sending the painting *Pastoral* of 1965. Michael Compton of the Tate Gallery comments upon Cohen's artistic success: "From about 1952 until 1968, Harold Cohen built up a reputation as a painter equal to that of any British artist of his generation."[10]

9. David Carrier, "The Arts and Science and Technology: Problems and Prospects," *Leonardo* 21 (1988): 341-42.

10. M. G. Compton, "Harold Cohen," *Harold Cohen* (London: Tate Gallery Publications, 1983), p. 19.

FIGURE 1. Harold Cohen (British, b. 1928), *Before the Event*,
1963, tempera and oil on canvas, 98″ × 116″.
Photo: Becky Cohen.

In 1968, Cohen spent one year as a visiting professor in the Department
of Visual Arts at the University of California at San Diego. Early in his visit
a graduate student in the music department offered to teach him how to
use a computer. He became fascinated with the computer and its possibilities for art making. At the time Cohen felt disillusioned with painting.
Wanting to develop a theory of representation, he believed that after twenty
years of painting he had done little to develop such a theory. Although at
the height of his career as a respected modern painter, he turned to the
computer because it "opened the way to a completely new set of perceptions."[11] Cohen became involved with a group of computer scientists at
Stanford University working in artificial intelligence, initially Edward

11. Harold Cohen, personal interview, 17 November 1986, pp. 18-19.

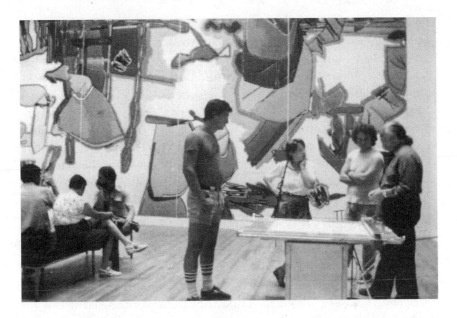

FIGURE 2. Harold Cohen, *Untitled*,
AARON drawing, 1983, mural, hand painted by Cohen,
Tate Gallery, London, and a view of Cohen with plotter
executing an AARON drawing at the Tate Gallery.
Hardware: Digital Equipment Corporation Micro Vax II.
Software: by the artist.
Photo: Becky Cohen.

Feigenbaum and later Feigenbaum's mentor Herbert Simon, and changed his focus from canvas painting to the computer, using canvas, ink, and paint as his "primary output" media (Figure 2).[12] This transition provided Cohen with a more satisfactory means to explore how the cognitive formation of visual structure yields meaning to the viewer.[13] During the last two and a half decades his work has been mainly computer-based imagery. This imagery has received only a small amount of serious criticism from visual arts

12. Harold Cohen, "Corrections and Comments on the Text," unpublished, February 17, 1992, p. 2, in response to the original draft of my dissertation.
13. This thesis is developed and argued in my 1992 Ph.D. dissertation "From Canvas to Computer: Harold Cohen's Artificial Intelligence Paradigm for Art Making," Ohio State University, 1992.

critics and art historians. The lack of critical attention contrasts sharply with the more than two hundred articles written about Cohen's abstract expressionist paintings of the 1960s.

In the foreword to the Cohen exhibition catalogue, Alan Bowness, director of the Tate Gallery at the time of Cohen's 1983 exhibition, suggests a disparity in art historical discussion between Cohen's earlier modernist works and his later computer-generated imagery.[14] Cohen's abandonment by the visual arts community's critics and historians illustrates the problem pointed out by Carrier. With Cohen's move to the computer, he entered an uncharted theoretical territory for the visual arts that crosses art making and contemporary computer technology. His interdisciplinary art, incorporating the new discipline of computer science, caused difficulty for art critics and art historians of the 1960s and 1970s, especially those trained as formalists. The Late Modernist Formalist criteria,[15] stemming from the writing of Clement Greenberg, were helpful in making judgments about the form, color, and flatness of modern abstract works of art (for example, the work of Barnett Newman, Clifford Still) and somewhat useful for discussing Cohen's abstract expressionistic paintings, but these criteria proved inappropriate and ineffective for criticizing and historically locating his computer-generated imagery. Formalist art criticism could discuss the formal elements of Cohen's work but could not provide a fuller understanding of both abstract expressionist and computer-based works. With Cohen's transition from canvas to computer, the art historical community lost interest in a critical discussion of his art making. Reflection on his work was picked up by the artificial intelligence component of the computer science community.

The problem of the art critical and art historical disparity between the Cohen abstract expressionist paintings and his computer-based imagery calls for an interpretive approach that includes frameworks for criticizing computer-based imagery and locating it in an art historical manner. Cohen's abstract expressionistic field paintings of the 1960s — for example, *Before the Event* (Figure 1) — exemplify well the components embodied in Clement Greenberg's Late Modernist Formalist critical theory. Greenberg built his theory on Immanuel Kant's notion that design is what is essential

14. Alan Bowness, foreword, *Harold Cohen* (London: Tate Gallery Publications, 1983), p. 5.

15. Clement Greenberg, "Modernist Painting," *Art and Literature* 4 (1965): 193-201.

to painting, sculpture, and all the fine arts, and he claimed that the irreducible feature of painting is flatness situated in abstract form.[16] *Before the Event* and other Cohen imagery of the early 1960s present flat, boldly colored forms encased in softly ridged lines. His imagery of the early and mid-1960s adheres well to the coordinates of Greenberg's Late Modernist Formalist critique; Michael Compton thus acknowledges Cohen's reception and acclaim within the circle of Modern British painters.[17]

Difficulty arises in criticism of the body of Cohen's imagery, however, for although his abstract expressionist paintings seemingly fit the Greenbergian paradigm, Greenberg's aesthetic misses a central direction of Cohen's abstract paintings and his computer-generated imagery. A constant concern for Cohen has been the process of art making. This focus on process provides a view of art-making that is not primarily concerned with the art object, for it incorporates Cohen's concern for how the structuring of an image yields meaning to the viewer. Throughout his artistic development, from his years as a student at London's Slade School of Art, he sought to answer a question raised by his teacher Rudolph Wittkower: How does the visual symbol yield meaning to the viewer?[18] Both bodies of Cohen's work, in differing ways, search out how the cognitive formation of visual structure conveys meaning to those viewing the artwork. Cohen addresses this question through a developing theory of representation embodied in the artificially intelligent drawing program AARON that renders Cohen's computer-based imagery. Compton believes the more recent computer-based work to be Cohen's strongest visual contribution to date.[19] Greenbergian critical analysis, however, completely fails to capture the deeper concern that permeates all of Cohen's art making. And the question remains: How do we go about art critically and art historically analyzing Cohen's body of work, including the computer-generated imagery that has alluded serious

16. Immanuel Kant, *The Critique of Judgment,* translated, with an Introduction by Werner S. Pluhar (Indianapolis: Hackett, 1987); and Howard Risatti, "Art and Aesthetics: Late Modernism and the Formalist Debate," *Postmodern Perspectives: Issues in Contemporary Art,* ed. Howard Risatti (Englewood Cliffs, N.J.: Prentice-Hall, 1990), pp. 1-5.

17. Compton, pp. 19-23.

18. This is a central thesis argued in my 1992 Ph.D. dissertation.

19. He makes this comment in a personal letter to the author in 1989. Compton wrote an essay in the 1983 *Harold Cohen* catalogue that accompanied an exhibition of the same title held at the Tate Gallery. Compton knew Cohen from his days as a student at London's Slade School of Art and followed the development of Cohen's career.

art critical consideration? A brief review of photography criticism will assist in locating an evaluative approach to electronic, computer-based imagery.

## Photography and Electronically-Based Visual Arts

Walter Benjamin's essay "The Work of Art in the Age of Mechanical Reproduction" (1936) provides an insightful framework for understanding the impact of technology-based media on the fine arts.[20] Benjamin argues:

> Mechanical reproduction emancipates the work of art from its parasitical dependence on ritual. To an even greater degree, the work of art becomes the work of art designed for reproducibility. From a photographic negative, for example, one can make any number of prints; to ask for the "authentic" print makes no sense. But the instant the criterion of authenticity ceases to be applicable to artistic production, the total function of art is reversed. Instead of being based on ritual, it begins to be based on another practice — politics.[21]

Although Benjamin's analysis concerns photographic reproduction, it can also be applied to electronically-based visual arts. The development of photography provides a basis for the consideration of electronically-based imagery.[22] Benjamin's assessment holds six immediate consequences for the mechanically, or electronically, reproduced work of art. First, the aura, or halo of originality, a primary criterion for the art object in the development of Western art, has dissipated. Second, the originality of an artwork has dissolved because many copies or editions of a single image can exist. Third, the concept of the artist as a genius, a tenet of Western art from the Renaissance through modernity, is undermined. Fourth, the art work's

20. Margot Lovejoy, "Art, Technology, and Postmodernism: Paradigms, Parallels, and Paradoxes," *Art Journal* 49 (1990): 257.
21. Walter Benjamin, "The Work of Art in the Age of Mechanical Reproduction," in *Illuminations,* ed. Hannah Arendt (New York: Schocken Books, 1978), p. 236.
22. In the 1970s, Hans Rookmaaker, an art historian at the Free University of Amsterdam who worked in the Dutch Reformational tradition, questioned the validity of photography as a visual art. The next generation and more contemporary artists, art historians, and art critics, working in the light of the Reformed heritage, are engaging the developing visual arts forms incorporating film, video, and computer. For example, Canadian visual artist Betty Spackman uses video and the computer in her recent installations pieces.

independence from originality, singularity, and genius stimulates new challenges and possibilities for our understanding of the visual field. Fifth, the art work's reproducibility helps reverse the view of art as an elitist commodity, reinstates the reproduced work as art available at relatively low costs to the masses, and thus brings about a democratization of the art marketplace. And sixth, these changes bring possibilities for a new social meaning of art. Benjamin's analysis gives a legitimate place for art critical and art historical consideration of both photography and electronically-based visual arts. In light of postmodern considerations, both photography and electronically-based visual arts should hold a more central position in contemporary visual arts discourse. This repositioning of the visual arts will be dealt with more fully in the following section.

Although Benjamin's prophetic assertion provides a framework to differentiate between the original work of Western art and mechanically and electronically produced and reproduced artworks, there exists a striking and key difference between photographic and electronically-produced imagery. The photograph normally depends on a prior real-world subject towards which the image points, giving the viewer a sense of having been there.[23] The electronically-based digital image, however, comprised of small pixel units that represent precise numerical values, refers to an event that could possibly be, to a potentially totally fictive construction. As symbol-manipulating machines, computers differ radically from conventional approaches to art-making. The work of the artist becomes one of manipulating symbolic order through the writing of code rather than through the more conventional interaction of material and the artist's senses.[24] The digital image, whose construction could be fully fictive, moves towards a world that could be, rather than representing a world that we know. Benjamin presents a starting point for assessing electronically-based imagery. With its possibility for constructive fiction and its location in cyberspace, however, electronically-based visual art requires theoretical considerations that move beyond Benjamin's assessment.

23. George Legrady, "Image, Language, and Belief in Synthesis," *Art Journal* 49 (1990): 267.
24. Legrady, p. 267.

# A Postmodern Shift

Both photography and electronically-based imagery, little considered in the deliberations of Modern Art, have taken a central position in contemporary Western culture, a culture often categorized as postmodern. Before focusing specifically on electronically-based visual arts in relation to art historiography, let us consider specific concerns of postmodernism that relate to these two discussions.

The concept of postmodernism was introduced in 1934 by Spanish writer Federico de Onis in his *Antologica de la poesia española e hispanoamericano,* using the idea to delineate a reaction from within modernism.[25] The concept resurfaced in several discussions throughout the mid-twentieth century; by the 1970s the term had received new currency as one encompassing a variety of trends that do not rely on traditional philosophical underpinnings. My own discussion of the term "postmodern" incorporates three differing points of reference noted by Margaret Rose: understandings of the term developed in relation and in reaction to (1) the meaning of modernism in architecture and the visual arts, (2) twentieth-century economic and technological developments of industrial and capital-based expansion that characterize modern societies, and (3) modernity, the sum total of modern, modernism, and modernization.[26]

In *The Postmodern Condition,* the French philosopher Jean-François Lyotard, a dominant figure in shaping a deconstructionist vein of postmodernism, criticizes Western culture for its construction of "grand narratives of legitimation." Lyotard uses this phrase in reference to overarching philosophies of history — for example, the Enlightenment march towards reason and freedom, and Marxism's emphasis on human productive capabilities, progress through class struggle, and the rule of the proletariat. These meta-narrative approaches, according to his critique, illustrate a modern approach towards self-legitimation. He contends that each formulates a "first-order" discursive practice of inquiry and politics within a larger totalizing meta-discourse which then sustains and legitimatizes itself, while guaranteeing a standard for right pragmatics and right practices.[27] Lyotard's

25. Charles Jencks, *What is Post-Modernism?* (New York: St. Martin's Press, 1987), p. 8.
26. Margaret A. Rose, *The Post-Modern and the Post-Industrial* (Cambridge: Cambridge University Press, 1991), pp. 1-2.
27. See Linda J. Nicholson's discussion in "Social Criticism Without Philosophy," *Feminism/Postmodernism* (New York: Routledge, 1990), pp. 21-26.

sharp critique focuses on the meta-component, pointing out that we can no longer rely on these meta-claims for capturing truth. He notes that in the nineteenth and twentieth centuries we have paid a high price for the nostalgia of the whole.[28] He then asks where legitimation abides, and suggests that there will be many discourses of legitimation, plural, local, and immanent, distributed among the plurality of discursive practices. Lyotard's analysis holds definite implications for the charting and discussion of a meta-narrative project, namely Modern Art, as well as the art critical and art historical mapping of contemporary visual arts that include postmodern components.

A second publication of the mid-1980s that takes a prominent position in the art historical charting of the modern and postmodern eras is Charles Jencks' *What is Post-Modernism?* More specific to the areas of art and architecture than Lyotard's philosophical reflections, Jencks poses his questions in the context of modern and postmodern architecture. Jencks's discussion of the postmodern information world contributes more to the charting of electronically-based arts than do his broader analysis of modern, late modern, and postmodern and his frail attempt to redefine as "late modern" what Lyotard, Baudrillard, Foster, and Jameson often classify as "postmodern."[29] Helpful specifically for art critical and art historical approaches to electronically-based visual arts is Jencks's mapping of the postmodern information world and the rise of the cognitariat.[30] Jencks argues that contemporary culture is shifting into a new era of culture and social organization that Daniel Bell called the Post-Industrial Society; others have labeled this transition the "Third Wave," or the "informational society."[31] Jencks points out that this alteration towards an informational society was apparent in the United States by the early 1970s, for only thirteen percent of its work force was involved in the manufacture of goods, with sixty percent engaged in the manufacture of information.[32] This fundamental shift, symbolically represented by the launching of Sputnik at the end of the 1950s, came about through the development of electronic technologies,

---

28. Jean-François Lyotard, "Answering the Question: What is Postmodernism?" *The Postmodern Condition: A Report of Knowledge* (Manchester: Manchester University Press, 1986), pp. 71-82.
29. Jencks, pp. 32-38.
30. Jencks, pp. 43-56.
31. Jencks, p. 43.
32. Jencks, p. 44.

especially the computer, and continues to expand through rapid and efficient telecommunications networks residing in cyberspace. Incorporated in the shift to an information-based culture is the revolutionary growth of those who develop and manage the information, an emerging class that Jencks labels the cognitariat.[33] The cognitariat includes clerks, secretaries, stockbrokers, teachers, advertisers, writers, managers, bankers, governmental bureaucrats, lawyers, technologists and technicians, programmers, and accountants, among others.

To illustrate the composition of the postmodern information world and its managing cognitariat, Jencks charts in a comparative diagram three types of society: pre-modern (1000 BC–1450), modern (1450-1960), and postmodern (1960-), a description that is linear and chronological in formulation. Further, he subdivides the three dated groupings into five classifications of production, society, time, orientation, and culture and illustrates the changes of each with the movement from pre-modern to modern to postmodern.[34] For example, Jencks's discussion of his category of production elucidates the transition from a pre-modern agricultural neolithic revolution to a mass-production industrial revolution to our contemporary computer-based information revolution, thereby clarifying the importance of electronic technologies in our contemporary culture.

Jencks's linear categorical analysis of modern and postmodern also assists art critical and art historical considerations of electronically-based visual arts. First, he distinguishes between modern linear time and a more vertical postmodern shaping of time in which world events affect each other in an almost simultaneous chain reaction; for example, the televising of political conflict can lead to rapid international political intervention. Andy Warhol emphasized the speed and democracy that the new media brings with his prophesy that everyone would have their fifteen minutes

33. Jencks, p. 44.

34. Jencks, p. 47. Stone in "Will the Real Body Please Stand Up?", pp. 85-99, makes a different kind of distinction than does Jencks when she delineates four epochs in the development of "double presences" — the potential for a person to reside in two worlds at the same time, one of which is a real community and the other a chosen virtual community. Stone organizes virtual communities, that is people brought together by common beliefs and practices but separated by physical space, into four changing eras whose alterations result from a change in the way humans communicate: epoch one: texts (from the mid-1600s); epoch two: electronic communication and entertainment media (1900+); epoch three: information technology (1960+); and epoch four: virtual reality and cyberspace (1984+).

of fame.[35] Second, production shifts from an outworking of an industrialized base to one of information, with art-making possibilities also situated in an information base. Although much production in the 1990s is information-based, most contemporary art making still rests on an industrialized footing. Third, societal orientation changes from a more exclusive, nationalistic, modern, and centralized authority that could be categorized as a capitalist ruling class, to a threatened credibility of societal structures and classes that leads to a decentralized pluralism giving place to a global para-class, the cognitariat. Jencks's analysis reinforces Lyotard's critique of the grand modern meta-narratives. Fourth, the demise of centralized nationalistic authority leads to an emphasis on both world and local concerns, giving place to pluralistic, eclectic, and more inclusive orientations. And fifth, a unified culture exhibiting reigning styles, a dominant component of Modern Art, gives way to the simultaneous occurrence of many differing artistic genres. Electronically-based arts, native to the information society, fit well within the postmodern categories of Jencks's diagram. Jencks's differentiation between industrial and information production within differing conceptions of time provides a way to analyze visual arts that are electronically-based and that elude more traditional approaches to art criticism, including a Greenbergian formalist approach. This distinction also could assist analysis of video and performance arts that incorporate electronic components.

Lyotard's critique of modern meta-narrative projects and Jencks's depiction of an information-based society raise questions about Seerveld's cartographic methodology for art historiography.[36] Lyotard's appraisal raises a question concerning the validity of the apparent "meta-narrative" structuring of Seerveld's cartography. Jencks's detailed discussion of our information society brings to the foreground Seerveld's omission of a critique of our information society and electronically-based visual arts.

---

35. Jencks, p. 48.

36. Calvin Seerveld, "Toward a Cartographic Methodology for Art Historiography," *The Journal of Aesthetics and Art Criticism* 31, no. 2 (1980): 143-54; and a recent updating of the 1980 article in Calvin Seerveld, "Vollenhoven's Legacy for Art Historiography," *Philosophia Reformata* 58, no. 1 (1993): 49-79.

MARY LEIGH MORBEY

# Seerveld's Cartography in a Postmodern Shift

Calvin Seerveld's cartographic methodology presents a three-category model for art history. From the Dutch philosopher D. H. Th. Vollenhoven, Seerveld takes over four notions that shape his approach to historical methodology.[37] First, sound method sets appropriate limits to the field of investigation, in this particular case, art history. Second, Christian historiography works out the biblical confession that history is the story of God's creation and that Jesus's birth, death, resurrection, ascension, and coming triumph situate the major happenings on this earth. Third, attention is given to identifying typical philosophical categorical constructions that appear throughout the ongoing movement of history. And fourth, it is the historian's responsibility to delineate a just account of what took place, pointing out what is enriching and also what is wasteful. Seerveld works out these understandings in three categories that include the following: (1) lived and dated cultural periods; (2) a plurality of world-and-life visions that shape artistic traditions; and (3) the inheritance, or footprinted trail, that one generation gives over to the next, for good or ill. To illustrate his cartography Seerveld formulates a visual diagram that sets out the cultural period dynamics, combined with world-and-life visions.

What assistance does Seerveld's "three-dimensional" cartography lend to an art historical charting of the work of Harold Cohen? Although more current Seerveld scholarship makes overtures towards contemporary concerns,[38] and although his charting of recent art makers includes computer-generated art located under the cultural dynamic of pragmatism (with Cohen designated as having an idyllic worldview — see chart 1), Seerveld's cartography appears to continue the Enlightenment and modernist, first-order, discursive, and privileged meta-narrative project that Lyotard so sharply criticizes. Lyotard stresses postmodernism's severe critique of Enlightenment thought, with its notions of a unitary end of history and of a subject.[39]

---

37. Seerveld, "Vollenhoven's Legacy," pp. 50-53.

38. For example, see Calvin Seerveld's 1991 lecture "The Halo of Human Imagination" given at the C. S. Lewis Foundation Oxford Conference and Seerveld's Staley Lecture "Wicked Beauty and the Challenge of Modern Art" presented at Redeemer College in January 1993.

39. Jean-François Lyotard, "Answering the Question: What is Postmodernism?" *The Postmodern Condition: A Report on Knowledge* (Manchester: Manchester University Press, 1986), pp. 71-82.

CHART 1. Schematic conspectus for approximating several concurrent cultural dynamics and committed visions operative among human artists in the last few generations.

| cultural dynamic | Pragmatism 1890s– Cubism, Bauhaus, Abstract Expressionism Protest art, Computer generated art | Existentialism World War I– Surrealism, Theater of the Absurd, Art of the oppressed | Nihilism Dada 1917– Pop art 1950s Punk art Performance art | Reformational Christian 1920s– Black spirituals | Parodistic scepsis Serial music 1920s– Minimalist, op-art, colour-field, concept art of 1960s |
|---|---|---|---|---|---|
| committed vision of world and life | | | | | |
| mystic | Kandinsky 1921– | Kandinsky –1921 Matta | | Messiaen | Barnett Newman Rothko |
| heroic | Jackson Pollock | Anselm Kiefer | | | |
| picaresque | Rauschenberg | Miro Martin Disler? | Jean Tinguely | Flannery O'Connor | |
| scenic | Mies van der Rohe | | | late Henry Moore | Malevitch Mondrian 1917– |
| idyllic | Harold Cohen | Andrew Wyeth Damien Hirst Bergman, Kaufmann | Yves Klein Mark Prent | Peter Schaffer Peter Maxwell Davies | M. C. Escher Elsworth Kelly |
| paradigmatic | Braque | Edward Hopper de Chirico Magritte | Duchamp Warhol | Robert Bresson Henk Krijger Wladyslav Hasior | Vaserely Albers |
| hedonic | "Madonna" | | Xenakis Dennis Burton | | |
| troubled cosmic | | Pacheco | | Georges Rouault Alan Paton Barlach? | |

Seerveld's approach to historiography maps art history in terms of historical periods, and it works with models of historical periodization that derive from the project of modernity which Lyotard sharply questions. Fredric Jameson suggests that not only is this approach unfashionable, but also historical representation itself, even beyond the more traditional, narrative formulation presented in Seerveld's model, is in crisis.[40]

The structure of Seerveld's project, along with his omission of contemporary artists who emphasize electronic technologies, race, class, gender concerns, multiculturalism, and environmental considerations, could lead to criticism and invalidation because of its overt conceptual proximity to the modernist art historical enterprise. The Seerveld chart includes Jencks's characteristics of modernism — linear time, industrial production, capitalistic societies, exclusive orientations, and reigning cultural styles — while failing to address any of the features Jencks classifies as postmodern: cyclical time, information production, a global para-class society, pluralistic inclusiveness, and the existence of many simultaneous genres. Two areas important to the discussion of contemporary art and the art historical charting of Harold Cohen's work, namely, Lyotard's critique of historical meta-narratives and Jencks's discussion of artistic development in the age of information, remain unaddressed in Seerveld's development of his cartographic methodology.

Closer scrutiny of Seerveld's cartography reveals deeper concerns, however. Seerveld's scholarship, grounded in a Reformed view of history, is not determined by the innovation-progress model of modernism, but follows both the linear and spiral path of the biblical narrative in its creation-fall-redemption-restoration flow. On the one hand, Seerveld faces a tension created by the similarity of the biblical narrative and the grand meta-narrative of modernism, raising the question of how to talk about the biblical story in a milieu reacting against any form of overarching narrative. On the other hand, Seerveld wishes to engage, and to offer a "third way" to, the postmodern world and aims to address the myriad of issues that parallel Christian concerns — for example, a just treatment and care of one's neighbor — while at the same time maintaining and presenting a coherent bib-

---

40. Fredric Jameson, "Periodizing the Sixties," *The Ideologies of Theory: Essays 1971-86,* vol. 2: *The Syntax of History* (Minneapolis: University of Minnesota Press: 1988), pp. 178-208.

lical understanding of history and art history. Of course, the difficulty resides in how one goes about doing this.

To begin, one needs to make clear distinctions between the biblical story and a modernist grand narrative. The biblical narrative emphasizes that God crafted this universe and the men and women placed in it, and that God holds them; they do not hold, nor construct, nor shape God. Contrasting sharply with this belief is the modernist understanding that persons find their center in a human construct shaped by Enlightenment science, proclaiming that humankind can scientifically resolve its problems, and driven by the notions of innovation and progress, asserting that people shape, construct, and hold together their own worlds. Postmodern considerations — for example Lyotard's critique of the grand discursive metanarrative — are valid in criticizing the "modernist big story," but wrong in their critique of the biblical story, which encompasses faith and acknowledges that it is not a human construct. Postmodernism, although in reaction against Enlightenment rationalism and its outworking in the modernist project, grows out of modern rationalism. Jameson argues that we cannot simply put forward a position for or against postmodernism, for it has invaded everything and we cannot move to the outside to offer critique.[41] This is true also for the Christian living in contemporary culture and for current approaches to Christian-based art historiography.

Patricia Waugh suggests that grand narratives have been a way of formulating basic human needs and that the resulting grandness signals the urgency and intensity of need.[42] She further surmises that grand narratives will not just die but will be profoundly transformed, and that postmodernism will come to be seen as a strategy to expose the oppression of modernism rather than a condition to be embraced.[43] If Waugh's assessment is valid, we will see the continuance of narratives that meet basic human needs. Hence one wonders why those who embrace the biblical story hesitate in allowing it to address urgent contemporary needs, for example, environmental, multicultural and race, class, and gender concerns. Christians, understanding who they are and where they are going, need, however, to consider reflectively how one engages, dialogues, and puts forth a Christian voice in a pluralistic

41. Jameson, "Periodizing the Sixties," pp. 178-208.
42. Patricia Waugh, "Introduction," *Postmodernism: A Reader* (New York: Edward Arnold, 1992), p. 9.
43. Waugh, p. 9.

postmodern discourse. With this consideration in mind, how might Seerveld alter his art historiography to incorporate the more contemporary arts, including electronically-based visual arts, and, more specifically, to assist a more thorough charting of the work of Harold Cohen?

## Possibilities and Challenges

A reconstruction of Seerveld's art historical cartography could move from a mapping that appears to be fostered by the exclusive modernist project to a more open conception that gives place to the multiplicity of concerns comprising contemporary culture. His linear period dynamics could become multilayered to illustrate simultaneous developments — for example, a consideration of race, class, and gender moving parallel to and having equal weight with multicultural, environmental, and electronically-based visual arts concerns. Perhaps, and of even more importance, Seerveld might delineate how his Christian view of art history does not continue the modernist project, and further, demonstrate how it offers another way for contemporary art critical and art historical discourse.

Part of the dilemma faced by the Christian scholar in the arts is to gauge salient components of contemporary culture and to discern wisely which are in vogue and only temporary, and which contribute to the shaping of culture. Christian academics who are involved in the visual arts have stood back in hesitation as they observe deconstruction and computer-based electronic technologies entering the visual arts. It is becoming clearer that critiques such as Lyotard's and societal observations such as Jencks's are more than temporary fashion. These need to be taken seriously in our attempts to understand more fully the contemporary world. Christian scholarship in the visual arts is called to participate in contemporary discussion and to provide insight and understanding.

Let us consider, from this vantage point, the problem of the art critical and art historical exclusion of electronically-based arts, and in particular, the computer-generated imagery of Harold Cohen. A delineation of frameworks to facilitate meaningful discussion of electronically-based visual arts continues to be omitted from mainstream theoretical considerations in art criticism and art history.[44] It could be that electronically-based imagery,

44. Carrier, pp. 341-42.

tied more directly to the inheritance of photography than to traditional painting, is a "native" vehicle for art making in our contemporary culture. If this be the case, then how might art criticism and art history build and expand upon the ideas of Benjamin and Jencks?

An array of avenues can be investigated to locate fruitful bases on which to direct deeper discussion. First, theoretical models of computer-generated music can be studied to locate analogies to computer-generated art and thus contribute building blocks. Theoretical considerations concerning the relationship between the computer and music theory have been more thoroughly investigated, in part because the direct numerical correlation between computer algorithm and musical notation facilitates the investigation. The union of computer and music occurs in the medium of mathematical language, a point that remains problematic for the visual arts. Where visual arts making has stressed the physical interaction of the artist with tangible materials such as paint, the employment of symbol-manipulating machines brings about a radical rupture with the sensory experience of more conventional approaches to image making.[45] Second, the art historical canon can be examined to locate points on which to build discussion of electronically-based visual arts. For example, in addition to the development of photography, correlations can be found between computer-based visual arts and movements such as futurism, surrealism, and conceptual art. These connections, easily recognized within traditional art historical interpretation, may contribute to the discussion when they are reevaluated in relation to the new possibilities brought about by electronic technologies operating in cyberspace. Third, an investigation of the bases and development of contemporary Japanese electronically-based imagery would expand the discussion beyond the models and requirements of Western art. Last, as avenues are sought out for a more salient discussion of electronically-based arts, we need to avoid new hierarchical categories or parameters that recodify the visual arts into divisive power camps — for example, low art, high art, and possibly electronically-based arts.[46]

These four suggestions, building on the insights of Benjamin and Jencks, provide routes for intriguing discussion and critique of Harold

---

45. Legrady, p. 267.

46. My assistant at Redeemer College, Corina A. Bos, raised the point concerning different power camps within the contemporary visual arts. I thank Redeemer College Professor Hugh Cook and Messiah College Professor Paul Van Arragon for their helpful comments on an early draft of this essay.

Cohen's computer-generated imagery, and they facilitate a fuller interpretation of a central motif underlying both his modernist works and his computer imagery. Cohen's objective throughout his entire body of work — namely, to learn how the cognitive formation of visual structure yields meaning to the viewer — does not alter, even though the conceptual space and possibilities for his visual exploration do. An art historical charting of his exploration creates a tension for the cartographer: in Cohen's development from modernist painting to a postmodern inclusion of the computer and to a democratization that levels the hierarchical differentiation between high and low art, one finds concepts and ideologies embedded in both modernism and postmodernism.

These considerations, leading us further into the uncharted cyberspace of electronically-based visual arts, take seriously Calvin Seerveld's call for Christian scholarship and leadership in the development of contemporary art criticism and art history. This commission requires Christian scholars to analyze contemporary developments in the visual arts. Also, a Reformed conception of art history, which may be clear to more traditional thinkers, must look to different points of engagement within contemporary discourse. Postmodern pluralism, argues Diogenes Allen, gives an opening to the Christian voice alongside many other voices.[47] This opening needs to be considered carefully, however, for it could level all viewpoints, thereby flattening the transcendent emphasis of Christian belief. As Christians engage in critique and dialogue in a contemporary milieu, Roger Lundin reminds us, we need to take along an inheritance that encompasses sin and grace, death and resurrection. We need to develop a vocabulary and Christian practice that facilitate communication of the truth and richness of the biblical story.[48] A postmodern critique of Christendom also provides an opportunity for the Church and the Christian scholar. The critique gives the Church an opportunity to review failings, to reassess its "big story," and to reshape critically its voice and its communal work in the context of our contemporary pluralistic culture. This reassessment enables Christian scholars to understand more clearly their calling and voice in contemporary culture, and to recognize that the visual arts — painting, sculpture, elec-

47. Diogenes Allen, "Christianity and the Creed of Postmodernism," *Christian Scholar's Review* 23, no. 2 (1993): 117-26.
48. Roger Lundin, *The Culture of Interpretation: Christian Faith and the Postmodern World* (Grand Rapids, Mich.: William B. Eerdmans, 1993), p. 30.

tronically-based arts, video, and performance — play a dominant role in the current milieu. Our ongoing challenge is one of Christian engagement that brings freedom, moving carefully to avoid the captivity that has often accompanied Christian activity. Seerveld's challenge to Christian believers to be forthright, scandalous, humble, and open in their aesthetics remains constant in his scholarship as he endeavors to work out his cartographic methodology in relation to postmodern discourse. His leadership encourages his Christian colleagues and students who also struggle to find a Christian voice that engages our contemporary pluralistic culture.

# Serving Vintage Wisdom:
# Art Historiography in the
# Neo-Calvinian Tradition

HENRY M. LUTTIKHUIZEN

In a recent article written to honor the Dutch Neo-Calvinian philosopher D. H. Th. Vollenhoven, Calvin Seerveld tells us that "one commemorates, perhaps best, by carrying on reformingly the earlier service rendered."[1] Reflecting on the achievements of the past in a self-critical manner helps us pass on traditional values without idolizing them. A critical dialogue with the past can enhance our historical understanding, by making us more self-conscious of the words that the tradition has taught us to say, and will better enable us to share traditional insights and concerns with others. Commemoration, to my understanding, does not entail the putting of new wine into old wineskins but, as Seerveld has effectively shown through his own scholarship, the drinking of old wine from new glasses.[2] In other words, participation within a tradition calls us to present the fruits of the past to others in a pleasing manner that will encourage them to drink. Through the years, Seerveld has taught many of us that living in the Neo-Calvinian tradition is not supping with the dead; it is setting the table for the next generation. This essay, intended as a toast to Seerveld, searches for

1. Calvin Seerveld, "Vollenhoven's Legacy for Art Historiography," *Philosophia Reformata* 58 (1993): 70.
2. Calvin Seerveld, "Footprints in the Snow," *Philosophia Reformata* 56 (1991): 5.

78

a way to go about writing art history in the Neo-Calvinian tradition. By responding imaginatively to the work of Rookmaaker, Seerveld, and other Reformational scholars, I hope to discover a vintage of art historiography that I can call my own and can recommend to others.

Since the late nineteenth-century, when art history became an academic discipline, many scholars have wedded their interpretive strategies to positivism, claiming that their interpretations are value-free, that they let the facts speak for themselves.[3] Preoccupied with being understood as scientific researchers and seduced by what H.-G. Gadamer has aptly described as a "prejudice against prejudice," such art historians have lost sight of the commitments directing their interpretation, maintaining instead that their views are objective, unrooted in personal belief, philosophical presupposition, or communal tradition.[4] Recently, positivistic art historiography has been under attack by the so-called "new art history," a loosely organized conglomeration of feminists, Marxians, and post-structuralists out to expose hidden agendas within art historiography and the history of art, especially those operating on principles of exclusion.[5]

Although contemporary trends in art history have encouraged the development of methodological pluralism, there is still little room for religious commitment in art historical scholarship. Such beliefs are all too often relegated to the realm of opinion, as personal quirks best kept outside

---

3. For more on positivism's effect on art history, see Alois Riegl, "Kunstgeschichte und Universalgeschichte" [1898], in *Gesammelte Aufsätze*, edited by Karl Swoboda, with and introduction by Hans Sedlmayr (Augsburg and Vienna: Berno Filser Verlag, 1929) and Heinrich Wölfflin, *Kunstgeschichtliche Grundbegriffe* [1915], translated by M. D. Hottinger as *The Principles of Art History* (New York: Dover Publications, 1950). For a good introduction to their respective methodologies, see Michael Podro, *The Critical Historians of Art* (London and New Haven: Yale University Press, 1982).

4. Hans-Georg Gadamer, *Wahrheit und Methode* [1960], translated by Garrett Barden and John Cumming as *Truth and Method* (New York: Crossroads, 1976), pp. 235-74.

5. For more on the "new art history," see *Calligram: Essays in New Art History from France*, edited by Norman Bryson (Cambridge: Cambridge University Press, 1988); Norman Bryson, *Vision and Painting: The Logic of the Gaze* (New Haven and London: Yale University Press, 1983); *The New Art History*, edited by A. L. Rees and F. Borzello (London: Camden Press, 1986); Griselda Pollock, *Vision and Difference: Femininity, Feminism and the Histories of Art* (London and New York: Routledge, 1988); Donald Preziosi, *Rethinking Art History: Meditations on a Coy Science* (New Haven and London: Yale University Press, 1989); and Keith Moxey, *The Practice of Theory: Poststructuralism, Cultural Politics and Art History* (Ithaca, N.Y.: Cornell University Press, 1994).

the public arena of academic discussion. Religion, it is assumed, only gets in the way, bringing the conversation to a standstill.[6] Unfortunately, Christians have encouraged this reaction both by failing to talk, pietistically keeping their faith to themselves, and by failing to listen, turning a deaf ear to the thought-provoking insights of others, while giving dogmatic responses to complex questions. Hans Rookmaaker, Seerveld, and other Reformational scholars, refusing either to preach worn-out slogans or to suppress their own commitments, have effectively shown that academic discussion cannot really begin until participants acknowledge their starting points. Ideally, in art-historical debates scholars will be self-conscious of their own categorical framework and recognize its limitations, clearing space for methodological tolerance, as opposed to the desire for dominance or indifference.[7]

Within the Neo-Calvinian tradition, both the late Hans Rookmaaker, an art historian at the Vrije Universiteit in Amsterdam,[8] and Calvin Seerveld, an aesthetician at the Institute for Christian Studies in Toronto, have worked hard to free art historiography from its positivist heritage. Rookmaaker and Seerveld have effectively questioned the positivist claim of value neutrality by actively unveiling the implicit commitments informing various interpretive practices within the field of art history. Appropriating the thought of Abraham Kuyper, Rookmaaker and Seerveld have suggested that one's interpretation of the history of art is shaped by one's *levens-en wereldbeschouwing,* one's world-and-life-view.[9] In other words, they insist that art historians always confront art and history, and all aspects of human existence, from a certain pre-theoretical vantage point. Art historiography by necessity is informed by the prejudices of the art historian, just as a work

6. Richard Rorty, "Religion: A Conversation Stopper," Calvin College's *Dialogue: A Journal of Commentary and the Arts* (April/May 1994): 12-15.

7. Calvin Seerveld, "A Way to Go in Writing Art History," unpublished manuscript, presented at the Annual Meeting of the Universities Art Association of Canada/Association d'art des universites du Canada, Toronto, November 1987, pp. 1-2.

8. To learn more about the life of Hans Rookmaaker, see Linette Martin, *Hans Rookmaaker: A Biography* (Downers Grove, Ill.: Intervarsity Press, 1979).

9. Abraham Kuyper, *Lectures on Calvinism* [1898] (Grand Rapids, Mich.: Eerdmans, 1931) and Hans Rookmaaker, *Kunst en amusement* (Kampen, the Netherlands: J. H. Kok, 1962), esp. 55-98. Also see Albert M. Wolters, "On the Idea of Worldview and Its Relation to Philosophy," in *Stained Glass: Worldviews and Social Science,* edited by Paul Marshall, Sander Griffioen, and Richard Mouw (Lanham, Md.: University of America Press, 1989), esp. pp. 20-23.

of art is affected by the commitments of its maker. We cannot eradicate, avoid, or suspend our ultimate convictions. In honest scholarship faith and learning always intertwine, helping each other grow towards maturity. Consequently, the interpretation of artistic meaning and historical significance is never objective; rather it is subjective, projected from a given point of view.

Although Rookmaaker and Seerveld share the belief that art and its art-historical description are grounded in faith commitments, and have tried to write about art and its history in a manner guided by biblical wisdom, their respective art-historical methods differ in significant ways. This should not be understood as a weakness within the Neo-Calvinian tradition, but as one of its strengths. The differences between Rookmaaker and Seerveld are not to be lamented as in-house squabbling that potentially undermines the orthodoxy of the tradition. On the contrary, their differences reveal distinct possibilities within Neo-Calvinism, a tradition that embraces alteration and renewal. As this essay develops, it should become clear that, although sympathetic to many of the ideas and beliefs shared by Rookmaaker and Seerveld, I do not wish to follow directly in either of their footprints, nor do I suspect they would expect me to try. In what follows, I briefly address Rookmaaker's approach to art historiography, chart Seerveld's methodology, and provide an alternative.

## Rookmaaker

Art, according to Rookmaaker, is informed by the worldview of its producer and consequently loaded with religious meaning. The Christian art historian must look through the literal surface of the image, as if it possesses the transparency of a window, and witness the expression of personal and collective spirit. For Rookmaaker the materiality of the image is secondary to the message signified. This is not to say, however, that he is only interested in what is depicted, as opposed to how it is rendered. Both style and content come under the umbrella of the artist's interpretive vision, that is, her or his worldview.

In his book *Modern Art and the Death of a Culture*, Rookmaaker writes,

> Those who think that a painting must be a copy of nature to be realistic are mistaken: art never copies nature, but always portrays reality in a human way. That means that this painting does not copy nature as a

81

camera would, but depicts a human experience, a human understanding, an insight and emotion into what the truth about reality is. It speaks in an artistic way about reality. . . . It does not copy, it is about something that is of human relevance. In a way one can say that a painting gives a particular view of reality, a philosophy.[10]

This quote reveals Rookmaaker's failure to understand that photography is no more a neutral description of the world that painting is, but an interpretation of it. Not only is there a human perceiver guiding the camera, but the lens of the camera is itself myopic, making the photograph highly artificial. In other words, Rookmaaker seems to confuse the camera's ability to produce "reality-effect" with reality itself.[11] Photography is no less subjective than painting or sculpture, though its apparent naturalism may dupe insensitive viewers into believing that the photograph can substitute for the world. Although Rookmaaker does not seem to notice the photographer behind the camera, he recognizes quite readily the importance of the painter, whose interpretive vision is always expressed in artistic form. Because paintings do not merely mimic or imitate nature, they show the presence of the artist's worldview. Hence Rookmaaker calls viewers to consider not only the content of a given painting but also its pictorial form, for both are shaped by the artist's understanding of the world.

Worldviews, though personal, are not simply private affairs; they are communally shared. This is not to say, however, that they can ever be universal. The individuality of the point of view never disappears. As Albert Wolters has pointed out, "A worldview may be more than individual — it may be collective (that is, held by everyone belonging to a given nation or class or period). But even so it does not escape particularity, for it cannot transcend the experiences and perspectives of that particular nation, class, or period."[12] To understand the structure and direction of a specific worldview, Rookmaaker concentrates on the cultural conventions held in common within a particular time or place.

10. Hans Rookmaaker, *Modern Art and the Death of a Culture* (Downers Grove Ill.: InterVarsity Press, 1970), p. 21.

11. Roland Barthes, "The Reality Effect," in *French Literary Theory Today: A Reader,* edited by Tzvetan Todorov and translated by R. Carter (Cambridge: Cambridge University Press, 1982), pp. 11-17.

12. Albert M. Wolters, "On the Idea of Worldview and Its Relation to Philosophy," p. 19.

Broadly speaking, Rookmaaker's approach resembles that of Erwin Panofsky, whose iconological method has played a major role in the development of the art history on both sides of the Atlantic.[13] For Panofsky, as an art historian with neo-Kantian commitments, the mind constitutes the world. Consequently, works of art are interpretations of reality, produced from a certain point of view. The task of the art historian, according to Panofsky, is to unpack the meaning or message of a given work by exposing the artist's worldview, an act that demands a consideration of the cultural conventions guiding style, content, and perception itself.[14] Both Rookmaaker and Panofsky interpret works of art as symptoms or signs of worldviews. For them worldviews are more than mere mental habits, they are guiding principles — visions of how the world is, and visions of how the world should be. Artists and art historians not only look at art and life from a particular vantage point but also believe that their specific viewpoint alone is proper or normative. All worldviews are subjective, but ultimately one perspective provides greater clarity than all others.[15]

Although both Rookmaaker and Panofsky share a preoccupation with worldviews, their ultimate commitments differ. Rookmaaker's Neo-Calvinian convictions do not match Panofsky's humanist concerns. Simply put, Panofsky reads the history of art to cultivate humanity, to help us become more civilized. By contrast, Rookmaaker hopes to discover a biblical path, directing us towards God, while exposing avenues towards false idols as dead ends.

In *Modern Art and the Death of a Culture,* for instance, Rookmaaker outlines the close of Enlightenment culture. To his understanding, much of twentieth-century art aims to dismantle Enlightenment ideals of reason and nature. Dissatisfied with the norm of optical naturalism, modern artists began either, like Mondrian and Kandinsky, to look for a deeper truth beneath surface appearances or, like Duchamp and Schwitters, to destroy the notion that life has any meaning or value at all. Modern art, for Rook-

13. Erwin Panofsky, *Studies in Iconology: Humanistic Themes in the Art of the Renaissance* (New York: Oxford University Press, 1939), pp. 3-31. For more on Panofsky, see Michael Ann Holly, *Panofsky and the Foundations of Art History* (London and Ithaca, N.Y.: Cornell University Press, 1984).

14. Erwin Panofsky, "The History of Art as a Humanistic Discipline" [1940], in *Meaning in the Visual Arts* (Chicago: University of Chicago Press, 1955), esp. pp. 10-14.

15. Jaap Klapwijk, "On Worldviews and Philosophy: A Response to Wolters and Olthuis," in *Stained Glass: Worldviews and Social Science,* pp. 41-43.

maaker, alternates between intellectualism and irrationalism, between gnosticism and nihilism.[16] Although it has provided a powerful critique of the secular humanism of the Enlightenment, as a false optimism of the human condition, modern art's solution will itself function as road to ruins. The modern desire to recover the primitive or to arrive at nothingness is motivated by pseudo-religious motives, ones that fall flat and that Christians need to avoid.[17] Otherwise, the strength of a Christian perspective on art and culture will be forfeited, its purity lost in accommodation, contaminated by false belief. Although Rookmaaker is quick to call attention to the dangers of idolatry, he does not want Christians to ignore modern art: "Too many have bypassed modern art with a shrug of the shoulder, failing to see that it is one of the keys to an understanding of our time."[18] Studying twentieth-century art, in Rookmaaker's view, helps us discover signs of cultural crisis in the deconstruction of the Enlightenment worldview.

## Seerveld

In *Rainbows for the Fallen World,* Seerveld writes of modern art and the birth of a culture. As he puts it,

> Contemporary christian critics have sometimes slipped into the lazy opinion that "cubism" or "abstract" modern art is fragmented and defective, therefore a sure sign if not abetting cause of the breakdown of Western civilization. But that sweeping judgment about modern art is simply wrong. Braque and Picasso too, among certain other gifted artists, raised the painting consciousness of people by showing the painterly strength of allusive, styleful colour compositions that carried perspective, insightful meaning without using devices of mimetic illusions.[19]

For Seerveld, modern art opens up aesthetic possibilities by playfully exploring the various features of artistic form. For instance, by showing paint as paint, that is, by leaving brushstrokes unconcealed, modern artists help

---

16. Hans Rookmaaker, *Modern Art and the Death of a Culture,* pp. 104-33.
17. Rookmaaker, *Modern Art and the Death of a Culture,* pp. 226-27.
18. Rookmaaker, *Modern Art and the Death of a Culture,* p. 135.
19. Calvin Seerveld, *Rainbows for the Fallen World: Aesthetic Life and Artistic Task* (Toronto: Tuppence Press, 1980), pp. 175-76.

us discover anew the power of art as a rich opaque surface. Unconstrained by the limitations of naturalistic representation, artists can develop their imaginative insights to a greater extent.

Seerveld's critique of Rookmaaker extends beyond the meaning of modern art; it reaches out to examine Rookmaaker's categorical framework. Paintings, according to Seerveld, are not just faces that reveal particular worldviews. Like all of the visual arts, they speak to viewers. In other words, the visual arts function, says Seerveld, following the insights of the French phenomenologist Mikel Dufrenne, as "quasi-subjects."[20] Art should not be understood as a mere object for human consumption, for it actively produces viewer response, affecting beholders by its very presence. For Seerveld the history of art is unlike other histories, such as that of political or economic events, in that art continues to work, scrutinizing latecomers as we approach the presence of the past.[21] By contrast, Rookmaaker does not address the power of images per se; rather he points to the force of worldviews. In his view, art merely reflects the perspective that gave it shape and possesses no affective power of its own accord. Worldviews produce images, but images do not directly produce worldviews. Consequently, art history à la Rookmaaker can be quite easily subsumed under the general rubric of cultural history, along with all other human artifacts, which by necessity are also produced from a particular perspective.[22]

Although concerned with the affective power of art, Seerveld has not rejected the idea of worldview, only Rookmaaker's conception of it. Rookmaaker's use of the term suggests a close connection, if not fusion, between

20. Seerveld, *Rainbows for the Fallen World,* pp. 129-30. Cf. Mikel Dufrenne, *Phénoménologie de l'expérience esthétique* [1953], translated by Edward S. Casey et al. as *The Phenomenology of Aesthetic Experience* (Evanston: Northwestern University Press, 1973), pp. 145-46.

21. Calvin Seerveld, "Vollenhoven's Legacy for Art Historiography," p. 65. Cf. Hans Robert Jauss, "Literary History as a Challenge to Literary Theory" [1970], in *Towards an Aesthetic of Reception,* translated by Timothy Bahti, with an introduction by Paul de Man (Minneapolis: University of Minnesota Press, 1982), pp. 3-45.

22. This may partially explain Rookmaaker's efforts to avoid defining a specific nature of art, see *Modern Art and the Death of a Culture,* pp. 230-31. Cf. Graham Birtwistle, "Art and the Arts," in *Art in Question: London Lectures in Contemporary Christianity, 1984,* edited by Tim Dean and David Porter (London: Marshall Pickering, 1987), pp. 18-21. It should noted that earlier in his career Rookmaaker tried to define art, but later considered this an ill-advised project. For an example of his abandoned project, see Hans Rookmaaker, "Ontwerp ener Aesthetica op grondslag der Wijsbegeerte der Wetsidee," *Philosophia Reformata* 11 (1946): 141-67, and 12 (1947): 1-35.

worldview and period-style. To put it another way, Rookmaaker seems to treat worldviews as *Zeitgeister* and works of art as exemplary embodiments of temporal spirits. For Seerveld this interpretation is too simple. It implies that history can be packaged in nicely wrapped boxes. Such a view fails to account for change, the coming and goings of periods, even while it minimizes internal diversity, namely the significant stylistic differences within a given period.[23] Art-historical interpretation is no simple task, for although artworks of the past can affect us, augmenting our understanding of the world, we rarely confront images in full light. We usually face them, says Seerveld, in the moonlight of a cloudy night.[24] To help us grapple with the temporal character of artworks, Seerveld proposes that we follow three basic coordinates: the synchronic, perchronic, and diachronic.

His first coordinate, the synchronic, points to the driving force of a given period, such as the Enlightenment or the Renaissance. "Periods," writes Seerveld, "can be roughly dated somewhere; periods can run simultaneously, although they do not recur, and the more-than-individual hold on people, the principle of a period, is as historically real, as real a compelling force as Nazism, for example, or Hellenism."[25] These historical forces, framed by time and space, are pancultural in scope. The Enlightenment, for instance, includes artistic, philosophical, and economic phenomena and hence can be referred to as rococo in style, practicalist in philosophy, and physiocratic in business, without losing its core meaning, for all of these specific cultural practices and historiographic descriptions can be related to one another.[26]

Seerveld, contrary to most art historians, does not use periodization as a heuristic device.[27] To his understanding periods are not just figments of the imagination. They are historical realities, powerful forces as real as governments and other principalities. Many readers may smell the lingering

23. Calvin Seerveld, "Towards a Cartographic Methodology for Art Historiography," *Journal of Aesthetics and Art Criticism* 39 (Winter 1980): 143-45. Also see "Vollenhoven's Legacy for Art Historiography," pp. 54-55.

24. Calvin Seerveld, "Vollenhoven's Legacy for Art Historiography," p. 65. Cf. Kurt Badt, "Der Kunstgeschichtliche Zusammenhang" [1966-7], in *Kunsttheoretische Versuche,* edited by Lorenz Dittmann (Cologne: Verlag M. Dumont Schauberg, 1968), p. 161.

25. Calvin Seerveld, "Towards a Cartographic Methodology for Art Historiography," p. 148.

26. Calvin Seerveld, "Towards a Cartographic Methodology for Art Historiography," p. 149.

27. Norman Bryson, "Art in Context," in *Studies in Historical Change,* edited by Ralph Cohen (Charlottesville: University of Virginia Press, 1992), pp. 18-42.

aroma of Hegelian metaphysics in Seerveld's methodological presentation.[28] But Seerveld is quick to point out the differences between his understanding of periodization and Hegel's universal and unilinear progression of *Geist*. In Seerveld's view, periods are unpredictable, discontinuous configurations, and homogeneity, as we shall see, is not their key feature.[29]

This brings us to Seerveld's second coordinate, the perchronic. Complicating periodization is the conjunction of various perchronic types, that is worldviews that endure through time. Unlike Rookmaaker, who defines worldview roughly in terms of period-styles, Seerveld defines it in terms of stylistic types cutting across periods. Although perchronic types recur in different periods, they are not universal classes to be cast in a historiographic taxonomy of styles, but artistic traditions that can come and go.[30] Each type presents, according to Seerveld, a distinct cosmic vision. For instance, although the art of Michelangelo and Tiepolo belong to different periods, they share a heroic interpretation of the world around them, one that calls attention to the monumental struggles within human life. To take another example, the paintings of Correggio and Boucher, though from different timeframes, both provide an erotic understanding of the world, where frisky sensuality rules the day. Hence, for Seerveld there is no typical Renaissance or Rococo painting, but rather a variety of multiple and coexisting, though indefinite, perchronic types. Consequently, he writes, "a period needs to be read not as a one-line Gregorian chant melody but as a symphonic score. . . ."[31] Seerveld's concept of the perchronic also allows him to consider the diversity of a given period without losing sight of its assumed overall unity. For instance, one can discuss Renaissance paintings by Leonardo da Vinci and by Michelangelo without negating the significant differences between them. The idyllic style of Leonardo, his preoccupation with a nature perfected, can be shown to differ from the heroic style of Michelangelo.[32]

28. E. H. Gombrich, "In Search of Cultural History" [1967], in *Ideals and Idols: Essays on values in history and in art* (Oxford: Phaidon, 1979), pp. 24-59 and idem, "On Physiognomic Perception" [1960], in *Meditations on a Hobby Horse and Other Essays in the Theory of Art* (London and New York: Phaidon, 1978), pp. 45-55. Cf. David Summers, " 'Form,' Nineteenth-Century Metaphysics and the Problem of Art Historical Description," *Critical Inquiry* 15 (Winter 1989): 372-406, esp. pp. 380-84.

29. Calvin Seerveld, "Vollenhoven's Legacy for Art Historiography," p. 58.

30. Calvin Seerveld, "Vollenhoven's Legacy for Art Historiography," p. 62.

31. Calvin Seerveld, "Towards a Cartographic Methodology for Art Historiography," p. 148.

32. Calvin Seerveld, "Vollenhoven's Legacy for Art Historiography," pp. 59-62.

When discussing Seerveld's notion of the perchronic, one should keep in mind his interest in style, in how an artist frames her or his interpretation. Seerveld believes style is the best category for discovering an artist's worldview. Unlike genres (e.g., portraiture, landscape, and still-life), subject-matter (e.g., paintings of the Rape of Europa and depictions of the Last Supper), or iconographical motifs (e.g., lambs, bagpipes, and swings), the category of style explicitly reveals the perceptual understanding of the artist, the ways in which content is predicated and meaning is given.[33] It should be noted, however, that some art historians have questioned the notion of style, claiming that style is whatever you make it.[34] Seerveld is not willing to view style as a heuristic device. He does not believe that perchronic types are inventions of the art historian, but argues that they are ontic entities to be discovered and interpreted.[35]

In Seerveld's third coordinate, the diachronic, we see historical development, the dynamic changes within and between periods and styles. The continual alteration of time keeps art from becoming a static enterprise. Our interpretation of art history needs to be flexible enough, says Seerveld, to accommodate historical change, enabling us to chart the rise and fall of various trends and formats. That is to say, looking at diachronic coordinates allows us to see things such as the rise and fall of analytic cubism, Egyptian pyramids, and Catholic altarpieces. The diachronic coordinate reveals both the struggle between periods and the reformation within a given period, showing how artists respond to the work of previous generations. For Seerveld, the diachronic coordinate not only unveils the historical change within a particular period and between periods but also helps us to evaluate what an artist does with her or his inheritance, to see how the artist makes significant contributions within the past and for the present.[36] Interpreting art in relationship to these three historiographic coordinates, according to Seerveld, will provide a deeper understanding of art-historical matters.

33. Ibid., pp. 60-61. Cf. J. F. H. H. Vanbergen. *Voorstelling en Betekenis, Theorie van de Kunsthistorische Interpretatie* (Leuven: Universitaire Pers Leuven, 1986).

34. Svetlana Alpers, "Style Is What You Make It: The Visual Arts Once Again," in *The Concept of Style*, edited by Berel Lang (Ithaca, N.Y.: Cornell University Press, 1979), pp. 137-62.

35. Calvin Seerveld, "Vollenhoven's Legacy for Art Historiography," p. 6; "Towards a Cartographic Methodology for Art Historiography," p. 147; and "Footprints in the Snow," *Philosophia Reformata* 56 (1991): 1-34, esp. 5-9.

36. Calvin Seerveld, "Vollenhoven's Legacy for Art Historiography," pp. 64-65 and "Towards a Cartographic Methodology for Art Historiography," pp. 148-49.

The history of art should not be viewed, says Seerveld, as a logical progression nor as happenstance, but as a connected story full of surprises and insights. Like the flight of a firefly, it is directed, but not predetermined.[37] Interpretation should be performed playfully, in ways that respond imaginatively to art's affective power, pondering its past and present significance.[38] Rather than pigeonholing artistic events with pinpoint accuracy, which will only serve to silence and deaden art in name of objectivity, art historians need to clear an open space for art to make itself known, to show itself forth.

According to Seerveld, we should avoid interpretive practices, such as iconology, that limit the image's ability to speak. Instead of trying to decipher a single and precise meaning, art historians need to be open to the various subtle nuances an image makes. That is to say, art, unlike a sign, is connotative; it refers through ambiguity.[39] For instance, an emblematic reading of seventeenth-century Dutch still lifes as symbols of *vanitas* may miss the cunning ways they also make known the beauty and rich variety of God's creation.[40] In the project of identifying individual iconographical motifs, art historians may unwittingly misinterpret the relationship between motifs and fail to recognize their artistic dismantling at the hands of artists who attempt to alter their symbolic meaning.[41] To unpack the meaning of an image, viewers must respond to its allusive character in imaginative and insightful ways.

37. Calvin Seerveld, "A Way to Go in Writing Art History," pp. 6-7.

38. Calvin Seerveld, "A Way to Go in Writing Art History," p. 6 and "Vollenhoven's Legacy for Art Historiography, p. 63. For more on Seerveld's notion of the aesthetic, see *Rainbows for a Fallen World,* esp. pp. 104-37.

39. Calvin Seerveld, *Rainbows for the Fallen World,* pp. 125-35. Cf. Mikel Dufrenne, "Is Art Language?" *Philosophy Today* 14 (Fall 1970): 190-200.

40. Lawrence O. Goedde, "A Little World Made Cunningly: Dutch Still Life and Ekphrasis," in *Still Lifes of the Golden Age: Northern European Paintings from the Heinz Family Collection,* exhib. cat. (Washington: National Gallery of Art, 1989), pp. 35-44. For more on the multivalent character of Dutch painting, see Goedde's *Tempest and Shipwreck in Dutch and Flemish Art: Convention, Rhetoric, and Interpretation* (University Park and London: Pennsylvania State University Press, 1989; E. John Walford, *Jacob van Ruisdael and the Perception of Landscape* (New Haven and London: Yale University Press, 1991); and Reindert Falkenberg, *Joachim Patinir: het landschap als beeld van de levenspelgrimage* [1985], translated by Michael Hoyle as *Joachim Patinir: Landscape as an Image of the Pilgrimage of Life* (Amsterdam and Philadephia: John Benjamins, 1988).

41. For a good critique of static iconographical studies, see Calvin Seerveld, "Telltale Statues in Watteau's Painting," *Eighteenth-Century Studies* 18 (Winter 1980-81): 151-80.

# Critique

Like Seerveld, I hope to revive the art-historical imagination, while preserving the work of art as a vital presence. But I wonder whether his cartographic method will take us there. Let me outline four potential problems I see in Seerveld's approach to art historiography.

## 1. Dead Scholasticism

One danger of the cartographic method, one that Seerveld readily acknowledges, is that it can deteriorate into an approach that studies art only to see where it fits in the grand scheme. This unfortunate desire to pigeonhole stylistic types within an all-encompassing system not only encourages historiographic complacency but also drains the artwork's vitality by negating its affective presence. Consequently, Seerveld is always quick to say that one should read his art historiographic mappings with a sense of humor and recognize them as imaginative responses.[42] Although I admire Seerveld's efforts to maintain play, I fear the risks are too great, for ambiguity and nuance can be easily lost. Neat and tidy charts, like all systematic approaches, can effectively efface works of art by denying the work's affective presence.

## 2. Literary Imperialism

The cartographic method also seems to reduce images to words. For instance, Seerveld's perchronic types all derive from literary sources. Categories such as the idyllic, the heroic, and the picaresque were all applied to poetry before they were to painting. Non-linguistic features, such as size, medium, placement, are all treated as secondary to stylistic concerns, which are rooted in language.

42. Calvin Seerveld, "Vollenhoven's Legacy for Art Historiography," p. 72.
43. David Summers, "This is not a Sign: Some Remarks on Art and Semiotics," *Art Criticism* 3 (1986): 30-45; and Summers, "The 'Visual Arts' and the Problem of Art Historical Description," *Art Journal* 42 (1982): 301-10. For more on semiotic interpretations of art historiography, see Mieke Bal and Norman Bryson, "Semiotics and Art History," *Art Bulletin* 73 (1991): 174-208; and Keith Moxey, "Semiotics and the Social History of Art," *New Literary History* 22 (1991): 985-99.

To heighten our sensitivity to visual material we need to recognize the difference between words and images. Instead of interpreting works of art as stylistic signs, we should consider them in terms of their physical relationship to us, the ways in which they confront us in our space.[43] This would ensure that we discuss the materiality of the work beyond the sense-impression it makes as a signifier. In other words, if we are to understand the visual appearance of an artwork, then we need to transcend stylistic categories, for they reduce it to the status of signifier, the psychological imprint of the signified, the form of meaning. As symbolic modes, per-chronic types remain conventional, referring only to what one does with materiality. To see how the materiality of a work affects its production and reception we may need to look elsewhere, beyond stylistic features.

For instance, when comparing the graceful lines of Raphael's *Galatea* with sensual painterliness of Titian's *Venus of Urbino*, one needs to recognize the difference between fresco painting and oil on canvas. The former demands that the artist work quickly with a perceived idea of the project. The smoothness of the wall invites clarity of presentation. By contrast, oils permit the artist to work slowly and make changes. The rough texture of the canvas, though it hinders precision of line, fosters open brushstroke, producing greater psychological effect.[44] Seerveld's cartographic method allows for this type of discussion, but makes it less significant than worldview analyses.

## 3. Conceptual Purity

Although Seerveld defines periods and styles imaginatively, he does believe they are realities. Unfortunately, he is not persuasive on this point. Take for instance my own field of study, fifteenth-century Dutch painting: it has been called early Netherlandish painting, late Medieval painting, and Northern Renaissance art. The variety of labels is not per chance, but due to the cagey nature of historical continuity and change. Periodization has lost its legitimacy in art history, for it has proven to be impossible to keep periods distinct from one other. For instance, so-called medieval and byzantine features have been found in the Italian Renaissance, calling the very idea of rebirth into question. Because of the lack of clarity, it has become

44. David Rosand, *Painting in Cinquecento Venice: Titian, Veronese, and Tintoretto* (New Haven and London: Yale University Press, 1982), esp. pp. 15-26.

increasingly difficult to believe that particular periods or styles exist, except as useful framing devices.

Seerveld has tried to solve this problem by introducing a perchronic coordinate. Although this allows room for diversity within a given period, helping us to avoid some forms of oversimplification, it has produced new problems. A perchronic interpretation of worldviews runs the risk of reducing religious convictions to mere caricatures, by ignoring the differences between those who are said to hold the same worldviews. For instance, if we interpret Rubens's *Rape of the Daughters of Leucippus* as heroic-baroque, we may become more aware of his appropriation of Michelangelo's artistry, but the interpretation may hide the erotic elements of the work and the use of a Titian-like painterly technique.

## 4. The Archimedean Point

Seerveld, like Rookmaaker, concentrates his attention on the study of worldviews, a common Neo-Calvinian practice since Kuyper's famous Stone Lectures.[45] But as we shall see, worldview analysis may pose more theoretical problems than it is worth.[46] To show the troublesome character of worldview studies, we need to look back into the historical past, not just to Dilthey's use of *Weltanschauung*, as is commonly done, but back to fifteenth-century Italy, to Alberti's discussion of *perspectiva*, for "to view the world" one first had to "see through" something else.

To render the illusion of three-dimensional space, medieval artists tilted the ground plane upward and plotted out orthogonals, lines perpendicular to the picture plane, measured in equal increments from the bottom edge of the work and meeting together at a vanishing point on the horizon.

45. Abraham Kuyper, *Lectures on Calvinism;* Brain Walsh and J. Richard Middleton, *The Transforming Vision: Shaping a Christian World View* (Downers Grove, Ill.: Intervarsity Press, 1984); and Albert M. Wolters, *Creation Regained: Biblical Basics for a Reformational Worldview* (Grand Rapids, Mich.: Eerdmans, 1985).

46. For a useful discussion of the structure and conceptual status of worldviews, see *Stained Glass: Worldviews and Social Science,* edited by Paul Marshall, Sander Griffioen, and Richard Mouw (Lanham, Md.: University of America Press, 1989), esp. Jacob Klapwijk, "On Worldviews and Philosophy: A Response to Wolters and Olthuis," pp. 41-55; and William Rowe, "Society After the Subject, Philosophy After the Worldview," pp. 156-83. Although none of the authors in this collection reject the term "worldview," they do point out some of its problems.

Unfortunately, they did not know where to place the transversals, lines parallel to the picture plane. Alberti solved the problem by introducing a point of view. To measure the location of coordinates for drawing transversals, Alberti assumed a certain vantage point. The entire organization of spatial relations within the picture is determined by this point. Consequently, as Panofsky has shown, linear perspective is not objective, but incredibly subjective, a conventional construction dependent upon viewer placement, for we can only see how things are from a particular point of view.[47] Although it provides enough clarity to seem persuasively real, linear perspective is little more than an elaborate trick.

Alberti's picture-box has proven to be an effective means of concealing the picture plane and of unveiling a virtual world beyond. But, like its worldview counterpart, *perspectiva* is not without problems. As Leonardo first noticed, its assumptions do not correspond to the way we see things. Not only does it assume the placement of viewer, but also it presupposes a singular point of view, which does not exist. We do not see through a single cone of vision, for we have two eyes, making our vision binocular. Furthermore, our eyes are rounded and do not take in light from a single point. Finally, Alberti's model assumes that sight begins from a relatively static position, but in vision our eyes are constantly moving, and without micro-vibrations we would not see anything at all.

Worldview analyses rely on similar false assumptions. First of all, worldview studies begin from a particular point of view, that of the scholar, from which she or he interprets works of art, which are also assumed to derive from certain points of view. Although this stance is by necessity beyond the world it perceives, making it appear acontextual, this need not imply the presence of an underlying positivism, for what allows the viewer to see is not simply the result of objective distance, but an assumed interpretive lens providing clarity. Having the proper commitments, it is thought, enables the scholar to see straight. For instance, although Rookmaaker addresses non-Christian worldviews as historical positions, he seems to equate that of his own, namely Neo-Calvinism, with the biblical one.[48] Searching for an antithetical critique free of false religion, Rook-

---

47. Erwin Panofsky, "Die Perspektive als 'symbolische Form'" [1927], translated, with an introduction, by Christopher S. Wood as *Perspective as Symbolic Form* (New York: Zone Books, 1991).

48. Hans Rookmaaker, *Modern Art and the Death of a Culture*, pp. 243-52. Cf.

maaker seems to forget the historical roots of his own convictions. Neo-Calvinism is, after all, only a historical response to normativity, not normativity itself. Pure antithesis is impossible, for one's beliefs are always in flux, being shaped by one's cultural and historical context.[49] Consequently, we do not see the world from a single point of view.

The same danger seems to be present in Seerveld's cartographic method, for one must be off the chart to read it. If the interpreter is understood as being transcendent, beyond the contingency of the world viewed, then it is easy to confuse one's vision with that of God. Yet, Seerveld notes, "A pedagogical danger of the cartographic methodology . . . is to mistake the shorthand sketched overview to be the masterplan printout."[50] In an attempt to avoid such an erroneous identification, he has pointed out that historians do not possess a gnostic key to unlock future developments. To contextualize the proper perspective, Seerveld has introduced as one of his perchronic types the "troubled cosmic" style, which reveals deep need for reconciliation for a broken world along with glimpses of joy.[51] This stylistic category allows him to address commitments that affirm biblical truth without negating their differences with biblical religion.[52]

Like Seerveld, I want to affirm the fallen and finite character of my interpretations. The elimination of worldview jargon makes that easier, however, for we can discuss the active religious convictions presented in

---

Abraham Kuyper, *Lectures on Calvinism*, esp. pp. 17-40; and Herman Dooyeweerd, *Vernieuwing en bezinning: Om het reformatorisch grondmotief* [1959], partially translated by John Kraay as *Roots of Western Culture: Pagan, Secular and Christian Options* (Toronto: Wedge Publishing, 1979).

49. Jacob Klapwijk, "Reformational Philosophy on the Boundary between the Past and the Present," *Philosophia Reformata* 52 (1987): 101-34.

50. Calvin Seerveld, "Vollenhoven's Legacy for Art Historiography," p. 63.

51. Calvin Seerveld, "Vollenhoven's Legacy for Art Historiography," p. 62.

52. The differences between Rookmaaker and Seerveld on this point may roughly correspond the differences between the historiographic methodologies of Dooyeweerd and Vollenhoven. Rookmaaker seems to follow in Dooyeweerd's footsteps, looking to expose a person's Archimedean point, his or her religious standpoint in regards to a particular ground-motive. See Herman Dooyeweerd, *The Roots of Western Culture.* Seerveld, like Vollenhoven, prefers to speak of the Calvinist worldview rather than the Christian worldview, a telltale sign of his desire to stay within historical limits. For more on Vollenhoven's method, see his "De Consequent Problem-historische Methode," *Philosophia Reformata* 26 (1961): 1-34; and Calvin Seerveld, "Biblical Wisdom under Vollenhoven's Categories for Philosophical Historiography," *Philosophia Reformata* 38 (1973): 127-43.

works of art without assuming that artists have perspectives. In other words, the optical metaphor of worldview, whether applied to the artist or the beholder, is misleading, for it suggests a transcendent point of view that only God could possess.[53] Consequently, the discussion of religious beliefs and art-historical interpretation may be better served without it.

## Ideology

To describe the convictions embedded in particular works of art, the term "ideology," when properly defined, may prove to be more helpful than notions of "worldview." The benefits of ideology, however, hinge on its definition. Ideology, in traditional Marxism, is defined as false consciousness, as a distorted vision of real circumstances. As a defense of dominant class interests and as part of the superstructure reflecting society's economic base, ideology maintains the current mode of production. Ideology so defined resembles the appearance of worldview, for it implies both that perspectives stem from a particular vantage point and that from the proper viewpoint one can see the world clearly.[54]

My definition of ideology differs significantly from that of traditional Marxism. First, all works of art and art-historiographic interpretations are ideologically motivated. Ideology does not function like a rose-colored pair of hermeneutic glasses, as something one can wear or remove, rather it is one's interpretive blood, something that one cannot live without. Ideology is not something that can be escaped or suspended. Second, ideologies do not merely reflect or mirror historical circumstances, but actively shape the structure of cultural institutions and give it direction.[55] As a web of religious

---

53. Cf. Martin Jay, *Downcast Eyes: The Denigration of Vision in Twentieth-Century French Thought* (Berkeley: University of California Press, 1993).

54. Cf. Albert M. Wolters, *Creation Regained*, pp. 1-2.

55. For more on ideology, see Louis Althusser, "Ideology and the Ideological State Apparatuses," translated by Ben Brewster in *Lenin and Philosophy and Other Essays* (New York: Monthly Review Press, 1971), pp. 126-86; Terry Eagleton, *Ideology: An Introduction* (London: Verso, 1991); W. J. T. Mitchell, *Iconology: Image, Text, Ideology* (Chicago: University of Chicago Press, 1986), esp. pp. 160-208; Keith Moxey, *Peasants, Warriors, and Wives: Popular Imagery in the Reformation* (Chicago: University of Chicago Press, 1989); Moxey, *The Practice of Theory*, esp. pp. 41-50; Raymond Williams, "Base and Superstructure in Marxist Cultural Theory," *New Left Review* 82 (1983): 3-16; and Lambert Zuidervaart, *Adorno's Aesthetic Theory: The Redemption of Illusion* (Cambridge, Mass. and London: MIT Press, 1991), esp. pp. 68-70.

and cultural commitments, wherein theological and socio-political concerns are entangled, ideologies affect every aspect of human life. In some cases, ideological commitments are disseminated through the visual arts as a means to suppress opposition and reinforce the authority of the current institution in power, whether it be the State, the Museum, the Academy, or the Church. Worldview studies, like traditional Marxist accounts, tend to treat works of art as passive reflections and ignore their affective power. For instance, one can imagine a scenario in which a peasant painting by Pieter Bruegel the Elder is described simply as a picaresque perspective of rustic life. Such a view, however, is incomplete, if not misguided, for it does not take into consideration the ways in which Bruegel's moralizing satire affirms sixteenth-century Netherlandish humanist elitism, by characterizing peasants as vulgar *boers* preoccupied with immediate gratification of bodily pleasures. Not only do ideologies affect the production and reception of artworks, but the production and reception of artworks affect ideologies, by giving them shape and by reinforcing or altering their content.

To interpret the ideological character of the work, the viewer should look for the visual strategies employed, which were produced to persuade a particular audience to accept certain beliefs as their own. Interpreting the meaning of the work is not passive, for ideologies usually do not simply display themselves on the image's surface. Consequently, viewers must take on the responsibility to look, that is make the effort to see something.[56] In the dialogical relationship between viewer and work of art, each scrutinizes the other. Ideological prejudices are always in operation on both sides of this relation, for subject and quasi-subject alike, wherein the goal is not scientific explanation, an objective gathering of facts, but a deeper understanding of our humanity and the responsibilities that entails.

Historians who interpret works of art, whether they be paintings, sculptures, or even photographs, as documentary evidence illustrating a particular state of affairs without reference to the ways in which these affairs are

56. For more on active interpretation, see Roman Ingarden, "Phenomenological Aesthetics: An Attempt at Defining its Range," *Journal of Aesthetics and Art Criticism* 33 (1975): 257-69; Ingarden, *Vom Erkennen des literarischen Kunstwerks* [1937], translated by Ruth Ann Crowley and Kenneth R. Olson as *The Cognition of the Literary Work of Art* (Evanston: Northwestern University Press, 1973), esp. pp. 37-41; José Ortega y Gasset, *¿Qué es filosofía?* [1929], translated by Mildred Adams as *What is Philosophy?* (New York: W. W. Norton, 1960), esp. pp. 75-76; and Umberto Eco, *Interpretation and Overinterpretation* (Cambridge: Cambridge University Press, 1992).

represented, misunderstand the images confronting them and hence mis-interpret the respective historical circumstances that produced the images. But historians also need to be careful not to read works of art allegorically, by peeling away the literal surface of the image to some deep meaning behind it. Such a view belittles, if not denies, the image's materiality, that is, its physical presence as shaped by cultural tools. Rookmaaker, in his analysis of worldviews, preoccupied as he is with the religious intentions of artists, offers the materiality of the image little importance. By viewing art as a quasi-subject, Seerveld gives its materiality a greater significance. Following the insights of the art historian Kurt Badt, Seerveld is quick to point out the ways in which the artist's materials and instruments are disclosed in a given work of art.[57] The artist depends upon an artistic medium to make the artist's marks and remarks. Not only do images record their own making, their *facture,* but also they show their materiality.

The difference between Rookmaaker and Seerveld on this point may be highlighted by investigating their respective views on the Creator-artist analogy. For Rookmaaker, artists, in the image of God, create new things, though not out of nothing.[58] But Seerveld does not discuss the artistic vocation in terms of creating. As he puts it,

> Comparisons between God as capital A Creator Artist and man as small, image-of-God creator artist are only speculative and misleading. To turn analysis of "what now is human artistic activity?" into a theo-logical dis-cussion on the unique "creativity" of God is no help at all in determining the nature and place of art on earth. Such a would-be Christian approach is often caught in the age-old trap of *analogia entis.*[59]

The artist does not give materials value, for they had it prior to human intervention, as part of the goodness of Creation. Rather than providing meaning to meaningless stuff, form to matter, the artist builds upon the meaning already there.

---

57. Calvin Seerveld, "A Way to Go in Writing Art History," pp. 5-7. Cf. Kurt Badt, *Die Kunst Cezannes* [1956], translated by Sheila Ann Ogilvie as *The Art of Cézanne* (Berkeley: University of California Press, 1965), p. 247.

58. Hans Rookmaaker, *The Creative Gift: Essays on Art and the Christian Life* (Westchester, Ill.: Cornerstone Books, 1981), p. 113. Cf. Graham Birtwistle, "Art and the Arts," pp. 21-22.

59. Calvin Seerveld, *Rainbows for the Fallen World,* p. 26.

Though Seerveld respects the materiality of the image, it is difficult to see in his cartographic method how this materiality has any significance beyond its relationship to the formation of various perchronic types. In other words, it becomes hard to imagine how images possess power beyond the fact that they present worldviews. Consequently, although I agree with much of Seerveld's overall view concerning materiality, I would like to address the question in a different fashion, concentrating upon art's power to re-present, to enter into ontological communion with that which it shows.[60] Images, in my view, often function as substitutes, restoring the presence of something by replacing it, as they assume the guise of being something other than themselves.[61] Because I have posed the question in terms of representational power, the scope of my project is somewhat broader than that of Seerveld, for it includes visual items that represent prototypes but are not usually considered art. Although the specificity of art may be lost, this way of framing the discussion may heighten our awareness of the potency of visual images. For instance, a study of representational power may help us to understand the nexus in late medieval religious devotion between picture, relic, and eucharistic host, as interrelated images localizing the divine, miraculously revealing while mysteriously concealing its presence.[62]

As mentioned previously, the power of images does not originate in the act of making; rather the making of an image continues the power of materials at another ontological level. Images often function as "real meta-

60. Hans-Georg Gadamer, *Truth and Method*, p. 126. Cf. David Freedberg, *The Power of Images: Studies in the History and Theory of Response* (Chicago and London: University of Chicago Press, 1989); Hans Belting, *Das Bild und sein Publikum im Mittelalter: Form und Funktion früher Bildtafeln der Passion* [1981], translated by Mark Bartusis and Raymond Meyer as *The Image and Its Public in the Middle Ages: Form and Function of Early Paintings of the Passion* (New Rochelle, N.Y.: Aristide D. Caratzas, 1990); and Belting, *Bild und Kult: Eine Geschichte des Bildes vor dem Zeitalter der Kunst* [1990], translated by Edmund Jephcott as *Likeness and Presence: A History of the Image before the Era of Art* (Chicago: University of Chicago Press, 1994).

61. David Summers, " 'Real Metaphor': Towards a Redefinition of the 'Conceptual' Image," in *Visual Theory: Painting and Interpretation,* edited by Norman Bryson, Michael Ann Holly, and Keith Moxey (New York: Polity Press, 1991), pp. 231-59.

62. Barbara G. Lane, *The Altar and the Altarpiece: Sacramental Themes in Early Netherlandish Painting* (New York: Harper and Row, 1984); and Henry Luttikhuizen, "Meditation Bred in the Bones: The Relation Between Image and Relic in Fifteenth-Century Netherlandish Culture," unpublished manuscript, presented at the *Twenty-Ninth International Congress of Medieval Studies*, Kalamazoo, Mich., on 6 May 1994.

phors."[63] The term *metaphora* etymologically derives from the act of carrying something over or beyond, of transferring something. Images, in my view, are literally metaphors, carrying not just that which they represent, but also their media (their physical materiality as shaped by cultural tools) and handiwork (the signature of their maker). This metaphorical alteration begins prior to iconic resemblance, that is, before the image looks like anything else. Put differently, representation of any state of affairs is dependent upon this literal transference, for, as Meyer Schapiro has noted, iconic resemblance is impossible without a framed, relatively monochromatic, and smoothly prepared field.[64] The uniform planar surface of a painting makes illusionary space possible. Simply stated, one cannot view a depicted world beyond the picture plane without a picture plane. Although the materiality of an image can be concealed for the sake of naturalism, its presence is essential.

Materials affect the manner in which we make and receive works of art. Not only do they impose physical limitations on the maker, in terms of their durability, cost, accessibility, and their capacities to be shaped and transported, but also they may demand respect as sacred items, as do the precincts in which they reside. Consider the case of limewood. In pre-Christianized Germany limewood trees were believed to possess magical powers that could heal and protect human beings. In the fifteenth century, well after the introduction of Christianity, German sculptors continued to make their images of merciful Madonnas from limewood, reappropriating this miraculous material.[65]

Artists are in many cases not unlike magicians, who also do not make transfigurations occur *ex nihilo*. Both the artist and magician, though highly skilled, are, to a certain extent, dependent upon the powers of their materials and a space for make-believe. The magician cannot create an illusion, for example, of sawing a person in half, without a saw, a person, a box, an informed audience, and a special precinct (namely, a stage), nor without presenting a sense of the person's previous state of wholeness.[66] Otherwise, the trick will not work. The illusion of iconic resemblance has similar

63. David Summers, "Real Metaphor," pp. 245-49.

64. Meyer Schapiro, "On Some Problems in the Semiotics of Visual Art: Field and Vehicle in Image-Sign," *Semiotica* 1 (1969): 223-42.

65. Michael Baxandall, *The Limewood Sculptors of Renaissance Germany* (New Haven and London: Yale University Press, 1980).

demands, for to make present what they exhibit, images must place the absent in the already present.

The power of images does not diminish with intellectual prowess, for rational thought does not lessen the aura of the image. Works of art can affect anyone who confronts them, including "enlightened" viewers in western societies. The capacity to replicate images mechanically, not the capacity to perceive an image with clear reason, may diminish the aura of the image.[67] But if reproductions can be distinguished from originals, then the authenticity of the image may be preserved and its power enhanced.

Unlike speech, which can performed by nearly all, in most cases the making and ownership of marks, whether in writing or picture, is reserved for a cultural elite. In many cultures artists are shaman, powerful priests who mediate the sacred and the profane. Although we usually see this outside of western civilization, it is important to note the close connection between artist and priest in the western heritage. Not only have artists assumed magical powers, as in the stories of Daedalus and Pygmalion, but also they have been considered geniuses, chosen by God, a feature they shared with emperors and poets.[68]

Furthermore, the Latin words *auctor* (= author) and *augur* (= soothsayer) may also be related. In ancient Rome, only the *augur* had the *auctoritas*, the authority, to interpret the signs of the gods. Of course, the *augur* did not arbitrarily choose the sign's meaning, but was restricted by a strict and elaborate code of rules, by a given *decorum* for viewing. In a sense, the *augur* was devoted to bird-watching, *avispicium*. By consulting the *auspices* or birds, the *augur* discovered divine oration. This seeing of birds could not occur anywhere. It demanded the marking out of a sacred precinct, a *templum*. To make this space, the priest *drew* it out or *abstracted* it. This

---

66. Cf. E. H. Gombrich, "Leonardo and the Magicians: Polemics and Rivalry" [1983], in *New Light on Old Masters: Studies in the Art of the Renaissance IV* (Chicago and London: University of Chicago Press, 1986), pp. 61-88. For an interesting discussion of early Christian depictions of Christ as a magician, see Thomas Matthews, *The Clash of Gods: A Reinterpretation of Early Christian Art* (Princeton: Princeton University Press, 1993).

67. Walter Benjamin, "Das Kunstwerk im Zeitalter seiner technischen Reproduzierbarkeit" [1935], translated by Harry Zohn as "The Work of Art in the Age of Mechanical Reproduction" in *Illuminations* (New York: Schocken, 1968), pp. 217-51.

68. Ernst Kris and Otto Kurz, *Die Legende vom Künstler: Ein historische Versuch* [1934], translated by Alastair Laing as *Legend, Myth, and Magic in the Image of the Artist: A Historical Experiment* (New Haven and London: Yale University Press, 1979).

act of *contemplatio* or contemplation is the setting up of a sacred space, a *templum*, a place from which one can see all and be seen by all.[69] Through the Horatian dictum *ut pictura poesis* (= as in painting so in poetry) and Italian renaissance *paragone* (= competition between the arts, including that between the verbal and visual practices), entangled notions of artist, poet, and priest became highlighted.[70] As interpreters, all three had the authority to respond, under the direction of decorum, to the presentation of the divine. Without proper sensitivity and skill, signs cannot be understood nor their meaning communicated.

Substitutive images function by displacement, making the absent present, solving the defect of distance that separates prototype and viewer. By definition, images are not merely self-referential, but always refer to something else. Even in the case of images with assumed apotropaic power (= the ability to ward off evil), the source of power comes from elsewhere. Images present marks or traces of what they represent, not things in themselves. Thus, as the French philosopher Emmanuel Levinas might put it, in the image is one place where alterity can come to pass, for we can see the other in the image without reducing the other to the same, that is, to the image.[71]

If we address images in terms of substitutive power, it is easy to see why historically they have been so troublesome to Christians. The distinction between image and idol was necessary for the legitimation of liturgical art, and maintaining this difference became crucial for Catholic and Orthodox worship.[72] Unlike an idol, which is worshipped as an end in itself, an image is venerated as a means towards a prototype. Jean Calvin did not believe that there was a difference between veneration and worship, and

69. Martin Heidegger, "Wissenschaft und Besinnung" [1954], translated by William Lovett as "Science and Reflection" in *The Question Concerning Technology and Other Essays* (New York: Harper and Row, 1977), pp. 165-66; and William V. Rowe. "Our Simplicity," inaugural address at the Institute for Christian Studies, Toronto, on 7 November 1987.

70. Rensselaer Lee, *Ut Pictura Poesis: The Humanistic Theory of Painting* (New York: W. W. Norton, 1967); David Summers, *Michelangelo and the Language of Art* (Princeton: Princeton University Press, 1981); and Summers, *The Judgment of Sense* (Cambridge: Cambridge University Press, 1987).

71. Emmanuel Levinas, *Totaité et Infini* [1961], translated by Alphonso Lingis as *Totality and Infinity: An Essay on Exteriority* (Pittsburgh: Duquesne University Press, 1969), esp. pp. 187-219.

72. Michael Camille, *The Gothic Idol: Ideology and Image-Making in Medieval Art* (Cambridge: Cambridge University Press, 1989), esp. pp. 203-20.

consequently his followers stormed churches to destroy works of art.[73] Disenchanted with the presence of sacred images, they rendered them idolatrous. In many ways iconoclasm has given Calvinism its identity. One only needs to take notice of the white-washed walls in Reformed churches to understand this. Kuyper, Rookmaaker, and Seerveld have all worked hard to show us that art can be a legitimate calling, but we continue to struggle with role of liturgical art within our tradition. Although I do not pretend to have a solution to this problem, grappling with the substitutive power of images seems to be a good starting point.

To understand the history of art I encourage my students to focus on two questions: (1) What does the image look like? and (2) Why does it look the way it does? By concentrating on these two questions, I hope we will discover not just something about its visual appearance, but something about the ways in which it works. To disclose the intentions of the work, that is, to recognize its visual strategy, demands that we look at its historical context.[74] Looking at historical context can aid our understanding by providing a framework to moderate our conjectures, to keep our theses within limits.

For Seerveld and others, my approach to periodization or historical context may seem instrumentalist, as a view in which the visual arts have no specific nature and are just one set of many cultural tools. But I am not out to master the arts or teach people how to win favor and influence people through the use of images. Instead I want to look beyond encompassing power towards humility, to dwell with the image, preserving and caring for its presence. As Paul Ricoeur tells us, "To dwell is to be received as a guest. And construing is making, but in such a way that we do not make the world less worthy of dwelling in. Some kind of humility, accordingly, is entailed in the act of dwelling."[75] This presupposes an initial act of generosity, of openness. Through this act of circumcision, this cutting open the flesh, self-enclosure and self-withdrawal are eliminated. When we break out of ourselves in hospitality, we are at home in the world. As Emmanuel Levinas

73. Jean Calvin, *Institutio Christianae religionis* [1559], translated by Ford Lewis Battles as *Institutes of the Christian Religion* (Philadelphia: Westminster Press, 1960), vol. 1, pp. 99-116; Carlos M. N. Eire, *The War Against Idols: The Reformation of Worship from Erasmus to Calvin* (Cambridge: Cambridge University Press, 1986).

74. Umberto Eco, *Interpretation and Overinterpretation*, pp. 23-88.

75. Paul Ricoeur, "Review of Nelson Goodman's *Ways of Worldmaking*," *Philosophy and Literature* 4 (Spring 1980): 118.

puts it, "Paradoxically, it is as *alienus* — as stranger and alien — that humanity is not alienated."[76]

A responsible interpretation of art on these terms may appear to be weak and vulnerable, but to my understanding it is the most ethical one, for it recognizes the face of the image, while acknowledging its ideological commitments. This is not to say that I am willing to compromise my principles or suspend my values to accommodate a given image, but that I am willing to confront it humbly, keeping my religious convictions intact. As Jaap Klapwijk has shown, "it is only when the risks of communication are recognized that the challenge can be accepted responsibly. Aware of the risks we can, open to others and respecting them, truly render account of Christian hope."[77]

Antithetical critique, an all too common practice within the Neo-Calvinian tradition, rests on the false premise of a pure and single point of view. But as I have tried to show, we cannot obtain such a viewpoint, for one cannot remove oneself from time or space. Critique that does not acknowledge contextuality also can fall prey to ideological dogmatism, bringing us no closer to truth or justice.

Not only is the antithetical critique näive in terms of its contextuality, but also it may be unethical, leading to hypocritical slandering of others and to an arrogant ignoring of the self. At its worst, antithetical critique may judge the ideological commitments of others as merely a series of mistakes to avoid, failing to recognize the potential truths they may reveal. Promoting self-assurance in our own capacities to know biblical truth, antithetical critique also may conceal our finitude and our fallenness. Humility, not pride, should guide our studies. Consequently, we should search for a more responsible mode of critique, one that respects the self and others.

Dialogue is impossible without respect for religious difference. Loss of identity and polarization remain real concerns, but one cannot converse without accepting such vulnerability. If we choose to remain deaf to the ideas of others, we isolate ourselves from culture and fail to hear God's call

---

76. Emmanuel Levinas, *Le Dit et la Dire,* p. 48. Quoted in Theodor de Boer, "Beyond Being: Ontology and Eschatology in the Philosophy of Emmanuel Levinas," *Philosophia Reformata* 38 (1973): 25.

77. Jaap Klapwijk, "Antithesis, Synthesis, and the Idea of Transformational Philosophy," *Philosophia Reformata* 51 (1986): 138-54.

through the thoughts and deeds of others. Consequently, we need to look for more effective ways to talk about works of art, ways that, while acknowledging our interpretive limitations, consider the materiality of the image and its affective presence and avoid worldview jargon and the mirage of antithetical critique. Images, after all, are not passive illustrations of worldviews, but powerful re-presentations, actively tantalizing viewers to believe something. Their vivid presence may prove to be more persuasive than mere words can tell.

Although in this essay I disagree with Rookmaaker and Seerveld on some points, I do not consider my approach to art historiography an erasure of their respective methodologies. On the contrary, I have absorbed much of their thought. Rookmaaker and Seerveld do not offer us sour grapes, but robust flavor of the Neo-Calvinian tradition. Serving this fine vintage in tasteful and pleasing manner, Rookmaaker and Seerveld have taught us valuable lessons, helping us to see the religious direction of works of art. But the call for reformation continues. In my critique I have tried to show the need to look for new wine glasses, ones that, although shaped by the authority of the past, are not old-fashioned. To my understanding, Neo-Calvinian wine would taste best in a translucent, though not transparent, goblet, one that will show the fruits of biblical wisdom, while reminding us that we only see through a glass, darkly.

# II. PHILOSOPHICAL DIALOGUE

# Deconstruction and Christian Cultural Theory: An Essay on Appropriation

## MEROLD WESTPHAL

The prospects do not seem bright for an appropriation of postmodern insights in the service of a Christian interpretation and critique of contemporary culture. Philosophical postmodernism is widely seen as being, at best, the moral equivalent of leprosy and, at worst, the moral equivalent of AIDS. The need to demonize runs deep. How else persuade ourselves, in spite of the evidence to the contrary, that we are really good — the last, best hope of the world? So it is that the temptation to lump postmodernism together with Hitler and Stalin is simply irresistible to some.

For example, Michael Howard is enthusiastic about the "devastating attack on the forces of postmodernism in academic studies, literary, philosophical and historical" that he finds in Gertrude Himmelfarb's *On Looking into the Abyss.* She portrays postmodernists as the spiritual successors of John Stuart Mill's vision of a "value-free society" and of the Bloomsbury group that "poured mockery on the whole concept of moral commitment and regarded history, philosophy, and literature as vehicles purely for private pleasure." Sandwiching a reference to Jacques Derrida, probably the most widely influential of the French poststructuralists on the North American scene, we find this summary. "We know what happens when people actually put these 'value-free' principles into practice; we saw it only a generation ago on a horrific scale in the Holocaust. . . . At best [these

107

people] are frivolous game-players who make a virtue of their moral irresponsibility. At worst, they are set on destroying the standards that not only make their own activity possible but also enable society to survive at all."[1]

Apparently in dealing with the bad guys one is permitted to be scurrilous rather than scrupulous. When an Oxford historian praises a City University of New York colleague for deriving Fascism from Mill's vision of a liberal society, it would seem that the academy is truly in deep peril — to say nothing of the curious portrayal of Hitler's gang as a "value-free" society. I had thought their problem was in assuming that the quite particular values of which they took themselves to be the embodiment were absolute values; and I was reminded of Arthur Schlesinger's address in which he reminded us that the atrocities of modernity have been committed by moral absolutists.

A certain Francis Duke from Los Angeles was thinking along the same lines. His reply to the Howard review points out that the Holocaust, like the Inquisition and slavery, was perpetrated by those who took the values legitimating their power to be quite absolute. Acknowledging his own reservations about postmodernism, he adds, "But implicitly they are asking the right question: How do we make sure another Holocaust doesn't occur while we are busy listening to Bach and Mozart and congratulating ourselves on our wonderful eternal values?"[2]

Literary theorist Roger Lundin is as eager as historians Howard and Himmelfarb to protect the world from the postmodern menace. His defenses are activated by the suggestion that "postmodernism can be seen as an extended meditation on several Pauline themes whose repudiation all but defines modernity" as the claim to absolute knowledge. Reference is to the notion that we do not now see the eternal "face to face" but only "in a mirror, dimly" (1 Cor. 13:12) and that we hold the truth of the gospel "in clay jars" (2 Cor. 4:7), to say nothing of our tendency as sinners to "suppress the truth" (Rom. 1:18). "Philosophically speaking, the main motifs of modernism are the attempt to have done, once and for all, with Paul and his gloomy followers, from Augustine through Luther and Calvin to Kierkegaard and Barth."[3]

---

1. Michael Howard, "Facing the Monsters," *The New York Times Book Review,* March 6, 1994, pp. 11-12.

2. Letter to *The New York Times Book Review,* March 20, 1994, p. 31.

3. Quoted from Merold Westphal, "The Ostrich and the Boogeyman," *Christian Scholar's Review* 20, 2 (December 1990), pp. 115-16.

Lundin duly notes that the suggestion alleges an affinity between the hermeneutics of finitude and the hermeneutics of suspicion to be found in postmodernism and the Pauline understanding of the radical limits of our cognitive equipment. But rather than explore this curious convergence, he warns against misreading poststructuralist intentions, and counters, "To say that postmodernism is an extended meditation on Pauline themes is like saying that because Joseph Stalin shared Winston Churchill's fear and loathing of the Nazis, the Russian dictator's speeches to rally his country-men were extended reflections on political democracy and economic free-dom. It is accurate to say that, like Derrida, Augustine would assail the tenets of modernism, but it is misleading to imply that since the two of them would spurn Descartes, they would be eager to embrace each other."[4] Presumably Lundin does not intend for us to correlate Paul (and Augustine) with Stalin, leaving Derrida to play the role of Churchill.

In this Wonderland, as in an earlier one, things get "curiouser and curiouser." First of all, nothing was said about the intentions of the post-structuralists, whose radical secularism is obvious enough, while on the other hand, their "Pauline" dimension is something neither their friends nor their foes are eager to notice. One might have hoped that "can be seen as an extended meditation" would not be immediately translated as "is an extended meditation" in the sense implying that this is the writers' inten-tion. What about the possibility that what they help us to see exceeds their intentions:[5] that a hermeneutics of finitude will illumine the epistemic meaning of creaturehood and that a hermeneutics of suspicion will illumine the epistemic significance of sin, even if developed by those who do not speak the language of Creation and Fall? What happened to the notion that all truth is God's truth, even truth from the pens of atheists?

Nor was there the slightest suggestion that Augustine and Derrida would be "eager to embrace each other," only that the (not so obvious) similarity of substance between their critiques of what Augustine calls

---

4. Roger Lundin, *The Culture of Interpretation* (Grand Rapids: Eerdmans, 1993), pp. 205-7.

5. My strategy in dealing with philosophical postmodernism is the same as my strategy for reading the hermeneutics of suspicion in Marx, Nietzsche, and Freud. In *Suspicion and Faith: The Religious Uses of Modern Atheism* (Grand Rapids: Eerdmans, 1993), I argue that, contrary to their atheistic intentions, their religion critiques echo and illumine the biblical critiques of instrumental religion and make good Lenten reading for Christians willing to engage in serious self-examination.

philosophical "presumption" (*Confessions* VII, 20) is worth noticing and exploring, and not just the (quite obvious) difference of motivation that underlies the similarity. If there really is a similarity of substance, then the simile of Stalin only serves to obscure the possibility that those of us who trace our lineage through Augustine might find insights worth appropriating from Derrida in the pursuit of our own project.

Lundin is a serious scholar, not a talk show host trying to raise ratings or a televangelist trying to raise money with rhetorical reassurances that he will protect us from the bad guys. I assume the same about Howard and Himmelfarb. Why are they then so quick to link Hitler and Stalin with postmodernism? This assimilation of postmodernism to totalitarianism is especially ironic since the former is a sustained critique of the violent, totalizing discourses that absolutize their own insights, thereby legitimizing the violent, exclusionary practices congruent with those discourses.

Perhaps part of the reason is political: postmodern critique does not find such discourses and practices only in such safe places as communism and fascism. (The habit of labeling anyone who dares to criticize the West as either communist or fascist dies hard.) But the stated reason is ethical: postmodernism is seen as an nihilistic threat to what is good in our way of life, as a loss of moral compass that reinforces the moral wasteland of contemporary culture rather than challenging it.

Lundin, in particular, sees Derrida as providing philosophical aid and comfort to the therapeutic ideals so devastatingly analyzed by Rieff, Bellah, and MacIntyre. According to the latter, the implicit moral philosophy of a therapeutic culture is "emotivism," the view "that all evaluative judgments and more specifically all moral judgments are *nothing but* expressions of preference, expressions of attitude or feeling, insofar as they are moral or evaluative in character."[6]

We are familiar with emotivism from the logical positivism of the forties and fifties (even if most denizens of our therapeutic culture are not).[7] But postmodernism is not positivism. Both traditions are skeptical,

6. Alasdair MacIntyre, *After Virtue*, 2d ed. (Notre Dame: University of Notre Dame, 1984), p. 11. Cf. Philip Rieff, *The Triumph of the Therapeutic: Uses of Faith After Freud* (New York: Harper & Row, 1966) and Robert Bellah et al., *Habits of the Heart: Individualism and Commitment in American Life* (Berkeley: University of California Press, 1985).

7. For classic statements, see A. J. Ayer, *Language, Truth and Logic* (New York: Dover, 1946); Charles L. Stevenson, *Ethics and Language* (New Haven: Yale University Press, 1944); and Paul Edwards, *The Logic of Moral Discourse* (New York: Free Press, 1955).

to be sure, of the grand claims to absolute knowledge that accompany the metaphysical foundations of morality in much of the philosophical tradition. But beyond their irreverence toward metaphysical pretensions, there are at least two striking differences. The postmodern critique applies to all human knowledge, and not just to ethics and metaphysics. It is miles removed from the scientism of the positivist tradition. More importantly, in the present context, the positivists were the ones who insisted that their theories entailed moral subjectivism, while in the case of the postmodernists, it is their enemies who make this claim.

At least some postmodernists continue to think that while the Enlightenment project of providing absolute justifications for our ethical beliefs has self-destructed, their own work still has the character of morally significant critique, both of theory and of practice. Like almost everyone else these days, they reject the positivists' all or nothing approach: *either* we have absolute knowledge in ethics, *or* we have nothing at all and ethics is nothing but personal preferences, any one of which is as good as any other. Moreover, echoing Kierkegaard's lament that "the system has no ethics" and paraphrasing Kant's claim, "I have had to deny knowledge in order to make room for faith," they argue, in effect, "We have had to deny absolute knowledge in order to make room for moral responsibility." Then they add, "If we are to oppose the physical violence of political totalitarianism, we must oppose the epistemic or 'interpretative' violence of totalizing discourse."[8]

In this context, to assimilate the postmodernists to the positivists is doubly problematic. First, it attributes to them a position they explicitly repudiate; second, by assuming that since they deny we can have everything they must mean we have nothing, it invites the suspicion that one accepts the positivists' all or nothing approach, that one's own ethics stands or falls with claims to absolute knowledge that would have made the apostle Paul's hair stand on end. But why should a seriously Christian ethics be tied in this way to the epistemological extravagances of the not noticeably biblical projects of Plato, Descartes, and Hegel? Why not agree with Paul that we see "through a glass darkly"?

8. An especially lucid presentation of the first of these claims is to be found in John D. Caputo, *Against Ethics* (Bloomington: Indiana University Press, 1993). On the notion of "interpretative violence," see Jacques Derrida, "Force of Law: The 'Mystical Foundation of Authority,'" *Deconstruction and the Possibility of Justice,* ed. Drucilla Cornell, Michel Rosenfeld, and David Gray Carlson (New York: Routledge, 1992), especially pp. 6-7 and 13-14. Given as a lecture at Cardozo Law School, 1989.

I do not wish to claim that my account fits every thinker to whom the postmodern label has been applied. Perhaps there are some for whom the parallel with the positivists is perceptive.[9] Surely there are epigones who relish the image of local intellectual terrorist and who pose as moral nihilists. But I believe my account does fit, among others, Foucault and Derrida, the two French poststructuralist philosophers with the widest North American influence. (Derrida, it will be remembered, was the one assimilated first to Hitler and then to Stalin above.)

In a famous essay, "What Is Enlightenment?", Foucault insists that his own brand of critique is "rooted in the Enlightenment." But "I have been seeking to stress that the thread that may connect us with the Enlightenment is not faithfulness to doctrinal elements, but rather the permanent reactivation of an attitude — that is, of a philosophical ethos that could be described as a permanent critique of our historical era."

Seeking to characterize that ethos positively, he writes, "But if the Kantian question was that of knowing what limits knowledge has to renounce transgressing, it seems to me that the critical question today has to be turned back into a positive one: in what is given to us as universal, necessary, obligatory, what place is occupied by whatever is singular, contingent, and the product of arbitrary constraints? The point, in brief, is to transform the critique conducted in the form of necessary limitation into a practical critique that takes the form of a possible transgression."[10]

If we ask, "What are we being invited to transgress?", the answer is clear: the arbitrary constraints in which the singular and contingent, e.g., the German will to empire and fascist anti-Semitism, are taken to have ultimate validity. This genealogical form of critique is not emotivism but the hermeneutics of suspicion developed by Marx, Nietzsche, and Freud as an

9. Caputo suggests as much in distinguishing heteromorphic from heteronomic postmodernism. See especially Chapter 3 of *Against Ethics* and *Demythologizing Heidegger* (Bloomington: Indiana University Press, 1993), p. 59, where he speaks of "a certain prophetic postmodernism." Cf. pp. 187 and 201-5. A similar distinction is found in Peter Sloterdijk's *Critique of Cynical Reason,* trans. Michael Eldred (Minneapolis: University of Minnesota Press, 1987). I suggest a Kierkegaardian reading of the distinction in "Postmodernism and Religious Reflection," forthcoming in *International Journal for Philosophy of Religion.*

10. Michel Foucault, "What Is Enlightenment?," in *The Foucault Reader,* ed. Paul Rabinow (New York: Pantheon Books, 1984), pp. 42-45. Cf. "The Subject and Power," Foucault's Afterword to Hubert L Dreyfus and Paul Rabinow, *Michel Foucault: Beyond Structuralism and Hermeneutics,* 2d ed. (Chicago: University of Chicago Press, 1983).

(unintended but theologically profound) commentary on the Pauline notion that sin produces distorted truth. It highlights one way this happens: the confusing of our particular interests with the universal good. And, like the Pauline version of this theme, the postmodern version resists the comforting assurance that this happens to "them" but not to "us."

In a similar fashion, Derrida takes his stand with the Enlightenment, at least with regard to the necessity of critique. "We cannot and we must not — this is a law and a destiny — forgo the *Aufklärung*, in other words, what imposes itself as the enigmatic desire for vigilance, for the lucid vigil, for elucidation, for critique and truth, but for a truth that at the same time keeps within itself some apocalyptic desire . . . to demystify or, if you prefer, to deconstruct apocalyptic discourse itself. . . ."[11]

Even more dramatic is the claim that what is at work in the negations of deconstruction is nothing other than justice. In a lecture given at Cardozo Law School in 1989, Derrida argues that although positive law at its best seeks to be the embodiment of justice, it is always a human construction and thus liable to deconstruction. "The fact that law is deconstructible is not bad news. We may even see in this a stroke of luck for politics, for all historical progress." Historical progress! So much for the notion that since nothing historical is absolute and final, everything historical is of equal value. Derrida continues, "Justice in itself, if such a thing exists, outside or beyond the law, is not deconstructible. No more than deconstruction itself, if such a thing exists. Deconstruction is justice. . . . The undeconstructibility of justice also makes deconstruction possible, indeed is inseparable from it."[12]

The language of "justice in itself" evokes both Plato's and Kant's notions of what is truly transcendent. Derrida finds such a notion highly problematic; hence the "if such a thing exists." But he also finds that he cannot work without it. He employs a crucial distinction between positive law and a justice to which it is responsible. He is claiming, in effect, that the natural law tradition survives the collapse of excessive epistemological claims ("we hold these truths to be self-evident") traditionally accompanying it.[13] Per-

---

11. Jacques Derrida, "Of an Apocalyptic Tone Newly Adopted in Philosophy," *Derrida and Negative Theology*, ed. Harold Coward and Toby Foshay (Albany: SUNY Press, 1992), p. 51. The French original was first given as a lecture in 1980 and published in 1981. On p. 59 Derrida writes, "So we, *Aufklärer* of modern times. . . ."

12. Jacques Derrida, "Force of Law," pp. 14-15.

13. For an analysis of Derrida's relation to this tradition, see my "Derrida as Natural

haps this is why Derrida can say, "Nothing seems to me less outdated than the classical emancipatory ideal," teasing Habermas, as it were, to see deconstruction as akin to Habermas's own critical theory, a parallel attempt to salvage the Enlightenment commitment to philosophy as critique after the fall of absolute knowledge.[14]

Like the laws, I am responsible as an individual to that which precedes my desires and even my insights. In another recent essay, Derrida invokes Levinas's notion of the trace. The trace recalls Gilbert and Sullivan's modern major general who is not now an orphan and, moreover, never has been; it signifies something at work in my thinking that is not now and never has been fully present to my thinking. No matter how far back I go in memory or (Platonic) recollection, it has always already been there and departed. "Language has started without us, in us, and before us. This is what theology calls God. . . . Order or promise, this injunction commits (me), in a rigorously asymmetrical manner, even before I have been able to say *I* [so much for the primacy of the self and its desires], to sign such a *provocation* in order to reappropriate it for myself and restore the symmetry. That in no way mitigates my responsibility; on the contrary. There would be no responsibility without this *prior coming (prévenance)* of the trace, or if autonomy were first or absolute. Autonomy itself would not be possible, nor would respect for the law . . . in the strictly Kantian meaning of these words."[15]

A full gloss on this passage would involve a detailed analysis of Levinas and of Derrida's appropriation of him.[16] But this much is immediately clear: (1) the reference to Kant makes it clear that we are talking about ethical and not just grammatical responsibility; (2) Derrida associates him-

---

Law Theorist," *International Philosophical Quarterly* 34 (June 1994): 247-52. In this essay the similarity and difference between Derrida's justice in itself and Kant's regulative ideas is briefly explored.

14. "Force of Law," p. 28.

15. Jacques Derrida, "How to Avoid Speaking: Denials," *Derrida and Negative Theology*, p. 99. French original, 1987.

16. Key texts would include: Emmanuel Levinas, *Totality and Infinity*, trans. Alphonso Lingis (Pittsburgh: Duquesne University Press, 1969); Jacques Derrida, "Violence and Metaphysics: An Essay on the Thought of Emmanuel Levinas," *Writing and Difference*, trans. Alan Bass (Chicago: University of Chicago Press, 1978); and a second round of discussion, Levinas's "Wholly Otherwise" and Derrida's "At this very moment in this work here I am," the opening essays of Robert Bernasconi and Simon Critchley, eds., *Re-Reading Levinas* (Bloomington: Indiana University Press, 1991).

self with the Levinasian thesis that heteronomy precedes autonomy;[17] and most importantly, (3) the deconstruction of Kantian ethics seeks to preserve moral responsibility, not obliterate it. Derrida joins Levinas in saying, "We have had to deny autonomy in order to make room for responsibility."

How is it possible for presumably responsible scholars to find Hitler and Stalin in this?

Well, that isn't exactly what happens. When demonization takes place the silence on these themes in thinkers like Foucault and Derrida is deafening. In the case of Derrida, attention is almost invariably directed to his notion of play. Thus, in Howard's summary of Himmelfarb, postmodernists are "frivolous game-players who make a virtue of their moral irresponsibility."[18] Similarly, Lundin dates the "deadly opening salvo in the Continental invasion of American universities" to Derrida's lecture, "Structure, Sign, and Play in the Discourse of the Human Sciences."[19] According to Lundin's Derrida "there is nothing behind or beneath [language] save the *free play of desire*." His (Derrida's) ideal is "a world in which intellectual history becomes a great video arcade, and every character or idea in that history is but one more game meant to heighten the pleasure of *the postmodern player at the controls*."[20]

Just about everything is wrong with this account. In the first place, nothing is more distinctive of postmodern analyses than the vigorous denial that we are or can be in control. With Freud, who describes psychoanalysis as a "most bitter blow" to human self-love because it endeavors to show "to the 'ego' of each one of us that he is not even master in his own house";[21] with Heidegger, for whom "*die Sprache spricht*" in and through the human speaker, who is a kind of mouthpiece;[22] and with the structuralist account of how it is that language speaks and not "man," postmodernism is a sustained assault on the dialectical illusion of a self in control. Under such

17. Cf. the discussion in Caputo's *After Ethics* of "heteronomous" postmodernism.
18. Howard, p. 12.
19. Lundin, p. 189. Derrida's lecture was given at Johns Hopkins University in 1966 and published (in French) in 1967. Its English translation appeared in 1978.
20. Lundin, pp. 192 and 194. My emphasis.
21. Sigmund Freud, at the conclusion of the Eighteenth Lecture of his *Introductory Lectures on Psychoanalysis, Standard Edition*, Vols. 15 and 16.
22. Martin Heidegger, *Poetry, Language, Thought,* trans. Albert Hofstadter (New York: Harper and Row, 1971), pp. 197-98; cf. *On the Way to Language*, trans. Peter D. Hertz (New York: Harper and Row, 1971), p. 124.

headings as "the death of the author," "the death of man," and "the end of humanism," it seeks to show the variety of ways in which we are not in charge, especially in the realm of language.[23] Unless the video arcade image is meant to evoke the frustration rather than the pleasure of the player who is at the controls but unable to control what happens on the screen, it is highly misleading.

More specifically, in Derridean diction the human subject is not the subject of the verb to play. Thus, in the essay cited by Lundin, Derrida speaks of "the *play* of the structure" and "the play of the world" but not of the play of the subject of desire.[24] Ironically, Lundin quotes both of these passages,[25] one of them twice; but this does not keep him from offering an interpretation of Derridean play wholly at odds with their import.

For Derrida as for Gadamer play is out there. The game is happening, and if we become players it is because we are drawn into a game we did not originate and cannot control.[26] Derrida does indeed bring the "play of the structure" into relation to human desire. But instead of speaking of the free play of desire, he portrays desire as hostile toward the play of the structure and the play of the world. Desire is for "a reassuring certitude, which itself is beyond the reach of play." This certitude is to be the cure for the anxiety that is "invariably the result of a certain mode of being implicated in the game, of being caught by the game, of being as it were at stake in the game from the outset." The subject for whom the controls are a means to personal pleasure is not the postmodernist who rejects the notion of "a full presence which is beyond play," but the devotee of the metaphysics of presence, one name for the tendency of the philosophical tradition to

---

23. For an overview of this theme in relation to "the death of the author" in Barthes, Foucault, and Derrida, see my "Kierkegaard and the Anxiety of Authorship," *International Philosophical Quarterly,* 34 (March 1994): 5-22.

24. Jacques Derrida, "Structure, Sign, and Play in the Discourse of the Human Sciences," *Writing and Difference,* pp. 278, 292.

25. Lundin, pp. 190, 194, 200.

26. For Gadamer's interpretation, see Hans-Georg Gadamer, *Truth and Method,* trans. Joel Weinsheimer and Donald G. Marshall, 2d ed. rev. (New York: Crossroad, 1991), especially pp. 101-31. For discussion see Fred Dallmayr, "Hermeneutics and Deconstruction: Gadamer and Derrida in Dialogue" and Neal Oxenhandler, "The Man with Shoes of Wind: The Derrida-Gadamer Encounter," in *Dialogue and Deconstruction: The Gadamer-Derrida Encounter,* ed. Diane P. Michelfelder and Richard E. Palmer (Albany: SUNY Press, 1989). Cf. Martin Heidegger, *The Principle of Reason,* trans. Reginald Lilly (Bloomington: Indiana University Press, 1991), p. 14.

seek a fixed center for every structure that "permits the play of its elements . . . [but] also closes off the play." In short, play is not the fulfillment of the subject's desires but precisely what must be brought to a halt if those desires for control and security are to be fulfilled.[27]

Similarly, when Derrida speaks of the "play of the world" it is to present play as "the disruption of presence" and what presence signifies, namely, the "reassuring foundation" in which we can assume a godly position above the play of the world, standing at "the origin and the end of play" as its Alpha and Omega. In short, the play of the world, so far from putting the postmodern player at the controls, deprives us of the security of being in control. *It is what makes it clear that we are not God.*[28]

Among the other early essays of Derrida that reinforce this understanding of play is "Plato's Pharmacy."[29] There one will find reference to the play of schemas, of thematic oppositions, of traces or supplements, of differences, of chains of signification, and of language. Writing will be the subject of the verb to play, but the subject of desire who would be seated at the controls of the world shows up only as a Platonism that is "the repression of play."[30]

It can come as no surprise that Derrida is no friend of Plato's demand and promise of absolute, pure presence, meanings and truths apprehended in an eternal now above the possibility and need of revision that comes in the wake of time. But it will come as a surprise to those who read Derridean play as a commentary on the "God is dead — everything is permitted" theme, to hear (whoever has ears to hear, let them hear) how emphatically he denies that he is engaged in some "back-to-the-sophists" project. What interests him is the possibility of "some entirely-other of *both* sophistics

27. "Structure, Sign, Play," pp. 278-80. These passages are the immediate context of the passage about the "play of the structure" that Lundin quotes.

28. "Structure, Sign, Play," p. 292. Again, these passages are the immediate context of the cited passage about the "play of the world."

29. Jacques Derrida, "Plato's Pharmacy," *Dissemination,* trans. Barbara Johnson (Chicago: University of Chicago Press, 1981). This essay was first published in 1968. I emphasize the early dates of these two essays (see note 19 above) because some would suggest that the reasonably tame, Enlightenment- and responsibility-loving Derrida of the eighties (see notes 8, 11, and 15) is a move, under pressure, away from the dangerous, wild, irresponsible Derrida of the sixties. My counter-suggestion is that this latter Derrida is a figment of the imagination of those whose readings of his work from the sixties is wildly irresponsible. This is wonderfully ironic, for whatever one ultimately makes of his work, one cannot deny that he is a meticulous reader of the texts he deconstructs.

30. "Plato's Pharmacy," p. 156.

*and* Platonism, some resistance having no common denominator with this whole [opposition between Platonism and sophistry]."[31] Derrida explicitly rejects the assumption, apparently shared by his critics and attributed to him against the evidence, that we have to choose between Platonic absolutism (in some form, the history of metaphysics) and sophistic relativism. From the very beginning, his project, whether one calls it humanism or anti-humanism, is the attempt to find an alternative to sophistry that does not forget that we are not God. For he sees the history of metaphysics as a set of variations on the Platonic theme, each of which demands and promises an absolute knowledge in which we would be able to see the world *sub specie aeternitatis,* to peek over God's shoulder from a standpoint securely outside the play of the world, above the temporal flow of both signifiers and signifieds which, like a rolling stream bears all its sons (and daughters) away. It is ironic that this flight from incarnation is sometimes carried out in the name of the Word who became flesh and lived among us.

At the outset, I mentioned the possibility of appropriating postmodern insights in the service of a Christian interpretation and critique of contemporary culture. If the argument to this point is convincing, it has shown that what we might call the immoralist objection to even the possibility of such appropriation is unsound, at least (1) with reference to the general posture of some postmodernists, who present themselves as moralists rather than immoralists, and (2) more specifically with reference to the Derridean theory of play, which is sometimes seen as evidence that deconstruction reduces all morality to arbitrary preference.

But even if such *a priori* objections against the possibility of learning something from postmodernism can be deflected,[32] there remains the question whether there is anything worth appropriating. If I am asking whether a certain food will be good for me, I need a stronger answer than, "Well, it won't kill you." Since the focus to this point has been on Derrida, I will stay with him as I suggest an affirmative answer to the question.

31. "Plato's Pharmacy," p. 108.

32. My own sense is that the other attempts to dismiss postmodernism or, more specifically, Derrida wholesale are variations on the immoralist objection and rest on the same kind of misreading. This is not to suggest that Derrida and company should be considered immune from critique, but that such critique will have to occur at the retail level and on the basis of careful reading.

Derrida regularly insists that the issues he is discussing are theological, and we have already seen that *deconstruction is the denial that we are divine.* At the heart of the metaphysical tradition, Derrida sees a Heraclitophobia that begins with Parmenides and Plato. Like both Nietzsche and Kierkegaard, he sees the flight from flux and flow as endemic to the speculative impulse of Greek and hellenized Christian thought, a flight rooted in anxiety in the face of a world, whether factual or semantic, too changeable to be under our control. The longing for Absolute Knowledge, which presents itself as the love of Truth, is less a desire to submit one's thought to the way things are than a desire to compel the world to submit to our conceptual mastery. The attempt to put a halt to the play of the world or the play of our structures of signification, is the attempt to find a location for our own discourses outside of that play which is primarily, but not exclusively, the flow of time. This is a theological issue, because the identity of Thought and Being that is both required and promised as Absolute Knowledge is one of the classical definitions of God, who sees everything in an Eternal Now unconditioned by either past or future. As the desire and demand to see things *sub specie aeternitatis,* metaphysics is the not terribly subtle desire and demand to be God, and *deconstruction is the continuous reminder that we are not God.* In fact, it claims, we cannot even peek over God's shoulder.

Derrida's arguments are quasi-transcendental arguments about the conditions of the possibility of human meaning. When they are successful (quite frequently, I think), they show that we cannot have Absolute Knowledge, cannot stand at the Alpha or Omega points to look in on time from the security of a *pou sto* outside of it. Properly construed, Derrida's arguments have Kantian limits. They show us something about human thought and language, but nothing about what else, if anything, there may be. Derrida ought to speak like Kierkegaard's Johannes Climacus, who knows that reality may very well be a system for God even if it cannot be for us.[33]

But Derrida does not speak this way. He does not so much argue for the unreality of God as assume it, so when he shows that *we are* not the Alpha and Omega he talks as if he has shown that *there is* no Alpha and Omega. This is a *non sequitur,* and my primary criticism of Derrida is that he regularly falls into it. My complaint is not that he assumes atheism, but

---

33. Søren Kierkegaard, *Concluding Unscientific Postscript,* trans. Howard V. and Edna H. Hong (Princeton: Princeton University Press, 1992), I, 118.

that he forgets that he has done so. He has the same right to assume that no one inhabits the Eternal Now as Kierkegaard has to assume that someone does. That either must first prove theism or atheism before thinking within that framework is a prejudice of Enlightenment evidentialism. But then they need to remember that conclusions into which their assumption essentially enters remain hypothetical.

When Derrida forgets to make this distinction and talks as if he has shown that there is no Alpha and Omega, we could point out that he has not established this and then reject deconstruction as bad philosophy. But that would be to throw out the baby with the bathwater. What if he has strong quasi-Kantian arguments that do show that we are not God?[34] Might not Christian thinkers draw on them in their own work? Would it not be useful in the interpretation and critique of contemporary culture to be on the lookout for its "Luciferian" dimensions, the ways in which its Day Star brilliance says, in effect, "I will make myself like the Most High" (Isa. 14:14)?

*"But we already know this. And if, from time to time, we need to be reminded, can we not turn to Augustine, Luther, Calvin, and, if all else fails, Kierkegaard?"* The point is well taken insofar as it indicates that Derridean thought is scarcely the Columbus who first (or second) discovered this truth. Moreover, it raises the important question whether Derrida's way of showing and saying that we are not God is sufficiently distinct to merit our attention and possible appropriation — we who trace our lineage through Augustine.[35]

I want to suggest three ways of saying yes to this last question. First, with reference to the acknowledgement that we are not God, Derrida is especially sensitive to the difference between the saying and the said (Levinas), the how and the what (Kierkegaard), the *modus significandi* and the *res significata* (Aquinas). He knows how easily the propositional content of such a saying is undermined and for all practical purposes neutralized by the performative mode of our speech act. If irony ("For Brutus is an honorable man") is the cancellation of what is said by the how of its being

---

34. The Kantian character of Derrida's thought is especially emphasized in Rodolphe Gashé, *The Tain of the Mirror: Derrida and the Philosophy of Reflection* (Cambridge: Harvard University Press, 1986) and Irene E. Harvey, *Derrida and the Economy of Différance* (Bloomington: Indiana University Press, 1986).

35. I see Aquinas, Luther, Calvin, and Kierkegaard as representing different species of Augustinianism and focus on the Protestant forms in this essay addressed primarily to a Protestant readership.

said, Derrida knows that irony and self-deception easily accompany each other, or, in other words, that not all irony is intentional. We can manage not to notice that in and through the very act of saying that we humans are not God we can enact the Luciferian project.

We do this, for example, (1) when we treat the theological framework within which we place this affirmation as final and ultimate, (2) when we react defensively/aggressively to criticisms of our own framework and tradition, (3) when we seek to deflect such criticisms by discrediting the critic (denying in effect that all truth is God's truth and committing the genetic fallacy at one and the same time), (4) when cultural theory becomes the vehicle for making "them" look bad in relation to "us" — in short, (5) when we act (no matter what we say) as if our own religious culture were an impregnable fortress from which to sally forth against the enemies of the Good who lurk in secular culture (or in religious cultures different from our own).

*"But we speak, however fallibly, on the basis of the infallible Word of God to a culture that simply ignores the Word of God."* This objection leads us to a second reason to look especially closely at Derrida's version of the "we are not God" thesis. Of course Derrida doesn't think there is any infallible Word of God. But his arguments, if successful, only establish a weaker claim about divine revelation which, properly formulated, would go something this. "It is not that the voice of God is nowhere to be heard, but only that this voice [if there is such a thing] is always and already couched in human terms. . . ."[36] This distinction, which echoes Barth's between religion and revelation and Levinas's between the saying and the said,[37] is the stubborn refusal to allow the objector's "however fallibly" to function as a vacuous Shibboleth. It is the reminder that even if God has spoken to us, whenever we try to say what we have heard, the formulation is our own and thus human, all too human. Just as the legislation that sincerely seeks to enact justice results in positive law that is deconstructible, so the theology that sincerely seeks to echo the Word of God may be a somewhat muffled sound.

36. Caputo, *Demythologizing Heidegger*, p. 100. This formulation derives from Caputo's attempt to read Heidegger against Heidegger, but I believe it fits just as well into my attempt to read Derrida against Derrida.

37. Karl Barth, *Church Dogmatics*, Vol. I, 2, trans. G. T. Thomson and Harold Knight (Edinburgh: T & T Clark, 1956), §17, "The Revelation of God as the Abolition of Religion." Emmanuel Levinas, *Otherwise than Being or Beyond Essence*, trans. Alphonso Lingis (Dordrecht: Kluwer, 1991).

It is a bit like that game in which a statement is whispered from one person to another to see how it gets transformed in the transmission.

The distinction between those who seek to speak on the basis of the Word of God and those who do not is beyond challenge. The problem is that it is no reliable index of who is right. The secular critics of Christian anti-Semitism, of slavery, and of apartheid, for example, were right. And those who purported to speak on the basis of the infallible Word of God but tolerated or championed these evils were wrong. As Al Verhey puts it, secular culture

> may challenge and judge certain claims made on the basis of Scripture. Scripture has, after all, been used to justify racial and sexual discrimination; it has been used to justify "holy wars," crusades, and inquisitions; it has been used to justify the abuse of power and the violation of the rights and integrity of others in order to pursue what has been taken to be God's cause. Secular moral wisdom, and especially the principle of justice, has sometimes challenged such uses of Scripture and led the church to consider particular practices and to repent of them. We must note that it is not the authority of Scripture itself that comes under criticism and review here, but authorizations for the use of Scripture in moral argument and moral claims made employing such authorizations. In the churches, Scripture itself has sometimes finally corroborated the judgments of secular morality and has been vindicated against both its detractors and its so-called defenders in such cases.[38]

Perhaps we once learned from a rather Kierkegaardian Karl Barth, "It was the Church, not the world, which crucified Christ."[39] Today we can be reminded of this by a somewhat Nietzschean Derrida. He is a thinker, in the Enlightenment tradition, for whom interpretation and critique cannot be separated, and for whom the culture of the critic is just as vulnerable to critique as any other culture the critic may wish to critique.

38. Allen Verhey, *The Great Reversal: Ethics and the New Testament* (Grand Rapids: Eerdmans, 1984), p. 193.

39. Karl Barth, *The Epistle to the Romans,* trans. Edwyn C. Hoskyns (New York: Oxford University Press, 1977), p. 389. In the Preface to the Fourth Edition (pp. 20-21), Barth notes that "the literary organ of the Dutch Reformed Church" warned its readers against his book on the grounds that it was "foreign to their piety." For an interesting juxtaposition of Barth and Derrida, see Walter Lowe, *Theology and Difference: The Wound of Reason* (Bloomington: Indiana University Press, 1993).

So far the Derridean argument that we are not God is a double reminder that a Christian interpretation and critique of contemporary (secular) culture is an open invitation to the critique of Christian culture itself, its theories, practices, and institutions. First, there is the distinction between the propositional content and the performative mode of saying that human beings are not God. Second, there is the observation that the sincere attempt to express some transcendent Truth or Justice does not elevate us above the human condition. We do not become God by purporting to base our discourse on divine revelation. Nor are we anything but confused when we act as if our attempt to point to the Absolute somehow made our pointing absolute. This confusion is perhaps the greatest temptation of Christian intellectuals. And there stands St. Jacques, inadvertently working his hardest to protect us from Wormwood and Screwtape!

This second point can be phrased as a gloss on the (in)famous Derridean claim, *"There is nothing outside of the text."*[40] It would go something like this: If there is anything, such as God or Justice in itself, that might be said to be outside the text, saying that or anything else about it would bring it within the text. This is the Kantian point that we have only phenomenal language for talking about any possible noumenal world, and it is the reason for the discussion about the relation of deconstruction to negative theology.[41]

But the textuality of Derridean thought means more than that anything we talk about thereby gets incorporated into human discourse, explosive as that truism may be. Derridean textualism is an extension of the notion of text beyond language in the usual sense.[42] Like Paul Ricoeur, who extends the notion of text so as to treat meaningful action as text,[43] Derrida extends the notion of writing so that "things" we would not normally refer to as texts can be seen to have textual structures.

One advantage of this strategy for cultural theory is that it provides a

40. Jacques Derrida, *Of Grammatology*, trans. Gayatri Chakravorty Spivak (Baltimore: Johns Hopkins University Press, 1974), p. 158.

41. For an introduction to this issue, see my essay, "Faith as the Overcoming of Ontological Xenophobia," forthcoming in a *Festschrift* for Robert Scharlemann.

42. After quoting *"There is nothing outside of the text"* in its immediate context, Barbara Johnson makes this point nicely in her introduction to *Dissemination*, p. xiv.

43. See "The Model of the Text: Meaningful Action Considered as a Text" in Paul Ricoeur, *Hermeneutics and the Human Sciences*, trans. John B. Thompson (New York: Cambridge University Press, 1981).

common frame of reference for discussing such different cultural artifacts as theories, practices, and institutions; and, within cultural theory in the narrower sense, it provides a common grid for discussing explicitly textual practices, such as philosophy, literature, and history, alongside practices that transcend textuality in the usual sense, such as theater, cinema, music, painting, sculpture, and architecture.[44]

But what especially concerns me here is the relational or contextual character of textual structure. To be (in) a text is to be inextricably inter-related, and in many directions at once.[45] Here we meet a third way in which Derrida's way of saying that we are not God deserves the careful attention of Christian scholars. He joins Hegel and structuralism in denying the maxim of Bishop Butler that G. E. Moore liked to quote, "Everything is what it is, and not another thing."[46] The semantic principle of Spinoza, that every determination is a negation, becomes the semantic/ontological principle that everything (at least everything finite) has its meaning and its being by virtue of its relation to the others that it is not; these others, consequently, enter essentially into the meaning and the being of the self-same. The same does not merely stand over against the other but has the other essentially within it. Nothing stands alone. Nothing (at least nothing finite) is a Spinozistic substance that exists in itself and is conceived through itself. Everything is and is understood through its others.[47]

The importance of this for cultural theory is that it helps to underscore the radical relativity of everything finite, and thus of all cultural processes and artifacts. They are and they mean only in contexts they neither create nor control. And since these contexts are in continuous historical flux, the being and the meaning of culture and its components is never final or

---

44. There is also the danger of neglecting the import of the differences among the various forms of cultural expression.

45. Simon Critchley's reading of "There is nothing outside of the text" makes it equivalent to "There is nothing outside of some context." See *The Ethics of Deconstruction: Derrida and Levinas* (Oxford: Blackwell, 1992).

46. G. E. Moore quotes this maxim on the frontispiece of *Principia Ethica* (Cambridge: Cambridge University Press, 1962), and again on p. 206.

47. For classical theism, finite creatures are relative because they are essentially related to God; but God is absolute because the divine being is not essentially related to creatures, since creation is a free act, and thus contingent. Hence the qualifier, "at least nothing finite." This notion that the other is internal to the same is developed by Levinas in *Otherwise than Being* and by Ricoeur in *Oneself as Another,* trans. Kathleen Blamey (Chicago: University of Chicago Press, 1992).

finished.[48] The term "cultural relativity" is pleonastic, for to be or belong to a culture is to be inextricably related.

But Derrida refuses to identify this relativity with relativism. He does not withdraw his repudiation of the sophists. He sees that unless one distinguishes the relativity ("textuality") of all phenomena from the relativism that seeks to render arbitrary preference immune from critique (and thus reduce human life to a conflict among various wills to power), one will have no alternative to that relativism but some variety of Platonism. Absolute Knowledge (in some form) will become such a necessity that its impossibility will be overlooked, no matter how much bad faith that takes. Even when we deny it propositionally, we will affirm it performatively. If we wish to escape nihilism, we will have to play God. But, Derrida says, we are not God, and any genuine overcoming of nihilism will have to be honest about the human condition. Does this preclude grace? No, but it does preclude realized eschatology, the claim that we have reached the heavenly city, have put the journey behind us, and now see Truth face to face.

The deconstructive theory of textuality is, perhaps above all else, an attempt to point toward an overcoming of nihilism that is willing to remain human. To that end it seeks to articulate the coexistence of relativity and critique. In terms of its own critique of finality it can hardly expect to be or be taken to be the last word on this problem. But it is not a theory that Christian cultural theory needs to fear and to demonize. There just may be some gold to be mined in its disturbing texts.

48. On this point Derrida is more Hegelian than structuralist. This is one reason why he can describe himself as an Hegelian without closure or totality. See *Of Grammatology*, p. 26.

# Poetry and Poeming:
# John Dewey and Calvin Seerveld
# on Norm and Process

## CARROLL GUEN HART

Calvin Seerveld has done the Reformational community a great diaconal service. Working within a religious tradition which has long been suspicious of anything not discrete and clearly defined, he has successfully made room for the "allusive" and the "nuanceful" as typically aesthetic ways of praising God and culturally developing our world. Seerveld has shown great pastoral sensitivity and patience in trying to nudge Christians away from sentimentalized or moralizing art and toward a deeper, more bruised, but also more redemptive art. He has also sensitized us to the spiritual allegiances at work in art, while giving artists the tools to understand and counteract those spirits with a crafted, historically up-to-date, Christian aesthetic commitment.

In articulating his systematic aesthetics, Seerveld characteristically identifies polar opposites, each of which he rejects in favor of a "third way." Quite often, John Dewey figures as one extreme against which Seerveld identifies himself. For example, discussing contemporary culture's substitutes for God, Seerveld first identifies *Angst* as Heidegger's "highest moment of revelation." The opposite to this, says Seerveld, is "the American do-it-yourself world and trust-to-luck of technologist Dewey, almost blushworthy in its optimistic superficiality, but dismayingly successful — In Experiment We Trust!" Seerveld's Scylla and Charybdis thus take shape as

126

Heidegger's "chagrined fearless despair" on the one hand and Dewey's "irrational action" on the other.[1]

In a different context, Dewey is implicated in Seerveld's indictment of what he calls pragmatist nominalism with respect to normativity. Nominalism here is again an extreme, namely, the polar opposite of an equally mistaken idealism. Seerveld thinks that idealists are on the right track when they delimit, in an open-ended way, certain "irreducible features of things that cannot be conceptually determined." Unfortunately, idealists go astray when they hypostatize such features — "As if *modes* be *things* — which they are not." Pragmatists, however, in their attempt to undo such hypostatization, go to the opposite extreme and, by a "perverse, kenotic logic," dissolve "defining typicality" into "circumstantial functionality." It then becomes impossible to pinpoint a "centrally cohering, irreducible feature" of something; an irreducible core of this sort "must remain permanently indeterminate, the protean object of an ongoing process of approximation."[2] This would mean that one is prevented, in principle, from any serious theorizing about art. For if one cannot identify art in its defining qualities, then a theory of art has nothing on which to build.

Dewey also surfaces as a conspicuous example of how *not* to do aesthetic theory. Seerveld says, for example, that "pragmaticist Dewey" has tried, "democratistically, to break down the peculiar cachet won by art-as-such and to dissolve art back into ordinary experience."[3] Seerveld coins the pejorative term "democratistically" to suggest that Dewey is a leveller who, in the name of democratic populism, rejects the snobbery of "fine art" but also, in effect, the developed nature of art itself. Seerveld hears Dewey saying that, in a historically regressive way, we should take art back to a less developed form so that it can be accessible to all; presumably this means the lowest common denominator. This levelling is not Dewey's only fault,

---

1. Calvin G. Seerveld, *A Christian Critique of Art and Literature* (Toronto: Wedge, 1964), p. 13.

2. Calvin G. Seerveld, *Rainbows for a Fallen World* (Toronto: Tuppence Press, 1980), pp. 106-7. I realize that in these passages Seerveld is speaking not specifically of Dewey, but of thinkers like W. B. Gallie, in "Art as an Essentially Contested Concept," *Philosophical Quarterly* 6 (no. 23, April 1956): 97-114. However, there can be no doubt that, since Dewey is the pre-eminent theorist of pragmatist aesthetics, Seerveld tacitly includes him in these criticisms. This criticism is echoed in a different context when Seerveld accuses Dewey of dissolving art back into ordinary experience; part of this criticism (though not all of it) is that Dewey tries to dissolve the art object into its functions.

3. Seerveld, *Rainbows*, p. 113.

however: "Though John Dewey fabricates a philosophy beyond revelation and demons, it is significant that he too, pragmatically, seeks for the key to knowledge and even the salvation of humanity in imagination and art."[4] Seerveld goes on to say that "These idolatrous celebrations of imagination show a disenchantment with scientism which is not peculiar to our irrational age; trusting to imagination today, however, with so much gunpowder, seems extra dangerous, romantically forlorn."[5]

For the purposes of this essay, I shall focus on just one major criticism, namely, that Dewey's aesthetic theory "dissolves" differentiated art back into undifferentiated organic experience. If true, in the sense in which Seerveld intends it, this would mean that Dewey's aesthetic theory is both reductionist and historically regressive. I shall argue that Dewey does dissolve art back into experience, but only temporarily, and for the purpose of understanding aesthetic development. For although differentiation may be, on the whole, a good historical development for art, an understanding of art in its less differentiated stages is important for aesthetic education. I call these two approaches "grounding" and "emergence," referring to different *foci* on the continuum of differentiation. Section 1 will explore, in general terms, the grounding and emergent dimensions of Dewey's concept of experience. Section 2 will focus on the direction of "emergence" by examining the ideal function of "aesthetic art" in human culture. Section 3 will consider the direction of "grounding" by looking at Dewey's articulation of a developmental theory of aesthetic activity. Section 4 will bring these two dimensions into interaction as they shape an experimental strategy for aesthetic education both aesthetically responsible and sensitive to the needs of the learner.

## 1. Grounding and Emergence in Deweyan Experience

The irreducible unit of human experience, in Dewey's conception, is a combination of biology and culture, what Dewey calls "body-mind" or "cultural naturalism." As organic beings, we exist in continuity with all other living creatures, but we are not purely organic creatures. We are also cultural creatures, capable of shaping our biological existence (within certain limits)

4. Seerveld, *Critique*, p. 65.
5. Seerveld, *Critique*, p. 65.

for communally determined human purposes. Our natural/cultural lives exhibit a lateral, interactional dynamic and a longitudinal, developing dynamic which together constitute the spiral that characterizes organic life, but rises to a level unique to human creatures.

As organic beings, then, we belong to that larger ecological system which we call life. The whole system, inclusive of environment and organisms, itself has "organic" character, in the sense of being a "self-conserving" and "expanding" whole whose differentiated parts develop and maintain its characteristic pattern of functioning.[6] Life in this systemic ecological sense exhibits the "lateral" push-pull of coordinating energies:

> A pond moving in ripples, forked lightning, the waving of branches in the wind, the beating of a bird's wing, the whorl of sepals and petals, changing shadows of clouds on a meadow, are simple natural rhythms. There must be energies resisting each other. Each gains intensity for a certain period, but thereby compresses some opposed energy until the latter can overcome the other which has been relaxing itself as it extends. Then the operation is reversed, not necessarily in equal periods of time but in some ratio that is felt as orderly.[7]

Any event, whether we commonly ascribe it to the organism or to the environment, is in fact a cooperation of energies within and without. For "natural operations like breathing and digesting, acquired ones like speech and honesty, are functions of the surroundings as truly as of a person. They are things done *by* the environment by means of organic structures or acquired dispositions. . . ."[8] Take breathing, for example. Of course creatures use their muscles to breathe, but changes in environing air pressure also "breathe" organisms; thus one might say, in fact, that the ecology itself breathes. This ecological notion of experience reminds one of the artist's notion of "composition," in which the focus falls less on the "recognition and identification of material forms" than on "the tension between forms,

---

6. John Dewey, "Contributions to a *Cyclopedia of Education*," in *The Middle Works: 1899-1924*, Vol. 6: *1910-1911*, ed. Jo Ann Boydston (Carbondale: Southern Illinois University Press, 1985), p. 437.

7. John Dewey, *Art as Experience*, in *The Later Works: 1925-1953*, Vol. 10: *1934*, ed. Jo Ann Boydston (Carbondale: Southern Illinois University Press, 1987), p. 159.

8. John Dewey, *Human Nature and Conduct*, in *The Middle Works: 1899-1924*, Vol. 14: *1922*, ed. Jo Ann Boydston (Carbondale: Southern Illinois University Press, 1988), p. 15.

the effects of movements on shapes and qualities, the active spaces which surround solid masses."[9]

The longitudinal dynamic involves the increasing inclusivity and richness of such coordinations. Humanly speaking, our most important example of this is the acquisition of "meaning," as the product of language.[10] Language, for Dewey, is the "communication of intent" from one person to another around a common object. When the second person incorporates an understanding of that intent into her own actions, thereby acting cooperatively with the other so as to fulfill the original intent, the three together have established a "common, inclusive undertaking," in which the object functions as means. "Meaning" is this inclusive undertaking, this participation in intent, which, once named, crystallizes into a potentially universalizable way of acting toward objects. In this way meaning transforms primary human "associations" into "communities" based on emergent shared purposes, and catches up objects into these shared human purposes. Originally verbal as names for interactions, meanings subsequently attach themselves to the objects which function as means, and act as reminders of their potential for entering into these interactions. These reminders identify and preserve "connections" or "sequential bonds in nature,"[11] enabling us to act "in deference to the *connections* of events."[12] Once we have meanings (and the interactions they recall), we have the distinctively human features of "culture," with all of the emergent interactions it makes possible. Language, the "cherishing mother of all significance,"[13] is our "cultural matrix,"[14] the vital core to human life from which more differentiated human experiences arise.

Our cumulative store of meanings results in a sort of cultural "deposit" which Dewey calls "mind" — that "body of organized meanings by means of which events of the present have significance for us." Mind in this sense is both instrumental and final: as a deposit of meaning-connections, it preserves

9. Allen S. Weller, quoted in Lee Nordness, ed., *Art U.S.A. Now* (New York, 1962), p. 12. Cited in John J. McDermott, "Deprivation and Celebration: Suggestions for an Aesthetic Ecology," in *New Essays in Phenomenology: Studies in the Philosophy of Experience*, ed. James M. Edie (Chicago: Quadrangle Books, 1969), p. 116.

10. See Dewey, *Experience and Nature*, in *The Later Works: 1925-1953*, Vol. 1: *1925*, ed. Jo Ann Boydston (Carbondale: Southern Illinois University Press, 1981), pp. 132ff.

11. Dewey, *Experience and Nature*, p. 101.

12. Dewey, *Experience and Nature*, p. 143.

13. Dewey, *Experience and Nature*, p. 146.

14. John Dewey, *Logic: The Theory of Inquiry*, in *The Later Works: 1925-1953*, Vol. 12: *1938*, ed. Jo Ann Boydston (Carbondale: Southern Illinois University Press, 1986), p. 28.

both our cumulative experience of interacting with our world and those shared activities and purposes which constitute community in the richest sense. Mind is constitutive for peculiarly human experience: "the experience enacted is human and conscious only as that which is given here and now is extended by meanings and values drawn from what is absent in fact and present only imaginatively." This means that imagination is crucial: "Imagination is the only gateway through which these meanings can find their way into a present interaction; or rather . . . the conscious adjustment of the new and old *is* imagination."[15] Thus mind takes experience to a qualitatively new level. The re-activation of mind through imagination gives us, eventually, our whole inner landscape of memory, anticipation, and desire.

The emergence of community and meaning defines an increasing role for human responsibility. Though experience is not primarily and exclusively ours, yet it is important for us to accept responsibility for our role in experience. And our role is defined specifically by that "tensive," dramatic, historically unique combination of lateral and longitudinal dynamics which Dewey calls a "situation." A situation, though based on the organic pattern of loss and rediscovery of equilibrium, is peculiarly "tensive"[16] for human experience in that the coordination of energies, having reached a crisis of indeterminacy, defines a space for human choice. The specific quality of the situation is defined by the energies, environmental and subjective, which constitute it, as well as the cumulative experience (in the form of "mind" and "self") which define its history and limit its future possibilities. These energies, working together, restore that lateral equilibrium which is essential to life and growth. We also become increasingly aware of our responsibilities in the longitudinal dynamics of our experience. As humans responsible to our sustaining ecologies, we make choices affecting the future development of our historically unique situation. We determine which values to realize in this situation. We decide which sort of action the situation calls for and how we should respond. We choose whether or not to discipline our actions in response to the situation. These are not one-time discrete actions, but rather a series of choices embedded within processes of doing/undergoing in response to the dynamics of the situation and the requirements of our chosen values.

15. Dewey, *Art as Experience*, pp. 276-77.
16. I take the term "tensive" from Thomas Alexander; I agree that it better names what Dewey means by "problematic." See Thomas M. Alexander, *John Dewey's Theory of Art, Experience and Nature* (Albany: State University of New York Press, 1987), p. 147.

This cultural naturalism is the basic way in which humans negotiate the crucial matters of life or death, of communal flourishing or destruction. In Dewey's conception, the body-mind, being itself two-layered, faces in two directions — on the one hand toward the basic conditions of existence which we share with all other living creatures, and on the other hand toward the higher functions which are distinctive to humans. These two directions I call, respectively, "grounding" and "emergence."

If we begin with this fundamental unit of human experience and look in the direction of grounding, says Dewey, we see the basic context and conditions of our existence. The direction of grounding exhibits relatively more stability and relatively less differentiation, and our dependence on our ecological context is tighter and less flexible. In addition, the communal and systemic are more prominent than the individual. The direction of grounding reminds us that we come out of an organic and communal "matrix" to be honored and respected as the source of our own life. It also reminds us that the communal undergirds all of our individual qualities and actions, and that ultimately the office of these is to serve the common good. Looking at things from the perspective of grounding, we become aware of the existential dimension of our lives which is both good in itself and a "means" for realizing the ideals we choose. Understanding the ecological dynamics of grounded experience helps us to respect the distinct normativity of process, so that, even when we choose to develop human experience in a chosen direction, we honor that experience for its own sake and for its further potentialities. Dewey articulates a fundamental principle of grounding when he says that "to entertain, choose, and accomplish anything as an end or consequence is to be committed to a like love and care for whatever events and acts are its means."[17]

If we look at the basic unit of human experience in the direction of emergence, however, we see a different set of characteristics. Here we can play imaginatively with meanings and find new combinations and arrangements.[18] This is the process of discourse in which meanings "copulate and breed new meanings," generating surprising "new objects."[19] Thus in the direction of emergence we see relatively greater flexibility in responding to our environment: we can temporarily step back and use our imagination

17. Dewey, *Experience and Nature*, p. 275.
18. Dewey, *Experience and Nature*, p. 152.
19. Dewey, *Experience and Nature*, p. 134.

and intelligence to project possible courses of action before committing ourselves to the risks of existential action. On this level we find greater individuality, and with it choice and freedom. In turn, we find an increased emphasis on human responsibility and a far more nuanced way of responding to the world. Looking at things from the point of view of emergence, we envision the ideals for human life, and the highest development of human functions. By the same token, we find greater potential for ignoring, to our own detriment, the life-giving connections with our shared matrix.

Hence Dewey has two different but complementary ways of looking at human experience — in the direction of grounding and in the direction of emergence. In the direction of grounding, he surely does emphasize our interconnectedness rather than our individuality. If he took grounding on its own, apart from emergence, he would indeed be guilty of reductionism and "organicism." Seerveld's warnings on this head are not mistaken. However, Dewey emphasizes that grounding must be understood only together with emergence. Thus grounding reminds us that even our most individual actions are ecologically rooted and are "ours" only in a relative and limited sense. Moreover, grounding indicates that if our actions are to bear fruit in the world and to nurture our own human community, we must respect the often lowly beginnings and processes which bring about such flourishing. Together these two aspects of experience articulate what Dewey calls the "logical" dimension of experience, "the finished map that is constructed after the country has been thoroughly explored."[20] When constructed from the perspectives of both grounding and emergence, of both norm and process, the map acquires both richness and reliability.

## 2. The Role of Aesthetic Art in Human Culture

Let us now consider the emergent dimension specifically with relation to the aesthetic moment of experience. Dewey identifies the defining traits of the "peculiarly and manifestly aesthetic"[21] moment of experience as focusing on

20. John Dewey, "The Child and the Curriculum," in *The Middle Works: 1899-1924*, Vol. 2: *1902-1903*, ed. Jo Ann Boydston (Carbondale: Southern Illinois University Press, 1976), p. 283.
21. John Dewey, "The Philosophy of the Arts," in *The Later Works: 1925-1953*, Vol. 13: *1938-1939*, ed. Jo Ann Boydston (Carbondale: Southern Illinois University Press,

what he calls "aesthetic art," or "the formed matter of aesthetic experience."[22] The basis for specifically "aesthetic art" is Dewey's notion of "art" in the general sense. An "art" is any "action that deals with materials and energies outside the body, assembling, combining, refining, manipulating them until their new state yields a satisfaction not afforded by their crude condition."[23] Through art we convert this raw experience into "refined" experience — that is, experience particularly suited to a specific purpose. The difference is between raw ore and a copper cooking vessel, or between a juicy grape and the fermented wine. Artful refining characterizes a wide variety of things, from hammers ("industrial art"[24]) to logical objects ("intellectual art"); it also includes those objects which are designed particularly for the purpose of that "delightful perception" we call "aesthetic" ("aesthetic art"). Dewey says that the aesthetic is "the delight that attends vision and hearing, an enhancement of the receptive appreciation and assimilation of objects."[25]

The peculiar focus of the aesthetic experience is the unique quality of an individual entity or event. Something about it reverberates in our memory and desire. Here Dewey agrees with Whitehead, who says: "When you understand all about the sun and all about the atmosphere and all about the rotation of the earth, you may still miss the radiance of the sunset. There is no substitute for the direct perception of the concrete achievement of a thing in its actuality. We want concrete fact with a highlight thrown on what is relevant to its preciousness."[26] Dewey insists that aesthetic appreciation and art are not "luxuries," for they represent "the only ways in which the individualized elements in the world of nature and man are grasped," and these elements comprise "the most characteristic as well as the most precious thing in the real world."[27] If we do not engage in aesthetic expe-

---

1988), p. 358. In his later works, Dewey prefers the form "esthetic," but to conform with standard usage I shall stay with the form "aesthetic." In all Dewey quotes which follow, I shall change "esthetic" to "aesthetic" without further notation.

22. Dewey, *Art as Experience*, p. 277.

23. Dewey, *Experience and Nature*, p. 267.

24. Dewey, *Art as Experience*, p. 151.

25. Dewey, *Experience and Nature*, p. 267.

26. Alfred North Whitehead, *Science in the Modern World* (New York: Macmillan, 1925). Quoted in John Dewey, "Art in Education — and Education in Art," in *The Later Works: 1925-1953*, Vol. 2: *1925-1927*, ed. Jo Ann Boydston (Carbondale: Southern Illinois University Press, 1988), p. 111.

27. Dewey, "Art in Education," pp. 111-12. I should note at this point that, although

rience, we run the risk of what Whitehead calls the "celibacy of the intellect."[28] For though the qualitative individuality of things is ultimately a "mystery" that we cannot grasp conceptually,[29] we can experience it imaginatively and highlight it so that other people can share its meaning. Hence, in any experienceable object which is definitely aesthetic, an imaginative quality dominates: "The work of art . . . is not only the outcome of imagination, but operates imaginatively rather than in the realm of physical existences. What it does is to concentrate and enlarge an immediate experience."[30] The peculiar term "aesthetic art" means that the distinctively aesthetic moments of life clearly include not only an experience but also its correlative object. Dewey is concerned with both the authentically aesthetic perception and the object which is formed precisely to evoke such experiences.

The fully developed aesthetic object, designed for aesthetic perception, manifests "rhythmic form." This is a peculiarly aesthetic version of that stable, moving "equilibrium," that "felt harmony" which characterizes the consummation of any experience. Moreover, a finished aesthetic object has an expressiveness deepened by the visual and kinetic rhythms wrought into it. For an object's expressiveness occurs when "meanings and values are . . . extracted from prior experiences and funded in such a way that they fuse with the qualities directly presented in the work of art."[31]

---

Dewey, as was the custom in his time, uses the term "man" as a generic term for humankind, he also went one step further and acknowledged the male bias in all of his own thinking. In this connection he writes that "Women have as yet made little contribution to philosophy. But when women who are not mere students of other persons' philosophy set out to write it, we cannot conceive that it will be the same in viewpoint or tenor as that composed from the standpoint of the different masculine experience of things." ("Philosophy and Democracy," in *The Middle Works: 1899-1924*, Vol. 11: *1918-1919*, ed. Jo Ann Boydston [Carbondale: Southern Illinois University Press, 1982], p. 45.)

28. Quoted in Dewey, "Art in Education," pp. 113.

29. Dewey, "Time and Individuality," in *The Later Works: 1925-1953*, Vol. 14: *1939-1941*, ed. Jo Ann Boydston (Carbondale: Southern Illinois University Press, 1988), pp. 111-12. Dewey says that "The mystery of time is . . . the mystery of the existence of real individuals. It is a mystery because it is a mystery that anything which exists is just what it is. We are given to forgetting, with our insistence upon causation and upon the necessity of things happening as they do happen, that things exist as just what they qualitatively are."

30. Dewey, *Art as Experience*, p. 277.

31. Dewey, *Art as Experience*, p. 104.

Henry Moore's piece *Internal and External Forms* uses the warmth and grain of the wood, complemented by the sculpture's enfolding visual-kinetic rhythms, to suggest the human warmth and tenderness of many things gently held. For me, certainly, the piece explores and deepens my understanding of holding and being held, in pain or tenderness or joy. Here the preciousness of a human activity is highlighted, fused with the complex patterns of meaning — of memory and desire — that it has for us. This object is so meaningful that it is worth experiencing all on its own, apart from any ulterior purpose. In this sense it is legitimately "final." It "does" nothing but meet that "characteristic human need" which is "the possession and appreciation of the meaning of things."[32] Such an aesthetic object communicates to us, in artistically heightened form, the peculiar feel of this highly valued human relationship. It stands as a symbol with no purpose other than to be experienced as a symbol. We do not analyze it; we experience it, with deeper insight than we would otherwise have had. And once we have experienced *Internal and External Forms,* we can never again experience either wood or the human activity of holding in quite the same way again.

Like all "refined" forms of experience, however, aesthetic art objects are not absolutely "final" in the sense of being cut off from the rest of human experience. Such refinements must circle back upon our ordinary communal experience; as the "fruit" of our ordinary experience, they have an ethical obligation to return and enrich it, dropping "seeds" in our cumulative store of cultural experience. Thus the Moore sculpture stands as a reminder to our human community of the depth of human relationships which we wish to preserve in all our human purposes and activities. Although this is a form of "instrumentality," it is indirect, not the short-range instrumentality of the moral lesson, still less as a "compensating transient pleasurable excitation."[33] Rather, the indirect instrumentality of the artwork lies in its ability to refresh and enlarge our communal experience of the world. As Dewey says, the work of art is "useful" in the sense of "contributing directly and liberally to an expanding and enriched life."[34] Artworks are "celebrations . . . of the things of ordinary experience."[35] It is precisely

---

32. Dewey, *Experience and Nature,* p. 272.
33. Dewey, *Art as Experience,* p. 16.
34. Dewey, *Art as Experience,* pp. 33-34.
35. Dewey, *Art as Experience,* p. 16.

because artworks evoke communal human meanings so vividly and freshly that they can function so well in building and maintaining a sense of community in a culture. And because the quality of experience is so balanced and integrated, such objects can also help us to recover the unity of our lives in the midst of our specialized activities, and the freshness of our perceptions in the midst of life's exigencies.[36]

Works of art also show us what genuinely balanced, fully integrated ecological experience is like. For it is not routine, focused on motor action apart from thought and perception; indeed the work of "aesthetic art" in its richness reveals to us what work can be when it is not focused on "special and limited ends," but is "an experience in which the whole creature is alive and . . . possesses . . . living through enjoyment," so that the resulting work contributes directly to an "expanding and enriched life."[37] And aesthetic experience is not intellectualist, teaching a moral lesson apart from perception and emotion; still less is it "sentimental," allowing us to enjoy the feeling of having feelings instead of enjoying the scene or the material of our experience.[38]

Genuinely aesthetic experience preserves for us the consummation of human experience. As Dewey says, "Art is the living and concrete proof that [humanity] is capable of restoring consciously, and thus on the plane of meaning, the union of sense, need, impulse and action characteristic of the live creature."[39] The aesthetic object and the aesthetic perception which it evokes give shape to the educational process by embodying the selective end which we wish to cultivate in all persons.

Despite Seerveld's criticisms of Deweyan "democratism," there is much he could endorse in Dewey's account of "aesthetic art" as emergent from communal experience. At the same time, it is understandable why Seerveld has his reservations. Seerveld gives us a very fine, normative description of art and aesthetic life, crystallized in its most distinctive form — and not only this, but a vision of what a distinctively Christian worldview can bring to the human activity of artistic forming. It is important that Seerveld take the highest Christian ground possible, and use as his illustrations the very best and most profound examples of Christian art, because he is trying to

36. Dewey, "Philosophy of the Arts," p. 366.
37. Dewey, *Art as Experience*, p. 34.
38. Dewey, "Philosophy of the Arts," pp. 362, 363.
39. Dewey, *Art as Experience*, p. 31.

make a case for art in God's service. Moreover he is trying to convince a religious and cultural tradition which has long assumed that "Christian art" is an oxymoron:

> The arts are even urgently needed in our day (*if* they are transformed by human consciousnesses made communally new in Jesus Christ). Why? Not only because God's people need to experience, practice, and give away to their neighbours earnests of the Jubilee! Biblically understood, "the arts" are a most splendid, ordained vehicle for expressing "sabbath joy," the respite and anticipatory celebration of our Lord's final return and of [God's] covenantal closeness to us even now in our believing sufferings and in our believing merry-makings.[40]

This vision of imaginative arts as earnests of the Jubilee, as respite, and as anticipatory celebration of our Lord's final return and covenantal closeness, though expressed in different language, is not all that far removed from Dewey's insistence that imaginative arts are "the best proof of the existence of a realized and therefore realizable, union of material and ideal."[41] And surely Seerveld is so very interested in envisioning a distinctively Reformational art precisely because of art's crucial role in forming the tastes and perceptions of a Christian community. The question, though, is whether this concern skews his reading of Dewey's aesthetics.

## 3. From Seeds to Fruits: A Developmental Theory of Art

It is true that Dewey dissolves differentiated art back into undifferentiated human experience. The dissolution is temporary, however, and specifically aimed at understanding the emergence of aesthetic experience. His fundamental questions are these: "How is it that the everyday making of things grows into that form of making which is genuinely artistic? How is it that our everyday enjoyment of scenes and situations develops into the peculiar satisfaction that attends the experience which is emphatically aesthetic?" He goes on to say that "The answers cannot be found, unless we are willing to find the germs and roots in matters of experience that we do not currently regard as aesthetic. Having discovered these active seeds, we may follow the

40. Seerveld, *Rainbows*, p. 180.
41. Dewey, *Art as Experience*, p. 34.

course of their growth into the highest forms of finished and refined art."[42] This retracing of the development of art is what Dewey sets out to do in his theoretical formulation. Here we have the other angle on the "logical" dimension of experience, namely, as viewed from the perspective of grounding.

In keeping with Dewey's ecological view of experience, the germs of aesthetic art are both objective and subjective — namely, qualities in objects and impulsions in persons. On the objective side, the structure of meaning provides a basis for aesthetic experience. For once meanings (understood as communal human purposes) attach themselves to objects, we can never return to a pre-meaning involvement with them. Whenever we meet those objects, we experience them not only as unique individuals but also as participants in communal human relationships and purposes. This is so pervasive, says Dewey, that such meanings inhere even in the lines that enter the objects: "Different lines and different relations of lines have become subconsciously charged with all the values that result from what they have done in our experience in our every contact with the world about us." Thus the lines, textures, energies, colors, and so on which may be abstracted from meaningful objects themselves express those meanings. "For *this* reason," says Dewey, "lines are waving, upright, oblique, crooked, majestic; for this reason they seem in direct perception to have even moral expressiveness. They are earth-bound and aspiring; intimate and coldly aloof; enticing and repellent. They carry with them the properties of objects."[43]

On the subjective side, both aesthetic experience and artistic making are fundamental human "impulsions" available to all persons, and not just professional activities available to those with extraordinary talents.[44] Such impulsions meet their correlative energies in the resistant/enabling energies

42. Dewey, *Art as Experience*, p. 18.
43. Dewey, *Art as Experience*, pp. 106-7.
44. "Impulsion" is a technical term which refers to Dewey's ecological theory of experience. An "impulsion" manifests what I have called the lateral ecological dynamic. An impulsion is a primal ecological urge, distinct from a flickering and evanescent "impulse"; for an impulse is a specialized part of the larger impulsion which is "a movement outward and forward of the whole organism" into the environment. Dewey says that impulsion is "the craving of the living creature for food as distinct from the reactions of tongue and lips that are involved in swallowing; the turning toward light of the body as a whole, like the heliotropism of plants, as distinct from the following of a particular light by the eyes" (*Art as Experience*, p. 64). Thus the movement as a whole has priority and defines the function of its specific parts.

of the environing world into which we venture; if the process is successful, it results in a "felt harmony" between organism and environment.[45] Dewey insists that, although most obvious in the heliotropism of plants, the same dynamic ecological rhythm prevails in human experience. An impulsion on this level represents a human need. It is ecologically directed toward maintaining and developing the life of the human community and of the individuals within it. More specifically, a primal impulsion toward aesthetic activity would be, on the one hand, the collecting of vividly meaningful experiences or objects, and, on the other hand, the urge to express a vivid emotion in material terms.

Let us first deal with the collecting of vividly meaningful experiences or objects. Dewey says that we have experiences which "hold the attentive eye and ear," arousing our interest and affording us enjoyment, even if these are mundane events like machines excavating enormous holes in the earth.[46] If this seems *too* mundane, think of Henry Moore collecting shells and bones because something about them fascinates him and resonates in his experience. And occasionally we have what Dewey calls "*an* experience" — one in which we are fully alive to ourselves and our world, so that the experience has reached consummation, thereby touching some chord in our memory and desire and finding in the world some objective resonance for those meanings.[47] In such events we have a "total overwhelming impression," of what Dewey calls "the mystical aspect of acute aesthetic surrender."[48] This is aesthetic experience "in the raw,"[49] aesthetic experience as it naturally occurs, embedded in the fabric of our lives.

However, humans have never long been content with such experiences "in the raw," since they are too rare and fleeting. One of our primal "impulsions" is the need to "express" the meaning of such an experience in objective form.[50]

45. Dewey, *Art as Experience*, p. 50.

46. Dewey, *Art as Experience*, p. 11.

47. Dewey describes such experience in these terms: "Experience in the degree in which it *is* experience is heightened vitality. . . . Because experience is the fulfillment of an organism in its struggles and achievements in a world of things, it is art in germ. Even in its rudimentary forms, it contains the promise of that delightful perception which is aesthetic experience" (*Art as Experience*, p. 25).

48. Dewey, *Art as Experience*, p. 150, 35.

49. Dewey, *Art as Experience*, p. 10.

50. Dewey says that "the work of art develops and accentuates what is characteristically valuable in things of everyday enjoyment. The art product will then be seen to issue from the latter, when the full meaning of ordinary experience is expressed, as dyes

Originally, expression is just an organic "boiling over"[51] without conscious intent or shaping; it may be expressive to others but it is not intentionally expressive on our part. But at some point (and these times are all too rare for most people not trained to pay attention) we may begin to use this spontaneous "boiling over" as the raw material for a shaped object. The first rudimentary form of the aesthetic object is the emotionalized image: "when excitement about subject matter goes deep, it stirs up a store of attitudes and meanings derived from prior experience. As they are aroused into activity they become conscious thoughts and emotions, emotionalized images."[52] But the emotionalized image cannot be enough; fully developed aesthetic experience requires an object, for while physical materials and energies are not sufficient, they are necessary for an aesthetic experience.[53] While an emotionalized image may satisfy for a time, it is too transient to enable us to explore the aesthetic experience. "What is kindled must either burn itself out, turning to ashes, or must press itself out in material. . . ."[54]

Following Dewey's ecological pattern of experience, an aesthetically focused "art" experience involves both doing and undergoing, as well as an enrichment and deepening of meaning. "While there is no expression, unless there is urge from within outwards, the welling up must be clarified and ordered by taking into itself the values of prior experience before it can be an act of expression. And these values are not called into play save through objects of the environment that offer resistance to the direct discharge of emotion and impulse."[55] The processes are aesthetically specified versions of feeling, thinking, and "art" or making. "Aesthetic emotion" is an imaginative sensitivity to whatever is qualitatively congenial to the "emotionalized image" we are developing. It operates like a "magnet," drawing to itself those lines, shapes, colors, and so on which express a particular meaning.[56]

---

come out of coal tar products when they receive special treatment" (*Art as Experience,* p. 17).

51. Dewey, *Art as Experience,* p. 67.
52. Dewey, *Art as Experience,* p. 71.
53. Dewey, *Art as Experience,* p. 151.
54. Dewey, *Art as Experience,* p. 71.
55. Dewey, *Art as Experience,* p. 67.
56. Dewey, *Art as Experience,* p. 75. For Dewey, such "aesthetic emotion" is a specifically aesthetic version of our more generalized tacit ability to sense appropriateness and fit.

Henry Moore has written that "the human figure is what interests me most deeply," but that such work has been deeply informed by the meaningful forms of bones and shells.[57] Implicit in this is a Deweyan view of aesthetic experience as ecological. Hence an initial forming is succeeded (ecologically speaking) by a period of "taking in" (specifically, "aesthetic perception") during which we experience the meanings evoked by the emerging object, rather than using them as "signals" and moving on. Such perception involves not just an additive "placing something on the top of consciousness over what was previously known" but a transformative "reconstruction which may be painful."[58] Such perception develops the emotionalized image, which in turn requires more shaping. Thus "the physical process develops imagination, while imagination is conceived in terms of concrete material."[59] According to Moore, "The artist will sometimes start with a scribble, a piece of clay perhaps, and in the process of working out his initial idea — the impulse that led him to start — fuller ideas will come to him, so that the forms carved out from a piece of wood may become susceptible of interpretation say as a mother protecting her child, or as an embryo."[60] This process is what I might call "aesthetic thinking," for although "thinking directly in terms of colors, tones, images, is a different operation technically from thinking in words," it is still a way of intuitively understanding the effects of colors, and so on, a way as "intent" and "penetrating" as that of the scientist.[61] In this process, successive attempts to realize the image deepen its imaginative and emotional resonance. Dewey says that "the making comes to an end when its result is experienced as good — and that experience comes not by mere intellectual and outside judgment but in direct perception."[62]

Although Dewey's developmental theory of art emphasizes process, the aesthetic process is still, properly speaking, part of the "logical" articulation of experience, viewed from the ground up rather than from the top down. As a cumulative deposit of a great many critically sifted experiences, an understanding of aesthetic process forms part of our "map." It uncovers what a person might need at any given time in order to carry the process

57. Henry Moore, *Henry Moore on Sculpture*, ed. Philip James (London: MacDonald, 1968), p. 70.
58. Dewey, *Art as Experience*, p. 48.
59. Dewey, *Art as Experience*, pp. 81-82.
60. *Moore on Sculpture*, p. 117.
61. Dewey, *Art as Experience*, pp. 80, 52.
62. Dewey, *Art as Experience*, p. 56.

forward rather than retarding it. Dewey's ecological theory of experience highlights the interactional dynamics which must be honored if the aesthetic experience is to bear fruit.

Dewey works with a continuum of aesthetic experience, ranging from the aesthetic as a "primary phase" ("in the raw") to the aesthetic as an intentionally cultivated artistic object shaped especially for aesthetic perception. He has no intention of denying the developed character of art, nor of forcing art to regress to a populist lowest common denominator which would deny its own aesthetic integrity. But he does think that "fine art" has developed in the direction of elitism and segregation and thus may have severed the life-giving connections between art and human experience in general. In order to reconceptualize a more integrated development of art, Dewey does wish to dissolve "fine art" back into ordinary experience, in the sense of returning to aesthetic experience "in the raw" — but only for the purpose of retracing its differentiation in a way which also maintains continuity with the rest of our experience. Thus this is not a one-way or permanent "dissolution" of art, a denial of its legitimate cultural differentiation, as Seerveld's reading seems to imply. For Dewey still maintains both ends of the aesthetic spectrum, from the side which emphasizes its emergence out of experience as a whole, to the side which emphasizes its full differentiation and distinctiveness; he thinks that both ends are necessary to maintain a balanced view of aesthetic life.

Seerveld, in fact, makes a very similar point:

> Art, Christianly conceived, is not something esoteric. Art is no more special (nor less special) than marriage and prayer and fresh strawberries out of season. Like acrobatics and careful thought and running a business well, artistry takes training. It is more difficult than falling off a log. To sing with modulated tones, controlled breathing, and fine phrasing, or to take shopworn words and cast them into the necklace of a sonnet form and make them fresh again, or to walk across a stage and slump on the ground in such a way that every eye is struck by the despair cursing the person: all that takes special gifts and knowledge of execution. But art is not, therefore, suddenly mysterious or supernatural.[63]

Dewey's point is exactly this: art is not, therefore, suddenly mysterious or supernatural. And, like Seerveld, Dewey insists that art is not ultimately a

63. Seerveld, *Rainbows*, p. 25.

world unto itself but enriches the whole of our lives. The somewhat misleading phrase about "dissolving art into ordinary experience" is but an attempt to restore this sense of connectedness and integration to art, in tandem with its legitimate differentiation and development.

Of course there are differences here too. Just as Seerveld thinks that Dewey dissolves objects into functionality, Dewey might think that Seerveld's understanding of the aesthetic is so object-oriented that it leaves too little room for process and function. That is, Seerveld may be so concerned with the structure and quality of finished artworks that he gives too little attention to the way in which such works arise out of experience and function within it.

## 4. Norm and Process in Aesthetic Education

Viewing experience from the perspectives of grounding and emergence, Dewey has articulated a two-dimensional map of aesthetic art, emphasizing both norm and process. This map, as I have suggested, is extremely valuable. We make maps because we believe that they can help us on our journey by making available to us the results of past journeys. But a map is not a journey; still less is it an individual person who is on a very individual journey. The map envisions our goals and our best ideas as to how to get there, but the person who is on the journey begins wherever she begins and struggles with very individual obstacles on the way. Although maps of journeys provide invaluable help, there will be wrong turns and mistakes. If we focused only on the goal, we might become overly strict and judgmental, while if we did not value maps at all we might take a "hands-off" position toward human journeys, waiting passively for normative experiences to emerge and abdicating our own cultural responsibility.

This is why Dewey says that, for purposes of teaching, the "logical" dimension of curriculum needs to be "psychologized" — "translated into the immediate and individual experiencing within which it has its origin and significance."[64] Thus what concerns the teacher, as opposed to the theorist, is

> the ways in which that subject may become a part of experience; what there is in the child's present that is usable with reference to it; how such

64. Dewey, "The Child and the Curriculum," p. 285.

144

elements are to be used; how [the teacher's] own knowledge of the sub-ject-matter may assist in interpreting the child's needs and doings, and determine the medium in which the child should be placed in order that [the child's] growth may be properly directed.[65]

If we return to the map image, the teacher's job is to utilize her or his knowledge of the journey and the goal in order to help the student discover it all for the first time. In order to do this, the teacher must take infinite pains to understand the student's needs. Still more important, the teacher must look at the student with a loving and cherishing eye, believing that the roots of aesthetic experience are there and searching them out.

Since Dewey believes that properly developing experience is both in-teractive and continuous, he suggests that these two dimensions define the office of the teacher. First, the principle of interaction. Since ecologically structured experience involves not only person but environment, it is the teacher's responsibility to "recognize in the concrete what surroundings are conducive to having experiences that lead to growth," and, further, to "util-ize the surroundings, physical and social, that exist so as to extract from them all that they have to contribute to building up experiences that are worthwhile."[66] Since the desirable environment must be tailored to the needs of the students involved, "responsibility for selecting objective con-ditions carries with it . . . the responsibility for understanding the needs and capacities of the individuals who are learning at a given time."[67] And since the actual students, being individuals in a specific situation, will never be exactly like any other group of students in a different situation, this will require close observation joined with all of the teacher's cumulative expe-rience.

Based on Dewey's understanding of the subjective aesthetic experience and objective aesthetic object, the teacher will try to develop these in tan-dem. This means that answers must not be provided to questions which are not being asked. Nor must objective quality be developed in isolation from the child's authentic aesthetic experience of that object. For if the child manages, perhaps by a lucky stroke, to produce an artwork valuable

65. Dewey, "The Child and the Curriculum," p. 286.
66. John Dewey, *Experience and Education*, in *The Later Works: 1925-1953*, Vol. 13: *1938-1939*, ed. Jo Ann Boydston (Carbondale: Southern Illinois University Press, 1991), p. 22.
67. Dewey, *Experience and Education*, p. 27.

to adult sensitivities, without participating in the aesthetic process of producing it, that experience is useless to the child. It only leads her, as Dewey says, to value objects more than her own experiences, and at worst to fake experiences which she thinks she should have. Because it is the child's aesthetic experience which must be nurtured, a first effort must not be dismissed because it is not "art" the way a cultivated adult may understand it. But when the aesthetic experience is present and developing, the teacher can also help the student acquire the discipline of working with a material medium. If a teacher understands the mutually interactional pattern of aesthetic perception and artistic making, the teacher can help the child know when it is time to work at the piece and when it is time to let it rest. A teacher will also help the child to reflect on the emerging work and to recognize what does and does not develop the child's imaginative experience. The teacher must know how and when to encourage technical facility, within the context of realizing an imaginative experience. While there is room for systematic teaching of technical ability to provide the "habitual coordinations" of eye and hand which enable a child to respond to an imaginative experience, technical facility divorced from realizing an imaginative experience may stifle the growth of the child's aesthetic experience.

Secondly, the principle of continuity. Since this principle means that experience is always tending in some direction or other, it is "the business of the educator to see in what direction an experience is heading."[68] The teacher then has the responsibility to make possible and encourage those experiences which, in the long run, lead to the inclusive and continuing growth of enriched experience. Again, the teacher must not decide this in the abstract, but combine a commitment to the valued "ends" of such education with a sensitivity to the natural rhythms and processes in the child.

In more concrete terms, the teacher's job is to keep an eye out for those primal "impulsions" toward imaginative expression which are the beginnings of any authentic experience. These "roots and germs" of aesthetic life may not look very aesthetic in themselves, but an experienced teacher, knowing the "leadings" of experience, must recognize them. They may be less visible than the child's statement, "I want to write a poem." They may be just some evidence of deep emotional turmoil which, in the teacher's judgment, might be the beginnings of an aesthetic and artistic experience.

---

68. Dewey, *Experience and Education*, p. 21.

The teacher may then suggest making an object, and subsequently must provide a nurturing environment for such rudimentary impulsions, discriminating what is conducive to the full development of authentically aesthetic experience.

But the teacher's responsibility to the student goes further. It should, I believe, involve modifying the abstract ideal to make it accessible and welcoming at different stages of the learning process; after all, Christians who believe in the incarnation have ample warrant for this. I have suggested above that Seerveld is particularly eloquent when he envisions the ideal of Christian art and the contribution it may make to the Christian community. Dewey alerts us, however, to a potential weakness in this approach — namely, its potential for ontologizing normativity in abstraction from the human lives which are its normal context. Without a corresponding emphasis on the imperfections and processes of embodied normativity, this remains a potential difficulty.

Seerveld's strategy — of taking the high ground in terms of aesthetic norms and standards — works to a degree when he talks about training in aesthetic awareness, for indeed we should learn to discriminate aesthetic values and religious spirits in art. However, the strategy may break down when he comes to the extremely important notion of aesthetic education. For a strong emphasis on norms and standards may encourage us to denigrate those learners who do not come up to the standards, for whatever reason. It may also encourage critics to elevate themselves as the judges of those who struggle (and perhaps fail) fully to embody these aesthetic norms.

Robert Hull discusses the pedagogic consequences of using the highly developed definitions of "poetry" which are found in aesthetic and literary theory, but also in many teaching resources. An example is Sybil Marshall, who worries that children's writing may not be authentically poetic: "To literature lovers, the word poetry implies organization, discipline, and imagery beyond the range of children to achieve."[69] Other writers suggest that, since only a very few children have such technical aptitudes, "the teacher should guide each line of the poem."[70] The result, Hull says, is the sense

---

69. Sybil Marshall, *Creative Writing* (London: Macmillan Education, 1978), p. 16. Quoted in Robert Hull, *Behind the Poem: A Teacher's View of Children Writing* (London and New York: Routledge, 1988), p. 244.

70. S. M. Lane and J. Kemp, *An Approach to Creative Writing in the Primary School* (Glasgow: Blackie, 1967), p. 40. Quoted in Hull, *Behind the Poem*, p. 244.

that "for children to write poems involves reaching up to a preconceived technical threshold." This only fosters nervousness, presumably for both children and teachers. The deeper curse, however, is that a teacher's expectation can also *create* the problem it imagines; that is, if a teacher takes every stumble to mean that "Children don't have technical skill" (rather than "We are not at a point where their technical skill has emerged"), the teacher will act on that assumption, and the children will never receive the opportunity to develop skill. Moreover, as Hull says, this becomes "a judgment on a child" rather than just a "comment on a process."[71] As anyone who has been through this will know, such judgments are curses. They can stifle aesthetic life for years into the future. Witness the many books currently being written to help those who believe that they cannot write and have nothing worth saying.

Dewey's answer to this over-emphasis on abstract normativity is not to get rid of normativity but to utilize both the logical and psychological dimensions of normativity, for purposes of teaching. Abstract logical normativity — that is, our ideal conception of what we think poetry should be — remains extremely important because it gives us a criterion for selecting what in the child's experience needs to be encouraged and what needs to be moved beyond. If teachers do not have this logical conception of normativity, they end up with a *laissez-faire* attitude which refuses to take responsibility for choice. This attitude allows students to flounder with no direction and only causes frustration.

However, logical normativity on its own, although it may provide a view of the goal, will not help us know how to get there step by step. For that we need a psychologized understanding of normativity which enables us to appreciate the texture of the process from its beginnings. Such psychologization will take place on two fronts: seeing how the child's experience "contains within itself the attitudes, the motives, and the interests which have operated in developing and organizing the subject-matter to the plane which it now occupies," and interpreting the subject-matter as "outgrowths of forces operating in the child's life" in order to discover "the steps that intervene between the child's present experience and their richer maturity." A psychologized normativity will help us see the developmental steps leading from the germs of aesthetic experience to the highest forms of art we can envision. This developmental understanding can then help

71. Hull, *Behind the Poem*, pp. 244-46.

us see "what step the child needs to take just here and now," and should also make us more patient with the "uncertain and tortuous," as well as the "efficient and successful."

The implication is that a necessary step at any given time — one which may be normative in that educational situation — may well be deficient when compared to abstract normativity. Or an aesthetic experience which represents an important developmental breakthrough may not come up to our abstract standards for aesthetic experience. Dewey would argue that this compromise is necessary — more, it is developmentally responsible — if we are to begin with a child's actual aesthetic experiences and develop them, as opposed to applying an alien normativity from outside. Abstract normativity still provides an ideal which enables us to discern "the promise contained in feelings and deeds which, taken by themselves, are unpromising and repellant [*sic*]" and to see whatever in the child's experience is "germinating seed, or opening bud, of some fruit to be borne."[72] But it will help us nurture that germinating seed only if it is translated into the realities of developing aesthetic experience.

This is what Robert Hull means when he suggests that teachers need a more functionalized understanding of poetry, as well as a conception which is "broader" and "less mean-spirited."[73] Thus Kenneth Koch, in helping nursing-home patients learn to write poetry, uses as his models the poetry of William Carlos Williams and D. H. Lawrence because, with its combination of "prosiness, talky quality, repetition, and lyricism," such poetry is closer to speech rhythms than more complex poetic and rhythmic forms. Although it may not be something many writers can master, he says, it is not completely unapproachable, and "a modestly educated, unliterary old person can have a chance of writing something like it."[74]

In addition, a more generous conception of poetry (or of art in general) would include not only a vision of poetry in its optimum forms but also a welcoming attitude toward the whole process that gives rise, here and

---

72. Dewey, "The Child and the Curriculum," pp. 278-83. An abstract ideal prevents us from absolutizing or finalizing what is transitional in a child's development and making it complete in itself (p. 282). Such absolutizing would lead us to neglect what the child may become in favor of what the child is now, and thereby lead to arrested development.

73. Hull, *Behind the Poem*, p. 247.

74. Kenneth Koch, *I Never Told Anybody: Teaching Poetry Writing in a Nursing Home* (New York: Random House, 1977), p. 8.

there, to poems. This means that we love the process of writing itself and even acquire the ability to see "bad" poems as poems which do not yet know how to become good, rather than as simply "bad." Not that we abandon our standards and insist that bad poems are as good as good ones; obviously that makes no sense. But we do need to appreciate the good in whatever is being done and to see its possibilities for becoming better. This is why Brenda Ueland says that

> when you write, if it is to be any good at all, you must feel free, — free and not anxious. The only good teachers for you are those friends who love you, who think you are interesting, or very important, or wonderfully funny; whose attitude is: "Tell me more. Tell me all you can. I want to understand more about everything you feel and know and all the changes inside and out of you. Let more come out." And if you have no such friend, — and you want to write, — well then you must imagine one.[75]

A generous conception of poetry will love a bad poem as a good effort which can — and should — be better. A bad poem is still a poem and as such is to be treated with tenderness and respect. It may well need improvement, but a bad poem will not get better if it is not first welcomed and accepted, just as it is.

In the title of this essay, I use an unfamiliar word: "poeming," in contrast to "poetry." This term comes from Robert Hull, who suggests, in a Deweyan fashion, that although teachers need a working conception of "poetry," even more they need a working appreciation of the process of "poeming." For the goal of such education, as Hull (and Dewey) would see it, is not just the production of "good" poems in an abstract critical sense, but the authentically aesthetic experience of working to produce a poem out of (and for) one's experience. Still, though, in teaching the question also emerges: "But is it poetry?" As a teacher, what can one say about a really bad poem? Hull says that "even if one cannot find anything good to say about a poem, some demonstration of faith is needed in any commitment that has gone into it. . . ." He continues:

> It might be better to take the emphasis on poetry as activity one stage further and think of "poem" as a verb masquerading as a noun. The pupil

75. Brenda Ueland, *If You Want to Write* (St. Paul, Minn.: Graywolf Press, 1938), p. 8.

has, perhaps, been poeming, but hasn't discovered the things that one looks for when one goes poeming. . . . The empty lines where the poem might have been invite awareness that the writer may have been looking in the wrong places, or in the wrong way. "This isn't a poem" asserts baldly that there has been no journey, no visit.[76]

Denise Levertov, an accomplished poet, speaks of the arduous process of "poeming" in similar terms, likening the journey in art to the journey in faith: "Every work of art, even if long premeditated, enters a stage of improvisation as soon as the artist moves from thinking about it to beginning to form its concrete reality. That step, from entertaining a project for a poem . . . to actually . . . writing it, resembles moving from intellectual assent to opening the acts of daily life to permeation by religious faith."[77] "Faith" here speaks not only to the content of poetry but to the "demonstration of faith" needed to begin and to continue the risky and anxious process of writing. Levertov's distinction is, in part, between our love for finished poetic ideals and the love which we must develop for the seeds of poems in our own experience.

Similarly, Alicia Ostriker says that becoming conscious of oneself poetically is "hard labor." It involves pushing past the "interior censor that stands at the threshold of every important truth about ourselves, forbidding us to enter. . . ." And once we enter the "authentically deep," we discover that it is "always a tumult, shifting sands, never simple."[78] Such is the hard labor in store for all those brave enough to try to write poetry; and the anxiety is such that these persons, at whatever level, need all the pastoral support, respect, and encouragement they can get. They do not need to be told simply that their work does not come up to certain standards for poetry.

This is not to say that such standards are not themselves necessary and important. But for pedagogic purposes we need to be able to contextualize, relativize, and developmentalize such standards so that they become blessings rather than curses. The contextualized standard is just as real and good as the more abstract one — good for a different purpose. The abstract ideal is a crucial reminder of the high standards we have for redemptively Chris-

---

76. Hull, *Behind the Poem*, pp. 257-58.

77. Denise Levertov, "Work that Enfaiths," in *New and Selected Essays* (New York: New Directions, 1990), p. 249.

78. Alicia Suskin Ostriker, *Feminist Revision and the Bible* (Oxford, UK and Cambridge, Mass.: Blackwell, 1993), p. 111.

tian art; but the embodied, imperfect, journeying normativity of creaturely processes is also crucial as we broken creatures seek to help each other on our difficult journey toward our communal ideals. I am not suggesting that we lower our standards all around; but that, for someone who is just beginning or who is struggling against huge obstacles, we may need a more generous and flexible normativity which affirms, for developmental purposes, something we may not wish to affirm as our ultimate standard. This deep respect for creaturely reality is, paradoxically, one of Dewey's most valuable contributions to a Reformational aesthetic theory. I say "paradoxically" because I believe that this is (alienated Congregationalist) Dewey's way of getting at the riches of the doctrine of creation.

For Christians, there is an ethical issue here which we must not miss. It is all very well to envision Christian poems as providing us with a rich, honest, compassionate view of broken creatures in the process of being redeemed. But this vision is useless without a compassionate and understanding educational approach which welcomes and honors the human process of poeming, whatever its anxieties and wherever it needs to be at a given time. As Marion Milner says, "In order to experience such a tenderness for nature outside, in all her forms, one had surely to have found some way of coming to terms with nature inside; or rather, with those parts of nature inside that one had repudiated as too unpleasant to be recognised as part of oneself."[79] Having standards for good Christian poems without the Christian compassion and honor for those who are in the process of poeming risks becoming an ideology which curses creaturely poeming with a sense of guilt, anxiety, and inadequacy. Dewey's insight is that norm and process, responsible poetry and the all-too-human process of poeming, mutually inform and critique each other. For only when Christian compassion redemptively encompasses not only the creatures enpoemed but also the creature poeming can Christian aesthetic theory encourage Christian artists to bring redeeming love into the world of contemporary art.

79. Marion Milner, *On Not Being Able to Paint* (New York: International Universities Press, 1957), p. 44.

# Thinking in the Image of Need:
# The Language of *Ereignis* in
# Heidegger's Nietzsche Lectures

## DONALD L. KNUDSEN

One must enter the study of the history of Western philosophy with caution. It is an arena filled with disputation. Truths are asserted in the name of truth, which itself is subsequently reviewed for the sake of considerably different findings. Awareness of such variegation can lead one out of the sphere of philosophical inquiry entirely. By no means, however, does such a move preclude a return. The philosophical questions remain durable over time, whether or not the individual chooses to engage them. The student's task is to decipher the extent to which one or another of the established philosophers can serve as a teacher.

I shall introduce here a minute portion of the thought of Martin Heidegger (1889-1976), the German philosopher whom many still regard as the foremost representative of European philosophy in the twentieth century. Heidegger is known as an existentialist, though he repudiated such a label for himself. Whereas the humanist view of existential thought locates the primary source of truth in the individual, Heidegger repeatedly searches for what the name of that source might be in its Being. What can Heidegger teach us about philosophy during that period of time, the mid-1930s, when he elaborated a meditative turn *(Kehre)* to poetry and the work of art?

With this turn, Heidegger begins to develop a new language. It is expressly devoted to history as a process whose design is not subject to human ratiocination for purposes of subjective re-direction. A term begins to appear in Heidegger's writings at this time: *Ereignis,* meaning "event" or "emergence." The term signifies both the end of an entire tradition of philosophizing and the beginning of something new.

Heidegger's attempt to revolutionize the meaning of history focuses on the culmination of traditional philosophy in Nietzsche's aesthetics of the will to power, and on the creative exploration of meditative thought in, especially, the poetry of Hölderlin. Among the texts available for study from this period, I have selected one from Heidegger's Nietzsche lectures on art, delivered at the University of Freiburg during the 1936-37 academic year.

To my knowledge, this text has not yet been presented systematically in the English language. After providing an interpretive summary of the passage, I shall account for its connections to central themes of Heidegger's argument on Nietzsche and then discuss the place of Hölderlin and poetry in Heidegger's thought. My critical assessment considers Heidegger's way of thinking at the level or depth of terms that he himself employs. The text of Heidegger's discourse shows his effort to address a new spiritual need in Germany and overcome the supposedly nefarious effects of traditional Western philosophy by plumbing its nihilism to the depths of metaphysical anguish. In the way that Heidegger turns within the genesis of this reticulated nihilism — with its inner desiccation and self-overcoming — I find a mythologizing tendency oriented redemptively to the German people and their language. For guidance in understanding what a category such as "mythologizing" might mean for work in the history of philosophy, I am indebted to the writings and teaching of Dr. Calvin Seerveld.[1]

My concluding remarks should bear results for the current debate about the timing and structure of Heidegger's supposed turn *(Kehre)* of the mid-1930s. In particular, I apply the category of "mythologizing" to Heidegger's own process of self-imaging. In this process, Heidegger transcends the category of individual will, yet, resolutely and in need, he maintains the image of "whole consciousness" in the effort to help realize Being within the being of the Germans.

---

1. Calvin Seerveld, "Biblical Wisdom underneath Vollenhoven's Categories for Philosophical Historiography," in *The Idea Of A Christian Philosophy: Essays in Honour of D. H. Th. Vollenhoven* (Toronto: Wedge Publishing Foundation, 1973), pp. 127-43.

## Heidegger's Text as Document

The text for our discussion can be found only within an edition of Heidegger's works published after his death. The passage was omitted — presumably by Heidegger himself — from the 1961 publication of *Der Wille zur Macht als Kunst* in the first of the *Nietzsche* volumes.[2] According to Heidegger's own testimony, he did not withdraw or supplant substantive material during his editing of the 1936-37 lectures for the 1961 publication.[3] The 1985 *Gesamtausgabe* version of Heidegger's *Nietzsche: Der Wille zur Macht als Kunst* presents the passage as of such significance that it is mentioned in the editor's afterword. Bernd Heimbüchel explicitly notes the part of it where Heidegger mentions his 1933 *Rektoratsrede*, a speech delivered when he assumed the rectorship of the University of Freiburg.[4]

The question of "why" Heidegger deleted this passage after the war might be answered simply by pointing out Heidegger's reference to that *Rektoratsrede*, in which he had promulgated National Socialist principles and programs. There is no denying the plausibility of such an explanation, given that Heidegger himself provided none. But this response would verge on speculation if it did not probe other issues and thereby set a context for philosophical elucidation.

The passage missing from Heidegger's authorized version compels us to consider the role of scholarship. This instance of textual recovery by a scholar is not the only one to have occurred regarding Heidegger and his Nietzsche lectures.[5] In the case at hand, the document is found in the *Gesamtausgabe* series of which Hans-Martin Sass, compiler of an extensive bibliography and glossary of Heidegger's works, asserts that it fails to meet generally accepted standards of historico-critical work.[6] Yet, although

---

2. Martin Heidegger, *Nietzsche: Erster Band* (Pfullingen: Günther Neske, 1961), p. 183.

3. Heidegger, *Nietzsche: Erster Band*, pp. 9-10, and Martin Heidegger, *Nietzsche. Vol. I: The Will to Power as Art*, trans., with notes and analysis, by David Farrell Krell (San Francisco: Harper & Row, 1979), pp. xv-xvi.

4. Martin Heidegger, *Nietzsche: Der Wille zur Macht als Kunst*, ed. Bernd Heimbüchel for the *Gesamtausgabe, Band 43* (Frankfurt am Main: Vittorio Klostermann, 1985), p. 295.

5. Richard Wolin, *The Politics of Being: The Political Thought of Martin Heidegger* (New York: Columbia University Press, 1990), p. 198.

6. Hans-Martin Sass, *Martin Heidegger: Bibliography and Glossary* (Bowling Green, Ohio: Philosophy Documentation Center, Bowling Green State University, 1982), p. 2.

Heimbüchel, editor of the volume under consideration here, does not provide critical notes for textual sources potentially available for public scrutiny, he does account for the way by which the passage mentioning the *Rektoratsrede* was obtained. The restoration was made possible by access to a stenographic record of Heidegger's original lectures prepared by Dr. Wilhelm Hallwachs, a member of the audience. According to Heimbüchel, the transcription of this record reads word-for-word with much of Heidegger's own manuscript.[7] The preliminary result of Heimbüchel's editing — if contrary information does not surface with regard to either Hallwach's record or its transcription — is that the insertion is verifiable and thus open for discussion of its contents.[8]

Heidegger omitted from publication an entire passage consisting of over two full pages of German text, of which the referral to the *Rektoratsrede* is "only" the concluding statement. The text maintains an internal coherence through its attention to the development of the *Ereignis* language. Its connections to its chapter setting are obvious. Moreover, the vocabulary of *Ereignis* and closely related terminology occupy a crucial place within Heidegger's mid-1930s language, as this appears in texts from the same period.

These factors provide further impetus for presenting the restored document in its entirety. Its intrinsic value for the purposes of Heidegger scholarship cannot be doubted. The text, as now restored, is not the product of any re-editing by Heidegger. Furthermore, the matter of its having been unavailable at one time for open scrutiny raises questions about Heidegger's motives for having presented it in his original delivery of the lectures.

Such questions often occur within the context of textual study that allows for a communication of evidence concerning the completeness, context, and relative truth-value of textual sources. In *Sein und Zeit* (1927), Heidegger himself had contributed to an understanding of the hermeneutical circle of interpretation by transferring its focus from textual study to the meaning of the Being by which the human being *(Dasein)* interprets itself. The supposed neutrality of textual study has disappeared altogether from Heidegger's 1936-

---

7. Heidegger, *Nietzsche: Der Wille zur Macht als Kunst,* p. 294.

8. Domenico Losurdo, "Heidegger and Hitler's War," in *The Heidegger Case: On Philosophy and Politics,* ed. Tom Rockmore and Joseph Margolis (Philadelphia: Temple University Press, 1992), p. 144. Otto Pöggeler, "Heidegger, Nietzsche, and Politics," in *The Heidegger Case,* p. 132. Tom Rockmore, *On Heidegger's Nazism and Philosophy* (Berkeley: University of California Press, 1992), p. 173.

37 Nietzsche lectures. Concern with a "circle" as figure remains, though now for a process of thought in which the emergence of full-fledged truth is occurring. According to Heidegger, history itself is being re-made in the language of *Ereignis* within the structure and direction of his own thinking.

Heidegger utilizes the *Ereignis* language only on one, extended, occasion within the course of these Nietzsche lectures on art, namely, in the text which also incorporates the single reference to the *Rektoratsrede*. Heidegger is putting the statements made in the 1933 speech on new ground with direct historical implications. It is in particular the language of *Not* ("need"), fundamental to the *Rektoratsrede,* which is transformed into that of the "metaphysical need" of our text. Metaphysical need, elucidated by a background of Hölderlin's poetry and the politics of Germany in the mid-1930s, is what Heidegger means by the *Ereignis* language in the lecture segment presented here. The authenticity of Heidegger's discourse on need is marked by his whole-hearted resolve to lead in realizing essential dimensions of Being (state, poetry, thought) for the German people.

Thinking with Heidegger in rejection of theoretical neutrality by no means entails an absorption into the mythologizing tendency which fuels his deliberations. A pattern of thought obtains depth in the full appropriation of its own terms. If the core of Heidegger's thinking remains impervious to propositionally-guided criticism from the interpreter, it still can be deciphered and elucidated from a position of transcendence that recognizes the durability of philosophical problematics and the means for their resolution. An ethical directive will lead the interpreter who realizes that presuppositions of ultimate significance mark the signposts and carry the language for philosophical reflection.

Heidegger's discussion should be rendered as closely as possible to the relatively coarse, adamant style which he himself adopted. What follows is a reading and, given the text as it stands, will by no means provide an immediate explanation for Heidegger's 1961 deletion.

## The Hidden Passage

The David Farrell Krell translation accurately reflects the 1961 German edition with this rendering of our passage: "One of the essential formulations that designate the event of nihilism says, 'God is dead.' (Cf. now *Holzwege* 1950, pp. 193-247.) The phrase 'God is dead' is not an atheistic proclamation: it is a formula for the fundamental experience of an event in Occidental history."[9]

The 1985 Heimbüchel version for the *Gesamtausgabe* begins along the same lines: "One of the essential formulas for the knowledge of the emergence *(des Ereignisses)* of nihilism runs: 'God is dead.'"[10] Yet the Heimbüchel edition enters new territory with a footnoted quote by Heidegger from Nietzsche: "(Cf. XIII, 75: 'The *refutation* of God: actually only the moral God is refuted.')."[11] In 1961 Heidegger extirpates this material and what follows it in order to make reference only to his own *Holzwege*.

Heimbüchel confirms the next sentence of the Neske edition/Krell translation found above — except that he finds it at the virtual close of the passage involved, where Heidegger makes personal mention of his 1933 *Rektoratsrede*:

> "God is dead" is therefore not an atheistic teaching, but the formula for the ground-experience of an emergence *(eines Ereignisses)* in Western history. I have with whole consciousness appropriated *(Mit vollem Bewusstsein habe Ich . . . aufgenommen)* this sentence from my rector's speech of 1933.[12]

The formerly hidden text lies inclusively between the initial formulation of nihilism and the concluding mention of the *Rektoratsrede*, as can be found in Heimbüchel's edition.

9. Heidegger, *Nietzsche, Vol. I: The Will to Power as Art*, p. 156. Krell notes "that the 'event' of nihilism, cited four times in this and the following paragraphs, occasions perhaps the earliest 'terminological' use of the word *Ereignis* in Heidegger's published writings" (fn., p. 156). Krell's observation slights the occurrence of *Ereignis* within systematic settings in texts generally available at the time of this writing *(Hölderlin und das Wesen der Dichtung* and *Der Ursprung des Kunstwerkes)*. Moreover, because he relies upon the 1961 Neske edition, Krell completely bypasses the *Ereignis* language in the text under our consideration.

10. Heidegger, *Nietzsche: Der Wille zur Macht als Kunst*, p. 190. This and all further translations from the Heimbüchel edition are mine.

11. Heidegger, *Nietzsche: Der Wille zur Macht als Kunst*, p. 190.

12. Heidegger, *Nietzsche: Der Wille zur Macht als Kunst*, p. 193. For translation of the passage from the *Rektoratsrede* to which Heidegger refers, see Richard Wolin, ed., *The Heidegger Controversy: A Critical Reader* (Cambridge, Mass.: MIT Press, 1993), p. 33: "And if our ownmost existence itself stands on the threshold of a great transformation; if it is true what the last German philosopher to passionately seek God, Friedrich Nietzsche, said: 'God is dead'; if we must take seriously the abandonment of man today in the midst of Being, what then does this imply for science?"

Heidegger protectively circumscribes Nietzsche's word of the "death of God" with his own statement that such a formula is essential in the knowledge of the event of nihilism. He thus assumes control of the dialectic that will be required to appropriate Nietzsche for this section of his lectures. Heidegger first clears the ground of those believers who take Nietzsche's word at its most obvious face-value. Heidegger casts blame on those who grossly misinterpret Nietzsche as an atheist. Their problem could be general stupidity, the desire for disputation, or a fear of not knowing how to make sense of things.

According to Heidegger, Nietzsche's meaning is much different from what the Christian dogmatists have supposed. The basic knowledge on which late nineteenth-century Nietzsche stood prohibited a form of human existence without some kind of God or gods. At that time, human beings could relate effectively only to the God who arrives and who must arrive with presence among them. Such a coming is possible only when judgment of the last things, especially with respect to the hazard of death, is placed at God's discretion, thus creatively implanting within humans the fear of what might happen if they refuse obedience while alive. But what if fear mingled with awe of the ultimate as value no longer presses upon the human heart? Then it might be possible to speak of "God" with whatever language one has at one's disposal.

Accusation of atheism isolates the negativity of Nietzsche's proclamation and fails to notice its possibly productive effects. Heidegger invites the comparison between the truly engaged Nietzsche, who devoted his life and health totally to the exploration of the demise of "God," and the folks who speak headily with beer in hand of "God, Freedom, and Fatherland." For these latter, it is possible to speak of "God" in whatever manner suits them. Such emptiness and deceitfulness reaches its full expression, according to Heidegger, between 1914 and 1918, when friend and foe could each appeal for mercy from the "same" loving God in order to help save the "Christian, Western world." Heidegger intends to draw his audience's attention fully to his remarks: "Pay complete attention: A glance at this emergence *(Ereignis)* deals always with the whole, not with the still possible composure of a few in their breeding *(Art)*; but, therefore, with whether or not this God is and can be still a world- and reality-forming principle."[13] In this, Heidegger's first use of the *Ereignis* language within the parameters of the previously

13. Heidegger, *Nietzsche: Der Wille zur Macht als Kunst,* p. 191.

hidden text, he indicates that the issue of reality-formation is fundamentally true as an historical event within the whole. Truth can be questioned because it is historical.

At the core of Heidegger's questioning is the naming of a temporal turning which divides nihilism according to its destructive effects and constructive possibilities. Heidegger is driven within the dialectic of this opposition to search for new, historically-rooted structures of reality in which nihilism is eventually overcome. *Ereignis,* as the emergence of truth in the world, is Heidegger's word for that which opens up possibilities for human existence, if they can be seized in time, as well as that which closes matters down. *Ereignis* is the site for the encounter between that which, being finite, is given over to the fate of death, and that which, being the source of finitude itself, is, with a law of its own, the origin of new meaning for the German people in their Being. We recognize here what Heidegger means by the language of the "whole" *(Ganze)* in anticipation of his eventual reference to the "anguish of Being in its totality." The restructuring of "reality" is not a matter of decision-making by a well-bred, politic few. Heidegger is tracking *Ereignis* for its ontological pith, as it is built on historically-based questioning.

Heidegger recalls Nietzsche's word as it is proclaimed self-sacrificially before the "dying God." Heidegger approves of Nietzsche's resisting simple "No"-saying to find, according to a newly-engendered trajectory,[14] the resources for saying "Yes" to possibilities for human beings beyond his own time. Heidegger's next, restored, reference to *Ereignis* specifies how to gauge affirmatively Nietzsche's contribution to the understanding of nihilism:

> Nietzsche was sufficiently honest to call himself a nihilist, which does not indicate: one who says only "No" and would transport everything into Nothing; but, rather, one who stands within the emergence *(Ereignis)* of the dying God and imposes nothing of himself; who by all means says "No" to untruthfulness at large; who says "No," however, because he has already said "Yes" earlier and more strictly and more earnestly than his "Christian" contemporaries, who themselves, with a tremor in the voice at the banquet, call out to the true, good, and beautiful.[15]

14. Pöggeler, "Heidegger, Nietzsche, and Politics," p. 132: "Heidegger said: When Nietzsche spoke about the death of God or the death of the God of morality, he was not only standing before the 'event of the dying God'; he was also waiting for the coming (Dionysian) God."

15. Heidegger, *Nietzsche: Der Wille zur Macht als Kunst,* pp. 191-92.

Historical knowledge within the "emergence of the dying God" requires a truth-claim from a temporal source. The Christian God rises (or, emerges) into God's own death according to a self-declaration — such as Nietzsche's — different from those that God had formerly received from the people.

Heidegger does not claim that the collapse of the Christian God has resulted simply from the ostentatious activities of Christianity's adherents: even with banquets to attend, they by themselves do not determine the course of world- and reality-forming events. Nevertheless, Heidegger follows the human line for evidence of the "self"-ruination attendant upon the core of Western history's most revered entities. These might be divined "with a tremor in the voice" by Christians and humanists, but are otherworldly representations of the calumny, mendacity, and untruthfulness *(Verlogenheit)* present in human "self"-valuation. Heidegger appropriates Nietzsche within the rhetoric of spiritual difference: Nietzsche, in judgment of the interior intimacies of the God-believers, maintains his unflinching stance at the locale of the "dying God."

Nietzsche's sincere and genuine figure serves as grounds for the appeal which Heidegger raises to his audience on behalf of "the greatest" *(das Grösste)*. The special aspect of this appeal is evident as Heidegger here refers also to Hölderlin for the similar believability to be found in him. As for Nietzsche, Heidegger quotes him once again and attributes to him an original signature of the *Ereignis* language: "Nietzsche once wrote (XII, 416): '*The great event (Ereignis):* God is dead. It is just that people don't notice that they are feeding off dying values. The general laxity and dissipation.'"[16] Nietzsche's insight is that the highest values are those which devalue themselves. The Platonism of the "true, good, and beautiful" dissects the world in which human beings live. An ideal realm thus emerges — in time, paradoxically — with the form of self-dissipating eternity. Heidegger finds Nietzsche, who spent his mature philosophical years attempting to overturn such Christianly-baptized Platonism, at the culminating edge of that same tradition.

*Ereignis* shall be realized only through the crucible of radical critique, even though equivocators will certainly seek replacements for genuine sparring. Heidegger has one such writer in mind, as one who siphons off from dying values a slovenly and wasteful word of praise for the brave and believable ones who have applied their words to diagnosing Western cul-

---

16. Heidegger, *Nietzsche: Der Wille zur Macht als Kunst*, p. 192.

tural disease. Heidegger refers here to Stefan George, who should have known better because of his thoroughgoing reliance as a poet and aesthete upon the metaphysical analyses prepared by Nietzsche. George wavers at the prospect of a full commitment to the process of thought that Nietzsche spurs. George writes, as Heidegger quotes him: ". . . — nun ist not:/sich bannen in den kreis den liebe schliesst. . . ."[17] Heidegger here demurs, inasmuch as George fails to *see*[18] the *metaphysische Not* (metaphysical need) in Nietzsche's word for nihilism. George would rather retire into the inner circle where love is protected from outside dangers. For the thinker who does what is great and can do nothing other, however, there can be no support for George's prevarication: "No, this claim is still not valid for the thinker, because it has not yet achieved the most extreme plight *(Not)*, which is the need *(Not)* of Being in its totality *(die Not des Seins im Ganzen)*, out of which the cry for God becomes the most creative call on earth. The greatest *(Grösste)* do only that which others cannot."[19] Heidegger's selection from George's poem is opportune, inasmuch as it permits the comparison of spiritual dimensions available for usage of *Not*. Stefan George, whom Heidegger read carefully, could not penetrate through superficiality even in a song dedicated to Nietzsche.

The investigation of fundamental need is not open to the multitudes in the fashions of democracy. A battery of castigating remarks is delivered against this perversion inflicting Europe. Heidegger quotes Nietzsche in critique of the "rise of the mob," "the social mishmash," the "all-the-same-man," as the products of a decomposition of "value"-systems that are politically grounded in the minds of the calculative, peering, flatulently individualistic representatives of the everyday. The "greatest" ones, who

17. Heidegger, *Nietzsche: Der Wille zur Macht als Kunst*, p. 192: "now is misery:/to banish oneself within the circle that love locks. . . ."

18. Heidegger's use of language referring to "sight" anticipates underpinnings for *Ereignis* in *eräugnen*, which implies setting before the eye *(Auge)*. The element of "placing before" must be included in the experience of *Not* as a realized event. Cf. David Halliburton, *Poetic Thinking: An Approach to Heidegger* (Chicago: University of Chicago Press, 1981), p. 184, for the analysis of Heidegger's *Unterwegs zur Sprache* (1959). Halliburton recognizes by footnote Hofstadter's introduction to *Ereignis* language in *Poetry, Language, Thought*, trans. Albert Hofstadter (San Francisco: Harper & Row, 1975), pp. xviii-xxii. Here Hofstadter mentions the preliminary connection already in *Der Ursprung des Kunstwerkes* (1935-36) between truth, clearing, lighting, and sight (as in perception of the Greek temple).

19. Heidegger, *Nietzsche: Der Wille zur Macht als Kunst*, p. 192.

know of the scourge that encircles the earth, find in democracy's bombastic excesses a dissolution of what pertains to the need of Being. The mere successes of democracy as a political and economic form are no more than a surface deviation within the inexorable rise of nihilism throughout Europe.[20]

If Heidegger can denigrate without exception the values of democracy and the kind of mind that extols them, then he, by contrast, as one who belongs to the community of the great *(Grösste)*, can thoughtfully refer to the whole consciousness *(Mit vollem Bewusstsein . . .)* with which he has appropriated *(habe Ich . . . aufgenommen)*, from the *Rektoratsrede* of 1933, the quote from Nietzsche on the death of God. That quote is transformed and completed in Heidegger's new-found language for the ground-experience of an emergence *(eines Ereignisses)* of nihilism in the West.

## Nietzsche's Aesthetical Metaphysics

Heidegger's discourse occurs within a chapter that has been editorially entitled "Platonism and Nihilism." Having established the priority of the metaphysical need for understanding over the hackneyed forms of democratic value-making, Heidegger immediately proceeds to elucidate the goals that must be realized if Europe is to be master of itself. Such mastery will happen only within individual nations. Struggle within and between them will determine the shape of the great politics to which the peoples are advancing.

In the background of Heidegger's discussion of Nietzsche's word, however, lies Heidegger's consideration of the poetry of Hölderlin. It is to this poet that Heidegger first credits his own use of the *Ereignis* language. Heidegger's lectures of the mid-1930s on Hölderlin, the work of art, and truth as event are companion pieces to the text just presented.

But this passage is a critical moment in the course of Heidegger's lectures on Nietzsche. I propose to investigate Heidegger's relationship to Nietzsche in terms of "the ontological difference." We have encountered this category, without naming it, in Heidegger's appropriation of the "whole" for questioning. At issue is reality-formation, the emergence of a new articulation for the positioning of human beings in their response to

20. Heidegger, *Nietzsche: Der Wille zur Macht als Kunst*, p. 193.

Being. Nietzsche, with his word of "God's death," has shattered the vessels that have transported "divine wisdom" to humans for generations. The relationship of Being to the human being has been thus freed of tradition. Such freedom is not easily won. It is built on the recognition of plight (*Not*) in the most radical way: thoroughgoing disinheritance from the tradition to which one is still indebted.

According to Heidegger's reading of Nietzsche's word, the "God" of the Christian/Platonist tradition is an entity, a being, and is thus subject to the principle by which its "That it is" (Being) is manifest within the realm of beings as a whole. Settled, then, in the background of Heidegger's discourse is the ontological difference between that which "is" and "That" by which any being, as discretely formed over time, can be interrogated for its mode of being. Heidegger has already based the full thrust of his Nietzsche lectures on this ontology.[21]

Heidegger introduces "Being" in 1936-37 as a question for the meaning of what is. It is meaningless to ask what Being itself is. The ontological difference indicates the mystery by which the meaning of Being has been veiled from Western, metaphysical view.[22] Not only, therefore, does the history of metaphysics have an inner necessity conditioned by forgetfulness, but the meaning of Being itself can be rendered destitute, needy, subject to the dictates of time.[23] Heidegger grants Nietzsche's partial insight into the ineluctable finitude of Being with his doctrine of eternal recurrence of the same.[24] Nietzsche thus returns to the early, pre-Platonic Greeks for renewed questioning, as if possibly there to locate the sources for a new beginning. Heidegger maintains that Nietzsche simply borders on the origin for those sources, however, given Nietzsche's metaphysical view of truth in extremity, as will to power.[25] Nietzsche still would posit the definition of a being in the ultimate reflection of his status within the whole.[26]

For Heidegger, who sees an intimate connection between the questions of Being and of truth, the category of "truth" carries the weight of evidence for that which has happened and is happening within the tradition of

21. Heidegger, *Nietzsche, Vol. I: The Will to Power as Art*, pp. 4, 18, 20, 22, 31, 37, 39, 44, 59, 63, 67-68, 105, 131, 135.

22. Heidegger, *Nietzsche, Vol. I: The Will to Power as Art*, p. 4.

23. Heidegger, *Nietzsche, Vol. I: The Will to Power as Art*, p. 20.

24. Heidegger, *Nietzsche, Vol. I: The Will to Power as Art*, p. 19.

25. Heidegger, *Nietzsche, Vol. I: The Will to Power as Art*, pp. 117-18, 120-23, 130-31.

26. Heidegger, *Nietzsche, Vol. I: The Will to Power as Art*, pp. 138-40, 142-56.

Western philosophy. Heidegger asks how the occasional word *is* revealed, such as with the early Greek word for truth in *aletheia*.[27] *Lethe*, fate, remains preserved within the history of the Greek word for truth as a sign that truth eventually will become a meaningless factor, tucked away under the fold of death. Yet the *"a"* of *aletheia* shows opposition to that which is ultimately concealed. The *"a"* is negatively oriented in the early Greek language. It indicates a refusal to let that which is remain utterly mysterious.

The search for truth takes definitive form, however, in the early history of philosophy, especially with regard to the concern for representation of the real as "truly" real. Just as, for Heidegger, the philosophy of Plato is the classical point of departure for such a view of truth, so too he takes Nietzsche's persistent effort to "overturn" Platonism as a clue to Nietzsche's place in the history of tradition. With his doctrine of the will to power, Nietzsche exhausts the possibilities that had still remained open for Western philosophy in representing the real. The assault upon the entity for its definition as held within the human memory for recall, testing of propositions, and experimentation with words thought to represent reality — this form of assault, which reached profound proportions with Plato and Aristotle, obtains the necessity of its own law historically, and it shall be exposed in time.[28]

The form by which truth is judged in representation reaches its apotheosis in Nietzsche's radical turn to the source of all definition, i.e., the metaphysics of subjectivity.[29] Nietzsche seizes upon the human will and finds it a life-enhancing principle filled with the processes of power. The will to power is Nietzsche's Being of beings. The implications of this metaphysics are considerable if thought through with regard to Nietzsche's effort to overturn Platonism.

Heidegger recognizes that the Platonism to which Nietzsche applies his efforts is not to be confused with Plato's dialogues in their entirety. Nietzsche, the educated classical philologist, was not so much hindered by his knowledge of the texts as he was irremediably influenced by the doctrine which developed from a facet of them.[30] Platonism signifies the split be-

27. Heidegger, *Nietzsche, Vol. I: The Will to Power as Art*, pp. 67-68. Cf. Martin Heidegger, "The Origin of the Work of Art," in *Poetry, Language, Thought*, pp. 51-81, for an extensive discussion of truth as *aletheia*. Heidegger constructs a non-representational language by which the work is established in the event of truth.

28. Heidegger, *Nietzsche, Vol. I: The Will to Power as Art*, pp. 200-210.

29. Heidegger, *Nietzsche, Vol. I: The Will to Power as Art*, pp. 148-49, 153.

30. Heidegger, *Nietzsche, Vol. I: The Will to Power as Art*, pp. 155-56.

tween the supersensuous as Form and the sensuous as merely participatory, and, correlatively, the exaltation of theoretical knowledge at the expense of artistic creation. The attempt at overturning, however, becomes for Nietzsche a stringent positivism, in which what is placed before the percipient subject in experience is defined as the true. Even if, for Heidegger, Nietzsche eventually breaks through this positivism to deny the realm of appearances as well, he still grants priority to the modes of scientific knowing with respect to truth, that is, truth as judged within the measures of subject/object representation.[31]

The consequence for art production as a form of life-enhancing creation is that it is rootless with regard to the question of truth. One might say that the only purpose of creation in art, on these terms, is creation itself, which, given Nietzsche's positivism, is reduced to feelings of rapture, to physiological states that remain isolated from and discordant with the communicability of worldly truth. The only available option for art as free creation is an aesthetics of individual expression, which entails an exceedingly solitary kind of existence verging on solipsism.[32] Although such isolated art production has value within the privatized life of sensuousness, it merely passively counters the weight of Platonism, and, in fact, amounts to the most extreme effort to draw values of all sorts — including its own — into a void.[33] Yet, one wonders what kind of transformation is possible in a void.

Heidegger finds Nietzsche's attempt to overturn Platonic values accompanied by the step into nihilism. As the quote from Heidegger's discourse has shown, however, Nietzsche's nihilism is not meant to transport everything into a "Nothing." Nietzsche seeks to overthrow all forms of nihilism, which he understands as precisely the self-devaluation of the highest values. Artistry is conceived as the countermeasure to Christian/humanist nihilism. The sincere and genuine figure of Nietzsche, especially before the "dying God," is the mark of his affirmation made prior to any criticisms rendered against those perceived to be in error. Yet Nietzsche's spirit is still found at

31. Heidegger, *Nietzsche, Vol. I: The Will to Power as Art*, pp. 151-54.
32. Heidegger, *Nietzsche, Vol. I: The Will to Power as Art*, pp. 138-41.
33. Such a voice is the *nihil* of nihilism. The reduction to absurdity of Platonism — itself the highest value that is to be ruined from "within" — brings Nietzsche into the full effect of "historicism." Cf. Johan van der Hoeven, "History and Truth in Nietzsche and Heidegger," in *Life Is Religion: Essays in Honor of H. Evan Runner*, ed. Henry Vander Goot (St. Catherines, Ont.: Paideia Press, 1981), pp. 61-82.

the site of personal value — where truth and artistry vie in raging discord, epistemologically internalized as the ecstasy of self-dissection.

At the beginning of his lectures, Heidegger declares that his attitude toward Nietzsche will be that of *Auseinandersetzung,* or, elucidation and confrontation. Heidegger places the relatively isolated Nietzsche into the context of Western philosophy in its entirety. Thus, Nietzsche is the last metaphysical thinker of the tradition. Consolidating the law (nihilism) which undergirds Western philosophical history, Heidegger confronts Nietzsche precisely with the failure to fulfill the gesture of overturning Platonism. The clue to this failure occurs in Nietzsche's subscription to the proposition as the ideal form of truth-declaration. For Heidegger, the effect of Nietzsche's word of "God's death" must be applied to the standards of logical activity as well as to personal creativity.

Even though Nietzsche proceeds only so far along the path of dismantling the tradition, however, he is an essential figure for Heidegger's appropriation.[34] The factor of inward strife that Nietzsche has imparted to philosophical reflection is a signpost for those, such as Heidegger, who would overcome nihilism from within on a thoroughgoing, systematic basis. The culminating nihilism of Nietzsche opens up the mystery of Being in the event of its metaphysical need. Nietzsche's use of the *Ereignis* language is prescient, inasmuch as it provides Heidegger support for just that language which can be employed to transform the ontology of being human.

The emergence of metaphysical need or anguish controls the center of Heidegger's ontological difference.[35] Being itself does not appear in the

34. *Ereignis,* the word, maintains the etymological connection to *sich aneignen,* which means "to appropriate." Cf. Robert Bernasconi, *The Question of Language in Heidegger's History of Being* (Atlantic Highlands, N.J.: Humanities Press, 1985), pp. 86ff: "*Ereignis* is the fundamental word of Heidegger's later thinking. In ordinary German it customarily means 'event.' In Heidegger it has another meaning and is usually translated 'appropriation.' . . . It is essential to recognize that *Ereignis* is not a word for Being. *Ereignis* is the word that arises from the experience of *the lack of a word for Being.* . . . With the entry into *Ereignis,* the truth of Being appears within the history of metaphysics, but no longer prevails as it once did." Although Bernasconi refers here to texts that include ones written after 1961, "appropriation" occurs in elemental form in the 1936-37 text we are discussing, where the horizon for Heidegger's appropriation includes the specific figure and word of Nietzsche. Heidegger includes Nietzsche within the community of "the great" that can provide leadership for the Germans in their cultural distress.

35. In *An Introduction to Metaphysics* (Garden City, N.Y.: Doubleday, 1961), trans. Ralph Manheim, Heidegger finds new ground in Nietzsche for questioning the meaning

manner of a thing to be handled, possessed, and trumpeted. The human being is known within the encompassing range of a source that cannot be grasped. Under these conditions, Heidegger turns radically in a regressive direction to the origin of the rise of achieved knowledge in philosophy and the sciences. In questioning the origin of Western philosophy, Heidegger names the forgotten issue, the mystery, in terms of intrinsic neediness: Being is *not* a being. The ontological difference marks the absence of any ultimacy that can be truly defined. Yet, in articulation of the ontological negativity at the root of all "things," Heidegger proceeds freely from the origin to grapple with the history of metaphysics as a whole. In the dialectic of this overcoming of and return to the origin, Heidegger displays a marked mythologizing tendency in thought.

A typical aspect of mythologizing thinking is the preoccupation with the structures of "genesis." In the regressive move to the origin, Heidegger does not abolish the metaphysical tradition into the realm of sheer illusion. He clearly recognizes that the Being for which he seeks is not *a* being. It therefore encompasses the entire range of beings without direct interference. The ontological difference, in its negativity, provides the very possibility of meaning for human existence. Hence, the mythologizing mode of Heidegger's remains a transcendental investigation of the sources of that which, on its own terms, is doomed to dissolution *and* of that which promises the coming of a new time for humans in their Being.[36] The

---

of Being. In this book (hereafter IM), delivered as lectures during the 1935 summer semester yet published only in 1953, Heidegger prepares the interpretation of Nietzsche that will prevail in the 1936-37 discourse on Nietzsche's word of "God's death." Nietzsche's protest against a supposedly empty metaphysical realm shows the need that prods Heidegger's introduction of the question "Why is there something, rather than nothing?" (IM, pp. 1, 30). Victor Farías notes that Heidegger at this time was repeatedly subjected to the criticism "that his philosophy was nothing more than an expression of destructive nihilism, a kind of by-product of Jewish thinking that the Nazis regarded as 'subversive.' " (*Heidegger and Nazism*, ed. Joseph Margolis and Tom Rockmore [Philadelphia: Temple University Press, 1989], p. 252). In *An Introduction to Metaphysics*, Heidegger opposes the notion that his thinking moves toward destructive nihilism: "The being after which we inquire is almost like nothing, and yet we have always rejected the contention that the essent in its entirety *is not*" (IM, p. 29). Rather, even when his thinking needs to be violent, it holds that *logos* occurs redemptively.

36. A mythologizing tendency appears in *An Introduction to Metaphysics*, prior to the 1936-37 Nietzsche lectures, in Heidegger's concern for the reality that surpasses objectivity: "The need *(Not)* of being and the greatness of its beginning are no object of a merely historical observation. . . . We know from Heraclitus and Parmenides that

opposition of corruption, forgetfulness, and fall to redemption in primordiality originates non-logically within the whole circle of Heidegger's own self-imaging. Criticism and construction work cooperatively in Heidegger's reading of Nietzsche's word of "God's death" for the analysis of both Nietzsche's self-desiccation and his self-overcoming in metaphysics. Dialectical thinking in Heidegger thus operates by way of non-objectifying motive-analysis at the metaphysical level. Nietzsche is assessed for his doctrine of the will to power; he is also considered the last metaphysician. The mythologizing thrust prompts Heidegger's constant insistence that he is in process, en route, despite the obstacles that can be and have been posed by the substantializing of truth in traditional form.

## Hölderlin's Poems as Sacred Source

The structure of Heidegger's approach does not change from that of mythologizing in the turn to Hölderlin. Heidegger thinks of Nietzsche and Hölderlin together within the community of the "greatest." The difference between them is simply one between philosophy and poetry in their various susceptibilities to the "anguish of Being in its totality." Still, Heidegger indicates a need for Hölderlin's poetry that is not of the same order as Nietzsche's analyses. Heidegger's way of thinking is not structured autonomously in the manner of the Enlightenment. Hölderlin's poems have become a sacred source in the development of Heidegger's thought. Heidegger is indebted to Hölderlin for his own use of the *Ereignis* language. The mythopoetic language of Hölderlin gives presence to Heidegger's consciousness in the imagery of soil, bread, and wine. The mythologizing of Heidegger's self-awareness requires constant grounding in time.

I suggest a brief word study of Heidegger's usage of the *Ereignis* language prior to the 1936-37 Nietzsche lectures. Heidegger's customary word for "history" is *Geschehnis*. *Ereignis* as a word is no less ordinary in German usage. Yet, with Heidegger, the manifestation of a word in his thinking assumes significance by the way he has appropriated it.

In the 1934-35 lectures on Hölderlin's poems *Germanien* and *Der*

---

the unconcealment *(aletheia)* of being is not simply given" (IM, p. 160). Heidegger's 1936-37 discourse on *Ereignis* is his mode of providing *logos* for the event of Nietzsche's word of "God's death" — contrary to traditions of Christian humanism.

*Rhein,* Heidegger quotes from the poet's *Mnemosyne:* ". . . Lang ist/Die Zeit, es ereignet sich aber/Das Wahre."[37] The quote occurs in Heidegger's remarks on what it means for a people to determine their own time. The time has been "long" for truth to come to pass. Emptiness and haste bury the recognition of how much time it takes for the people *(Volk)* to achieve their unique revelation of Being in truth.[38] When will the *Vaterland* be realized in its Being *(Seyn)?*[39]

Heidegger continues the language of *Ereignis* in *Hölderlin und das Wesen des Dichtung,* delivered as a lecture in Mussolini's Rome of 1936 and published in 1937.[40] Language is not simply a tool at human disposal, he says. It gives, rather, the opportunity to exist as human beings within a world. Human beings are not self-sufficient before language, since it is the event *(Ereignis)* which compels and orders the supreme possibility of existence.[41]

The basis of human existence is that of a conversation into which humans have been led by the gods, and to which they (pre-Platonic Greeks) have responded with a world in which divinities were named. In such naming human beings have come to exist historically. The truth-saying of the poet on behalf of the people identifies language as the ultimate event *(Ereignis)* of existence, as that by which existence acquires its meaning and foundation.[42]

*Ereignis* thus opens up the realm between the signs of the gods and the

---

37. Martin Heidegger, *Hölderlins Hymnen "Germanien" Und "Der Rhein,"* ed. Susanne Ziegler for the *Gesamtausgabe, Band 39* (Frankfurt am Main: Vittorio Klostermann, 1980), p. 55.

38. Heidegger, *Hölderlins Hymnen "Germanien" Und "Der Rhein,"* pp. 55-56.

39. Heidegger, *Hölderlins Hymnen "Germanien" Und "Der Rhein,"* pp. 120-23.

40. Martin Heidegger, "Hölderlin und das Wesen der Dichtung," in *Erläuterungen zu Hölderlins Dichtung,* ed. Friedrich-Wilhelm von Herrmann for the *Gesamtausgabe, Band 4* (Frankfurt am Main: Vittorio Klostermann, 1981), pp. 33-48. Martin Heidegger, "Hölderlin and the Essence of Poetry," in *Existence and Being,* intro. and analysis by Werner Brock (South Bend: Gateway Editions, 1949), pp. 270-91.

41. Heidegger, "Hölderlin und das Wesen der Dichtung," p. 38. Note Heidegger's footnote for the second edition of this page in 1951: "deliberately ambiguous — it must say strongly enjoined 'but the event, that as such." In comparison, the first rendering of *Ereignis* is less specific: "Language is not a tool at human disposal, but it is that event which orders the supreme possibility of human existence." (My translations.) Heidegger, "Hölderlin and the Essence of Poetry," p. 276; this translation produces only Heidegger's first version of the *Ereignis* language.

42. Heidegger, "Hölderlin und das Wesen der Dichtung," p. 40. "Hölderlin and the Essence of Poetry," p. 280.

voice of the people. The poet is the one thrown into this middle terrain. Heidegger finds Hölderlin thrown in this way, especially because of Hölderlin's concern with the meaning of the poet as such and not with an individual poem as a specifically human creation. Hölderlin is Heidegger's "poet of the poet."[43]

Hölderlin projects poetical meaning for a new time. Now, however, is the time in which the gods have disappeared *and* that in which preparations are being made for their return on German soil. It has been a long time of destitution *(dürftige Zeit)* for the poet and the poem. It is a time of need, with a shaped negativity as in Heidegger's emergent language of *Ereignis*. In this time of fundamental transition, Hölderlin is seen by Heidegger to speak of the essence of poetry as historical in the most radical sense.[44]

*Der Ursprung des Kunstwerkes,*[45] delivered by Heidegger in 1935-36 in lectures and expanded late in 1936 while he was presenting the first material on Nietzsche and art, is testimony to the effort to transcend human subjectivity for the event of truth in the work of art.[46] The work has an origin not of human making. Heidegger's shift away from subjectivity is clear: he finds that the event *(Ereignis)* of the work's "being created" not only reverberates through the work but also adheres to the "eventful fact" *(Ereignishafte)* that the work *is* such as it is.[47] He insists upon the nuances of *ereignen* as verb, indicating both a happening and a specific region for its occurrence.[48] In this instance, he writes that the individual poem *(die Poesie)* occurs *(ereignet sich)* as a human product only because its own language "preserves the original nature of poetry."[49] And, poetry, in its essence "the

43. Heidegger, "Hölderlin und das Wesen der Dichtung," pp. 46-47. "Hölderlin and the Essence of Poetry," pp. 288-89.

44. Heidegger, "Hölderlin und das Wesen der Dichtung," p. 47. "Hölderlin and the Essence of Poetry," pp. 289-90.

45. Heidegger, "Der Ursprung des Kunstwerkes," in *Holzwege* (Frankfurt am Main: Vittorio Klostermann, 1980), pp. 1-72. "The Origin of the Work of Art," in *Poetry, Language, Thought,* pp. 17-87.

46. Jacques Taminiaux, "The Origin of 'The Origin of the Work of Art,'" in *Reading Heidegger: Commemorations,* ed. John Sallis (Bloomington: Indiana University Press, 1993), pp. 392-404.

47. Heidegger, "Der Ursprung des Kunstwerkes," p. 52. "The Origin of the Work of Art," p. 65.

48. Halliburton, *Poetic Thinking,* p. 184.

49. Heidegger, "Der Ursprung des Kunstwerkes," p. 60. "The Origin of the Work of Art," p. 74.

founding of truth," remains beyond the calculative sweep of human designs. The work of art sustains its own being over time in a way that human artifacts, such as tools, do not.

Reconsideration of the questions of truth, poetry, being, and time in the interconnective language of *Ereignis* leads Heidegger to the grounding of the work of art in a realm ontologically prior to the fissure opened up by Nietzsche between personal creativity in subjectivity and truthful form in worldly objectivity. In that realm, which is the (mythologizing) origin of its own genesis, Heidegger discerns the emergence of a kind of truth that is not made with human hands. Human history is subject to a law beyond the measure of mortals.

Heidegger closes the main body of *Der Ursprung*'s text with a quote from Hölderlin: "Schwer verlässt/Was nahe dem Ursprung wohnet, den Ort."[50] What abides near the place of the origin departs reluctantly for a destination that is uncertain. The only certainty is the necessity of the departure. Heidegger's meditation on the metaphysical uncertainty of the work of art is also preparatory. The work has not been realized yet within the world of the German people of the mid-1930s. However, Heidegger charts a way through the dominating categories of truth, origin, work, and history under the sign of time (as destitute) in order to locate new ground.[51]

---

50. Heidegger, "Der Ursprung des Kunstwerkes," p. 64. "The Origin of the Work of Art," p. 78.

51. "Ground" imagery for philosophical elucidation finds its counterpart in "Der Ursprung des Kunstwerkes" with the introduction of "earth" as an elemental factor in the constitution of the work of art. See, for instance, Joseph J. Kockelmans, *Heidegger On Art and Art Works*, Phaenomenologica #99 (Dordrecht: Martinus Nijhoff, 1985), p. 78: "The term 'earth' has a mystic and even gnostic ring to it and seems to belong in theology and poetry rather than in philosophy. Heidegger must have discovered the importance of this concept for his own thinking in his meditations on Hölderlin's poems. . . ." Since Victor Farías published *Heidegger and Nazism*, the conflict for the interpretation of Heidegger has intensified greatly. Without granting the aura of "a mystic and even gnostic ring" to Heidegger's rendering of "earth," Farías places it squarely within the spiritualization of political factors which Heidegger underwent by 1936 with his notion of the truth as embodied in the work of art. The "work" indicates for Farías fundamentally the explanation of the origin of the state. The historic life of a specific people in its form of social organization crystallizes the interplay of its world and its earth in its work of art (*Heidegger and Nazism*, hereafter HN, p. 240).

Farias writes that Heidegger published his essay "Ways to Language" in 1937 in a collection edited by Kerber, the mayor of Freiburg and a member of the SS, entitled *Land of the Alemammani: Book on the Fatherland and its Mission* (HN, p. 241). Kerber

## Heidegger's Cultural Politics

The weight of Heidegger's lectures on Hölderlin and on the work of art presses emphatically upon his use of the *Ereignis* language in the passage on Nietzsche's word of "God's death." Heidegger's reference to his "whole consciousness" is not the free expression of personal subjectivity. Rather, he achieves an awareness of that "wholeness" by means of submission to a law which represents "the anguish of Being in its totality." Heidegger is resolved to gather together all the aspects of his own being on behalf of the project that would transform the German people. The event of Being in its transcendental direction is occurring within the circuit of Heidegger's thinking. Evidently, in projecting this self-image, Heidegger mythologizes the relationship that he has to himself and to the world. His whole consciousness reflects the whole of the realm of beings in the event of the new, that is, the experience of nihilism as a fundamental event in the history of the West.

---

is quoted by Farías as follows concerning the political purpose of the volume: "The political question of the upper Rhine has been clearly settled by our Führer. . . . But what does remain . . . as our particular task is the conservation . . . of our autochthonous element, linked to the land and entrusted to us . . ." (HN, pp. 242-43). Hitler's forces had already secured territory on March 7, 1936, in the demilitarized zone of the Rhineland in violation not only of some clauses of the Versailles Treaty but also of the Locarno Pact, freely negotiated by Germany in 1925. The task of Hitler's government became to maintain order in the conquered land. The requisite dialogue with France over the sensitive territorial issue was provided "intellectually" by Kerber's book. No synthesis, however, was desired between the "different minds" of the "two cultural nations" (HN, p. 244).

Heidegger's contribution, "Ways to Language," shows how dialogue necessarily displays the elemental factor of *polemos,* the combat out of which the truth emerges. With the rules for political victory established, the only remaining question for Heidegger is to show for the French and the German people what their respective characters could be or are, such that dialogue can emerge. While the French think about nature inadequately with their reliance on the mathematical theory of Descartes, the Germans, for Heidegger, understand nature as earth for its mission within history (HN, p. 244). Leibniz must be counterposed to Descartes. Moreover, Heidegger insists that the poets and thinkers of German Romanticism (including Hölderlin) must be thanked for their metaphysical understanding of the historical life of a people (HN, p. 245).

Whatever the difference of political emphasis between Farías and Kockelmans, they agree on Heidegger's "spiritualization" of earth. I note Heidegger's condition of need *(Not)* in its totality, "out of which the cry for God becomes the most creative call on earth," from the *Ereignis* discourse in the first Nietzsche lecture series.

173

In mentioning his 1933 *Rektoratsrede,* Heidegger recapitulates the temper of *Not* which dominated that speech and the other speeches he delivered as rector on behalf of the Nazi Party.[52] Heidegger's idea at the time was that the experience of most extreme distress *(Not)* (including abrogation of civil rights beyond the appeal to law, as found in the Civil Service law enacted April 7, 1933) must precede the formation of a collective will to power that transforms history. Nietzsche's metaphysics moves in the spirit of Heidegger's words in his speeches of 1933 and 1934.

By 1936-37, Heidegger had removed himself from immediate political concerns to focus on those dimensions of Being — poetry and thought — which he could teach. Heidegger still faced acrimony from his Nazi competitors in the interpretation of philosophy and, especially, of Nietzsche. In fact, Heidegger had simply transmuted elements of his previous political program into the status of principle, the truth and greatness of which could be understood by the community of the great. Heidegger's affirmation of "whole" consciousness signals his resolve to lead in every way possible according to the example of the Führer.[53] The category of Heidegger's "mythologizing" tendency is significant, however, in reading the signal of his resolve. Heidegger would rather be political as the sage who lectures, writes, and converses for that struggle in which Germany would be itself again.

By recognizing Heidegger's "mythologizing" tendency around 1936-37, one can follow clearly the political component of his turn *(Kehre)* to poetry, language, and the work of art. Heidegger's turn is perpetually in process, it is

52. "Science and German fate must come to power at *the same time* in the will to essence. And they will do this then and *only* then when we — the teachers and students — expose science to its innermost necessity, *on the one hand,* and, *on the other,* when we stand firm in the face of German fate extreme in its extreme distress *(Not)*" ("The Self-Assertion of the German University," in Wolin, ed. *The Heidegger Controversy,* p. 30). "What the real gravity of the new situation *(des Neuen)* calls for is the experience of affliction *(Not),* is the active engagement with real conditions. Only *that activity is justified that is performed with full inner commitment to the future*" ("The University in the New Reich," in ibid., p. 45). "So-called 'intellectual work' is not spiritual because it relates to 'higher spiritual things.' It is spiritual because, *as work,* it reaches back more deeply into the afflictions *(Not)* that are part of a people's historical existence and because it is more directly — because more knowingly — beset by the hardness and danger of human existence" ("The Call to the Labor Service," in ibid., p. 54).

53. Note the suggestive phrasing of A. v. Sch. in July, 1933 in "Arbeitsdienst, Wehrdienst, Wissendienst," with: "Mit vollem Bewusstsein. . . ." See Guido Schneeberger, *Nachlese zu Heidegger* (Bern: Suhr, 1962), p. 84. The phrase might have been a code language for certain people in leadership.

never finished. The political aspect of his transcendental turn cannot be established without conflict about what is appropriate to read off the hieroglyphics of Being in the event of truth in the world. To reduce the timing of Heidegger's turn to "simply" political matters as understood by the politicians and gangsters of his day, however, would be to confuse what is empirical and what is otherwise, namely, mythologizing, in his processes of thought.[54]

54. The contest for Nietzsche in the mid-1930s was heated: cf. Steven E. Aschheim, *The Nietzsche Legacy In Germany, 1890-1990* (Berkeley: University of California Press, 1992), pp. 262-71. A primary competitor with Heidegger for the interpretation of Nietzsche was Alfred Bäumler, former ally of Heidegger and interpreter of Nietzsche for Alfred Rosenberg within Hitler's own circle. Heidegger might have conceded something to Bäumler in the 1936-37 Nietzsche lectures, inasmuch as he used Bäumler's critical edition for reference. Hugo Ott mentions that Heidegger defended himself in 1945 before the denazification committee by claiming persecution from Bäumler for Heidegger's interpretation of Nietzsche (*Martin Heidegger: A Political Life*, trans. Allan Blunden [New York: Basic Books, 1993], p. 196.) Moreover, Heidegger indicates in a 1945 letter to the rector of the University of Freiburg that his effort at spiritual resistance to the assimilation of Nietzsche to National Socialism began with his 1936-37 lectures. Heidegger says that "the debate with Nietzsche's metaphysics is a debate with nihilism as it manifests itself with increased clarity under the political form of fascism" (in Wolin, ed., *The Heidegger Controversy*, p. 65). Heidegger's retrospective apparently confuses his ongoing strife with principal figures in the National Socialist movement with National Socialism itself, many of the principles of which Heidegger was easily attuned to in the mid-1930s — denigration of democracy, advocacy of international struggle, territorial self-identity by means of re-conquest, submission of personal subjectivity to law for the people *(Volk)*, etc.

Farías reminds us of the connection Heidegger saw between Nietzsche and National Socialism in the culture of the popular mind and its leading representatives. Heidegger, however, interpreted Nietzsche's nihilism against the reigning ideologies in the assertion that (1) nihilism was more than a random occurrence of special circumstances in the history of the West, and that (2) Nietzsche's philosophy was essentially a response to the nihilism which he diagnosed (Farías, *Heidegger and Nazism*, pp. 252-53). In *An Introduction to Metaphysics*, Heidegger protects Nietzsche even from those who advocate National Socialism: "The works that are being peddled about nowadays as the philosophy of National Socialism but have nothing whatever to do with the inner truth and greatness of this movement (namely the encounter between global technology and modern man) — have all been written by men fishing in the troubled waters of 'values' and 'totalities'" (IM, p. 166). Yet Heidegger places Nietzsche within the history of Western metaphysics insofar as Nietzsche's doctrine of the re-evaluation of values still turns to subjectivity in assessing the Being of beings (IM, p. 167).

It is highly unlikely that Heidegger's above-mentioned note in parentheses concerning global technology was contained in his original delivery of the lectures. Cf. Richard Wolin, *The Politics of Being*, p. 105; consult also "Only a God Can Save Us," in The *Heidegger Controversy*, pp. 103-4. Heidegger's tendency to insert or delete significant material from the mid-1930s is itself a concern that only independent scholarship can weigh.

In his 1936-37 Nietzsche lectures, Heidegger presented an extremely concentrated discourse on Nietzsche's word of "God's death." Heidegger in 1961 authorized the passage deleted from publication, even though its thematic of nihilism perfectly summarized the only journey that Nietzsche could have possibly undertaken, on his presuppositions, through the Scylla and Charybdis of Platonism and Positivism to a new, radically human, beginning. Heidegger's *Ereignis* language for the double-edged, historical aspects of nihilism is uniquely disclosed in a presentation that is itself an event. He testifies here to the work that he had been doing elsewhere on Hölderlin, language, and the artwork. The passage, now available only through the efforts of scholarship, is integral to the movement of Heidegger's thought from Nietzsche's "metaphysical anguish" to the question of the great politics that Germany must ground according to its needs in the mid-1930s — i.e., struggle on the international level, self-assertion, consolidation of territory (in both soil and culture).

I, for one, can only surmise that Heidegger had the passage deleted because of its reference to his "whole" consciousness in conjunction with the mention of the *Rektoratsrede*. But I hope I have shown "why" Heidegger had to remove the entire two pages of German text from publication if he were to take away even a portion. The *Ereignis* language permeates the passage both in text and in spirit. If jagged in its implications for the political use of Nietzsche's word, of *Ereignis* as key term, of the contest for truth, and of the artwork, the document still is a gem of meditative thinking upon the question of the event of language.

The interpreter of Heidegger might wonder how it is possible even to deal with such a thinker as this. Heidegger is a central figure in twentieth-century philosophy because he thinks seriously, from his position, upon durable issues that are of transcending philosophical significance. Truth, history, work, art, and artistry: the list of fundamental issues could be continued without a doubt. It is at least *possible* to think through Heidegger's considerations as they return to and proceed from the origin. This possibility is granted through an ethical principle that declares the basic equality of human beings in the liberty which has been granted them, ultimately, as a free gift. At least in the mid-1930s, Heidegger knew neither that gift nor the liberty which it provides. Nor did he realize, in his authoritarianism, that it is legitimate within the terms of civil constraint for people to engage in the battle between views. Philosophy articulates the course of this strife in dialogue.

# III. CULTURAL CRITIQUE

# Suffering in High and Low Relief: War Memorials and the Moral Imperative*

## JOHAN SNYMAN

"One should be . . . acutely suspicious of the meanings artists convey through works of public art. We need a critique of monuments," was an aside Calvin Seerveld made in one of his lectures on a visit to South Africa in 1969. Of all his impassioned, erudite pleas (in themselves masterful cameos of imaginative allusiveness) for a Biblically directed vision on the importance of the arts, that remark on public art lodged in my mind. He

* The presentation of this paper was made possible by a grant from the Human Sciences Research Council, Pretoria, and a research fellowship from the Kulturwissenschaftliches Institut in Essen, Germany. Further financial support was given by the Slovenian Society of Aesthetics. I would also like to express my indebtedness to Mr. Neels Nieuwenhuizen and Ms. E. Wessels of the War Museum of the Boer Republics in Bloemfontein, and to colleagues at the Rand Afrikaans University for their invaluable assistance in drawing my attention to, obtaining, and reproducing archival material. I owe Prof. Jörn Rüsen of the Bielefeld University, Prof. Detlef Hoffmann of the Oldenburg University, and Prof. Jonathan Webber of Oxford University a great deal for drawing on their resources and participating in their project on *Die ästhetische Inszenierung der Demokratie*. Last, but not least, a word of special thanks to Dr. Ales Erjavec of the Institute of Philosophy at the Slovene Academy of the Sciences for being instrumental in getting me to start thinking about the "aesthetics of war."

179

reiterated this in a lecture twenty-three years later, at the same venue: "It would be good for a government not only to protect reproduction of art by copyright, but also to foster public artworks, not mega-projects, but neighbourhood, site-specific art and street theater, festival events, so that artistry be poured like perfume over the body of the least of the civic inhabitants, who could never afford to go to the theatre or opera."[1]

Following Seerveld's suit, this essay is a "little narrative *(petit récit)*" in the Lyotardian sense.[2] It has extremely "local" origins: the remote past of the Anglo-Boer War of 1899-1902 in South Africa. After a study of Theodor W. Adorno's social philosophy and aesthetics, enlivened by debates on the *Aufarbeitung der Vergangenheit* (reinterpreting the past) in the former Federal Republic of Germany, a part of my own past became upset. If Adorno's philosophy can be viewed as a coming to terms with that past which is historically signified by Auschwitz[3] and as culminating in a new moral imperative, namely, to prevent a repetition of Auschwitz,[4] what exactly happened in the world of the Afrikaner? How is it possible that the political system of apartheid was instituted, repeating some of the atrocities the Afrikaner people suffered in the concentration camps of the Anglo-Boer War? Why did the intellectual life of the Afrikaner in general lack the kind of moral imperative that the thought of Adorno affords?

I shall approach these questions in the following way. After the function of public art such as war memorials is outlined, three specific war memorials are analyzed, namely, the Vietnam Veterans Memorial in Washington D.C., the Dachau memorial near Munich, and the Women's Memorial in Bloemfontein, South Africa. In each case the specific interpretation of history that is embodied by the monument is deciphered in terms of the attendant culture of representation and expression: whereas the Dachau memorial augments an already existing "tradition" of Holo-

---

1. Calvin Seerveld, "Necessary Art in Africa; a Christian Perspective,", in C. Seerveld et al., *Art in Africa* (Potchefstroom: Institute for Reformational Studies [Series F1, no. 312], 1993), p. 10.

2. Jean-François Lyotard, *The Postmodern Condition: A Report on Knowledge* (Manchester: Manchester University Press, 1984), p. 60.

3. Carl-Friedrich Geyer, *Kritische Theorie: Max Horkheimer und Theodor W. Adorno* (Freiburg/Munich: Alber, 1982), p. 142; also Joseph F. Schmucker, *Adorno — Logik des Zerfalls* (Stuttgart: Frommann-Holzboog, 1977), p. 118.

4. Theodor W. Adorno, *Negative Dialektik* (Frankfurt a. M.: Suhrkamp, 1967), p. 356.

caust art, and the conceptualist nature of the Vietnam Veterans Memorial turns it into a political indictment of the military establishment, the Women's Memorial had to make good for a lack of artistic representation and expression. In all three cases, the edifices have an alienating effect that upholds a social imperative. But differences in approach to the subject matter as well as in the function of the memorials, informed by different cultures of representation and expression, cause them to point to two contrasting, even opposing social imperatives. War memorials usually imply an oath: on behalf of the dead, and on behalf of the visitor, they say "Never again!" But this oath is not as unequivocal as it may sound. Sometimes it is understood in a very restricted sense: This may never happen to us and ours again! Or it may be understood in a more expansive sense: This may never happen to us and ours again, and we ourselves may never be party to anything similar happening to others. I propose to call the first understanding the ethnic imperative. The second understanding is reminiscent of the so-called moral imperative. Because this "reading" of war memorials poses the question of a renewed interpretation of the sublime as an aesthetic category, the last part of the paper sketches a "genealogy" of the sublime, taking into account Paul Crowther's reformulation and Adorno's critique of the Kantian sublime.

## 1. The Social Function of the War Memorial

What is the function of public art in society? More specifically, what is the role of war monuments and war memorials? According to Arthur C. Danto, there are "tacit rules that govern the distinction between monuments and memorials,"[5] and that amount to the following:

> We erect monuments so that we shall always remember, and build memorials so that we shall never forget. . . . Monuments commemorate the memorable and embody the myths of beginnings. Memorials ritualize remembrance and mark the reality of ends. The Washington Monument, vertical, is a celebration, like fireworks. The Lincoln Memorial, even if on a rise, presses down and is a meditation in stone. Very few nations erect monuments to their defeats, but many set up memorials to the defeated

---

5. Arthur C. Danto, *The State of the Art* (New York: Prentice Hall, 1987), p. 115.

dead. Monuments make heroes and triumphs, victories and conquests, perpetually present and part of life. The memorial is a special precinct, extruded from life, a segregated enclave where we honor the dead. With monuments we honor ourselves.[6]

The fact that in the postwar Federal Republic of Germany (and even in the German Democratic Republic) no monument to the German defeat was erected, not even a memorial to the German dead, seems to accord with Danto's view. The former West Germans inaugurated a new kind of memorial instead: the shelled remains of some prominent prewar public building as *Mahnmal*, as a perpetual sign of warning against the horrors of war.

One could wonder whether the *Mahnmal* succeeds in making its point as time lapses. For the second and third generation, the scarred *Mahnmal* easily becomes a scar in the mind. The ever-present sign of warning turns into an ominous sign of humiliation — unless the *Mahnmal* is regularly attended with the ritual of remembering and mourning *all* the unnamed victims, and unless this occurs in a way that allows the present generation to empathize with the victims by considering the paradoxical and remote possibility that they themselves might fall victim to some ineffable and as yet unforeseeable catastrophe.

## 2. The Vietnam Veterans Memorial

Danto's distinction between a memorial and a monument is poignant: with the memorial we honor the dead, with the monument we honor ourselves. The memorial asks for sobriety and humility on the part of the survivors and the living. The monument, by contrast, is a license for self-indulgence, for aggrandized vanity. This distinction is borne out by considering the differences between the Washington Monument as an obelisk, "a monumental form with connotations of the trophy in Western art" and the Vietnam Veterans Memorial, "which carries no explicit art-historical references."[7] In its original conception by Maya Ying Lin and as dedicated in 1982, the Veterans Memorial consists of two black granite walls holding back the sides of a pointed 132-degree depression in the ground. The walls of the monument contain only the names of the more than 58,000 dead

6. Danto 1987, p. 112.
7. Danto 1987, p. 113.

Americans of the Vietnam War in the order of the dates of their deaths. To this "special precinct, extruded from life, a segregated enclave where we honor the dead," a bronze statue of three servicemen by Frederik Hart was added as a concession to part of the public who demanded some kind of "exacting" heroic realism.

Danto describes the Veterans Memorial thus:

> Like innocents . . . [the three servicemen] see only rows and columns of names. They are dazed and stunned. The walls reflect their obsessed gaze. . . . The gently flexed pair of walls, polished black, is like the back of Plato's cave, a reflecting surface, a dark mirror. The reflections in it of the servicemen . . . are appearances of appearances. It also reflects us, the visitors, as it does the trees. Still, the living are in it only as appearances. Only the names of the dead, on the surface, are real.[8] (Figure 1)

If one disregards the bronze statue for a moment, this memorial, as an instance of conceptual art, serves its purpose well. Structurally, it is nearly the exact opposite of an obelisk. Its principal axis is horizontal instead of vertical.[9] Instead of soaring up into the limitless sky, it descends into the earth, obstructing the descent with two walls meeting in a corner where the names of the first and the last fatal casualty of that war are juxtaposed on two separate panels. According to Lin, "thus the war's beginning and end meet; the war is 'complete' . . . yet broken by the earth that bounds the angle's open side, and contained by the earth itself."[10]

In itself, the memorial commemorates no heroes and no heroic event. Given its present setting, situated as it is between the Washington monument and the Lincoln memorial, the American public can have it both ways. On the one hand, the memorial serves a "cathartic function," "easing trauma into memory. In this, especially, the Vietnam Veterans Memorial is a stunning success. It is the continual witness of tearful homages to the deceased. Flowers and mementoes are regularly left there. These visible expressions of grief are eloquent demonstrations that the individual and collective wounds of Vietnam are still raw, and in need of remedy."[11] On the other

---

8. Danto 1987, pp. 113-14.
9. Cf. J. Beardsley, *Earthworks and Beyond: Contemporary Art in the Landscape* (New York/London/Paris: Abbeville Press, 1989), pp. 124-25.
10. Quoted in Beardsley 1989, p. 124.
11. Beardsley 1989, p. 125.

FIGURE 1.   Maya Ying Lin. *The Vietnam Veterans Memorial.* 1982.
Photo: Bert de Vries.

hand, the memorial confronts the visitor with the stark results of war: people reduced to cold statistics, columns of faceless names of dead people. The memorial itself mourns the fate of the dead. Small wonder it evoked such controversy before its dedication. As anti-representational, conceptual art, it indicts the wielders of political and military power, urging them to consider the wages of war.

I do not know of any other memorial which underscores the tragedy of war so effectively by its understatement of grief and its stubborn, even iconoclastic abstinence from heroism. Fifty-eight thousand meticulously recorded war casualties overwhelm the spectator. The magnitude of this visual record incites the viewer to imagine the face of each single victim — an impossible task that quickly stuns the imagination. Each name then becomes an abstract, depersonalized instance of the universal voiceless victim of the modern war industry.

184

## 3. The Dachau Memorial[12]

The Dachau Memorial by Glid Nandor in the late sixties also fits Danto's "tacit rules that govern the distinction between monuments and memorials," but for different reasons from the Vietnam Veterans Memorial. Although it shares the Veterans Memorial's decided anti-monumentalism, it is not iconoclastic. Like the sponsors of the Vietnam Veterans Memorial, the founders of the Dachau Memorial are people who survived the events commemorated here. They organized themselves into the Comité Internationale de Dachau to raise money internationally. The former West German government also contributed 300,000 marks towards the memorial. Like the Vietnam Veterans Memorial, this memorial commemorates something which did not take place on the exact spot of the memorial.

Dachau was indeed the first concentration camp built by the National Socialist government after its rise to power in 1933, and it served as a model for other camps such as Buchenwald and Sachsenhausen. The camps were intended to house political prisoners or *Schützhaftlinge*, people taken into so-called preventive custody. The National Socialist regime instituted a policy of social and political hygiene right from its inception: politically deviant people (i.e., opponents of National Socialism) were isolated together with criminals, and later on with so-called social deviants (i.e., homosexuals), for the sake of society's health.

After the governmentally initiated pogrom against the Jews on November 9, 1938 (the *Reichskristallnacht*), Dachau became a place of detention for a further category of "undesirables," namely, the Jews. The inmates performed hard labor. As the Second World War proceeded, Dachau became a prisoner of war camp, and hard labor crossed the imperceptible line to slave labor. Starvation, illness, and hard labor, combined with extreme forms of maltreatment, took their toll among the prisoners. Summary executions for the most spurious of trespasses abounded. Some categories of prisoners, such as the Russians, were singled out for *Sonderbehandlung* (special treatment, a euphemism for torture and death). By the end of the war, trainloads of dead and dying prisoners from other camps were literally dumped on Dachau. The point to bear in mind is that Dachau was never an extermination camp like Belzec, Treblinka,

12. James E. Young, *The Texture of Memory: Holocaust Memorials and Meaning* (New Haven: Yale University Press, 1993).

Sobibor, and Auschwitz in conquered Poland, where the Nazis systematically murdered people in calculated batches. In Dachau people from twenty different ethnic backgrounds died due to political power that knew no bounds.

The camp was liberated on April 29, 1945. What the Allies found in the camp confirmed the worst reports by refugees and served to bring these atrocities to public attention. Within a few months the American forces changed Dachau to a detention camp for members of the German SS awaiting trial. By 1948 the camp was transformed again, this time to a camp for returning German refugees. In less than ten years, Dachau bore little trace of what happened there during the war.

One of the former detainees of Dachau, Pater Leonhard Roth, took the initiative to have a proper memorial built on the site. According to Roth, the postwar transformation of the site showed an appalling indifference to the suffering that had occurred there. The site as such, as the victims experienced it, should be preserved, and the process of integrating it into the everyday life of postwar Germany should be stopped. The survivors insisted on a recollection of an indescribable experience of suffering by restoring the camp to an observable document of the atrocities perpetrated there. A memorial would help to forestall historical forgetfulness. But the memorial should not be a mere re-presentation of suffering. Rather, it should contain a clear message to break with the past. The memorial should refer beyond itself.

The whole memorial is in the form of a camp fence, but the barbed wire is formed by the grotesque and partially dismembered skeletons of Nazi concentration camp victims (Figure 2). The original design required the visitor to approach the memorial from the right or the eastern side, where a wall bearing an inscription from Job 38 would have been erected. Passing this wall, the visitor would descend into an excavated space, flanked on the one side by the memorial. After coming to the central feature of the memorial, a group of emaciated and contorted figures viewed from underneath, the visitor would ascend to a wall on the left where an urn with the ashes of the Nameless Prisoner was interred.

The original design was only partially realized. The flanking walls with the inscription and the urn with the ashes were left out. Although the inscription from Job 38 is absent from the present precinct, it remains an important key to understanding and experiencing the edifice. The inscription should have read as follows (Job 38:16-17):

FIGURE 2.   Glid Nandor. *The Dachau Memorial.* 1960.
Photo: Johan Snyman.

. . . [H]ast thou walked in search of the depth?
Have the gates of death been opened unto thee?
Or hast thou seen the doors of the shadow of death?

This quotation from Job constitutes the frame of reference, that of a descent into a valley of death, invoking associations of a trench, a mass grave, and the pits where murdered victims of Nazi gas chambers were cremated. At the same time, a longing for redemption from above is suggested.

How does such a dialectic of threat and redemption work in this memorial? The visitor descends into the depths of despair, to be confronted and overwhelmed by the suffering victims of the Nazi system. The presentation of the victims follows the medieval tradition of the triptych, with the center-piece alluding to the Crucifixion. The portrayal of suffering is grotesque: victim and instrument of torture are fused into one. The skeletons *are* the barbed wire. Nandor's sculpture is expressive of the unthinkable horror of the Second World War — the co-optation of the victims in their process of destruction.[13]

13. Cf. Zygmunt Bauman, *Modernity and the Holocaust* (Cambridge: Polity Press, 1989), pp. 117-50.

187

In this sense this memorial bears witness for the suffering in *all* Nazi concentration camps. The location as well as the styling of the sculpture alienates the visitor from the portrayed victims. The victims are barely recognizable as human shapes. Not only are they (and were they, once upon a time, in the past) physically maimed, but they are sculpturally mangled as well. Empathizing with the victims is prevented by showing them stripped of their humanity and dignity: their suffering is complete, beyond comprehension even in the portrayal thereof. Not a semblance of human dignity remains. In front of this memorial one can only mourn the ineffable suffering. As Adorno intimated, to accord the suffering of these victims any positive meaning would have amounted to an insult.[14]

The Dachau Memorial far exceeds Pater Leonhard Roth's expectations. Indeed, it is in line with what one can call Holocaust art: artistic renditions of the suffering of Holocaust victims, especially at the time of the event. Contemporaneous with the experienced horror, Holocaust art initially served the purpose of crudely recording events for posterity where all other means of recording were ostensibly lacking. But even these crude reports are not mere recordings: the drawings utilize the expressive qualities of variedly accentuated and toned line to convey melancholy and despair about a heap of decomposing bodies. The remarkable thing about Holocaust art is that it did not remain in the realm of recording. It functioned as a means of interpreting the events to the victims themselves, whether by invoking childlike images and portrayals of impending danger or by using mannerist conventions to depict the threat of a Stoic world catastrophe that at the same time shrouds the Jewish victims in a halo of sacredness. Such representations tried to come to terms with the immediate effects of the Holocaust.

An interesting feature of Nandor's work is the treatment of the crucifixion motif. The figures in his sculpture refer to incidents which occurred in the concentration camps when prisoners committed suicide by falling onto the electrified camp fence, electrocuting themselves. The few photos of such incidents have become icons of Nazi atrocities. Nandor stylized these incidents to a unity of victim and instrument of torture. Iconographically, Nandor has his precursor in Jean Vebér, a French caricaturist at the beginning of this century who drew political cartoons for a French newspaper of the British war effort to conquer the two Boer republics in South

---

14. Adorno, 1967, p. 352.

Africa. Because he did not report on-site, but rather commented on events, Vebér portrayed his views of the progress of the war in terms of well-known works of art. He frequently "quoted" Gericault's *Disaster of the Medusa* and Käthe Kollwitz's *The Revolt of the Weavers*. One portrayal of British war strategy under the heading *Les Progrés de la Science* shows Boer prisoners of war trying to escape but becoming crucified in a camp fence.[15]

Art historically, this is the first transposition of the crucifixion motif to a part of modern industrialized warfare. [This distinguishes Vebér's cartoon from Goya's portrayals of atrocities of war in *Los Desastres de la Guerra*, especially no. 37 in this series of aquatint plates, entitled "Esto es peor" ("This is worse").[16]] As far as can be ascertained, Nandor was not acquainted with Vebér's cartoon. When one looks back from Nandor's work to Vebér's cartoon, however, the latter becomes part of the history preceding the Dachau memorial, and it represents a step in the process of creating icons of suffering by connecting the horrors of war with the well-established crucifixion motif, eliciting the same reverence for war victims as for the crucified Christ.

## 4. The Women's Memorial

As a memorial for (some of) the victims of the Anglo-Boer War, the Women's Memorial drew on a different iconographical and iconological tradition. Instead of the crucifixion motif, the Women's Memorial utilized the motif of the Piéta. Several reasons from the monument's history can be found for this preference in motif.

Danto's "tacit rules" seem not to have existed or not to have been acknowledged in the construction of the Women's Memorial in Bloemfontein, unveiled in 1913 (Figure 3). Like the Vietnam Veterans Memorial, it was funded by public donations. The driving force behind the completion of the memorial was a foreigner, Emily Hobhouse. "That Englishwoman" was a vociferous member of an anti-war, mainly Whig-inspired faction of the British public during the Anglo-Boer War. She did much to alleviate

---

15. Jean Vebér, "Les Camps de Reconcentration au Transvaal" (*L'Assiette au Beurre*, no. 26, 1901), p. 396.

16. Francisco Goya y Lucientes, *The Disasters of War*, with a new introduction by Philip Hofer (New York: Dover, 1967).

the suffering of Boer people during the war, involving herself very closely with relief aid in the former Boer republics of the Transvaal and the Orange Free State, to the ire of the British colonial and military authorities and much of the British public. The design that won the public competition came from the German architect Frans Soff, who proposed a monumental obelisk to be erected on a hillside outside Bloemfontein. The obelisk would be adorned by a bronze statue of a Boer woman with two children. The original maquette did not satisfy Emily Hobhouse, however, and she was asked to supervise the making of the statue by the Dutch-South African sculptor, Anton van Wouw, who was sent to Rome for that purpose.

Van Wouw was not left to his own devices: not only had he to tear his own work down several times, but "that Englishwoman" insisted on van Wouw's changing his whole original concept. She related to him an incident she experienced during her relief work in the concentration camps:

> . . . I was called to see a sick baby. The mother sat on her little trunk with the child across her knee. She had nothing to give it and the child was sinking fast. I thought a few drops of brandy might save it, but tho' I had money there was none to be had. . . . There was nothing to be done and we watched the child draw its last breath in reverent silence.
>
> The mother neither moved nor wept. It was her only child. Dry-eyed but deathly white, she sat there motionless looking not at the child but far, far away into depths of grief beyond all tears. A friend stood behind her who called upon Heaven to witness this tragedy. . . .
>
> The scene made an indelible impression upon me. . . . Years after, when Mr. van Wouw came to Rome to carry out the monument, . . . I described to him this scene as it seemed to me to hold in itself the centre and core of the tragedy: broken-hearted womanhood, perishing child-hood.[17]

Hobhouse also left us a record of van Wouw's progress under her supervision. I quote at length, for her description and judgment are telling:

> I . . . went to criticize his first clay model at his desire. I did not like it and had to tell him so. He is too easily satisfied and will have, I think, to rub shoulders a bit with the sculptors here who are capable of expressing their ideas in stone and bronze — and of composition — and are not content with mere portrait work such as Mr. van Wouw has chiefly done.
>
> It is a great subject — a grand opportunity — and since he has appealed to me for help I shall do my utmost to keep him up to the pitch and not let him be satisfied too easily. But of course he may not have *greatness* in him. I do not yet know. I always thought only Rodin could treat that subject worthily.[18]

17. Emily Hobhouse, *Boer War Letters*, edited by Rykie van Reenen (Cape Town: Human & Rousseau, 1984), p. 112.
18. Hobhouse 1984, p. 513.

She expressed her final judgment in a letter dated April 5, 1912: "The standing woman seems to me very good, full of feeling and the sitting mother is better, though still far from satisfactory. The child on her knee is nicely modelled though still only appears to me a *sleeping* child and neither sick nor dead. I suggested he should get leave to go to a hospital and study one or two dead figures,"[19] and (from a memoir): "Mr. van Wouw as you know reproduced the scene in bronze. Had he seen it with his own eyes, the child would have borne more directly the aspect of emaciation and death."[20]

## 5. The Aesthetic Ideology of the Women's Memorial

What is the point about the Women's Memorial? Should one regard it as an unsuccessful attempt at a memorial, one both executed by an incompetent sculptor and blurring the borders between a monument and a memorial?

Let us attend to the second problem first. The sandstone obelisk, situated on a hillside as it is, conveys something dignified and celebratory. The sculpture's placement on a four-meter-high pedestal in front of the obelisk transforms the tragic group into something heroic, something elevated above the ordinary. It aggrandizes suffering. This is not so much a memorial dedicated to the suffering of the dead, as a monument for the grief of those left behind. The facial expressions of the two women are not properly visible because of the elevation of the statue (Figure 4). So they do not communicate with any onlooker. And, as Emily Hobhouse correctly observed, the child does not "directly [bear] the aspect of emaciation and death." The statue does not confront one with the suffering of victims of war, but rather conveys the longing for an abstract restitution. The elevation of the group alienates them from a public.

The bas-relief side panels bear this out. The right hand panel portrays the chaos of the destruction of farms and forced removals to concentration camps (Figure 5). The composition has no focal point: it is in high relief, and the sun always casts long shadows on it, making it a not very discerning piece of sculpture. The composition of the left hand panel is intriguingly

19. Hobhouse 1984, pp. 513-14.
20. Hobhouse 1984, p. 112.

FIGURE 4.
Detail of figure 3.
Photo: War Museum of
the Boer Republics,
Bloemfontein.

classical: it has a receding focal point in low relief (the dying child in the tent), with the foreground figures, the survivors, in high relief and framing the picture (Figure 6). There is a spatial continuity between the onlooker outside the picture and the spectators outside the tent in the picture: both categories of "public" partake in the grievous event of a child dying in a concentration camp. But, once again, the emaciation of the dying child is not clear to see. For all the uninformed visitor might know, people are just looking at a sleeping child in a tent. What is emphasized sculpturally, however, is the grief-strickenness of the onlookers. They stand immobilized, they can only look on, they cannot relieve anything. The spatial continuity

FIGURE 5.   Anton van Wouw.
Right hand side relief panel: *Forced Removal Scene.* 1913.
Photo: War Museum of the Boer Republics, Bloemfontein.

FIGURE 6.   Anton van Wouw.
Left hand side relief panel: *Concentration Camp Scene.* 1913.
Photo: War Museum of the Boer Republics, Bloemfontein.

between the onlooker and the figures in the bas-relief (linked with the chronological continuity between the onlookers and the figures in the picture at the time of the memorial's unveiling), taken together with the elevation of the main statue, makes this memorial to "broken-hearted womanhood" and "perishing childhood" a *monument* to endurance through and in spite of grief. It is a monument not only to, but also *for* the grief-stricken survivors.

This becomes clear when one reflects on the sculptor's alleged incompetence. If Rodin could have carried out the commission for this memorial, the statue would not have landed on a pedestal. As in *The Burghers of Calais*, the onlooker would have confronted at eye-level the expression of various dimensions of human suffering. To achieve this communication of the expression of suffering, Rodin's figures would have been more dynamic (instead of being completely immobile like van Wouw's), utilizing the expressive features of the anatomy of the body in different kinds of postures. Rodin's figures would have been less heavily clad and much more tense.

Van Wouw's inability to render suffering in such terms as Rodin's accorded well with the cultural background of the public for whom this memorial was commissioned. If Rodin's Balzac memorial caused an outrage in France, and if his Calais memorial was controversial, his possible portrayal of Boer suffering would not have been acceptable in South Africa at that time. A significant reason was the conflict of interest between Emily Hobhouse's urge to commemorate the victims, and the Boer people's need for a monument. A tug-of-war ensued: to whom did (the recollection of) the dead belong? Where should they be located in history — on the side of the Boer people, or on the side of humanity? For what cause did they die?

Emily Hobhouse was, for her time, a very emancipated woman and, although from a religious background (she was the daughter of an Anglican vicar), a free thinker. Knowing that the practice of concentration camps during the Anglo-Boer War contravened the Hague Convention of 1899, and that the British military authority was covering up many atrocities and committing many other atrocities unwittingly through neglect and logistical incompetence, she recorded meticulously incidents and even statistics about the camps. She could be called the initiator of investigative journalism for having photographs taken to record the extent of famine and illness in the camps. Publishing them in Britain could persuade the British electorate to press for an early end to the war (Figure 7). In the course of the war, approximately 26,000 women and children died in these concentration camps — that is approximately 10 percent of the white population of the former Boer republics at the time. Emily Hobhouse also started to keep a record of concentration camps for blacks, but, under colonialist (i.e., racist) rule, the facts were inaccurate and very hard to uncover.

The Boer women, acting against an unwritten rule of Victorian society to have respect for the dead and make no effigy of them, also had photographs taken of their dead children, but only if they were not emaciated. The purpose of these photographs was to preserve a recollection of the child, especially for the father and husband who was fighting on commando or was in exile in Bermuda, St. Helena, India, or Ceylon. Understandably the women wanted to retain the most positive recollection of the children possible under the circumstances (Figure 8).

Victorian composure prevailed in grief, as is also evident from many letters from the concentration camps. Most letters illustrate the fact that

FIGURE 7.
An unidentified occupant of the Bloemfontein Concentration Camp.
Photo: War Museum of the Boer Republics, Bloemfontein.

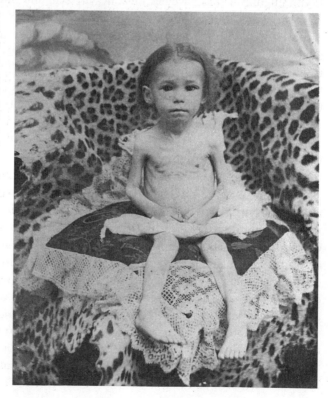

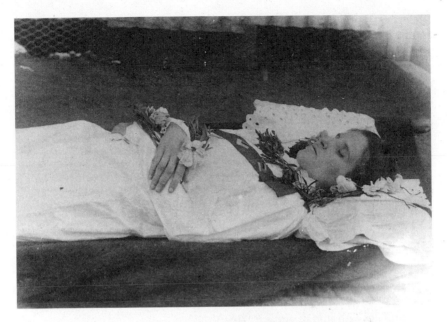

FIGURE 8. Photo of a girl aged 18 who died in the Bloemfontein Concentration Camp. It was her last wish that a ribbon embroidered by herself with the flag of the Zuid-Afrikaansche Republiek (Transvaal) be tied to her breast, and that her corpse be photographed in this way. The photo had to be sent to her exiled father in Ceylon.
Photo: War Museum of the Boer Republics, Bloemfontein.

the Boer people were by and large an agricultural, non-urbanized community who could not avail themselves of the amenities of urban culture such as artistically appropriate expressions of emotions. That accounts for the fact that there are virtually no artistic renditions or representations of concentration camp experiences by the victims themselves. One has also to take into account the effect of military censorship on letters from the concentration camps: the precise conditions of these camps were not to be mentioned to the outside world. Therefore the letters were very stereotyped, and conceived only as a form of rudimentary communication.

The rhetoric of Victorian society dominated the letters, some of them with excruciatingly sad news. In a sense the form suppressed the content. The first page was usually framed in black, so the addressee knew he (usually he) was receiving bad tidings. But the greater part of the letter was taken up by writerly formalities. A letter from a concentration camp sounded much like the following (in translated form):

> My beloved and never forgotten husband,
>
> I am allowing myself to take up the pen to inform you about the well-being of all our beloved ones, hoping to hear the same from you. Thank you for your last letter which reached us two months after you wrote. (Alternatively: I have not heard anything from you since . . . , but got some news about you from Uncle X who saw you last at. . . .) Do you still have enough money? There is not much news to relate from the camp. (What followed then was usually an extensive report on the health and well-being of relatives and friends. On the last page of the letter the real news was broken:) A week ago our little son/daughter/children/old father/old mother died after a terrible suffering of inflammation. Now I must say good bye with the pen, but never with the heart, and with a kiss of love.
>
> Your never forgetting wife/mother/aunt. (In the Dutch-Afrikaans of the time this was written in the formal mode, and the letter was signed formally with initials and surname.)

The inability to give rhetorically appropriate expression to grief was reinforced by a very pious, albeit fatalistic, religiosity pervading the Boer population. The news in the letters is regularly interspersed with phrases interpreting their fate as a punishment from God for unspecifiable sins. The correspondents acquiesce like Job in their fate: "The Lord gave, and the Lord hath taken away; blessed be the Name of the Lord," or "Shall we receive good at the hand of the Lord, and shall we not receive evil?" This pious acquiescence is most dramatically illustrated in a poem by a member of the first generation of Afrikaner intellectuals, J. D. du Toit, who fought for a time with the Boers and obtained a doctor's degree in theology in Amsterdam in 1903. The poem comes from his first volume of verse, *Bij die Monument (At the Foot of the Monument)* published in 1908.[21] Du Toit must have known the poem *Verspätung* from Von Arnim and Brentano's *Des Knaben Wunderhorn*. (After all, he attended the German school at Kroondal near Rustenburg in the Transvaal, and he might have heard Mahler's version of *Verspätung* in the *Wunderhorn*-cycle in Amsterdam in

---

21. J. D. Du Toit, *Versamelde Werke, Deel VIII* (Johannesburg: Dagbreek-Boekhandel, 1962), p. 165.

1903). A comparison between these two poems reveals different aesthetic responses to the same set of dramatized experiences. I quote the two poems in full:

### Verspätung

Mutter, ach Mutter! es hungert mich,
Gib mir Brot, sonst sterbe ich.
  Warte nur, mein liebes Kind!
  Morgen wollen wir säen geschwind.

Und als das Korn gesäet war,
  Rief das Kind noch immerdar:
Mutter, ach Mutter! es hungert mich,
Gib mir Brot, sonst sterbe ich.
  Warte nur, mein liebes Kind,
  Morgen wollen wir ernten geschwind.

Und als das Korn geerntet war,
  Rief das Kind noch immerdar:
Mutter, ach Mutter! es hungert mich,
Gib mir Brot, sonst sterbe ich.
  Warte nur, mein liebes Kind,
  Morgen wollen wir dreschen geschwind.

Und als das Korn gedroschen war,
  Rief das Kind noch immerdar:
Mutter, ach Mutter! es hungert mich,
Gib mir Brot, sonst sterbe ich.
  Warte nur, mein liebes Kind,
  Morgen wollen wir mahlen geschwind.

Und als das Korn gemahlen war,
  Rief das Kind noch immerdar:
Mutter, ach Mutter! es hungert mich,
Gib mir Brot, sonst sterbe ich.
  Warte nur, mein liebes Kind,
  Morgen wollen wir backen geschwind.
Und als das Brot gebacken war,
Lag das Kind schon auf der Bahr'.

199

## Too Late

Mother, mother, I am hungry.
Give me bread, or I shall die!
    Wait, just wait, my darling child!
    Tomorrow we shall quickly sow the corn!

And when the corn was sown,
    The child still kept on crying:
Mother, mother, I am hungry.
Give me bread, or I shall die!
    Wait, just wait, my darling child!
    Tomorrow we shall quickly reap the corn!

And when the corn was reaped,
    The child still kept on crying:
Mother, mother, I am hungry.
Give me bread, or I shall die!
    Wait, just wait, my darling child!
    Tomorrow we shall quickly thresh the corn!

And when the corn was threshed,
    The child still kept on crying:
Mother, mother, I am hungry.
Give me bread, or I shall die!
    Wait, just wait, my darling child!
    Tomorrow we shall quickly grind the corn!

And when the corn was ground,
    The child still kept on crying:
Mother, mother, I am hungry.
Give me bread, or I shall die!
    Wait, just wait, my darling child!
    Tomorrow we shall quickly bake the bread!
And when the bread was baked,
the child was laid out on the bier!

*Suffering in High and Low Relief*

**In die kamp**

*Als zich hun ziel uitschudt*
*in de schoot hunner moeders.*

Klaagl. 2:12

My moeder, my moeder, ek het tog so honger;
kom gee my tog gou-gou 'n klein stukkie brood!

My kindjie, jou moeder die weet jy het honger,
Maar kom eers en rus op moeder se skoot.

My moeder, ag, help my, ek kan nie meer loop nie,
ek voel tog so moeg al; my honger is groot.

My kindjie, jou moeder die weet al dat jy moeg is,
maar slaap bring versterking op moeder se skoot.

Maar, moeder, hoe huil jy en snik jy so baie?
En waarom is moeder se oë so rood.

My kind, dit is trane wat jy nie verstaan nie;
kom, slaap net 'n bietjie op moeder se skoot.

My moeder, ek kan nie, ek het tog so honger,
gee eers aan jou kindjie 'n klein stukkie brood.

Nee, kom maar my liefling, rus eers in my arme,
en as jy ontwaak, help die Heer uit die nood.

Ek kan nie meer wag nie van honger, my moeder;
maar waarom tog so? Het die Heer ons verstoot?

Nee, liefste, verstoot sal die Vader ons nimmer,
maar hier in die tent is geen krummeltjie brood.

Geen brood nie, my moeder, ek kan nie meer hou nie,
Moet ek dan verhonger op moeder se skoot?

Nee, kindlief, die son is al amper weer onder,
En dit is weer awend, dan kry ons weer brood.

&ast;  &ast;  &ast;

201

Haar kindjie slaap in by die soete gedagte:
    as ek weer ontwaak help die Heer uit nood.
Die moeder ontvang met vermagerde hande
    haar deeltjie oplaas — maar die kindjie was dood.


## In the Camp

*When their soul was poured out*
*into their mothers' bosom.*

                    Lam. 2:12

Mother, dear mother, I am so terribly hungry;
Quickly, give me a little piece of bread!

My child, your mother knows that you are hungry,
But, first, come and take a rest on your mother's lap.

Mother, oh, help me, I cannot walk any more,
I am feeling so tired; my hunger is so enormous.

My child, your mother already knows that you are tired,
but sleep will refresh you on mother's lap.

But why, mother, do you cry and sob so much?
And why are your eyes so red?

My child, it is tears that you do not understand;
Come, just sleep a little bit on my lap.

Mother, I can't, I am too hungry,
first give your child a little piece of bread.

No, but come my darling and rest in my arms,
and when you awake, the Lord shall help in distress.

I can't wait any longer, mother, I am hungry;
but why is this? Did the Lord reject us?

No, love, the Father will never reject us,
but here in the tent there is not the smallest crumb of bread.

No bread, mother, I cannot take it any more,
Must I then starve on mother's lap?

No, darling, the sun is setting,
and then it is evening again, then we shall receive bread.

    *     *     *

Her child falls asleep with the sweet thought:
 when I awake the Lord shall deliver me.
The mother receives with emaciated hand
 her share, at last — but the child was dead.

The *Wunderhorn* poem is a very terse ballad. The terseness heightens the "sting in the tail" at the ballad's end. Especially in Mahler's setting of this poem, the last line (unaccompanied, in ascending scale) is an angry cry against the absurdity of the child's death. There is a built-in irony: the mother's rational long-term nurturing that does not heed the immediate need of the child protests against imposed order that stifles life by comfortable and apparently inevitable procrastination, heightened in Mahler's score with a *perpetuum mobile*. Life cannot be saved by following prescribed steps. This little ballad is an allegory of (Western) life — hence Mahler's change of title: *Verspätung (Too Late)* becomes *Das irdische Leben (Earthly Life)*.

Du Toit's poem is not as terse. It is didactic and sentimental, as can be expected from a first-generation intellectual. Du Toit's poem retains some of the irony of the *Wunderhorn* poem, but softens it. Calvinist decorum dictates that God cannot be the object of anger and protest. Whereas the *Wunderhorn* poem evokes anguish, Du Toit, in spite of the allusion to Jeremiah, changes the lamentation of the original into an acquiescing, elegiac poem in which anguish is suppressed. This is achieved by the more indirect style of narrative. Throughout the poem the omnipresent narrator obtrudes, whereas in the *Wunderhorn* poem the events are not mediated through a third person perspective. Du Toit's poem leaves the reader with an unsolved tension: despite a belief in Providence, salvation came too late, but Providence is not to blame. In a true lamentation, God's presence would have been invoked paradoxically by an outburst against Providence. By venting feelings of outrage, even against God, one invokes God's patience as a sympathetic and listening parent, and the lamentation becomes a cathartic experience.

It is safe to conclude that grief and mourning were suppressed rather than vented in the Calvinist Boer culture of the times. What remained and was fostered, especially after the war, was a sense of injury and humiliation. Under the reconciliation policy of Louis Botha, the former Boer general who became Prime Minister of the newly created Union of South Africa in 1910, this sense of loss developed into a subterranean eternal grudge: instead of being used to inculcate remembrance of the dead, the war experience of the Boer people was politicized and transformed into an index of indelible harm done by the imperialistic British, thereby extracting a terrible price for the country.

The idea, then, of a memorial to the women and children who "paid" with their lives in the concentration camps was received favorably as an opportunity for the survivors to "pay" their "debts" to the perished generation. One way of "making good" to those who had lost their lives was to elevate them to the rank of martyrs for freedom, and thereby to alleviate (at least for the survivors) the inflicted humiliation of being robbed of everything dear. Tormented and emaciated figures confronting one at a memorial would have offended the taste of the public who supported the erection of this edifice. In a very short time the memorial was converted, despite a pervasive iconoclastic Calvinism, into a shrine: not only were the ashes of Emily Hobhouse interred at the foot of the obelisk, but the "father of the nation" (the last president of the Orange Free State, Marthinus Theunis Steyn), the "hero of the war" (General Christiaan de Wet), as well as the "man of God" (Reverend J. D. Kestell) were buried within the precincts of the memorial. Their graves, and the authentic presence of their remains, serve to remind the visitor of a trinity of civic virtues: love of the fatherland, bravery, and unwavering faith. The lives of the people commemorated are enshrined in the memorial as the ideals of the survivors. The survivors participate in the lives and deaths of the people commemorated by having the latter re-presented and re-cast in the image of their experience of hardship. Thus is the experience of hardship transformed *ex post factum* into the virtues of endurance, of hope, and of restitution. The memorial becomes a nationalist shrine.

## 6. From Aesthetic Ideology to Moral Imperative: Saving the Women's Memorial from Its Institutionalization

I mentioned previously a clash of interests between Emily Hobhouse and the Boer people. She wanted a memorial to "broken-hearted womanhood" and "perishing childhood," they wanted a vehicle of restitution. Emily Hobhouse understood this well. In her dedication speech she mentioned compassionately "the supreme offering [that] was made, the supreme price [that] was paid." "[The Dead] will live within us *not* as memories of sorrow, but of *heroic inspiration*." And she exhorted the Boer people: "When you remember the ill done, remember also the atonement made."[22] Her text for the occasion allowed for popular sentiments.

But her text conveyed other sentiments as well. The climax of her speech contains these words:

> Your visible monument will serve to this great end — becoming an inspiration to all South Africans and to the women in particular. . . .
>
> For remember, these dead women were not great as the world counts greatness; some of them were quite poor women who had labored much. Yet they have become a moral force in your land. . . .
>
> And their influence will travel further. They have shown the world that never again can it be said that Woman deserves no rights as Citizen because she takes no part in war. This statue stands as a denial of that assertion. . . .
>
> My Friends: Throughout the world the Woman's day approaches; her era dawns. Proudly I unveil this Monument to the brave South African Women, who, sharing the danger that beset their land and dying for it, affirmed for all times and for all peoples the power of Woman to sacrifice life and more than life for the common weal.[23]

What strikes one as remarkable is Emily Hobhouse's elegant, unabashed feminism and the consequent direction of her particularization and universalization. Although hardly novel, that is philosophically the interesting point about her interpretation of the suffering of the Boer women and children. Emily Hobhouse elevates the Boer woman to the ranks of the Universal Woman's struggle for recognition. And the Boer woman forms

22. Hobhouse 1984, pp. 404-5.
23. Hobhouse 1984, pp. 406-7.

part of a whole which transcends herself: she fights along with other women in that part of the world. The meaning of her struggle is not parochial, but universal. It is a contribution towards a greater solidarity of humankind. That is what makes her struggle moral, and what allows the Boer woman to teach others a lesson in history which speaks across the political divide between Boer and British, between white and black.

But it is exactly this point that has, very significantly, been censored — omitted — in later commemorative issues of Miss Hobhouse's dedication speech. I quote the censored passages (indicated by brackets) at length:

> In your hands and those of your children lie the power and freedom won; you must not merely maintain but increase the sacred gift. Be merciful towards the weak, the down-trodden, the stranger. Do not open your gates to those worst foes of freedom — tyranny and selfishness. [Are not these the withholding from others in your control, the very liberties and rights which you have valued and won for yourselves? . . .]
>
> . . . [We in England are ourselves still but dunces in the great world-school, our leaders still struggling with the unlearned lesson, that liberty is the equal right and heritage of every child of man, without distinction of race, color or sex. A community that lacks the courage to found its citizenship on this broad base becomes a "city divided against itself, which cannot stand."]
>
> [We too, the great civilized nations of the world, are still but barbarians in our degree, so long as we continue to spend vast sums in killing or planning to kill each other for greed of land and gold. Does not justice bid us remember today how many thousands of the dark race perished also in Concentration Camps in a quarrel which was not theirs? Did they not thus redeem the past? Was it not an instance of that community of interest, which binding all in one, roots out racial animosity? . . .]

Philosophically speaking, Emily Hobhouse takes the stand of a moral universalist. There are universal moral principles which imbue human actions in time and in places with moral meaning when the actions contribute towards the eventual realization of these principles. Such principles are, among others, the great ideals of the Enlightenment, including liberty as an equal right.

This morality legitimizes itself through its purported moral weight, its capacity to extend itself unreservedly. No exception should be allowed. What is good for the particular can only be good if it would be good for all. The morality of one specific event or action is contingent upon its relationship with the universal principle, i.e., whether it can be an instance, an exemplary embodiment, of that principle. When the action is without precedent, or unrelated to any universal principle, its moral relevance is difficult to assess. But when the action in its uniqueness sets an example which should be imitated, it embodies the moral principle in an original sense. This explains the preponderance of the hero as a cultural topos in Emily Hobhouse's thinking and in the culture of war memorials until after World War I. The idea of the hero embodies moral and aesthetic principles at the same time.

Emily Hobhouse framed the moral meaning of the Boer women's struggle within the modernist notion of the hero, invoking the notion of the sublime. She herself referred to George Eliot, who said: "Tragedy must represent irreparable collision between the individual and the general. It is the *individual* with whom we sympathize, and the *general* of which we recognize the irresistible power."[24] The thrust of Emily Hobhouse's interpretation of the Boer woman's suffering as a symbol of the universal woman is to hold the Boer woman up as an example not only for the surviving Boer people but also for the world to emulate, should similar circumstances obtain. Her conception of tragic heroism assumes a strength of the individual, the perseverance of the subject, despite the "irresistible power" of the "general." The individual — the hero — embodies a far greater and exalted substance that can transcend its own historical limitations.

But there is something ambivalent in the idealist conception of the hero (something Beethoven realized with the dedication of his Third Symphony to Napoleon and the subsequent revision of that dedication). Does the hero represent the attainment of universality, or is the hero only a symbolical embodiment of the universal? In the first instance the hero is monumentalized, in the second instance the hero serves the commemoration of the universal significance of an historical action. The reception of the Women's Memorial under the circumstances of 1913, and the subsequent institutionalization of that reception in Afrikaner culture, favored the trend of monumentalizing the suffering of the Boer women and children, turning it into a metaphor of sacrifice that gives the descendants a right to claim the land:

24. Hobhouse 1984, p. 112.

If one could call it sweet for the hero to fight for the fatherland, and, loaded with fame, sacrifice himself for freedom, nation, and country, what respect does the tender woman command who, herself already in the claws of death, sees one beloved after the other entering their graves! And yet, she exhorts her husband and sons proudly not to be concerned about her, but to persist in the struggle![25]

In this way the Women's Memorial expresses a universalized imperative: it mobilizes the Boer people to see a particular significance in the suffering of their kin. This is an understandable reaction, and it did indeed serve as a consolation, especially in 1913. But it is clear how this interpretation of the meaning of historical suffering is immediately restricted: it ignores the fact recorded by Emily Hobhouse in her war diaries, and explicitly referred to in her dedication speech, that according to official figures, 13,315 Africans also died in English concentration camps,[26] and it blots out the moral dimension of this commemorative sign, namely, to remind people of the horror that once was and that may never occur again, not only *to* them but also never *by* them.

The censored reprint of Emily Hobhouse's dedication speech in 1963 thus confirms a tendency that began with the process of institutionalizing the Women's Memorial, namely, to monopolize the meaning of the suffering of the war for whites only. Evidence for this can be found in Van der Merwe's undated brochure, written sometime between 1926 and 1941. The brochure shuns all references to the suffering of black people during the Anglo-Boer War. It is against this restriction that the true war memorial functions as *Mahnmal*. It speaks silently on behalf of a "we" regardless of gender, class, or race, and it seems to say that as a particular people we have come to know what suffering entails, and we shall never let it happen again, neither to ourselves *nor to any other human being*. The future course of history has to be different from what is commemorated by this monument.

But in order to rehabilitate the moral dimension of the idea of the hero, it is necessary to attend to the "genealogy of the sublime," as Paul

25. President M. T. Steyn, quoted in N. J. Van der Merwe, *Die Nasionale Vroue-monument*, S.l. p. 6. No date, probably written between 1926 and 1941.
26. S. B. Spies, *Methods of Barbarism? Roberts and Kitchener and Civilians in the Boer Republics January 1900–May 1902* (Cape Town: Human & Rousseau, 1977), p. 266; cf. Emily Hobhouse, *The Brunt of War and Where It Fell* (London: Methuen, 1902), pp. 350-55.

Crowther puts it. Immanuel Kant could afford himself the luxury of calling wars under certain circumstances sublime,[27] but since Kant's day the character of the sublime has taken different forms. According to Crowther, the Kantian sublime presupposes the substantiality of the subject: faced with the overwhelming forces of nature, the individual subject feels exalted above the tremendous powers of the physical world, for the individual has a moral destination that cannot be annihilated by this nature. As Crowther correctly observes, this type of experience shifted during the nineteenth century. Instead of nature, an industrialized and urbanized society became the overwhelming force against which the individual had to hold his or her own.

Along with Adorno, I suggest that a further chapter can be written: "the age of the liquidation of the individual."[28] The substantiality of the subject (its potential moral greatness) was systematically eradicated by modern processes of social control, up to the point where the literal death of the individual became a mere matter of accident statistics. An individual's death does not affect other individuals in any way anymore — people have become used to the death of the other and to death as such.[29] Against this, Adorno suggests that the sublime be rehabilitated to retain something of its original (Kantian) meaning. To save it from the theatricality and subservience to domination that come with celebrating human greatness, the sublime should be conceived as protest against domination, as approximating the expression of the inexpressibly silenced voices of the suffering in some kind of language. Adorno invokes the Kantian sphere of the aesthetic as an alternative discourse to the world of instrumentally rational procedures. Memorials should not continue to invoke the discourse of greatness by elevating victims to the purported height of their overwhelming victimizers and thereby offering false restitution. Memorials vow silently for the sake of future victims.

27. Paul Crowther, *The Kantian Sublime: From Morality to Art* (Oxford: Clarendon Press, 1989), p. 165; and Immanuel Kant, *Werke. Bd. 8: Kritik der Urteilskraft und Schriften zur Naturphilosophie,* edited by Wilhelm Weischedel (Darmstadt: Wissenschaftliche Buchgesellschaft, 1957), p. 351.

28. Theodor W. Adorno, *Gesammelte Schriften, Bd. 14* (Frankfurt a. M.: Suhrkamp, 1973), p. 21.

29. Theodor W. Adorno, *Aesthetic Theory,* trans. C. Lenhardt (London: Routledge & Kegan Paul, 1984), p. 283.

# "You Wouldn't Shoot a Brother in the Back": Images of Race in Neil Jordan's *The Crying Game*

## FRAN WONG

*The films I make are unusual and need special handling. They start with realistic premises and lead to seemingly unrealistic conclusions. And I'm interested in the way politics, racial issues, and sexual issues impinge on that journey.*

— NEIL JORDAN[1]

*The Crying Game* (1992) (hereafter *Game*) is one of Irish writer and director Neil Jordan's most provocative films. Dealing with politics, race, and sex — any one of which could be the subject for a whole film — *Game* amazed filmgoers[2] as it connected the three topics in surprising ways. Some recog-

1. Quoted by Mark Harris, "The Little Movie That Could," *Entertainment Weekly*, February 12, 1993, pp. 16-21; the quote occurs on p. 21.
2. I use the word "filmgoers" deliberately. Almost any other word one could use to describe people who engage with film privileges one sense over the other when in actuality *both* sight and sound are important in "receiving" a film. For instance, at least in their etymologies if not in their common usage, "spectator" and "viewer" relate to seeing, and "audience" relates to hearing. Of course in this day of VCRs "film*goer*" may not be accurate either, since many people do not go to a theater to "take in" a film, but

nition for his accomplishment came in the spring of 1993 when Jordan won an Academy Award for best original screenplay. I hope my own analysis will contribute to the growth of *Game*'s reputation as a well-constructed and fascinating work.

This essay will discuss race in *Game,* concentrating on the first third of the film where race is dealt with directly. Race is presented primarily in the sights (visual images) and secondarily in the sounds (aural images) of the film. *Game* depicts race relations in contemporary Britain in ways that encourage filmgoers to examine their own racial attitudes, their interracial relationships (if they have any), and their society's racial interactions.

In my writing on film, I am indebted to Cal Seerveld, who worked with me on understanding film as a medium distinct from other art forms closely related to it such as fiction and drama. "Cinematic" was the key word in our discussions: "What is cinematic about this film?" "How has the director achieved his or her effects and goals cinematically?" Foundational questions such as these continue to be helpful to me in determining the basic issues to examine when discussing film.

Physically, film is both sights and sounds, but *Game* presents race less in the sound than in the visual aspects of the film, which, because they are ambiguous, must be interpreted. Although the dialogue explicitly mentions race here and there, the music and sounds do not refer to it directly. The background music, however, does allude to race by emphasizing certain points in the action. A full treatment of the background music in *Game* would require a paper in itself; here, I will discuss only a few instances of its use in emphasizing the emotional content of what we are watching. How, then, does Jordan present race visually in the image track and aurally in the soundtrack (the dialogue and background music) of *Game*?

Race is a complex topic. During the last few decades immigration patterns and human mobility have turned the world into the "global village" predicted by Marshall McLuhan. But thirty or forty years is not long, especially when, within that period of time, the rate of change has increased exponentially. Thus we now have a situation where, as the world's racial groupings mingle in the various places that have permitted or encouraged immigration, many people are still in a state of racial culture shock.

One's race is part of who we are as human beings. Discussions of

---

go to a video store to rent one for "home consumption," to use metaphors of eating commonly employed to describe our relationship to film.

human identity always require an oversimplification of the actuality of real people. Artistic creations such as *Game*, however, move in the other direction: they show us imaginary people and reveal them more readily than we can come to know actual people. Thus we can ask "How does a character's race affect the character and others?" and "How does Jordan present race cinematically?" and expect to get answers.

Jordan's *Game*, then, is a vehicle for understanding race and racial attitudes. But art is not just a means to the end of interpreting sociological and psychological change. Jordan presents believable characters of different races interacting in ways that engage us. It is his ability to touch us that gives his art the power to transform: with Fergus in *Game*, we too go on a journey in search of our own identities.

To do justice to the theme of identity in *Game*, we would need to discuss each issue — politics, race, and sex — separately, then look at how they are interconnected, a project requiring a considerably longer piece of writing than this is. In comparison to the other issues in *Game*, race may seem secondary. But in a film which spends a great deal of time showing relationships, we need to think about race to understand how each character's identity is affirmed or undermined by the other characters' responses to his or her race.

Although race is a complex subject, we do know it physically: even if we do not know what to name it, often we can *see* a person's race. Pictures of, or personal encounters with other humans frequently reveal their racial appearance. As well as being one of the bases of our own identity, in our experience with others race is, at the very least, visual.

In *Game* the racial diversity of the British Isles is more than just a given of the setting. Jordan could have made all the main characters white. Instead he has them reflect the changing face of England, where many citizens of former colonies have immigrated to large cities, and thus, implicitly, he raises the subject of race relations and their impact on Britain. I say implicitly because Jordan presents black/white relations in *Game* in a very matter-of-fact way. In the dialogue, for in stance, he downplays the subject. Except for the occasional apparently casual comment, characters make little direct reference to race, their own or anyone else's. Therefore, how Jordan presents race has to be inferred mostly from the visual images, from how he has shot the film.

*Game* begins with an establishing shot, a long slow pan of a bridge, the water the bridge crosses, and a carnival on the shore beyond the water. Credits appear over the picture, and we hear a song, Percy Sledge singing "When a Man Loves a Woman." The action opens with a shot of the carnival from above, the camera focusing on the loudspeaker on a pole that is broadcasting Sledge's song, then gradually descending to zero in on a couple.

The two people are particularly striking because of the color contrast between them. Both have blue denim jackets on, but Jude is a platinum blonde dressed in pastel shades, all of which emphasizes her lightness of color compared to Jody's brown skin: he is the only black[3] among the whites at the carnival. Through sight — the actors he chose because of the characters he created — Jordan engages us in noting racial difference. And through sound — the song and the conversation — Jordan underlines the irony in their relationship, an irony which only deepens when more is revealed: Jody does not love Jude as the song describes because he does not even know her — "What'd you say your name was?" (179)[4]

Their not knowing each other is partly related to their difference in race. We soon find out that Jude lives in a society that is largely homogenous, and Jody comes from a multicultural one. Compared with London and its environs, a place like Belfast in Northern Ireland (the carnival is near Belfast) remains largely untouched by the demographic changes that have affected England. There are very few blacks, except among the British troops, and socializing with a British soldier is considered bad enough when the soldier is white, let alone black. Thus, unless the other IRA members told Jude to pick a black, or Jody in particular, we could speculate that she chose Jody because she would rather see a black kidnapped than a white. Or perhaps she chose him because, being black, even when he is out of uniform she knows he must be a British soldier.

Because of the distance the camera keeps from the couple as they move, we begin to sense they are being watched. Then we briefly see Fergus, the person watching and following them and the character we will gradually come to identify with in observing the world of the film. As Jody and Jude walk away from the camera, Jude twice looks back over her shoulder, then

---

3. In this paper I use the terminology to describe race that is most commonly employed, but under protest. My reservation is that it is not accurate in describing people's skin colors. So, for instance, Jody is called a "black" but is actually brown; Dil appears to be racially mixed — perhaps one "black" parent and one "white" parent — but is actually a tan color; and Fergus is called "white" but is actually pinkish beige.

4. The page numbers appearing in parentheses after quotations from the dialogue in *Game* refer to the screenplay published in Neil Jordan's *A Neil Jordan Reader* (New York: Vintage International, 1993).

she looks directly at Fergus while Jody is in the washroom tent. We are being shown a triangle — two whites apparently conspiring against a black, but we do not have enough clues or time to puzzle out what is going on before the action continues.

Jordan now subtly introduces the topic of race in the dialogue. When Jody tries to kiss Jude, she objects: "Not here." Jody suggests nobody cares, but Jude says "You never know" (180), implying there could be prejudiced people observing them. We soon find out that she is not really concerned at all about people being violent towards them from racist motives: Jude is acting, playing a role to ensnare Jody. Once they are away from other people, Jude offers herself, lying down on a net spread out on the ground. As Jody kisses her, a very uninvolved Jude casts her eyes upward looking for Fergus who arrives momentarily, followed by the other members of the IRA cell. They pull a hood over Jody's head and take him to a waiting car.

At the carnival, when he was drunk, Jody claimed never to be offended, but once he is kidnapped, we find out he can be angry. In the car Fergus courteously refers to his identity as a member of the British army rather than his race, and asks him, "So what's your name, soldier?" Jody answers, "Fuck you" (181).

Once the IRA and their prisoner have settled in at their hiding place, we and Jody learn more about the IRA cell members' roles. As leader of the cell, Peter explains to Jody why he has been kidnapped; as a recent recruit, Fergus indirectly apologizes to Jody for being aggressive when he and the others captured him, by ordering tea for him; and as the sole female member of the cell, Jude makes tea for everyone.

The cell is superficially polite to Jody: Peter says he is their "guest" (182). As Peter speaks, three times the camera cuts to Jody sitting absolutely still with the hood on. When Peter says "If they don't release [the senior IRA member] within three days, you'll be shot" (182), we are shown Fergus watching and listening to Peter, then looking down at a gun he is holding: the visual implication is that, if there is any shooting to be done, Fergus will get the job.

Jody's silence and stillness are ways of expressing anger and having some control over his life. These refusals affect us too. As we look at Jody we cannot see his face: we have no expression to interpret. Instead, there is the hood, puffy and diamond-shaped like an enlarged distorted head, with its slight indentations where Jody's eyes and the sides of his nose would be. These shots help us imagine how he must feel, that is, to encourage us to empathize with him.

214

During Jody's initial twelve hours as a prisoner, the balance of power slowly shifts. The IRA members think they are watching Jody, keeping him captive with their guns and superior numbers, but, the hood notwithstanding, it is actually he who watches them. The role of observer that Fergus and the others played earlier now becomes Jody's.

As the three days pass, Fergus is the one who shows the most concern for Jody, even asking Peter, on Jody's behalf, if he may remove the hood. Jody knows the hood dehumanizes him, and each time Jody asks, we *want* Fergus to take it off as much as both Jody and Fergus want to remove it. Its official purpose is to prevent Jody from seeing his captors, but it is also the IRA's method of depersonalizing him, reminiscent of the horrors of slavery in the Americas.[5] Yet, despite his being abused, we choose to identify with Jody because he seems emotionally open and does not play the role of victim.

In the first third of the film it gradually becomes apparent that Fergus, who feels a growing concern for Jody, is also the primary character in the film visually. Fergus is the person through whose consciousness we the filmgoers encounter the world of the film. The camera either looks at the other characters from his physical point of view, or else keeps him centrally on-screen, most frequently in a middle shot or close-up. This deliberate limitation enables us to learn about the people around him at the same time he does, to go with him on his journey from innocence to knowledge.

It is clearly Fergus's journey: except for the times of conversation between him and Jody, and later the snapshots of Jody in Dil's flat, we see Jody only as Fergus and the others see him. As Jody and Fergus talk about their lives, we see first one, then the other, in the usual shot/reverse shot cutting of a conversation. Such seeing through Jody's eyes only when he and Fergus are together emphasizes their intimacy, and it shapes our seeing of Jody: in some ways, this film is about how a white man sees black men.

In the claustrophobic intensity of their isolation — Fergus is virtually the only person who speaks to Jody, and Jody is the only one Fergus has

---

5. Many blacks have been killed by whites, both during and since the time when slavery was the rule in the United States. Lynching was a favorite method of killing. Sometimes the victim was hooded and sometimes not, but often the killers wore hoods. With the hood on, Jody reminds me of the Elephant Man in David Lynch's movie of that name. Just as I find the hood disturbing in that movie, so I do here, with its suggestion that what is under the hood is freakish or deformed, ugly, not human, and with its effect of making the person look ridiculous, a mockery of who they really are.

any kind of intimacy with during the three days, perfunctory sex with Jude notwithstanding — the two men forge a friendship. Theirs is an intimacy so great that, in a reversal of the Stockholm syndrome, Fergus gradually identifies with his prisoner.[6]

Ironically, it is Fergus more than Jody who belongs to the category of the oppressed: he is Irish and an IRA member, and therefore looked down upon by the British for both his nationality and his political allegiance. Without discounting his patriotism, we could speculate that Fergus has joined the IRA to prove to himself and others that he is worth something. Jody is a member of a visible minority against whom there is prejudice. Yet because he is spunky, he rises above the difficulties of being a black in a predominantly white environment, and even of being a prisoner. Fergus, on the other hand, although belonging to the white majority, is vulnerable because of his political stance based on ethnicity, a category closely related to race. His involvement in Jody's kidnapping means he will be subject to criminal charges and their consequences if he is caught.

Because Jody will not speak, he hears Fergus and Jude discussing him as if he were not there, an experience black slaves sometimes had as they served their owners:

Fergus: Hey — what's he like?

Jude: Horny bastard. (182)

Soon after this exchange, we at last have some indication of how Jody is feeling. Before he throws himself on Jude, just as Fergus says "Have a look at him" (182), the first background music in the film quietly enters. Violins play a high sustained note which evolves into a brief melody in a minor key. Then as Jude begins to lift the hood off Jody's head, we hear the musical interval of a second being held.

In Western music the second is perceived as unpleasant: since it is dissonant and harmonically unresolved, it suggests tension, ours and Jody's. The music puts us on edge to prepare us for what follows. As soon as Jude lifts the hood, Jody flings it off and, getting revenge on her for his capture, pins her down with his body tied to the chair.

6. The Stockholm syndrome occurs when a person who has been taken hostage begins to identify with his or her kidnapper(s); Patty Hearst identifying with her kidnappers is an example.

For a moment or two, before the others grab him, Jody is able to act on his anger, physically and verbally, taking it out on the person at whom it is directed. It is as if, because she described him as "horny," he decides to play the part. In the stage directions of the screenplay Jordan says "He writhes on top of her in a grotesque parody of love" (183). If Jude believes in the stereotype of the "black buck," then Jody will act it out for her.

What we see in this mimicry is the violence and misuse of the power of rape, without the sex. This scene recalls the history of its racial opposite — white men raping black women. That pairing was the basis for the stereotype of the black man as hypersexual, in that white men imagined the stereotype in the first place, projecting their own lust onto black men.

As the newest member of the cell, Fergus is apparently not as inured to feeling compassion as the others. Also, for reasons only hinted at, Fergus is unprejudiced. A person's race does not seem to be an issue for him. Instead the question is "Are other people treating someone well, irrespective of race?" Fergus may be involved in illegal activity, yet he is genuinely caring. He treats Jody more kindly than the others do, asking his name, checking to see if he wants tea or food, and wondering if he is all right after sitting still for so long. As the three days pass, we see him guiding the hooded Jody when he walks, taking the hood off, helping him go to the bathroom, telling him his name, and gradually becoming emotionally more open to him. Insight grounded in the need for self-preservation helps Jody to fix on Fergus, with his active conscience, as the cell's weakest link.

The only IRA member who speaks of Jody with distaste is Jude. Calling Jody a "fucking animal," Jude tells Fergus how much she disliked having to act as a sexual decoy: "I had him all over me" (183). At the same time, by describing Jody as sexually preoccupied, she stereotypes him as instinct-driven, always ready for sex. Ironically, it is actually Fergus — "Did you give him it?" (182) and Jude — "And you know what, Fergus? One of you made me want it . . ." (184) who obsess about sex.

Racism causes whites in a predominantly white society to perceive blacks and other people of color — incorrectly — as less powerful than themselves. People of color, then, must work at being smarter than whites: the "underdog" always has to know what the "master's" next move will be.[7] If Jody is to save his life, he needs to learn about his captors as quickly as

---

7. *Toward a New Psychology of Women* by Jean Baker Miller, 2d ed. (Boston: Beacon Press, 1986) discusses this phenomenon.

possible. Being able to discern the situation accurately and manipulate it to his advantage is a matter of life and death.

As a result of this need, Jody's behavior in relation to Fergus may be both spontaneous and calculating at the same time. Jody knows that, if there is to be any possibility of surviving his ordeal, he must involve one of the cell members with himself. Fergus, not only the kindest one, but also his guard, is the obvious one to choose. As he watches the cell, Jody intuits that, if the IRA shoots him, Fergus may get the job. He therefore works hard at establishing a strong connection with him.

Jody looks for issues on which he and Fergus might agree. He affirms Fergus as a person, and identifies with him to encourage Fergus to identify with him. He also uses reverse psychology: after they hear a helicopter flying over the greenhouse, Jody, unable at first to name the deed, asks: "You're going to have to do it, aren't you? . . . They're going to let that guy die. And you're going to kill me." Fergus replies, "They won't let him die" (188). Fergus denies what might happen because he is unable to think of himself as Jody's killer, exactly the response Jody wanted.

Knowing he may be shot, Jody works at controlling Fergus from beyond the grave. To take advantage of the sexual curiosity he heard him express earlier in talking with Jude, Jody insists on showing Fergus Dil's picture. Neither man refers to Dil's race which, from her picture, we can see is both white and black.

Jody: Now *she's* my type.

Fergus: She'd be anyone's type.

Jody: Don't you think of it . . . She's mine. Anyway she wouldn't suit you. (190)

Once Fergus admires Dil's beauty, Jody knows he has him hooked. Both the visual and the aural aspects of the film signal this fact. The image track tilts to the diagonal (a canted frame) as Fergus reaches into Jody's inside pocket to find the picture, and above the quiet musical interval of a second, this time suggesting suspense, a gentle melody, Dil's theme, enters in the background and continues as we see shots of Dil's picture while the two men discuss Jody and Dil's relationship. Along with the interval of the second, which composer Anne Dudley uses in a variety of ways throughout the film, the melody too suggests something intriguing, unfinished, because it never resolves to the tonic. Dil's theme hints at the mystery of Dil.

To be as certain as possible of achieving his end, Jody works on two fronts at once. He is realistic enough to know that, in spite of his best efforts, he may still be shot. As well as working to save his own life, therefore, he also tries to so organize things that Fergus will feel responsible towards Dil even if he, Jody, is no longer around.

Next Jody attempts successfully to engage Fergus's sympathy about the foolishness of racism by complaining about the prejudice of the Irish in Belfast — "The only place in the world they call you nigger to your face." Fergus commiserates — "Shouldn't take it personally" (191). Imitating a Belfast accent, Jody says: "'Go back to your banana tree, nigger.' No use telling them I came from Tottenham" (191).

Jody does not take the racism personally because he has a strong sense of identity based in part on his national and cultural heritage — Antiguan by birth and English by upbringing, and on his skill and love for cricket:

> In Antigua cricket's the black man's game. The kids play it from the age of two. My daddy had me throwing googlies from the age of five. Then we moved to Tottenham and it was something different. . . . Toffs' game there. But not at home. So when you come to shoot me, Paddy,[8] remember, you're getting rid of a shit-hot bowler. (191-92)

Fergus and Jody also bond because of their common interest in sports and Fergus's enjoyment of Jody's sense of humor. Together, they behave as playful "child," to Peter's serious "parent." When Peter scolds Fergus for laughing with Jody, Jody takes advantage of the situation by suggesting a "them versus us" perspective — "They giving you trouble, Fergus?" (196) — and offering sympathy for Fergus's difficulties with the other IRA members.

When Fergus does not answer, Jody reinforces his point with a story about a Frog and a Scorpion to illustrate his theory that people fit into one of two groups, "givers" or "takers." Jody then claims that both he and Fergus

---

8. Here Jody jokingly calls Fergus "Paddy." In London, Fergus, pretending he is Scottish, uses the name Jimmy or Jim (212). Later, his boss, Deveous, calls him Pat and Mick (213). These are generic names for Irishmen (Paddy and Pat from Patrick, patron saint of Ireland) and Scotsmen (Jimmy). By treating all the males of Ireland or Scotland as a group, the English characters exhibit *ethnic* prejudice toward people to whom they are close both geographically and culturally.

are "givers" rather than "takers," and that it is in Fergus's nature to be kind. In hopes of saving his life, Jody is promoting an altruistic value system which Fergus accepts, either simply because it comes from Jody whom he respects, or because it was already his. Jody appears to be as oblivious to racial difference as Fergus is.

Another reason Jody and Fergus bond is that they are both soldiers who live under military rule. Jody points out to Fergus that he too is oppressed, hoping Fergus will see how little he gains from being in the IRA and will distance himself from the cell members and their plan to kill him if their demands are not met: "You fellas never get a break, do you? . . . We do a tour of duty and we're finished. But you guys are never finished, are you?" (198)

The relationship between Jody and Fergus has been growing. Now, as a result of Jude's hitting Jody in the mouth with a pistol, they draw even closer together, each defending the other against her. The way the film is shot at this point — detailed close-ups of Jody's mouth with the blood in it, and of Fergus looking sad — underscores their closeness. As Jody speaks of the certainty of his impending death, and of his desire for Fergus to make contact with Dil, we grieve with Fergus over his approaching loss and ours.

Fergus's guilt may be even greater because Jody is black. We glimpse one aspect of Fergus's value system in his words to Jody the night before the execution: "When I was a child, I thought as a child. But when I became a killer man I put away childish things" (202). Fergus's changing of this Scripture quotation suggests some regret at having abandoned the moral standards of his youth, which, because of his ethnic background and political affiliation, we can assume were Roman Catholic. Fergus would have internalized the command not to murder, and the desire not to hurt someone of a race that in the history of the Western world had been more sinned against than sinning, would add weight to the prohibition.

Because he has a strong sense of who he is, Jody is attractive as a person, whereas Fergus, although he has recently committed himself to the goals of the IRA, is still seeking a purpose for his life. When Fergus is unable to console Jody the night before his execution, Jody criticizes him, "Not a lot of use, are you, Fergus?" and Fergus answers out of his low self-esteem, "Me? No, I'm not good for much . . ." (202). An ironic reversal of racist stereotyping occurs here: according to the stereotype, Jody, not Fergus, should have low self-esteem. In fact, Fergus values Jody because he has brought meaning in Fergus's life, but his dilemma is that now he must kill his new friend.

The first shot on the morning of Jody's execution is of the outside of the greenhouse where Jody has been imprisoned, and, in effect, Fergus with him. It is early, there is mist, and birds are chirping: the woods are coming to life. Like an angel of doom, Peter comes to the door, raises his eyebrows significantly at Fergus, then clicks the bullet chamber of his gun. Fergus looks down sadly, remembering what he must do, then gently wakes the hooded Jody, helps him to his feet, and directs him out of the greenhouse.

As they pass Peter, he puts his hand on Jody's shoulder, almost as a gesture of comfort, and begins to speak officially: "I wish to say on behalf of the Irish Republican Army — ." Fergus interrupts him fiercely: "Leave him be — " (203), and music enters strongly in the background, two repeated intervals of a second in a minor key, the first interval major, the second minor. Below the melody sounds the steady inevitable beat of a kettle drum. A snare drum rattles intermittently. These are the sounds to accompany a prisoner being marched to execution. When Fergus removes the hood, Jody's theme enters, a rising four note phrase on a horn, suggesting hope. Then the relentless melody in seconds continues, gradually starting higher and higher, emphasizing both the tension and the pathos of the situation.

As Fergus shoves Jody out of range of Peter, they walk through the woods, Jody ahead of Fergus, who seems to both push Jody away and hold onto him at the same time. Their movements are jerky, not coordinated with each other. Fergus has Jody by the left sleeve of his jacket, which is off his shoulder on that side. From the visual image alone, it is not at all clear that Jody is Fergus's prisoner.

As they slow down, the camera pulls in for a close-up as, for the last time, Jody asks:

Take the hood off, Fergus —

No.

I want to see a bit. Please, please. Don't make me die like an animal.
   (203)

Jody alludes here to the racist attitude some whites act on. They believe that, just as they kill animals, so it is all right to kill blacks because they are

221

subhuman anyhow. He is also appealing to the bond he has created with Fergus, and to Fergus's "better nature." When the hood comes off, Jody, his head tilted back, looks up at the trees, his expression a combination of relief and worry. He looks down, closes his eyes, and breathes deeply.

The next view of the two men is a long shot from the front of them talking and walking closely together, in rhythm with each other, their steps coordinated. They would look like two friends out for a stroll through the autumn leaves, except for our awareness of the gun Fergus holds pointed into Jody's back, and the music building tension in the background.

Jody tells Fergus he is glad he is "doing it." When Fergus asks why, Jody says, "'Cause you're my friend" (204). This is the first time either of them has used the word "friend" about the other. Jody then quickly alludes to the topics of their previous talks — Dil at the Metro, and how Fergus's game, hurling, is faster than Jody's game, cricket:

Jody: So if I ran now, there's no way I'd beat you, is there?

Fergus: You won't run.

Jody: But if I did . . . you wouldn't shoot a brother in the back — (204)

As he says the last words, Jody suddenly sprints and we lose sight of him at the same time Fergus does since he moves forward out of camera range. Fergus screams his name then runs after him. We see Jody's hands in close-up, loosening and discarding their ties. Then in a long shot moving gradually to a medium shot, we see Jody and Fergus running, carrying on a preposterous conversation as they run, with Jody at one point laughing out of sheer exuberance. In the background the music slowly builds to a climax. A picture of the forest floor increases the suspense: besides emphasizing the beauty of the landscape through which the men are running, it also shows a branch and a log on the ground, possible hazards for the runners.

Jody knows he cannot run away from Fergus indefinitely. He has to face him sometime and run the risk of being shot. He turns and looks at Fergus, and, as a consequence, does not see what is coming down the road. "Told you I was fast — " he says, to which Fergus responds with a semi-smirk as he points the gun at him. For a few moment there is no music, just the sound of Jody breathing hard. Then a quiet, discordant, tension-filled interval sounds in the background while Jody puts his hand out as if to fend something off, and says in a low serious voice, "Don't do it" (205). He turns to run again as a final climactic two notes of "March to the Execution" play, and he is hit by a Saracen, a British army vehicle.

Fergus screams, "Jody!" in denial of what his eyes are witnessing, and for a moment there are only sound effects — the wheels of the Saracen screeching as the driver tries to stop it quickly, the doors at the back of the vehicle banging open, an officer barking an incomprehensible order at the soldiers jumping out. Then to the accompaniment of a new piece in a minor key, "Dies Irae," the Wrath of God, we see Jody's body lying bleeding on the road, the British army attacking the farmhouse and greenhouse where the IRA cell is, and Fergus running away through the woods in fear for his life. For the filmgoers, the unbearable tension is temporarily over; nothing remains but grief.

The identity issue Fergus works through with Jody is the question, "What are the implications of being a particular race?" Jody called himself Fergus's brother: Fergus lives with the memory of three days of a friendship more real than any he had ever had with Jude or the other IRA members, a memory that gives substance to Jody's declaration. From now on, Fergus will feel differently about black people because of the one black man he knew intimately.

Fergus experiences culture shock in his own culture, although his identity as an Irishman and an IRA member had already put him part way into such shock. Rather like business people or missionaries who, because they live for a long time in another country, receive its ways deeply into their very being, and cannot readjust to their native land, so Fergus has identified with Jody. He is his brother's keeper, and since he was unable to save Fergus, he will at least do his best to help Jody's "special friend," Dil.

*Game* is not a ghost story, but, partly because of Fergus's association with Dil, Jody continues to be a presence in Fergus's life, to haunt him throughout the rest of the film. There are many shots of Fergus looking at the pictures of Jody at Dil's. Three times Fergus "dreams" of Jody in his cricket whites, with Jody's horn theme playing during the dream. The first time *may* be an actual night dream Fergus has while he is asleep. We know that Fergus imagines the second "dream" because it is based on the first one: the images are the same and he is awake.

In the third "dream," after Fergus has found out who Dil is, and thus more of who Jody is, he imagines Jody smiling, gently mocking him as he tosses and catches a cricket ball. At public showings of *Game* filmgoers laugh at this point, as they realize the joke is on many of them as well as Fergus. Outside the diegesis of the film, the joke is Neil Jordan's. Within the film the joke is Jody's, but the "dream" is Fergus's: it is he who creates the image of how Jody must be feeling now that Fergus knows what he did not know before about Jody and Dil. A white man is imagining a black man having a laugh on him, but Fergus does not imagine the laughter as malicious.

The most important aspect of this joke is that it is visual and non-verbal. Neither Fergus nor the imaginary Jody says anything, yet the editing, juxtaposing the disclosure scene with this third "dream," and Jody's behavior in the dream, tell all. In addition to the background music, there are sound effects in this dream but not in the first two. We can hear the plop of the cricket ball hitting Jody's hand each time he catches it. Thus, there could have been dialogue: Fergus could have imagined Jody saying something, but he did not. And that is the power of the humor. It works without words because we are forced to interpret the significance of the shot ourselves.

The final observation about Fergus's relationship with Jody is a verbal one, made very near the end when Fergus addresses Jody's photograph in Dil's apartment as he awaits the police. He says "You should have stayed at home" (266). Perhaps he is referring to politics: Jody should have stayed in England and not taken a job as a soldier for Britain, thus ending up in Ireland. Earlier Fergus had made it clear what he thought of Britain's presence in his country:

Jody: What do you believe in?

Fergus: That you guys shouldn't be here.

Jody: It's as simple as that?

Fergus: Yes. (198)

Fergus's remark could also refer to Jody's coming to Britain as an immigrant when he was five years old. Fergus may be saying, "You and your family should have stayed in Antigua with other blacks where you belonged." If this is a possible interpretation, it is an ironic one historically since it was whites who first brought blacks to Caribbean islands like Antigua.

Both of these meanings may pertain, plus another one: Fergus could also be suggesting: "If you'd stayed at home — that is, 'in your place,' whether England or Antigua — I wouldn't have met and got to know Dil and be in trouble with the police now." His statement may be analogous to sexist comments made by people who tell women what their "place" is, and how to stay in it.

Lastly Fergus could simply mean: "I didn't want to have to deal with you, Jody: you brought complications into my life." In actual fact, Jody, recognizing Fergus as a fellow "giver," gave him a life by becoming his friend and asking him to take care of Dil. Racial difference is irrelevant: as Fergus goes to London, he sets out to live the rest of Jody's unlived life, and makes fine progress until first Dil and then the IRA surprise him. For Fergus, Jody and Dil *may* be "exotics" in the British Isles — members of a visible minority, easy to spot in a predominantly white society. But, because they do not carry the cultural baggage of centuries of hatred between England and Ireland that Fergus does, they are politically and spiritually free as he is not, and therefore he admires and envies them.

"You should have stayed at home" is deliberately ambiguous. It may be as close as Fergus ever comes to expressing racial prejudice, a way of verbalizing his anger, albeit after the fact, about Jody's presence in his society and in his life. But it is not said with bitterness: rather the tone is a mixture of affection, sadness, irony, and perhaps even mild fatalism. Nor does the background music underline it especially. It is simply Fergus saying goodbye to Jody whom, in some fashion, he has "assimilated," as we see by Fergus's retelling of Jody's story of the Frog and the Scorpion to Dil in prison at the end of the film.

Fergus's doubts about whether it really was "in his nature" to be kind, as Jody had claimed, are now gone. He has accepted what Jody said about him as his own self-assessment. While having little life of one's own and needing to imitate someone else may not be the highest motivation for being kind and doing good, nevertheless, as a result of meeting Jody and Dil, Fergus ends up much more consciously "doing as he would be done by."

The quotation from Jordan at the beginning of this essay says in part: "[Jordan is] interested in the way politics, racial issues, and sexual issues impinge on the journey . . . [from] realistic premises . . . to seemingly unrealistic conclusions." At the beginning of the story Fergus is naive, not fully knowing with what or with whom he is involved. Stephen Rea, who acts the part of Fergus in *Game*, says about him: "He's an innocent because ideology has closed him off to a lot of things. And then suddenly, when somebody becomes available to him, the floodgates open. He's on a sort of a quest for redemption, but he ends up sullied."[9]

By the end of the story, however, the "seemingly unrealistic conclusion" is that Fergus has chosen personal sacrifice, sacrifice for people of a race different from his own. He is now a "deeper" human, a person more comfortable, more at home, with himself and others. For Dil's and Jody's sake, as well as for himself, even in prison, he will, as the song with the final credits recommends, "Stand By [His] Man."

9. Quoted by Owen Gleiberman, " 'Game' Player," *Entertainment Weekly*, December 11, 1992, p. 49.

# Senggih's *The Survivors:*
# An Exercise in Artwriting*

### PETER ENNESON

On a given day in the fall of 1972 Henk Krijger takes from his bric-a-brac the collection of soiled and tattered paint rags —

> detritus of the artist's workshop;
> survivors twice over;
> objects of intrinsic interest, both for their visual texture and for the
> fabric of associations around them

— and, without explicit intent, but perhaps recognizing in them an objective correlative to his inner state, his existential predicament, his physical condition, begins working with them, arranging them, and as he engages with these materials, these soiled paint rags with their corroded voids and frayed edges, an image appears on the shroud: a spectral human form, forsaken, *wanhopig*, full of despair, empty.

---

* The term in my title is used by David Carrier in his book *Artwriting* (Amherst: University of Massachusetts Press, 1987) to refer to texts by both critics and art historians. Carrier cites as precedents Walter Friedlander, *Caravaggio Studies* (Princeton: Princeton University Press, 1955), p. xi, which speaks of "an art writer of the seventeenth century," and Michael Fried, "Thomas Couture and the Theatricalization of Action in 19th Century French Painting," *Artforum* 8, no. 10 (June 1970): 46, which speaks of "evolution in nineteenth-century art writing." But unlike them, Carrier makes "artwriting" a single word.

I am using the term here to cover something more freewheeling and perhaps messier,

Henk joins the shadow police, the shamans on their sacred rocks, the nameless, anonymous makers of Sumbanese ikat textiles; on this shroud he traces a figure:

*donker van toon*
*een archaishe trek*
(somber in tone
an archaic trace).[1]

---

more anarchic, more improvisational, more case-specific (cf. Hans Frei, "The 'Literal Reading' of Biblical Narrative in the Christian Tradition: Does It Stretch or Will It Break?" in *The Bible and the Narrative Tradition,* ed. Frank McConnell [New York: Oxford University Press, 1986], p. 67). The above essay is the precipitate of a series of attempts to write spontaneously, without too many methodological and art-ideological encumbrances, about specific Krijger works; to write in a manner similar to his own way of discussing his work (see his comments on *Darkroom of a Silver Man* in *Contact* 1, no. 1 [October 1969]). The essay brings together comments, quotations, and fragments, assembled in a decade or more of maverick reading, that seemed to me to have a bearing on Krijger's artmaking. I was "writing to learn" (cf. William Zissner, *Writing to Learn* [New York: Harper and Row, 1989], esp. p. 49: "Writing is a tool that enables people . . . to wrestle with facts and ideas" — I would add: "and artworks"). I wanted to develop ways of putting things together about or around *The Survivors* that would enlighten a larger public (cf. Mark Roskill, *The Interpretation of Pictures* [Amherst: University of Massachusetts Press, 1989], p. vii). My essay aims to provide a considered text that causes *The Survivors* to be viewed in a certain light (cf. Roskill, p. xii). So while my aims are consonant with artwriting as conceived by Roskill and Carrier, my appropriation of the term is more inclusive.

It should be clear that what I have written is, like Dan Hofstader's *Temperaments* (New York: Alfred A. Knopf, 1992), "far too free-ranging to have anything to do with academic art history." It has no intention to be canonical or exemplary: "no comparisons are drawn between vying talents," and I don't claim to know where to place Krijger on "the vast totem pole of contemporary art" (see Hofstader, p. xiiff.). Sustained and direct scrutiny; "being clear about what lies before us"; "*showing* what the artist has put in place" (Ludwig Wittgenstein); the indefinite postponement of the hermeneutic impulse; catalytic comments encountered in decades of cross-disciplinary reading; probing memory and imaginative reconstruction, indulging the free-play of the cognitive faculties — all these things have gone into my writing.

At a time of excessive self-consciousness about artwriting, its faults, and its over-burdens; mindful of the risks associated with the desire to *speak* the work (see Louis Marin, *Art and Philosophy* [Parma: Novastampa, 1991], pp. 96ff.); mindful also of the Byzantine proliferation of commentary, I have tried to write with some abandon but also with exactitude.

1. These two phrases come from a 1949 review of Krijger's work ("Henk Krijger exposeert in de academie," an article initialed by C.A.S. and most likely from the 31

Henk is back in the mid-forties, the war years.

He positions more rags, now with a dawning sense of purpose. A second figure appears, a mate to the first; and then two more . . .

witnesses to the atrocities,
*survivors.*

*       *       *

Hendrik (Henk) Cornelis Krijger ("senggih") was, largely through the efforts of Calvin Seerveld, the first and only Master Artist of the Institute for Christian Art/Patmos Workshop and Gallery, a position he held between September 1, 1969, and October 31, 1973. Born in Karoengi, Indonesia on November 19, 1914, Henk lived until 1928 on Sumba, until 1969 in The Netherlands (Amsterdam and The Hague), from 1969 to 1973 in the United States and Canada, and from 1974 until his death on September 29, 1979, in Breda, The Netherlands. Krijger had been brought to the attention of Seerveld and Mary Steenland in 1966 by Hans Rookmaaker, whose "Reformational" outlook and interest in aesthetics and art history Seerveld and Steenland shared. At the time of their meeting Henk was in his early fifties, well established as a painter, sculptor, and book designer/illustrator. He had been working for more than a decade on large, government-subsidized architectural commissions, occasionally taking on free-lance book design and illustration assignments, and spending what time remained on his own free work. His efforts in book design had won him a series of national awards,[2] several

---

December 1949 *Dagblad van Amersfoort*) and are in reference to a series of dark and brooding pieces Henk painted in the 1940s: *Zieke boer,* 1940 ("Sick Farmer"), *De wanhopige schilder,* 1940 ("The Desperate Painter"), and *De verloren zoon,* 1943 ("The Prodigal Son"). *The Survivors* runs in the same vein as these early works and shows a dimension of his oeuvre — triggered perhaps by a 1938 exposition of *De vreemdeling* ("The Stranger") and *De onnutte dienstknecht* ("The Unworthy Servant") by the reclusive Dutch Protestant artist Marius Richters (see note 10 below) — which hardly surfaces at all in Krijger's North American works.

2. After the war, Henk worked as a free-lance artist and book designer, first in Amsterdam and from 1951 until 1954 in the Hague, where he served as special printing advisor for Dammen, and from 1954 until 1956 as art director for Samson in Alphen

opportunities to design books for the prestigious De Roos Stichting, assignments for J. H. Kok, and the art directorship of several literary/academic journals.[3]

Artistically, Henk was a maverick, an anomaly. Pieter A. Scheen's entry on him in an art lexicon contains the following: "Artistically: originally enamored by W. Schumacher, Dik Ket, etc., later by Gust de Smet, Permeke, Chabot, currently a bit cobra-like, but that is only external. Tries to be himself and to succeed in that with work of a more or less socio-religious sensibility."[4] Dik Ket worked in the cold, precise, realist style of "Nieuwe Zakelijkheid"; Gust de Smet and Permeke were Flemish expressionists who influenced the Dutch "Bergense School" to which Krijger sometimes referred. Henk described his own style as a kind of expressionism.[5] And indeed, aspects of the standard dictionary description of expressionism are certainly apropos.[6] But traces of Nieuwe Zakelijkheid of the thirties, CoBrA-like elements, surrealist touches, hints of de Stil, and Eastern influences (Sumbanese and Balinese) abound.

Henk thought of himself as a *christen-kunstenaar*, that is, a Chris-

---

aan den Rijn. Between 1948 and 1960 nineteen books designed and/or illustrated by Krijger appeared among *De 50 best verzorgde boeken.*

3. For De Roos Stichting Krijger designed an edition of J. van Vondel's *Lucifer* (1954); a collection of poems by Elizabeth Barrett Browning entitled *Sonnets from the Portuguese and Seven Other Poems* (1957); a collection of poems by the African American poet Waring Cuney entitled *Puzzles* (1960); and an edition of Charles Perrault's *Le petit poucet* (1969). Of special note are the books published by J. H. Kok that Krijger designed for his friend G. Theodoor Rothuizen: a three-part series of meditations on the Psalms, entitled *Landscap* (1965, 1967, 1969) and a study of Dietrich Bonhoeffer entitled *Aristocratisch Christendom* (1969). Krijger was art director for *Horizon: gereformeerd apologetisch tijdschrift* and *Regelrecht: Evangelische orientaties.*

4. *Lexicon Nederlandse Beeldende Kunstenaars (1750-1950)* ('s-Gravenhage: Kunsthandel Pieter A. Scheen, 1968).

5. See his interview with Sue VanderWeele and Gayle Venema, "Krijger on Art," *Contact* 1, no. 1 (October 1969): 2-3. (*Contact* was a student newspaper at Trinity Christian College in Palos Heights, Illinois.) Krijger gives an account of his particular use of the term expressionism in an article on Bert Bouman entitled "Bij het werk van Bert Bouman, Houtsnijder," *Ontmoeting* 1 (1946-47): 344-53; see 345ff.

6. The *Random House Dictionary* defines Expressionism as follows: 1. *Fine Arts.* (a) a manner of painting, sculpting, etc., in which natural forms and colors are distorted or exaggerated; (b) a style of art developed in the 20th century, characterized chiefly by heavy, often black lines that define forms, sharply contrasting, often vivid colors, and subjective or symbolic treatment of thematic material.

230

tian/artist,[7] but he was a bit of a *dwaarsligger;*[8] a *buitenbeentje;*[9] an outsider. His art was resolutely modern, experimental, solidly anchored in the artistic currents of his time and place. It frequently showed erotic overtones and often ignored or deliberately foiled Calvinist pietism. His sensibility was that of a wayfarer, a sojourner, a *miles christi.*

His closest associations at the beginning of his career were with members of the largely *gereformeerd* Ontmoeting group (Jaap Das, Piet Risseuw, Bert Bouman, Cornelius Rijnsdorp, and others) but also to some extent the more *hervoormd* and ecumenical Wending group (Klaas Heeroma, J. W. Schulte Nordholt, W. Barnard). He was befriended by the tragic poet and

7. See Krijger's essay "De Christen-Kunstenaar: tussen twee vuren," *Regelrecht* 2, no. 4 (April 1965): 105ff. The use of the hyphenated form is quite deliberate here, I suspect, and I've tried to bring its import across by using the slash mark to combine the words Christian and artist. Krijger objected strenuously to the deluge of talk about "Christian art," which he considered isolationist: "Ik wil solidair zijn met de totale gescheidkundige ontwikkeling van vandaag en ik wil niet gedrongen worden in een ontwikkeling van het knusse christelijke wereldje apart. Ik wil *in de wereld* staan (natuurlijk zonder van de wereld te zijn)." ["I want to be solidary with the entire historical development of today and I don't want to be pressured into developing a snug little Christian world apart. I want to stand *in the world* (naturally without being of the world)."] G. Th. Rothuizen writes: "Henk Krijger echter was bovendien en dat zeer bewust christen-kunstenaar . . ." *Voorlopig* 12, no. 1 (January 1980): 1. For the feelings of some of Krijger's Dutch contemporaries on this issue, including Cornelius Rijnsdorp, see G. Puchinger, *Christen en Kunst* (Delft: W. D. Meinema, 1971). Krijger's formulation in "Bij de Dood van Marius Richters," *Ontmoeting* 8 (1954-55): 321, is instructive in this regard: "Hij [Richters] was een 'stille figuur', die nooit op daverende publiciteit uit was. Hij exposeerde nu en dan en het was bij die gelegenheden dat wij merken dat hij er wàs, dat hij in alle teruggetrokkenheid meedeed, de moeilijke taak trachtte te volbrengen, die ook wij ons opgelegd wisten: Christen èn kunstenaar te zijn." ("He was a 'quiet figure', who was never after booming publicity. He exhibited every now and then and it was on those occasions that we noticed that he was there, that, despite his withdrawal, he took part and tried to fulfill the difficult task we knew to be placed upon us as well: to be Christian and artist.")

8. Literally, "cross-beam." In the Dutch language railroad ties or sleepers are called *dwaarsliggers*, and the word *dwaars* is frequently used to describe people whose opinions are at odds with the mainstream, are contrary. In a book by that title, H. Berkhof uses the term to describe people who are at odds with the mainstream but whose efforts lay the foundations for a culture's ride into the future.

9. In a personal letter (23 May 1981) Cornelius Rijnsdorp described Krijger, himself, and their fellow travellers as *buitenbeentjes* (outsiders) within their milieu. In "Boutade en Getuigenis," *Bezinning* 9, no. 4 (1956), Rijnsdorp defines "buitenbeentjes" as "mensen die zich wel wat de groote lijn van hun overtuiging betreft laten in delen, maar verder niet" ("people who, with regard to the main lines of their convictions, can be counted as belonging, but no further").

231

fiction writer Hein de Bruin in the late thirties,[10] engaged in dialogues with the likes of J. J. Buskes, Fedde Schurer, H. M. van Randwijk, and later in the sixties had ties with the *gereformeerd* avant garde (G. Th. Rothuizen and H. M. Kuitert, then the theological bad boys of the Dutch *gereformeerd* churches). Within the Ontmoeting group Henk gained a secondary reputation as a writer,[11] and at the opening of the Christelijke Academie voor Beeldende Kunst in 1978 he was hailed as a leading champion *(stugge voorvechter)* of the cross-pollination of Christianity and art.

As Master Artist at ICA/Patmos Krijger entered a sustained period of artistic free-play. He produced a string of major works, two series of gouaches, a series of prints on the psalms, an exquisite series of collages on death and dying, and several commissions.[12]

*  *  *

In the fall of 1972 Henk had begun work on his *Homage aux Saltimbanques I & II.* These two constructions are built around a pair of lino blocks Krijger had cut two years earlier for *Acrobaten,* a limited edition series of two-color prints. Flanking the blocks Krijger strung beads and fragments of jewelry on a network of piano wire against a backdrop of rags like the ones he might have used to wipe those very blocks. In the *Homages* the rags have a decorative flavor like pieces of tie-dyed cloth.

It is as if, in the course of handling these dark and mottled rags, in the course of Henk's spontaneous manipulation of these materials, his active mind sets off in a new and different direction, a direction that draws, like Alberto Burri's 1952 *Sacco* series, on the metaphoric potential and evocative power of old rags.[13] Henk, ever attentive to the workings

---

10. See Henk Krijger's "Hij en Ik," *Ontmoeting* 4 (1949-50): 412-18.

11. Krijger published a novel titled *De Witte Duiven* (1952), a series of short stories, a novella, a piece of historical fiction, book reviews, art criticism, and reflective essays — more than two dozen pieces in all, mostly for *Ontmoeting* — between 1946 and 1956. To date only one of these pieces has been translated: "Zacchaeus," in *Homage à Senggih* (Toronto: Patmos Gallery, 1989). Also see Mark Vander Vennen, "Henk Krijger: The Writer," ibid., pp. 42-54.

12. See "Appendix F," *Homage à Senggih,* pp. 73-74.

13. Of Burri's *Sacco,* Werner Haftmann comments: "In 1952 an Italian painter, Alberto Burri, showed work consisting merely of old rags and scraps of sacking. . . . With their diverse structures the crumbling, spotted scraps of sacking formed a desolate field; the heterogeneous fragments were fastened together with thread and string and

of his visual unconscious, follows the new impulse to see where it might lead.

*   *   *

*Sur • vi • vor* (from the Latin *supervivere,* to live beyond) — a person or a thing that endures or lives on in spite of an affliction, adversity, or misery, in spite of a mortally dangerous occurrence or situation.

We speak of holocaust survivors, survivors of physical and sexual abuse, children of survivors, AIDS survivors, survivors of breast cancer, an entire panoply, each with its own stigmata, its own clew of secret wounds, physical and psychological.

Henk himself was a survivor, forced into hiding in 1942. For three years, through the Siege of Amsterdam and the Hunger Winter of 1944-45, he lived a fugitive existence, smuggling potatoes through the streets of Amsterdam, dodging the secret police, guarding his anonymity. And here, fifty-eight years old, at Patmos Workshop and Gallery, in the midst of floundering finances, under personal strain, in declining health, disconcerted, needing to get back, haunted by images of the past, it is as if all that the war meant for Henk, all that he has seen and felt, has been distilled and recombined, the entire chaotic welter of impressions has been allowed to surface, triggered by these tattered, stained, psycho-active rags.

It is as if the apocalyptic horsemen of Krijger's *We Played The Flute for You* . . . have done their bit, and here now are the survivors.

---

arranged into an unstable melancholy geometry. . . . Where fire or rot had made holes in the sacking, a nocturnal ground shone through, or a golden glow or an eloquent colour appeared. Here again the textile surface seemed to conceal something which nevertheless — despite the attempt to create a conforming beauty, a kind of order, from these tragic remnants and their colour modulations — peered through everywhere. The tatters seemed to conceal a mortal wound. . . . The power of scraps of rubbish to evoke the world's wounds and the threat of the void can no doubt be explained by the psychological mood of our time, by our cruel experience of life, and by the metaphysical anguish of contemporary [humanity]. . . . In decaying sacks and tatters he found the appropriate material in which to express, in terms of the crudest reality, this pictorial metaphor for the world's wounds and [humanity's] terror of the void." See Haftmann's *Painting in the Twentieth Century,* vol. 1 (New York: Frederick A. Praeger, 1965), p. 362. There are clear analogies between these works of Burri and Henk Krijger's *The Survivors.*

\*          \*          \*

We see here the darker side of an oeuvre that travels across the entire "bipolar spectrum";[14] we see here the troubled side of an oeuvre that runs the cosmic gamut of "reformatorische kunst" ("reformational art"),[15] that ranges freely through the array of typiconic formats, varying from lyrical-romantic to monumental and illustrative.[16] We are in the year that saw the completion of *Homage aux Saltimbanques I & II*, the year that saw the playful lyricism of *Well, Butterflies* and *Flight Patterns of Three Happy UFOs* and *Homage à Debussy*, the year that saw the quiet melancholy of the exquisite trio: *Charon, Sweet Chariot*, and *A man goin' roun' takin' names*.

\*          \*          \*

14. Cf. "Art of Darkness," *The Sciences*, 29, no. 6 (November/December 1989): 2-5. Like the work of the gifted Protestant writer J. K. van Eerbeek (Meindert Boss, 1889-1937), Henk's oeuvre alternates between the dark, brooding, and serious, and the relaxed, playful, and uncomplicated, between Marius Richters and Massimo Campigli. See H. J. van Boekhoven's comments on van Eerbeek in "Cirkels om J. K. van Eerbeek," *Ontmoeting* 1 (1946-47): 340, especially the following: "Het karakter van deze romans wekt de indruk, dat van Eerbeek telkens na zich verdiept te hebben in het probleem waarin hij zichzelf gevangen wist, zich van zichzelf afwende, om bij het schrijven van een verhaal over minder gecompliceerde mensen die verder van hem afstonden, ruimer adem te halen."

15. Cf. Hans Rookmaaker's article on "Reformatorische Kunst" in *Christelijke Encyclopedie* where he characterizes as follows the essentials of an artistic style unique to Calvinism: "Een grote vrijheid en openheid for al het geschapene, liefde voor het grote en kleine, besef voor een zekere hierarchie der waarden, vermijding van pracht en praal, nuchterheid die eenerzijds iedere idealisering vermijd, anderszijds iedere exaltatie der zonde vreemd is, nadruk op het menselijke zonder heroisering maar met erkenning van de betekenis van innerlijke en uiterlijke strijd, en met belangstelling voor de intiemere menselijke verhoudingen. . . ." ("Great freedom and openness to all of creation, love of the great and small, a sense of a certain hierarchy of values, avoidance of pomp and circumstance, a sobriety that on the one hand shuns idealizations of any kind, and on the other is a stranger to every exaltation of sin, emphasizes the human without heroizing, but with a recognition of inner and outer conflict, and with an interest in intimate human relations. . . .")

16. Cf. the comments on Leo Gestel (Bergense School) in the *Winkler Prins Encyclopedie:* "Zijn werken zijn lyrisch-romantisch tot monumentaal en illustratief." G. Th. Rothuizen's short essay "Bij een opening," *De Oude Man van Hoy: Figuren en landschappen* (Kampen: Kok, 1970), pp. 7-11, especially the final three paragraphs, evokes well the world that Krijger's works project.

Henk follows the impulse to see where it will lead. He is giving rein to a process he lauded two decades earlier in the work of his artistic fellow-traveller Bert Bouman.[17]

> Senggih is yielding to the free and primal flow of mental images.
> Senggih submits to the inclination to portray the associative images triggered by these rags.[18]

The process requires what Allen Ginsberg calls "a deconditioning of attitude — a deconditioning of rigidity and unyieldingness." It involves the "cultivation of tolerance towards one's own thoughts and impulses and ideas — the tolerance necessary for . . . acceptance of the mind's raw contents."[19]

17. In the article on Bert Bouman, *Ontmoeting* 1 (1946-47): 351, Henk notes that seeing a dying woman being transported with a handcart (during the "Hunger Winter") was the occasion for Bouman's cutting of *Hemelvaart*. In this print Bouman has, according to Krijger, yielded to "that peculiar modern inclination" *(neiging)* to represent mental associations. (The sentence reads: "In deze niet aan enig doel gebonden voorstelling, is meer ongeremd toegegeven aan die eigenaardige moderne neiging tot uitbeelden van gedachten associaties, die bij de beschouwers weer andere associaties moeten wekken . . ." (". . . which are to arouse other associations in the spectator . . ."). The emphasis here is on the phrase "ongeremd toegegeven" ("yielded without inhibitions" — "ongeremd" has to do with not applying the brakes).

18. Bric-a-brac is frequently the provocation for new works in Krijger's artmaking, as Willem Hart has noted in "A Box Full of Junk," *Vanguard* 10, no. 6 (November/December 1980): 15-17. This is the case in *That night the moon was completely different,* where a circular piece of concrete sends Henk back to a moonlit night in Spain some months after his first wife Nel had died, a night he associates with the Dutch romanticist religious ditty *'t Sheepje onder Jezus' hoede.* This is the case in *Darkroom of a Silver Man,* where an old door becomes the entrance to a visual meditation on male erotic fantasies. The door, the piece of concrete, are no longer objects of use, also not decorative elements in an artistic tableau, but "suggestion-rich," full of evocative potential. And so it is with *The Survivors. The Survivors* is a special case of the kind of assemblage that dominated Henk's work in North America. What is backdrop material in the *Homages* moves to center stage in *The Survivors.* While some of his pieces in North America are truly constructions made from found material — almost like assemblages or collages — Henk's procedure here, as in his *Annunciation* and *We played the flute for you,* is to use non-painterly material like rags as a base, or to incorporate fragments of foreign matter like tin cans, giving the painting the added density of secondary association.

19. See Allen Ginsberg, "Meditation and Poetics," in *Spiritual Quests: The Art and Craft of Religious Writing,* ed. William Zinsser (Boston: Houghton Mifflin, 1988), pp. 149-50. According to Ginsberg, "Major works of twentieth-century art are probes of consciousness — particular experiments with recollection or mindfulness . . ." (p. 147).

It is a process that accorded well with the "Eastern" dimension of Henk's nature, a process whose embattled prerogatives Henk sought to unleash and harness, harness and unleash, throughout his career.[20] It is a process he associated with *het verborgen omgang:* the hidden walk.[21]

So Henk takes what this flow of images offers up and begins to sketch.[22] He begins to sift through the flood of associations, to work them into four primal forms, to fix precisely the order and the gestures of the figures, to weave them into a tight new order.[23]

20. In a letter to Henk Melles dated 1975, Krijger spoke of his desire for a time of free creativity unencumbered by the expectations of others, without philosophies and theories, without "religious considerings," impelled only by his initial excitement as his two hands were chased exclusively by his most primitive art-guts. Krijger's attentiveness to the flow of mental images — he talks of the theater stage behind the eyes — , to the sometimes awkward offerings of the visual unconscious, and his desire for an unencumbered creativity, are continuous with his pleas in "Drie Overwegingen," *Ontmoeting* 2 (1947-48): 488ff., for breaking through old normativities and dogmas and for a habitus of existential dependence at the very core of artmaking.

21. Krijger uses the phrase "de verborgen omgang" in "Drie Overwegingen," p. 489. This phrase was used by Hein de Bruin as a provisional title for an unfinished novel, parts of which were posthumously published in a special issue of *Ontmoeting.* De Bruin had taken up an acquaintance with Krijger in 1936 to discuss some of the issues he wanted to tackle in this novel. The novel was to center around the problems encountered by an artistically inclined young man of orthodox Protestant extraction attempting to make his way in a largely unreceptive artistic milieu. The phrase is associated with the work of the Dutch theologian H. Miskotte, whose public lectures on the Apocalypse de Bruin and Krijger attended in the forties and whose writings include an article by the same title. For Henk, artmaking was frequently a vertiginous exercise in existential dependence coupled, at its best, with a sense of divine accompaniment.

22. See Rudolf Arnheim's illuminating comments on "the dialectics of sketching" in "Sketching and the Psychology of Design," *Design Issues: History/Theory/Criticism* 9, no. 2 (Fall 1993): 15ff. Sketching does not consist simply of representing on canvas the images held in the artist's mind; it consists rather in a dialectical process. Mental images are fugitive, easily wiped off the slate of memory; they offer a freedom not offered to optical precepts, especially in their dealings with space; they can ignore gravity. Being topological, they stand for a whole range of possibilities without being tangibly committed to any one of them. Being undefined in their specifics, they admit of distortions and deviations. Their pregnancy is what the artist draws on in the search for a final form. Sketches are the reflection of the guiding mental image. By making a sketch the artist supplies the mental image with the assistance of an optical image. It persists objectively, while mental images depend on the willfulness of the mind, which makes them come and go. A sketch stops the process and lets the artist examine what has been done and in what direction the work must proceed.

23. "The painter," says Maurice Merleau-Ponty, "rearranges the prosaic world and

236

\*   \*   \*

*The Survivors* (Figure 1) consists of a series of four figures, each shown frontally; the two outside figures are full length, the two inside figures are larger and cut off at the knees. Except for the position of the arms and hands, their stances are identical. Each figure occupies a space of his or her own in a visual field constructed from an array of paint rags, cut into rectangles and arranged on a piece of ¼-inch Masonite in a horizontal/vertical pattern characteristic of much of Senggih's work.[24] The figures are outlined in a black oil wash and modulated by varying degrees of brush work. The colors appear subdued and muted as on a cold and rainy November day. There is a hint of the Netherlandic landscape, of the architecture of the death camp — blue-grey sky, grass in autumn, asphalt, a series of black bars — but space, perspectival space is no more than a memory.[25] What is essential is the surface, the rags.

Krijger's arrangement of rags — Mondrianesque in its severity and sense of order; reminiscent of the modular exercises of Le Corbusier — replaces perspectival space with a structurally complex and highly textured field of action,[26] a module-based grid,[27] a rhythmic scaffolding, a melancholy geometry,[28] upon which a story, a cautionary tale, unfolds, narrated

---

... makes a holocaust of objects, but the disorder is always another order, a new system of equivalences . . ." ("The Indirect Language," in *The Prose of the World* [Evanston, Ill.: Northwestern University Press, 1973], p. 63ff.). Krijger makes analogous comments in "Krijger on Art," *Contact*, October 1969, pp. 2-3.

24. The two *Homages*, *The Survivors*, and *Serenade in Memoriam* have a horizontal/vertical composition more resolute, more rigorous, more consistently maintained than anywhere else within Krijger's oeuvre.

25. Cf. Haftmann, *Painting in the Twentieth Century*, p. 212, in reference to Massimo Campigli.

26. My use of the phrase "field of action" is an adaptation of the notion of William Carlos Williams that "an advance of estimable proportions is made by looking at the poems as a field rather than an assembly of more or less ankylosed lines . . ." (*Autobiography* [New York: Random House, 1951], p. 329). The notion is developed further, if somewhat indirectly, in his 1948 essay "The Poem as a Field of Action," *Selected Essays* (New York: New Directions, 1969), p. 280. It can, I believe, be profitably applied to all the arts, including the graphic arts.

27. Cf. Jack H. Williamson's essay, "The Grid: History, Use, and Meaning" in *Design Discourse: History/Theory/Criticism* (Chicago: University of Chicago Press, 1989), pp. 171-86, especially the section on "The modern grid."

28. Cf. Haftmann, *Painting in the Twentieth Century*, p. 355, in reference to Corneille.

FIGURE 1. Henk (Senggih) Krijger, *The Survivors*. 1972.
Rags and oil wash on masonite.
Courtesy of the Patmos Gallery and the Hendrik Krijger Estate.

through gestures from left to right. The array clearly demarcates four basic modules or panels, but also relates the first to the fourth, parts of the third to the second, and parts of the third to the fourth. The arrangement segregates and interrelates the four figures. It establishes a shifting network of visual relationships between the figures. Paradoxically, it ties them together and it holds them apart; they each state their point separately and in concert.

Except for the second figure from the left, the array also partitions individual figures vertically, drawing attention to individual gestures and specific bodily zones. They appear interchangeable, assembled from various sources. This partitioning is not random or ad hoc but well-considered, constructed on a human scale like the metrical canons underlying classical verse, like the panel exercises of Le Corbusier.

Structurally the second panel from the left controls the positioning of the rags. It is placed squarely across the golden mean of a golden section (Figure 2). To the left Krijger places a squarish rectangle centered just below the horizontal axis; to the right, centered slightly above the horizontal axis,

FIGURE 2.

he places another rectangle one-third as wide as it is long. Together these three patches are the fundamental co-ordinates, the dominant axes. Other pieces follow: two squarish patches for the third figure from the left, one for the head and one for the lower body;[29] smaller patches for the heads of the two outside figures (the patch on the fourth is, however, slightly smaller and placed somewhat higher than the one on the first); vertical scraps for their thighs and legs. Their placement seems governed by the impulse to create out of these rags, these tragic remnants and their color modulations, an ordered but asymmetrical counterpoint to the simple rhythmic repetition of the four almost identical figures. The result is a subtle richness of form in a desolate field.

Overall the piece reads across, but the horizontal flow accentuated by the black stripes is cut abruptly by the second panel from the left. The figure on this panel is in a space all its own, floating in an mottled grey abyss, unsupported by either vertical or horizontal.

29. At first glance it seems as if there are two rags here, but on closer inspection there is only one. Krijger painted them later in such a way that they look like two.

FIGURE 3.

In many places the cloth is creased and buckled, but nowhere more than in the second panel. Some of the pieces of cloth are tattered, and the white-painted Masonite shows through. In other areas unraveled strands and clumps of thread lie buried in oil impasto. Some of the holes appear corroded or charred while others are the results of spontaneous tearing. The most extensive tear coincides with the breast of the third figure.

It is evident that Henk had originally painted the "whitespace" around the head-cloths black, later filling in a blue-grey to leave black bars, and on some of these he applied additional scraps of cloth resembling black electrical tape. These bars are of three widths. A thick stripe seems to run from the far left of the first panel to the patch on the third (Figure 3); a second thick stripe seems to run from the far right of the fourth panel to the second panel. A third thick stripe bisects these two and ties the head of panel three to panel two. Two thinner stripes relate panels one and four, but the combination of thin/thin/thick in panel four is an inversion of their combination in panel one. On the one hand, the solemn, immobile forms, especially the two in the center, are just there in all their seclusion. On the other hand, they are linked, not just through homotaxis, contrast, alliterative form, but

240

also through the formal device of these rules functioning to establish an intimate texture of relationships.

The colors appear subdued and muted, yet the heads of the first and fourth figures are painted in vivid pinks; bright grass green — a dominant note in a series of chromatic chords punctuated by rust reds, deep blues, jet black — runs across the torsos of the first and last two figures.

Some areas, most notably the interior of the second figure, are altogether devoid of paint. Here, as in the head of the third figure, Henk directly offers the stained weave of the rags to our vision. He has painted the area surrounding this figure in places, but the interior space he has left virtually untouched. The inherent character of the rag is given full voice. Elsewhere paint is applied more heavily and the cloth is obscured, though never fully, and in those areas Henk's application of paint seems to follow a compositional logic rather than a semiotic imperative.

The linear flow from left to right underlines the narrative content of the piece, and the shifting visual relationships among discrete units embroider around this simple narrative a network of significant and effective linkages.

*       *       *

The rags then, supported by the horizontal rules and a well-defined palette of colors, set up a two-dimensional field of action that replaces perspectival space. The field separates/juxtaposes/contrasts/relates iconographic elements so that meaning is generated and multiplied through the placement of figurative structures in a contexture, through their play against each other. Just as the positioning of the rags constructs a two-dimensional field of action, so the positioning of these four figures and the sequence of their gestures construct a syntactic and semantic structure.[30] The understated gestures[31] articulated across the patterned array define a narrative thread

---

30. Cf. Louis Marin, "Narrative Theory and Piero as History Painter," *October*, no. 65 (Summer, 1993), p. 108.

31. Like Rembrandt's art, that of Henk Krijger is an art of gesture. See Henri Focillon, "In Praise of Hands," *The Life of Forms in Art* (New York: Zone Books, 1992), especially the following: "All great artists have paid close attention to the study of hands . . . , they have sensed the peculiar power that lies in them. Rembrandt shows hands to us in all the varied emotions, types, ages and conditions of life: the gaping astonished hand, thrust in shadow against the light, of a witness in the large *Raising of*

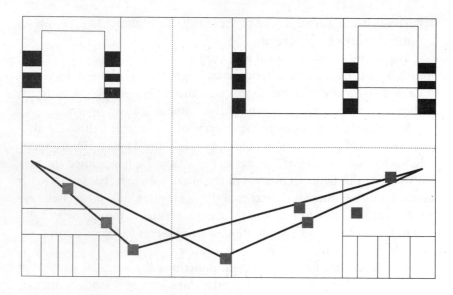

FIGURE 4.

running through the piece. They constitute a kind of pictorial writing reminiscent of hieroglyphs and Malaysian reliefs.

The method of arrangement is neither chronological nor episodic. The four figures are not involved in a unitary action like the figures in one of Jacques Louis David's historical tableaux. There is no orderly *fabula* underlying the work, no causal sequence, no disordering of particulars (as in Krijger's own *That night the moon was completely different . . .* or *Darkroom of a Silver Man*) for the sake of "making strange."[32]

The gestures don't so much arrest an action as distill.

---

*Lazarus;* the workmanlike and scholarly hand of Professor Tulp holding with a clamp a bundle of arteries in the *Anatomy Lesson;* the hand of Rembrandt himself in the act of drawing; the powerful hand of Saint Matthew writing at the angel's dictation; the hands of the aged paralytic in the *Hundred Guilder Print,* bent double by the coarse, inert mittens hanging at his wrist" (p. 158).

32. Cf. Meir Sternberg, "Time and Space in Biblical (Hi)story Telling: The Grand Chronology," in *The Book and The Text: The Bible and Literary Theory,* ed. Regina Schwartz (Oxford: Basil Blackwell, 1989), p. 81. Krijger himself used the term "making strange" in discussing his approach.

They range among expressive, iconic, and symbolic.

They belong to a global repertoire, a universal grammar.

They get their primary sense through their placement in this four-part sequence.

The gestures come in pairs: four distiches in a visual quatrain, signing, miming, semaphoric. They occupy three registers and are arranged along descending/ascending axes (Figure 4), one in the shape of a roughly symmetrical 'V' and the other with a more extreme descent than ascent: the opening and closing gesture in the top register; the left hand of the first, the right of the last, and the hands of the third in the middle register; the two hands of the second in the lowest, on which two hands the descending/ascending axis converge.

The narrative technique is concise, minimal, modern: a figure introduces the scene, his eyes cast a wary, furtive glance to his right;[33] another figure, appealing directly to the viewer, caps it off; they bracket the central action as it were; they mirror each other, but for the far right gesture and the far left gesture, which entail a small twist up of the hand and forearm — an inversion echoed in the stripes. This latter gesture is one of suppression, the shielding of the self from what has been shown, but it is simultaneously subtly benedictory, reminiscent of some medieval depictions of Christ. Like the raised right hand of Arnolfini in Van Eyck's famous double portrait, the final gesture "may recall by association the angel Gabriel's gesture at the Annunciation prognosticating an expected childbirth."[34] There is the simple cautionary tale, but also a countermovement where things are not what they initially seem. The introductory gesture recalls the gesture of the evangelist in Matthias Grünewald's *Ecce Homo,* but it has a double thrust: betrayal and disclosure. Also, note that the first figure has the palm of the left hand facing out, and the figure on the right has the left palm facing backward, the arm not limp as in the second figure, but slightly tensed as if to hold back what might be coming. Danger comes from behind in the psycho-geography of the upright.[35]

---

33. Actually the illusion of a sidelong glance appears only when *The Survivors* is viewed from the right with light coming in from the left. It is evident in the photo that I originally worked with. While probably not intended — actually all four figures look directly out to the viewer — the illusion is definitely there and unavoidable, a kind of gratuitous accident.

34. Cf. Mark Roskill, *The Interpretation of Pictures,* p. 67.

35. Cf. Erik H. Erikson, *Toys and Reasons: Stages in the Ritualization of Reality* (New

The figures are not the *"koddig"* (droll) and *"onbeholpen"* (clumsy) figures[36] that populate many of Krijger's constructions and that link him to Rembrandt and Breugel. These figures have a primal, almost tribal flavor. The handling of the massive heads is more severe than anything one finds up to this point in Krijger's oeuvre. There is a rejection of pictorial refinements — the playfulness of *Well, Butterflies,* the elegance and sophistication of the *Homages,* the linear intricacies of Henk's *Landscap* and *Lucifer* drawings — for a primeval direct expression. The figures are unadorned and naked from the waist up; the only markings are angular and oblong markings to indicate ribs and breasts.

Unlike the open-ended cry of anguish — the immediacy of Ossip Zadkine's *Ontwerp voor een monument van een gebombardeerde stad* (1947) and the raw expressiveness of Edvard Munch's *The Scream* — unlike the engorged symbolism of Picasso's *Guernica,* there's a traditional poetic closure to this piece, a closure similar to that of the antiphons sung in the Latin office of the dead, similar to lamentations, elegies, dirges. *The Survivors* is as highly structured as these formal expressions, mostly in verse or in song, of sorrow or mourning. Though not identical to an elegy (distich, with first line dactylic hexameter, second line pentameter), *The Survivors* has the same contextural complexity and rigor. *The Survivors* is like a quatrain, but not with alternating rhymes, rather with a ABBA structure and a complex internal contexture of echo and alliteration.[37]

---

York: Norton, 1977), p. 34: "The overall configuration of our construction expresses the truly basic developmental fact of childhood, namely, that the human being in growing up must learn to master to the point of unrestrained motion the evolutionary gift of an erect bipedal posture, and with it a basic space-time orientation. With his stereoscopic vision and his alert imagination, the human being learns to orient himself in his kind of space and time: looking forward to what is in front and what is ahead and *turning backward on what is behind and in back.* Combining values with directions, he learns to look up to what is above, higher and highest, and down to what is below, lower and lowest. But such upright orientation also creates a stark right and left; and eventually, strong connotations of social and sexual differentiation become attached to all these directions" (my emphasis).

36. See Rothuizen, *De Oude Man van Hoy,* p. 10.

37. One could perhaps say of Krijger's *The Survivors* what H. Van Der Leek says of Hein de Bruin: "Het dichten gaat hem niet gemakkelijk af. Een gedicht is bij hem een geboorte van iets dat langdurig en met voortdurende inwendige spanning is meegedragen, tot het zijn vorm vind. Van groote spanning getuigt ook deze vorm zelf. *Stark, tot springens toe samengetrokken, omsluit meestal een sonnet een golf van ontroert-zijn, die niet enkelvoudig te karacteriseeren is.* . . . . Hij beleeft de wereld der groote en kleine

\*       \*       \*

*The Survivors* is a tribal fresco of gesturing archetypical forms.

*The Survivors* is like the carved walls of the Toraja death-cliffs, lined with disintegrating tau-taus: "watchful armies of the waking dead."[38]

*The Survivors* is a series of dance notations for a visual requiem.

*The Survivors* is a somber, moving piece that narrates its sad lament through the sequential laconic gestures of four emaciated figures, survivors. The two figures at the heart of the narrative unfold, with great force, simplicity, and clarity, a tale of hunger, rape, death, and despair. In a sense these two enveloping figures are the real survivors.

\*       \*       \*

allusions, levels, depth:
   the planes shift,
   the facets multiply,
   latent aspects come to the fore,
the resonance of the piece deepens to a place beyond speech.

The figures are man and woman;
husband, wife, and children;
   an underground acquaintance,
   shot through,
   floating face up in the canal;

---

dingen vanuit een diepe, langzame, maar langaanhoudende en zijn heel wezen door-stralende en emoveerende ontroering. Een ontroering die niet zelden een inwendende crisis nabijkomt" (my emphasis). ("Writing poetry doesn't come easy for de Bruin. A poem is the birth of something carried along for a long time and with continual inner stress until it finds a form. The form itself testifies to great strain. Taut, compressed to the point of bursting, a sonnet often encloses a wave of emotion impossible to characterize in simple terms. De Bruin experiences the world of great and small with a deep, slow, enduring emotionality that irradiates his entire being, an emotionality that frequently approaches an inner crisis.") H. van der Leek, "Het Ingekimde Land," *Opwaartsche Wegen* 10 (1932): 98.

38. Tau-taus are shaman-carved wooden effigies found in balcony-like alcoves hewn into the Toraja death-cliffs. They are arranged in serial fashion in groups of four through ten across the entire face of the death-cliffs. The Toraja tribe is located on Celebes, near Sumba, where Krijger was born. The phrase "watchful armies of the waking dead" comes from Lawrence Blair, with Lorne Blair, *Ring of Fire* (New York: Bantam Press, 1988), p. 74.

detainees lined up in a concentration camp;
survivors, and children of survivors;
Lodewijk Brouwer,[39] 1942, exhausted isolated fugitive,
    wary observer, furtively passing on what he has been privy to,
    what no eye has seen, nor ear heard;
Senggih,[40] 1972, narrator, and cautioner
    holding it back, shielding himself and us.

The figures are *adam* and *eve*
    — through all the assaults on eve she has survived,
    through the barrenness, violation, abuse,
    through the *eenzame avontuur;*
    — through all the assaults on adam he has survived

The figures are
    his first wife, Nel, dead at 53,
    Henk himself, *een gehalveerde mens,*
    lesbian author, Anna Blaman,
    dutch painter, Marius Richters,
        *verloren zoon,*
        *unnutte dienstknecht.*

Structural rigor.
Narrative economy.
"... simplicity of syntax,
... extensive use of repetition and echo,
... symmetry of organization which adds dignity, and a variety in
repetition which adds interest"[41]
Suggestive power.
Density of allusion.
A socio-religious sentiment.

---

39. Lodewijk Brouwer was Henk's underground identity. Lodewijk Brouwer is credited as illustrator in the colophon of the first book put out by De Bezige Bij, *Dagboek Onder Het Kruis*, written by Evert J. Pot (W. A. P. Smit).

40. The name Senggih appears on all the works Krijger produced in North America and is linked to his childhood on Sumba.

41. Cf. Sean McEvenue, *The Narrative Style of the Priestly Writer* (Rome: Biblical Institute Press, 1971), p. 182. McEvenue explores the relation between priestly style and children's literature using Claudia Lewis's *Writing for Young Children* (New York, 1954). He highlights (p. 212ff.) the technique of writing in panels, or "panel writing" (see for example the children's story "The Little Red Hen"). *The Survivors* can profitably be viewed as a visual analogue to panel writing.

The work exhibits a truly remarkable concentration of artistic qualities.

\* \* \*

The use of non-arbitrary page proportions; the impulse to construct a well-defined grid within which to work; the habit of accommodating a hierarchy of elements into one view; the concern for closure; the striving for asymmetrical balance — all show Krijger's alliance with twentieth-century graphic design. The prominence of aesthetic considerations, the concern to put things in a new order, and the desire to elicit a dynamic life of forms show his alliance with modernist art. Everywhere there is a kind of neoclassicism: in the proportions, the vertical/horizontal arrangement of visual space, the functional and chordal use of color, the narrative closure of the piece. Henk orchestrates the vast array of possibilities served up by the artistic tradition into replete and ramified works.

\* \* \*

But at the same time, love impels the lament. *The Survivors* is profoundly expressive, deeply troubled, full of sadness about the world.[42] We can say of *The Survivors* what Peter Fuller says of Rouault's prostitutes: "His love is conspicuous. There is no heroism, no railing about the wages of sin."[43]

In a July 1979 letter to Cal Seerveld, Henk writes: "All my works are made out of a *huiveren voor de liefdegebod*" ("reverence for the law of love" — the word *huiveren* is best associated with the use of "fear" in idioms like "God-fearing").[44] In a series of notes which could well have been written at about this time, Henk states: "When I die, I want to know that, though

---

42. In a CBC television interview Helen Weinzweig mentioned in passing the fact that the artistic products of survivors of the Second World War are often marked by "a sadness about the world."

43. ". . . and yet, Rouault is neither a satirist sneering at raddled old powdered sluts; nor a strident moralist railing to us about the wages of sin. . . . His love . . . is conspicuous. . . . And this love gains material expression in the transfigurations of colour and form. The squalor of the woman's surroundings is metamorphosed into splendor through Rouault's relish in his painterly means and materials. Thus her hideous hues are transformed into translucent veils; and her sagging and degraded flesh is brought alive by the energy of his life-affirming line." Peter Fuller, *Images of God: The Consolations of Lost Illusions* (London: Chatto & Windus/The Hogarth Press, 1985), p. 43.

44. "Mijn *Fluitspeler,* en *Annunciatie,* en *Two couples boating,* en *Relics of a recent saint,* enz., zijn uit hetzelfde huiveren voor de Wet der Liefde ontstaan" (July 1, 1979).

247

my work has proven to fall short, I have in my own way lived the seven works of charity *in my art*."[45] In Vollenhoven's ontology, positive law "bridges the gap" between the law of love and the concrete situation,[46] but here we see that artistic actions do so as well . . .

From this work in particular we see how, in the artistic process, what begins as attentiveness to the self and its ravages becomes, in the course of play and an almost mystical involvement with the material, an act of empathetic human solidarity[47] — becomes an event in the life of a significant if isolated experimenter, striving to meet the joys and sorrows of his age with aesthetically worthwhile, multifaceted, existentially engaged and honest, vital and contemporary artistry.[48]

---

45. This is an abbreviated translation of "Als ik straks dood zal gaan *aan de ziekte van deze tijd, de kanker,* dan zal ik voor God en Jezus vershijnen en dan zal ik in het oordeel blijken *volslagen te kort geschoten te zijn,* maar ik wil op mijn manier weten dat ik de 7 werken van barmhartigheid heb nageleefd *in mijn kunst* en ook het gebod: *'Gij zult mijn getuigenis zijn.'"* (Krijger's emphasis.)

46. ". . . zij is een niet door willekeurige mensen, maar door ambtsdragers uit te vaardigen regeling die een brug dient te slaan tussen de liefdewet . . . , en het structureel bepaalde en naar tijd en ruimte beperkte samenlevingsverband waarvoor het betreffende ambt verantwoording draagt." (". . . it is a regulation issued by office holders that serves to build a bridge between the law of love and the structurally fixed, temporally and spatially confined societal relationship for which the office in question is responsible.") D. H. Th. Vollenhoven, "De Consequent Probleemhistorische Methode," *Philosophia Reformata,* 26, Jubileumnummer 1936-1961 (1961): 11-12.

47. Cf. Mark Edmunson "Prophet of a New Postmodernism," *Harper's,* December 1989, p. 70: "So, in Rorty's terms, the novel *(The Satanic Verses)* is an exercise in the widening of what he calls solidarity. It encourages the reader to bring more different kinds of people into the group that he or she refers to as 'we.'"

48. Cf. L. Yntema's comment in "-Ismen in de Letterkunde," *Philosophia Reformata* 12, no. 4 (1947): 191, that "een aesthetisch waardevolle, Christelijk-pluralistische, hedendaagse Hollandse roman is echter een zeldzaamheid" ("an aesthetically worthwhile, Christianly pluralistic, contemporary Dutch novel is rather rare" — my translation). Yntema uses the term pluralistic in a sense that is best covered by the more current term multifaceted. He contrasts it with "monistic," under which he places biologism, historicism, aestheticism, economism in the literature of class conflict, and psychologism in the psycho-analytic novel (p. 184). In "Prophet of a New Postmodernism," Mark Edmunson remarks: "Perhaps Rushdie's implications about America . . . are true, and we really are too weary and Alexandrian a culture, too self-conscious and too self-obsessed, to produce vital art that contributes to the sorts of human enlargements that a positive postmodernism would."

# Creation and Wholeness: The Poetry of Werner Bergengruen

## GUDRUN KUSCHKE

The coherence and richness of Werner Bergengruen's poetry have remained largely unexplored and therefore undiscovered. The neglect must be attributed to the restrictions of positivistic methods of interpretation, particularly in dealing with Christian poetry. Bergengruen constitutes the zenith of clandestine poetry during the Nazi era, and his poetic work possesses a uniquely congruent dimensionality that calls for holistic interpretations. It is therefore essential that an attempt be made to overcome the inadequacy of positivist methods with an integrated approach.

Bergengruen's importance as a poet must be evaluated against the particular situation in which he lived. He reached the height of his literary creativity during the twelve years of the Nazi regime. As one of the outstanding literary figures of the inner resistance, his poetry confronts the catastrophe of the Third Reich, facing the reality of inner and external destruction without evasion or adornment. It was precisely during the years 1933 to 1945 that Bergengruen revealed his virtual "need" of the fiery furnace of war in order to crystallize his poetic creativity.[1] Out of the crisis his poetry became a "gemeinstiftende Kraft,"[2] a community-building power.

---

1. Carl Jacob Burckhardt, *Über Werner Bergengruen: Porträt und Bibliographie* (Zürich: Arche, 1968), p. 17.

2. Theoderich Kampmann, *Das verhüllte Dreigestirn: W. Bergengruen, G. von le Fort, R. Schneider* (Paderborn: Ferdinand Schöningh, 1973), p. 14.

Although hardly able to arrest the catastrophe, it could nevertheless assist people in enduring and overcoming the crisis.

Needless to say, Bergengruen felt compelled to express himself all the more urgently and forcefully concerning the "heile Welt" (the world made whole) as the danger of de-Christianization loomed larger in Europe.[3] It is here that Bergengruen's poetry reveals its particular capacity to manifest an integrated Christian ethos. Significantly enough, Bergengruen shrank from explicit consolation and preaching. According to him the poet should not proclaim or even teach, but endeavor to "make visible."[4] His poetry proves to be the expression of a world-and-life-view, transformed into literary art.

The modern war-torn world, estranged from traditional values and Christian norms, could not continue to live in a demythologized atmosphere filled with the untruths that dominated the Nazi era. In this context, Bergengruen succeeded in re-establishing humanity's divine image, the revelation of eternal ordinances, and our relationship to God and creation. He showed respect for the poetic word as a reflection of reality in the light of the Word of God. Bergengruen's literary work was largely directed to a society in crisis and to the spiritual needs of the individual. Therefore his poetry discloses an intense and urgent quality of "engagement" with his time and for his country and its people. In order to communicate in such a world, Bergengruen utilized the word of nature, employing existential proofs to reintroduce the central truths of Christianity. Creation and its God-given laws are used to reveal humanity's integral part within God's plan.

## Hypothesis: A Christian Ethos

My hypothesis is that a Christian ethos, which is a visible manifestation of union with Christ, is the specific distinction characterizing the "Christianness" of Christian poetry. This ethos is not Christian *an sich*, but it is recognizable in the pure "Being" of a poem or person. The integrality of the Christian writer will be reflected in the integrated expression of the

---

3. Gerhard Arthur Zöllner, *Bergengruens Beitrag zur Deutung und Überwindung der Krisis des modernen Menschen* (Dissertation, Universität Bloemfontein, 1962), p. 132.
4. Werner Bergengruen, *Privilegien des Dichters* (Zürich: Arche, 1962), p. 79.

writer's literary creativity. If faith is present and powerful, it will flow into the poetry and permeate it. And as Christ pervades the whole person, so too does the Christian word aim at the totality of life. This total manifestation can be detected, analyzed, and evaluated in the concrete poem. The ethos is recognizable "in that which it makes of humankind, and thus in the artist and the art."[5]

My hypothesis requires an integrated structural approach. Such an approach will open up poetry in general, and Bergengruen's poetry in particular, in its multi-dimensionality and its coherent possibilities. The intention of this article is to show that a Christian world-and-life-view, which should be a fully integrated one, as well as the literary manifestation of this perspective, will surface in the integrated, objectified ethos of a text. For the purpose of this essay, only one of Bergengruen's poems will be discussed.

A Christian ethos ought to be Christ-centered and outwardly directed. This raises a question concerning its directionality. The answer is contained in the commission given humanity after the Fall to help redeem creation and thus to serve and praise God. In this light, the Christian ethos must reveal something of the reign of God in temporal life. But in order for this ethos to reveal, people must have knowledge of God's will for life, as it is disclosed in the world and creation. Only then can people direct their faith into all facets of life.

Although I believe that structural analysis will reveal the ethos of the person and his or her artwork, such rootedness of life in a commitment to God cannot be fully determined through a theoretical approach: it is only completely knowable through faith. In the final analysis, there is a quality of faith-bound sensitivity in any interpretation of culture, an intuitive layer which cannot be proved. The final intuitive judgement, largely based on faith, is "no psychic empathy nor mysterious metaphysical function, nor itself analytic cogitation, but is . . . a cosmic, transmodal bottom layer of consciousness which, ever present, makes all human knowledge possible [and] furnishes the spark of insight to scientific experiment."[6] At the same time, such scientific experiment must be tied to law-bound analysis in order

---

5. Reinhold Schneider, *Der Bildungsauftrag des christlichen Dichters* (Zürich: Arche, 1956), p. 8.

6. Calvin Seerveld, *A Christian Critique of Art and Literature* (Hamilton, Ont.: Guardian Press, 1977), p. 68.

to be normative. The problem now is to discover how the Christian perspective has been posited in a poem.

Here a normative clue comes from the knowledge that the total person, in the unity of body and soul, is involved in any act. According to Herman Dooyeweerd,[7] all acts arise from the human soul, which in its turn is governed by a religious basic attitude. This world-and-life-view which "hearts" the person also permeates the poetic structure. In the concrete completion of the act, the person's mentality is expressed.[8] This expression reveals the disposition of the person and the societal, cultural, and spiritual climate which color the concrete act. Human beings and their actions will mirror their "I." If the ethos reflects the Christian in the whole of life, in all human and all other relationships, then the ethos can be discovered through the reverse direction. In other words, the ethos, as the central condition of the human heart in its chosen stand towards God, does not remain statically encapsulated within the "I," but must come to fruition in an outward relation to others and the temporal world. Concrete "doing" will reveal the deepest dimension of one's subjective ethos.[9] It is this premise which I should like to demonstrate in the case of Bergengruen's poetry.

## Methodology: An Integrated Approach

The isolated studies of Bergengruen's poetry, the monotonous uniformity of preconceived opinions concerning the "Christianness" of his work, and the restricted formalism of analytical approaches have proved unsuccessful in unlocking the full dimensionality and ethos of his work. Such failures point out the need for a Christian literary methodology that discloses temporal reality in all its facets. An integrated approach, based on a Christian methodology, has therefore become essential for the reappraisal of Bergengruen's poetry, and of Christian poetry in general.

The crucial point of departure lies in the Word of God, which issues into the basic modes of existence. The Christian vision is an integrated and

---

7. In André Troost, *Casuïstiek en Situasie-etiek: Een methodologische terreinverkenning* (Utrecht: Drukkerij Libertas, 1958), p. 373.

8. Troost, p. 374.

9. Hans R. Rookmaaker, *Art Needs No Justification* (Leicester: Intervarsity Press, 1978), p. 46.

comprehensive one, including this world and the next. Because human beings turn these "givens" into visible manifestations, it should be possible to forge a method that successfully penetrates temporal reality and the objectified text as a totality.

My method of modal analysis assumes the intrinsic literary value of the text. As an integrated approach, it unfolds and evaluates the coherent totality of the poetic work in its spiritual vision. This method aims to open up the possibilities of a lingually based, aesthetically envisioned, and coherently portrayed experience. Herman Dooyeweerd's Philosophy of the Cosmonomic Idea, adapted by Hans R. Rookmaaker for the visual arts and Calvin G. Seerveld for literature, forms the basis of this analysis. I am greatly indebted to Cal Seerveld, not only for his valuable insights into literature, but especially for his significant contribution to my personal enrichment and spiritual as well as academic growth. In developing my model of analysis, I adhere mainly to Seerveld's interpretation of the order of the modal scale.

For the purpose of this paper, the modalities have been merged into three main levels of analytic interpretation: technical foundation (A), aesthetic imaginativity (B), and Christian ethos (C). The A1 and A2 levels of analysis have immediately been fused into a techno-interpretative unity.

A1. This level simply defines the lingual-formative basis of mechanical technicalities (from the numerical to the lingual), without any interpretative inferences being made.

A2. This is an interpretative level of the lingual-formative analysis, opened up by the aesthetic qualifying function; it unfolds the nuances and subtleties of the lingual element.

B. The second level of analysis is a refined interpretative one that attempts to analyze the guidance of the qualifying function of the aesthetic, where the higher aspects of the artwork are unfolded and revealed in their many potentialities. The artistic quality of the literary work is to be determined in direct correlation with the manner in which the aesthetic aspect has been expressed. It is here that allusive multidimensionality of the higher modalities will emerge (if they are present).

C. According to Seerveld, the crux to be interpreted in a literary text is the spirit that moves literature. The confessional belief of the implied artist will become evident in the expression of the ethos of the artistic product.

The quality of the whole will be determined by the quality of the parts, and aesthetic unity will be secured by a coherent fittingness among the various segments.[10] These three levels of analytic interpretation will now be unfolded with respect to "Nichts gib mir, Gott" ("Nothing Give Me, God"), a piece from Bergengruen's collection of poetry titled *Die heile Welt.*

### Nichts gib mir, Gott

1. Gib unser keinem, Gott, um was wir flehen,
2. Verworrne, die getrübtes Licht beriet!
3. Nein, einen jeden lasse nur geschehen,
4. wie in der Schöpfung alles Ding geschieht,
5. der Flug, der Fall, das Blühen und Verwehen,
6. der Berge Glühn, das Wachsen im Granit,
7. der Lachse Sprung, des Efeus Überstehen,
8. des Mondes Spiegelung im blassen Teich.
9. Nichts gib mir, Gott. Nein, lass mich nur geschehen,
10. dem Stein, dem Laube, den Gestirnen gleich,
11. und gönne mir, mit ihnen einzugehen
12. und mit den Kindern in dein Himmelreich.[11]

### Nothing Give Me, God

1. Give us not, God, that which we beseech,
2. confused, whom cloudy light has counselled.
3. No, let to each single one only be done,
4. as in creation to every thing is done,
5. the flight, the fall, the blossoming and scattering,
6. the mountain glow, the growth in granite,
7. the leap of salmon, the survival of ivy,
8. the reflection of the moon in the pale pond.
9. Nothing give me, God. No, let only be done to me,
10. as to the stone, the foliage, the stars,
11. and grant me to enter, with them
12. and with the children, into your heavenly reign.

(Author's own free translation)

10. Nicholas Wolterstorff, *Art in Action: Toward a Christian Aesthetic* (Grand Rapids, Mich.: William B. Eerdmans, 1978), p. 314.
11. Werner Bergengruen, *Die heile Welt: Gedichte* (Zürich: Arche, 1962), p. 118.

# A. The Technical Foundation

The twelve iambic pentameter lines resemble a sonnet. Furthermore, like a sonnet, the poem contains an octave concerned with a single thought. After the octave follows an extension of the thought in the form of a quatrain instead of a sonnet's usual sestet. The quatrain emphasizes the thought of the first four lines. It reintroduces examples from creation, but now on an individual and personal level: "lass *mich* nur geschehen" ("let only be done to *me*"), instead of the general approach of "*einen jeden* lasse nur geschehen" ("let to *each single one* only be done"). The last two lines of the quatrain introduce a new request, that of entering heaven with the children (of God) and inanimate creation.

The stanzaic division of eight lines and four can also be subdivided into a couplet, a sestet, and a final quatrain, which could again be subdivided into two thoughts. This division agrees with the poetic distribution, indicated by the capital letters in lines 1, 3, and 9. The three sentences also portray a classification and development of the content, for instance: (1) Give. . . . (2) Let that which is done to creation, be done to us. (3) Let us be done unto as to creation, and let us enter heaven. The request thus develops from the general to the specific.

## Rhyme

The rhyme scheme of abababacacac does not strictly correlate with the design of eight and four lines; the last quatrain is already introduced by a new rhyme in line 8, suggesting a coming transition in lines 9 to 12. The rhyme "a" runs in a continuous pattern throughout the poem, giving a sense of unity to the parts, whereas rhymes "b" and "c" assist in separating the thought pattern. Yet, the fact that the third rhyme scheme "c" is introduced immediately before the final quatrain, with its new thought, serves to tie the subdivided parts together internally; thus the breakup into parts is never complete.

The rhymed words are all passive except for the first "wir flehen" ("we beseech"). Thereafter they become "geschehen, Verwehen, Überstehen, geschehen, gönne einzugehen" ("be done, scattering, surviving, be done, grant to enter") and are all either verbs or nouns derived from verbs that indicate a passification of the subject. Thus the continuous rhyme "a" also carries the importance of "lasse . . . geschehen" ("let . . . be done") in the thought process.

## Rhythm

The poet immediately begins with metrical substitution: "Gíb únser" ("Give us") followed in line 4 by: "Néin, éinen jéden" ("No, . . . to each one"), and a sixfold accumulation of rhetorical stress in line 9: "Níchts gíb mír, Gótt. Néin, láss" ("Nothing give me, God. No, let"), thus emphasizing the threefold request of the three sentences. In addition, line 11 stresses "mít ihnen" ("with them"), which also corresponds to the previously indicated subdivision of the last quatrain into two parts.

The rhythm usually follows the punctuation, except in line 1, where the rhythm only halts after "Gott"; and in lines 11 and 12, where the twice-repeated start with "and" intends emphasis but also naturally restrains the flow of the rhythm, even though an enjambment is indicated. This causes the stress to be laid on both creation (in 10 and 11) *and* the childlike believers (12) entering eternity.

## Climax

The poem begins with an imperative request: "Gib," which is suddenly negated to "Gib . . . keinem . . . um was wir flehen" ("Give . . . not . . . that which we beseech"). In line 3 the negative is repeated in "Nein, einen jeden" ("No, to each single one"). Line 1 starts positively, negating in "keinem," while line 3 starts with a negative which, in the same line, is made positive. This negative is taken up in line 9 with "Nichts gib mir, Gott" ("Nothing give me, God"). While the negatives in lines 1, 3, and 7 are general injunctions, line 9 is very personal in "mir/mich" ("me"). This subjective stress is repeated in 11: "gönne mir" ("grant me").

The climactic development of the poem can perhaps best be expressed in key words: 1. Gib. 3. Nein. 4. wie. 9. Nichts. Nein. 11/12. und. In short it reads thus: "Gib . . . Nein . . . lasse geschehen . . . (wie in der Schöpfung). Nichts gib mir Gott. Nein, lass nur geschehen, und gönne mir dein Himmelreich" ["Give . . . No . . . let be done . . . (as in creation). Nothing give me, God. No, let only be done to me, and grant me your heavenly reign"].

Thus the first and last words form the crux: "Gib . . . Himmelreich" ("Give . . . heavenly reign").

The poem starts with an imperative in line 1, thus beginning from a high point and in downward gradation; the tension decreases in "Nein" (line 3), and another decrease occurs in 9 and 10: "Nichts . . . Nein." Lines 11 and 12 show a slight upswing with the repetitive "und." The first guttural imperative is also further neutralized by the introduction of the passively stated and softer labial use in "lasse nur." The imperatives climactically decrease, but also show a paradoxical quality: 1. Gib . . . keinem. 3. Nein . . . jeden. 9. Nichts . . . gib . . . Nein. 11. und gönne . . . und . . . Himmelreich. In line 9, the paradox is eliminated and a negative conviction takes its place, and in line 11 a softened imperative replaces the previous attitudes of "Nichts . . . Nein."

## Movement

A poem "breathes" through a metrical and rhythmic movement that visually and aurally expresses a perceptible pattern. Poems are thus rhythmically involved in the emotional content of the material represented. Line 6, the center of Bergengruen's poem, seems to be a rhythmic turning point. From here, there is a downward tendency in the rhythmic movement; then a stabilizing effect, and finally an upward rhythmic pattern can be detected. While the first half of the poem rhythmically vacillates between upward and downward movement, struggling to find an equilibrium, line 6 reaches a balance, which is fairly consistently maintained, except for a definite upward swing in line 7, and a final triumph of an upward reaching towards a simplicity of faith like that of a child, a faith rewarded in heaven. (See Figure 1.)

## Composition

The poem is divided into three parts: Lines 1 and 2; 3-8; 9-12. The rhyme, too, consists of three schemes: the ""a"-rhyme throughout the poem; the "b"-rhyme in lines 2, 4, 6; and the "c"-rhyme in lines 8, 10, and 12. The imperative requests can be triadically analyzed: part i. "Gib." ii. "Nein, lasse geschehen" ("No, let be done"). iii. "Gönne . . . Himmelreich" ("Grant . . .

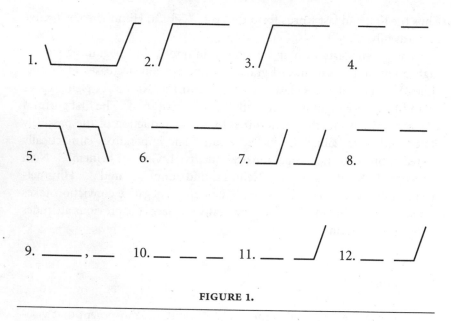

**FIGURE 1.**

heavenly reign"). The emphatic imperative of line 1, "Gib," is combined with a less emphatic "lasse nur geschehen." The second request is further reduced from "Nichts gib" ("Nothing give") to become "lass mich nur geschehen" ("let only be done to me"). The third request is one of quiet humility in "Gönne."

## Technical structure

The first line, which begins with an imperative request, appears fairly incomprehensible because of the tight concentration of apparently antithetical thoughts. The beginning of the poem suggests an improvisation of the Lord's Prayer, whereupon the speaker immediately seems to recollect himself or herself. The speaker continues from where he or she left off, but with a completely new attitude, negating the initial request. The original line, reminiscent of the Lord's Prayer ["Gib uns(er) tägliches Brot" ("Give us daily bread")] becomes "Gib unser keinem, Gott, um was wir flehen" ("Give us not, God, that which we beseech"). But God still takes a central position, situated in the middle of the line. The puzzling quality of the line is further supported by the sound effect of the repetitive w/v consonants in "wir . . . Verworrne" ("we . . . confused") as the subject of the request.

Compared with the imperative "Gib" in line 1, the "lasse nur geschehen" of line 3 is anti-climactically passive. In line 4, "wie" ("as") is the only directly expressed comparison in the poem. Lines 5-8 make use of examples from nature. While line 5 conveys the paradoxical in creation in "Flug . . . Fall . . . Blühen und Verwehen" ("flight . . . fall . . . blossoming and scattering"), line 6 presents a static image in "Berge Glühn" ("mountain glow"). In line 7, both "Lachse Sprung" ("leap of salmon") and "Wachsen im Granit" ("growth in granite") portray progress and growth; one image is taken from the animal world, and the other from the sphere of minerals.

"Efeus Überstehen" ("survival of ivy") seems to correlate with "Berge Glühn" ("mountain glow") and "Mondes Spiegelung" ("reflection of the moon") in that all three suggest a pause amid the paradox and growth as something which God causes to happen. They are creational examples, portraying quiet, unnoticeable growth (in stone), physical strain in overcoming obstacles (in salmon), and the evergreen rising quality of the ivy, uninfluenced by the changes of the seasons. Line 8 is like the final stage of the examples: from the paradoxes and overcoming of obstacles to the quiet reflection of the moon in a pond. The request of line 1 is repeated in line 9, but in a negative imperative twice repeated: "Nichts . . . Nein" ("Nothing . . . No"). Line 10 repeats the main components of creation (humankind, minerals, vegetation, and the heavenly constellation). Line 11 introduces another imperative "gönne" ("grant"), but much less emphatically then in "Gib" ("give").

The first line starts with a strong subjective request "Gib unser" ("Give us"), and then the subjective quality is repeated in "wir flehen" ("we beseech"), which highlights the subject-voice speaking. From line 5, the verbs are transformed into nouns, which nevertheless still maintain the active movement of the verb, even within the present substantive. Because the verbs change into nouns, the genitive becomes grammatically necessary in lines 6, 7, and 8. "Das Wachsen" ("the growth") has a double emphasis, not only as a noun from a verb, but also by means of the definite article. Thus the passive quality of the poem is strengthened through personification, which is nevertheless directly combined with inanimate creation: "das Wachsen im Granit" ("the growth in granite") and "des Efeus Überstehen" ("the survival of ivy").

259

# B. Aesthetic Imaginativity

In the specific belief of the "Zahlenmagie" (magic of numbers),[12] which is evident throughout the works of Bergengruen, the cipher three has particular importance. The number three envelops the entire world; it represents a whole and synthesizes antithetical tensions. It is a healing number and symbolizes the "heile Welt," an intact, whole world. With this historiographic knowledge (and even without it), the frequent triadic design in technique and content becomes revelatory. In this poem from the anthology *Die heile Welt*, God stands in the center, being placed literally in the center of lines 1 and 9, reflecting that all things are from, through, and to God (Col. 1:15-20).

The poem is divided into: humankind (lines 1-2); creation (3-8); and God (9-12). Humanity, as the lyrical subject, approaches God with a vision dimmed by sin and the Fall ["getrübtes Licht" ("cloudy light")]. Human beings, in direct relationship with God as stewards, are also related to creation and its divine laws. Creation offers us exemplary images of the obedient reflection of God's will (flight, fall, leap of salmon, survival of ivy). Thus humanity newly relates to God with a revised vision of obedient surrender (as exemplified in nature), and a new desire to be part of God-bound creation. One therefore has the impression of the parts (humankind and nature) being enclosed in a circle, indicating a process of completion: humankind relates to God and to nature and, through the exemplary character of the cosmos, reflects the image-bearing qualities of creation back to humankind and, thus newly visioned, to God, completing the circle. (See Figure 2.)

In addition, the central part of the poem (lines 3-8) represents a symbolic miniature of the cosmic whole. In line 4, the cosmos is in creational harmony, but within the whole are contained examples of the antithesis (in line 5). In lines 6 and 7 there is equilibrium ("der Berge Glühn" — "the mountain glow"), but also growth ("das Wachsen im granit" — "the growth in granite") and survival ("des Efeus Überstehen" — "the survival of ivy"), and finally all these images are a reflection of the cosmic whole and a reaction to God. (See Figure 3.)

These threefold divisions are further noticeable in the stanzaic design.

12. Max Wolfgang Weber, *Zur Lyrik Werner Bergengruens* (Winterthur: Verlag P. G. Keller, 1958). p. 15.

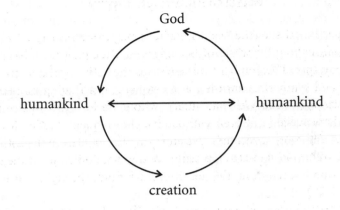

FIGURE 2.

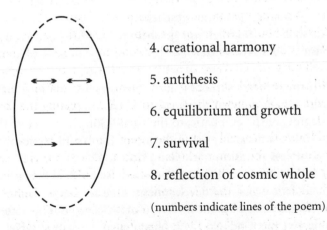

4. creational harmony

5. antithesis

6. equilibrium and growth

7. survival

8. reflection of cosmic whole

(numbers indicate lines of the poem)

FIGURE 3.

Humankind (1-4), creation (5-8), God and the reign of God (9-12). They reflect three stages of development in the petitionary quality of the poem: i. Emphatic imperative: "gib unser. . . ." This section represents humankind. ii. Negation: "Nein . . . einen jeden lasse geschehen . . . wie in der Schöpfung" ("No, let to each single one only be done, as in creation") stresses the part of creation. iii. "Lass mich nur geschehen . . . und gönne . . . Himmelreich" ("let only be done to me . . . and grant . . . heavenly reign") completes the third link in the circle which forms a whole.

The three elements of the cosmos are also emphasized: humankind, animate creatures (plants and animals), and inanimate things (minerals and heavenly bodies). There are also three levels of Being: humanity's conception (misleading because of "cloudy light"), creational obedience (lines 4-8), and the vision of the reign of God (lines 11-12). Even the rhyme falls into three schemes that suggest separate entities — humanity, creation, and the reign of God — firmly interconnected in a coherent whole. (See Figure 4.)

The rhyme thus stresses the three stages in the development of faith in this poem:

   i. Gib . . . Nein . . . lasse nur geschehen . . .
  ii. Nichts gib . . . lass mich nur geschehen . . .
 iii. Gönne . . . Himmelreich.

This maturing process simultaneously portrays a gradation of the movement from a high point in the first line ("Gib . . . Gott . . ."), in ever-lessening degrees of the emphatic, to the final "Gönne. . . ." Here the tone is different, but the insistence reminds one of Jacob's injunction: "I will not let you go unless you bless me" (Gen. 32:26).

These climaxes nevertheless reflect the existential antithesis even within the anticlimactic process of development: Line 1: "Gib ↔ keinem"; line 3: "Nein ↔ jeden"; line 9 has the inversion of "Nichts gib mir, Gott. Nein . . ." ("Nothing give me, God. No . . ."), plus a second negation which exemplifies the attainment of a certain measure of clarity. The paradoxes have been lifted in preparation for the final positive, but humble, request: "gönne" ("grant"). The sound effect of the hard guttural "g" running through the poem draws out a thought pattern: line 1: "Gib . . . Gott"; line 2: "getrübtes (Licht)"; line 3: "geschehen"; 4: "Schöpfung . . . Ding . . . geschieht"; 6: "Berge Glühn . . . Granit"; 9: "Gib . . . Gott . . . geschehen"; 10: "Gestirnen

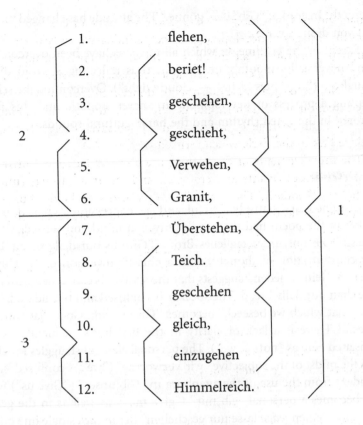

|   | Line |   |
|---|------|---|
| | 1. | flehen, |
| | 2. | beriet! |
| | 3. | geschehen, |
| 2 | 4. | geschieht, |
| | 5. | Verwehen, |
| | 6. | Granit, |
| | 7. | Überstehen, |
| | 8. | Teich. |
| | 9. | geschehen |
| | 10. | gleich, |
| 3 | 11. | einzugehen |
| | 12. | Himmelreich. |

**FIGURE 4.**

gleich"; 11: "gönne . . . einzugehen." A strong beseeching note sounds in the double use of an entreating imperative: "Gib . . . Gott."

Lines 3 and 9 with the twice repeated "lasse . . . geschehen" portray a more passive attitude, and yet the ever-present "g" sounds imply the process of growth ("Wachsen im Granit" — "the growth in granite"), of spiritual growth ("den Gestirnen gleich" — "as to . . . the stars") that is often invisible to the eye and usually not easy. After the paradoxes (flight, fall; blossoming and scattering — line 5), growth (line 6), and survival (line 7), the end proves the speaker to be more pliable and humble than was expressed in the imperative "Gib" of the beginning. Now the request is formulated differently. Instead of "Gib" it is "gönne." The attitude has changed to: grant what you desire for me.

Except in the last line, in which all tensions have been overcome, the sound never falls smoothly on the ear, thus reflecting a world divided through sin ("getrübtes Licht" — "cloudy light"). Overcoming the self and accepting a process of development are never smooth, and this fact is mirrored in the jolted rhythm and the harsh guttural sounds.

## Allusiveness

The first line is associatively forceful, and the impression is created that the speaker in the poem had the Lord's prayer in mind and started with the request: "Gib uns unser tägliches Brot" ("Give us our daily bread"). The tight concentration of thought, with a chiastic inversion of 1. "Gib . . . keinem 3. Nein . . . jeden," suggests that the speaker is concerned with much more than our daily bread. The speaker is confused and bewildered: "Give us . . . that which we beseech" becomes "Give us not, God, that which we beseech." There is a lack of clarity in the first line's "keinem . . . wir" (translated here as "not . . . we"). The personal element struggles for clarity from the midst of the subjective "wir Verworrne" ("we . . . confused"). This is evident from the use of the anaphora in "Gib unser" ("Give us") which later becomes a personal "gib mir" ("give me"), as well as in the general invocation "einen *jeden* lasse nur geschehen" (let *to each* single one only be done") and the specific "lass *mich* nur geschehen" ("let only be done *to me*").

The subjective "wir Verworrne" ("we confused") attains amplification in "die getrübtes Licht beriet" ("whom cloudy light has counselled"): the one ascribes the causality of the other. The sense of confusion and uncertainty is manifested in the accumulative effect of "Verworrne" and "getrübtes Licht." Although they express a cause and an effect, they are but modifications of a similar metaphor, namely opaqueness, a mental dullness owing to the impermeability of light.

In line 3, the imperative of line 1 is negated in an alliterative, chant-like repetition of n-sounds. The emphatic expletive "nur" ("only"), situated between the polar sound elements of the soft labial "l" and the harsh guttural "g," is significant as a synthesis of the two opposite attitudes of mind: "gib" and "lass geschehen." In this context, "nur" has the connotation of "solely, no more than just" (to allow the will of God to be done as in creation).

Line 9, reintroduces the original imperative "gib," but it is now negated by inversion, and it is personalized in "gib *mir*" and "lass *mich* nur geschehen." Thus the transition of attitude has been completed: now the "nur" ("only") strongly conveys the element of faith, because of which the subject is prepared for change.

In line 4, "wie" ("as") is the only direct conjunctive comparison, and unmistakably expresses an acknowledgement of the firm laws and ordinances in creation, which hold without the will of creation. The examples from nature reflect the ebb and flow, birth and death cycle as creational law. The verbs that become substantives in 5-8 symbolize nature's order and plan, and also enumerate Christian truths.

The manner in which God ordains the universe in its law and order is a visible reflection of divine concern for all of creation. Wishing to give a concentrated picture of the world, the speaker takes examples from the creational order, which include paradox, harmony, growth, progress, and survival. All of these are a dim reflection of the Creator (line 8).

The affirmation of creation's order is portrayed in lines 3 and 4. The speaker wishes to be a reflection of Christ and is prepared for unconditional commitment, as in the case of inanimate creation. The poem closes with a desire to enter God's reign — but it is a vision, stamped by faith, exemplified and strengthened by proofs from creation and temporal life. The dimmed light, whereby confused people have lived, is illuminated in the implication of the last line: ["und mit den Kindern" ("des Lichtes") — "and with the children" ("of light") — Eph. 5:9)]. Earthly life and earthly examples now obtain clarity and importance because of eternal life.

The key concept of the poem ("lasse nur geschehen"), which is repeated and thus emphasized, is amplified (in line 9) from a general creational obedience to a personal preparedness to submit to God's will. Line 3 strongly recalls the Lord's Prayer: "Dein Wille geschehe, wie im Himmel, so auf Erden" ("Your will be done, on earth as it is in heaven"). But it is significant that the earth is emphasized in line 4. Clearly the speaker is concerned with sanctified life in temporal reality ("wie in der Schöpfung" — "as in creation"). The speaker's perspective is an earthly and thus limited one, with creationally normative imagery (5-8). Such examples from creation call forth a renewed faith in God, who is the center of the cosmos, as God is the center of this poem. The overarching credo, which is summarized in the first and last words of the poem ("Gib . . . Himmelreich"), does not negate the present creation, but rather it unites earth and heaven, humanity and God, through the love and sovereignty of God evidenced in the order of nature. There is thus a closing of the gap between heaven and earth that was occasioned by the Fall. Creation points towards the reign of God ("Himmelreich"), and the ethos of this faith reverberates back into all creational life (line 10).

## C. The Christian Ethos

The Christian ethos of this poem is not to be determined only by the double invocation of God, in lines 1 and 9, nor only by the concluding mention of the reign of God. It emanates from the poem as a coherent whole; in the technical foundation, the semantic expressivity, the thought pattern, and the aesthetic coherence of all parts. The invocational design of the poem emphasizes our dependence on God and our responsibility to reflect God's image (line 8). The frequent stress of the symbolic number three represents the trinitarian concept of God. It is here manifested in the design, the content, and the technique.

The rhythm highlights the spiritual development of the lyrical "I" from a confused and incoherent member of a bewildered humanity (line 2), to someone able (despite "getrübtes Licht") to perceive creational symbolism and thus to attain a clarity of vision, which opens up the continued effectiveness of the hand of God in the order and glory of nature.

The rhyme scheme underlines the continuity and coherence of the universe (in the continuous "a"-rhyme), and the unity of humanity, nature, and the reign of God. The sound effects support the antithetical nature of humanity and the universe (in the "g" and "l" sounds), finally achieving a wholeness in which heaven and earth, humanity and nature (lines 11-12) are united in a new heaven and a new earth ("dein Himmelreich").

The semantic expressiveness stresses humanity's confusion (2), the image-bearing quality of the cosmos (5-8) that illuminates and renews humanity's dulled vision (2), and a final act of complete surrender (9-12).

The rhythmic movement reflects humanity's bewilderment in a frequent downward tendency (despite the iambic meter). Line 6, the center of the poem, brings about an equilibrium, which tends toward an upward rhythmic pattern in lines 7 and 12, reflecting a spiritual progress which results in the climax of lines 11 and 12:

und gönne mir, mit ihnen einzugehen
und mit den Kindern in dein Himmelreich.

The mood is one of achieved faith. In the order and ordinances of nature the lyrical "I" sees God's hand and care. The speaker comes to realize that complete surrender in faith, to God's plan and will, is necessary for God's will to be fulfilled. The speaker sees the continued effectiveness of the hand of God in the order of nature. The speaker's faith springs from life and creation (5-8). God is visible in the glow of the mountains, and an invisible God is revealed in the inner workings of granite.[13]

Although creation serves as rich symbolic proof of God's reliable ordinances, humanity on earth is still "verworren" ("confused") and thus sees and judges by "getrübtes Licht" ("cloudy light"), just as the moon is simply a reflection of the true light. In spite of eternal life, apparently far removed and distant, the continued use of earthly symbols, which reflect God's reign, helps to bridge the gap and strengthen the realization that life on earth must be lived with heavenly vision (9 and 10).

"Your will be done" is the eventual authorial stand. "Nothing give me, God," except what you will, is the confessional disclosure the speaker finally achieves. Although human beings are bewildered and see through a glass darkly (1 Cor. 13:12), often not understanding God's ways, the speaker is prepared to put oneself into God's hand unconditionally: "lass mich nur geschehen" ("let only be done to me"), whether this requires a quiet glowing, a hard process of growth like that of stone, or an "Überstehen" ("survival") — so long as one may enter the reign of God. The word "gönnen" ("grant") has the implication of grace, of a gift which cannot be gained by acts, but only asked for and believed. The scriptural truth of salvation for both cosmos and humankind is evident in lines 11 and 12. Thus, the New Testament eschatology, the renewal of the whole of creation, finds poetical expression in the Christian ethos of the lyrical "I."

## Conclusion

In this revitalization of both Christianity and the truthfulness of the word, Bergengruen's poetry unfolds a vast variety. His multifaceted gallery of

13. Weber, p. 41.

symbolical richness opens up and extends the main themes of paradox, continuance, and renewal. The challenge of faith, which knows humanity to be secure within the divine cosmic order, despite catastrophe and crisis, finds its literary expression in the unshakable affirmation of the "heile Welt." From this firm foundation of a manifested Christian perspective, Bergengruen is able to lead us, seeking order and our place in this order, to inner confrontation, and to an understanding of reality from the ever present eschaton.

## Additional References

Bergengruen, Werner. *Mündlich gesprochen.* Zürich: Arche, 1963.

Seerveld, Calvin. *Rainbows for the Fallen World.* Toronto: Tuppence Press, 1980.

# IV. RELIGIOUS ART

# The Maternal Mary:
## *Variazioni del Latte*

### BERT POLMAN

*The Roman Catholic veneration of the Virgin Mary is a splendid example of the provocative claim that Christianity is no doubt the most sophisticated symbolic construct in which femininity, to the extent that it figures therein — and it does so constantly — is confined within the limits of the Maternal.[1]*

Mary's womanhood as a female human creature is subsumed entirely by her motherhood. Mary's maternity, however, is certainly unusual: according to biblical record, she becomes pregnant by the power of the Holy Spirit without sexual intercourse,[2] and according to medieval tradition, she was

---

1. Julia Kristeva, "Stabat Mater" [orig. in French, 1977; translated by Arthur Goldhammer] in *The Female Body in Western Culture, Contemporary Perspectives,* Susan Rubin Suleiman, ed. (Cambridge, Mass.: Harvard University Press, 1985), pp. 99-100.

2. According to the apocryphal *Odes of Solomon* (second century), Mary became pregnant by drinking a cup of milk which the Holy Spirit had taken from the breasts of the Father; recounted in Marina Warner, *Alone of All Her Sex, the Myth and Cult of the Virgin Mary* (London: Pan Books, 1985), p. 195. Other Marian legends explain that Mary became pregnant by hearing the Word.

exempt from all labor pain, remained a virgin before and during childbirth (*in partu*), and thereafter as well. In 451 she was named *Aeiparthenos* (forever virgin) by the famous Council of Chalcedon. In Roman Catholic piety Mary experiences only one natural maternal process: she breastfeeds, and in that activity encapsulates all her motherhood.

Throughout Christian history, in theological works, in visual art and poetry, the *Theotokos* or "mother of God" is presented as *Maria lactans*, the mother who nourishes her child with breast milk. The imagery of the breastfeeding Madonna was borrowed by the early Christians from Egyptian depictions of the goddess Isis who suckles her infant Horus. Some scholars think that a painting of a woman nursing her child in the Roman catacombs of St. Priscilla (late second century A.D.), may well be the oldest painting of Mary nursing her child Jesus. In the fourth century, the Syrian hymnist Ephrem imagined Mary singing a lullaby:

> Shall I ope these milky fountains,
>   giving drink to thee the Fountain?
> Whence is this that I should feed thee,
>   feeding all things from thy table?[3]

That Christ on whom all creation depends should be nursed by a creature fascinated many of the early Christians. In his acrostic *Hymnus de Christo*, the Roman writer Coelius Sedulius (fifth century) pursues this biblical paradox:

> Behold! the world's creator wears
> the form and fashion of a slave;
> our very flesh our maker shares,
> his fallen creature, man, to save.
>
> He shrank not from the oxen's stall,
> he lay within the manger bed;

---

3. Excerpted from his Syriac "Nineteen Hymns on the Nativity of Christ in the Flesh," translated by W. H. Kent, in *I Sing of a Maiden*, Mary Therese, comp. (New York: Macmillan, 1947), 17; a prose translation by J. B. Morris and A. Edward Johnston of these lengthy hymns is available in *Nicene and Post-Nicene Fathers of the Christian Church*, Second Series, Vol. 13 (Grand Rapids, Mich.: Eerdmans, reprint 1979 [1890]), pp. 221-62.

and he whose bounty feedeth all
at Mary's breast himself was fed.[4]

Coptic Christians favored the *Maria lactans* imagery as evidenced, among others, in the paintings at Bawit, the manuscripts from Fayum, and frontispieces in other codices.[5] From Egypt this theme developed into "the nursing Virgin" or *Galaktotrophousa* iconography which spread selectively throughout the Byzantine world of the East into the Medieval cathedrals,[6] and eventually came to its greatest flowering in the West during the Renaissance. Influenced by Franciscan ideas of humility, the numerous *Maria del latte* paintings from fourteenth century Florence and Siena were the models that inspired many later European artists to continue to express the *Maria lactans* theme.[7]

The nursing Madonna connotes a range of meanings.[8] At a most basic level, breastfeeding is a powerful symbol of the gift of life, an empowering experience of nourishment that is essential for human life. That notion of life-giving is captured in the many paintings of the natural settings in which Mary nurses her child: the *Holy Family* miniature in the *Paris Hours of Rene of Anjou* (ca. 1415) with the midwife who prepares the bath water; the intimacy portrayed in Morales' *Virgin and Child* (sixteenth century) in which the child feels for the warmth of Mary's breast (Figure 1); or the

4. From his "A solis ortus cardine," translated by John Ellerton, in *Hymn Book* (Toronto: Anglican Church & United Church, 1971), no. 403:2,5.

5. See Alexander Badawy, *Coptic Art and Archeology, the Art of the Christian Egyptians from the Late Antique to the Middle Ages* (Cambridge, Mass.: MIT Press, 1978), pp. 227, 318.

6. See Penny Schine Gold's excellent treatment of Marian iconography in French sculpture of the twelfth and thirteenth centuries in her *The Lady & The Virgin* (Chicago: University of Chicago Press, 1985), pp. 43-75.

7. See Millard Meiss, *Painting in Florence and Siena After the Black Death* (New York: Harper Torch Books, 1964), p. 132ff.; and his "The Madonna of Humility" in *The Art Bulletin,* 18 (December 1936), pp. 435-64.

8. Margaret R. Miles discusses various meanings of the nursing Madonna in one historical context in her "The Virgin's One Bare Breast: Female Nudity and Religious Meaning in Tuscan Early Renaissance Culture" in *The Female Body in Western Culture, Contemporary Perspectives,* Susan Rubin Suleiman, ed. (Cambridge, Mass.: Harvard University Press, 1985), pp. 193-208; reprinted in *The Expanding Discourse, Feminism and Art History,* Norma Broude & Mary D. Garrard, eds. (New York: Harper Collins, 1992), pp. 27-37. See also Miles's *Image as Insight, Visual Understanding in Western Christianity and Secular Culture* (Boston: Beacon Press, 1985), esp. pp. 63-93.

FIGURE 1. Luis de Morales, *Virgin and Child*. Ca. 1570.
Reproduced by permission of the Prado Museum, Madrid.

charming domesticity in Rembrandt's *Holy Family* (ca. 1634) where Joseph admires Mary and her child. "No more bare flesh than was absolutely necessary surrounded this single nursing breast," says Ann Hollander, "the act was solemn and not sensuous. . . ."[9]

9. Anne Hollander, *Seeing Through Clothes* (New York: Viking Press, 1978), pp. 187.

Noting the change from earlier depictions of Mary who nurses as the queen of heaven to the Renaissance paintings in which the Virgin often nurses while seated on the ground, art historians have emphasized the humility of Mary in these later paintings.[10] While confirming that shift towards humility, I would also want to point out that even a representation of the humbly lactating Virgin is still an awesomely powerful image of a woman, an image of nourishing life that is shared with all other nursing mothers and which — notwithstanding that its power appears to be both craved and feared by many men — is an example of the biblical paradox whereby Mary's humility exhibits great power.

On a theological level, the breastfeeding of the infant Christ in these art works is initially a symbol of the full humanity of Jesus.[11] Incarnate in the "human likeness," Christ is completely human — but without sin, as we confess in the creeds of Christendom — and as a creature Jesus needed nourishment like all other creatures. The Jesus-child who glances at us while nursing not only narrows the distance between image and viewer in the *Litta Madonna* by Leonardo (ca. 1491) but also appears to say to us, "I live with food like you — would you doubt my humanity?"[12]

In meditating on the Virgin Mary who nurses her child Jesus, medieval mystics saw not only an historical event in the incarnation of Christ but also an eternal mystery whereby the Christian soul — and indeed the entire Christian community — is nourished by divine grace, of which Mary's milk is but the metaphor. Thus the Madonna is pictured by Rogier van der Weyden in his *Virgin and Child with Four Saints* (ca. 1450) nursing her child in the presence of various biblical saints who represent God's people (Figure 2); or she is portrayed nursing souls out of purgatory, as in *Virgin and Child with Souls in Purgatory* by Pedro Machuca (1517).

---

10. See Georgina G. King, "The Virgin of Humility" in *The Art Bulletin,* 17 (December 1935): 474-91; Millard Meiss, "The Madonna of Humility" in *The Art Bulletin,* 18 (December 1936): 435-64; and Victor Lasareff, "Studies in the Iconography of the Virgin" in *The Art Bulletin,* 20 (March 1938): 26-65.

11. The same emphasis on the humanity of Christ is also conveyed and reinforced through the depiction of the nude Christ-child's genitals. See Leo Steinberg's controversial *The Sexuality of Christ in Renaissance Art and in Modern Oblivion* (New York: Pantheon, 1984).

12. Steinberg, *The Sexuality of Christ,* p. 128. Jesus eating food is also a common event in the post-resurrection stories in the gospels as proof of the reality of the aliveness of Christ.

FIGURE 2. Rogier van der Weyden, *Virgin and Child with Four Saints.*
Ca. 1450. Photo © Ursula Edelmann. Reproduced by permission of the
Städelsche Kunstinstitut, Frankfurt am Main.

Mary's nursing is sometimes interpreted as an explicitly eucharistic symbol. As E. James Mundy has pointed out,

   . . . van Eyck's *Lucca Madonna* presents Mary as the altar on which Christ sits. Vessels to the right of the painting reinforce the suggestion that the

FIGURE 3. Robert Campin, *Madonna and Child before a Firescreen*. Ca. 1430.
Reproduced by courtesy of the Trustees, The National Gallery, London.

artist is depicting the Mass. Both baby and breast are the eucharist, presented to us. The two foods are assimilated. We the viewers are offered the
bread and wine that are God. . . . [In] Robert Campin's *Madonna and
Child before a Firescreen* [Figure 3] . . . Mary not only offers her breast;
she also presents her baby, as if he were bread fresh from the oven.[13]

13. Caroline Walker Bynum, *Fragmentation and Redemption, Essays on Gender and
the Human Body in Medieval Religion* (New York: Zone Books, 1991), p. 103.

In his *Rest on the Flight into Egypt,* Gerard David shows Mary nursing her Christ child in a grape arbor, which imagery relates to the eucharist[14] and to the biblical Song of Songs — a great source for allegorical interpretations in sermons, paintings, and lyrics, in which Mary becomes the woman of the Song.[15]

Such artistic works expressed the Roman Catholic dogma that grace came to humankind by way of Mary, "the Mediatrix of all graces," with a nursing metaphor that came from a long tradition of allegory. In the early eighth century, the Venerable Bede had already used this theological image when he addressed the Virgin:

> Thou whose blessed breasts,
> filled with a gift from on high,
> fed for all lands
> the unique glory of earth and heaven.[16]

In their paintings of *Maria lactans,* artists depict an exposed breast, of course. Partial nudity in paintings of biblical subjects — even more so than complete nudity — always creates a tension between erotic attraction and spiritual meaning, and this is certainly true of the nursing Madonna. The basic eroticism of many of these paintings is, as Anne Hollander says, "reassuringly transcended by the everyday sanctity of mother's milk. Breasts bring pleasure to everyone, and sight of them brings its own visual joy besides; and so images of breasts are always sure conveyers of a complex delight."[17] Erotic delight is a not uncommon experience of many mothers who nurse their children; in fact, some mothers report experiencing strong sexual arousal while suckling their babies.[18] It is striking that the Christian

---

14. E. James Mundy, "Gerard David's *Rest on the Flight into Egypt:* Further Additions to Grape Symbolism" in *Simiolus: Netherlands Quarterly for the History of Art,* 12 (1981-82): 211-22.

15. See Ann W. Astell, *The Song of Songs in the Middle Ages* (Ithaca, New York: Cornell University Press, 1990) pp. 42-72; and Maurice Vloberg, "The Iconography of the Immaculate Conception" in *The Dogma of the Immaculate Conception, History and Significance,* Edward Dennis O'Connor, ed. (Notre Dame: University of Notre Dame Press, 1958), pp. 463-512.

16. From Bede's "Adesto, Christo, vocibus," in *The Penguin Book of Latin Verse,* Frederick Brittain, translator and editor (London: Penguin, 1962), pp. 130-31.

17. Anne Hollander, *Seeing Through Clothes,* p. 186.

18. Marvin S. Eiger and Sally Wendkos Olds, *The Complete Book of Breastfeeding,* rev. ed. (New York: Workman Publishing, 1987) p. 194.

278

tradition is ecumenically united in permitting Mary to experience that sensuous delight of nursing, in view of the strong Roman Catholic position that holds Mary to be without sexual experience of any kind.

However, some artists unsettle the delicate balance between the sensual and the devotional in the "complex delight" of a nursing Madonna by emphasizing unduly the exposed breast. Various sixteenth-century paintings remind us of a hymn by Venantius Fortunatus (sixth century) in whose English translation it is literally Mary's "maiden breast [which is] by fullest heavenly grace possessed."[19] Sometimes the child's hands draw attention to Mary's breast, as in a *Maria Lactans* by Joos van Cleve (early sixteenth century), or sometimes it is Mary's own gesture that heightens the eroticism, as in the famous *Madonna and Child before a Firescreen* (Figure 3) by the Master of Flémalle (ca. 1425).

The most poignant example of this emphasis on the exposed breast is the *Melun Madonna* by Jean Fouquet (ca. 1450) for which the model was said to be Agnes Sorel, a mistress of King Charles VII (Figure 4). This piece of Renaissance erotica shocked viewers in its own time for the bold manner in which the artist painted the woman's upper body. This Madonna, as Hollander has noted, "contrary to pictorial custom, wears a very low decolletage and fashionable tight bodice, ostentatiously unlaced to liberate a most attractive large white breast. This breast bursts out of its confinement while the other one, for once equally visible under the dress, submits to its pressure with equally sexy effect."[20] Johann Huizinga remarks on this painting's "air of decadent impiety" and its "flavour of blasphemous boldness,"[21] while Francis Schaeffer refers to it as an early example of the autonomy of humanism which resulted in a loss of spiritual meaning.[22]

However, Mary nourishes not only her child Jesus, she is also shown nursing adults, an image that reminds us of the closing scene in Steinbeck's *The Grapes of Wrath* (1940) in which Rose of Sharon (a biblical name also commonly applied to the Virgin, as in the Litany of Loreto) suckles a poor

---

19. From his "Quem terra, pontus, aethera," translated by John Mason Neale; quoted in Charles Hartman, *The Life of Mary, Mother of Jesus* (New York: Guild Press, 1963), p. 8.

20. Hollander, *Seeing Through Clothes,* pp. 187-88.

21. Johann Huizinga, *The Waning of the Middle Ages* (Garden City, N.Y.: Doubleday Anchor Books, 1954 [1949]), p. 159.

22. Francis A. Schaeffer, *How Should We Then Live?* (Old Tappan, N.J.: Fleming H. Revell, 1976), pp. 68-71.

FIGURE 4.  Jean Fouquet, *Melun Madonna*. Ca. 1450.
Reproduced by permission of the Koninklijk Museum voor Schone Kunsten, Antwerp.

man. Medieval poets extolled incidents in which the Virgin nurses an anonymous monk:

> With much sweetness and much delight,
> from her sweet bosom she drew forth her breast,
> that is so sweet, so soft, so beautiful,

and placed it in his mouth,
gently touched him all about,
and sprinkled him with her sweet milk.[23]

The great theologian and founder of the Cistercian Order, Bernard of Clairvaux, was so devoted to Mary and to using the nursing imagery in his sermons on the Song of Songs that a legend developed later in which Bernard receives a vision of the Virgin who presses her breasts and lets drops of milk fall onto his lips. This legend demonstrates vividly the intimacy in which Medieval mysticism excelled. Though similar stories were told about some other Medieval saints, it was the Bernard legend that inspired *Maria allatta San Bernardo* paintings throughout the Renaissance and into the Baroque eras by artists such as Lippi, Fries, Poccetti, Murillo, Balestra, and Cano (Figure 5). The point of these paintings is that Mary encourages greater piety in her devotees with further nourishment of grace.

The symbolism of breastfeeding an adult, however, is complex: in the Medieval use of allegory, such paintings were intended to be devotional and didactic, but their erotic significance should not be ignored. It is probably helpful to note Bynum's warning in this regard:

> Twentieth-century readers and viewers tend to eroticize the body and to define themselves by the nature of their sexuality. But did medieval viewers? . . . I think we should be cautious about assuming that they did. . . . There is reason to think that medieval viewers saw bared breasts (at least in painting and sculpture) not primarily as sexual but as the food with which they were iconographically associated.[24]

But I still think it is appropriate to wonder what went through the minds of supposedly celibate monks (or any other persons) — in *any* historical era — as they meditated on the nursing Madonna and saw this theme in paintings, statues, stained glass, and their devotional and theological books. In the late nineteenth century, when western culture had eroticized the breast far beyond its intrinsic nature, the novelist Zola does not leave us wondering very long: he artfully depicts one priest's devotion to Mary through much sexual imagery and specifically through his attraction to her

---

23. From Gautier de Coincy's *Miracles de la Nostre Dame* (1223), quoted in Warner, *Alone of All Her Sex*, p. 199.
24. Caroline Walker Bynum, *Fragmentation and Redemption*, pp. 85-86.

breasts: ". . . he lived in Mary's beauty, was supported, hidden, lost without fear, left to drink milk of infinite love which fell drop by drop from the virgin breast."[25]

The lactating Virgin was so strongly promoted in both theology and art that it should not surprise us that many vials of Mary's presumed breast milk were venerated throughout the Roman Church, especially in the fourteenth and fifteenth centuries. Pilgrims flocked to shrines in Chartres, Paris, Rome, Venice, and Walsingham to pray to Mary for divine grace and healing in the presence of such relics. Popular piety nourished devotion to her breast milk as an object even apart from any of its intended metaphysical meaning. This abuse led John Calvin to remark caustically about the relics of Mary's milk,

> . . . there is no town, however small, no monastery or nunnery, however insignificant, which does not possess it, some in less, and others in greater quantities. . . . But had the breasts of the most holy Virgin yielded a more copious supply than is given by a cow, or had she continued to nurse during her whole lifetime, she scarcely could have furnished the quantity which is exhibited.[26]

The visual portrayal of the nursing Madonna declined noticeably after the Council of Trent. The fervor of the Counter-Reformation led to severe limitations on nudity in church art; it became indecorous for the Virgin to bare her breast to nurse, especially as the breast had come to signify more *eros* than nourishment. This restriction on breastfeeding still haunts western culture: men who bear arms to kill in public are venerated as heroes, but women who bare breasts to nurse in public get arrested![27] Though there were many European *Maria lactans* paintings available to Cynthia Pearl Maus, the compiler of a Marian anthology, *The World's Great Madonnas*, she chose not to include any of the great western works on this theme but only a few modern examples from the Third World, e.g., from India and

25. Emile Zola, *The Sin of Father Mouret*, translated by Sandy Petrey (Englewood Cliffs, N.J.: Prentice-Hall, 1969 [1875]), p. 73.

26. From John Calvin's satire, "An Inventory of Relics," in his *Tracts and Treatises on the Reformation of the Church*, translated by Henry Beveridge (Grand Rapids, Mich.: Eerdmans, 1958 [1544]), Volume I, p. 317.

27. Andrew Greeley suggests in a slightly different context, "The womanly breast is a masterpiece of design for which puritans will never forgive God . . . ," in his *God in Popular Culture* (Chicago: Thomas More Press, 1988), p. 165.

FIGURE 5.  Alonso Cano, *The Vision of Saint Bernard.* Ca. 1658/1660.
Reproduced by permission of the Prado Museum, Madrid.

Africa.[28] One wonders what paradigms of racism or other questionable attitudes caused this surprising choice. Is breastfeeding too sensitive a topic for the contemporary "Old World" mindset, but acceptable in the "develop-

28. Cynthia Pearl Maus, comp., *The World's Great Madonnas* (New York: Harper & Brothers, 1947), pp. 345, 470.

ing" cultures who are presumably not adverse to the empowering symbol of a strong, sensuous woman who offers life-giving nourishment?

Patriarchal fears of powerful nursing women notwithstanding, the image of the breastfeeding Virgin Mary continues to inspire human culture as a symbol of maternal nourishment, divine grace, and erotic pleasure, if not also of a humility which is sometimes wrongly focussed only on women. Today there is still a famous Marian shrine in St. Augustine, Florida, which honors *Nuestra Senora de la Leche y Buen Parto* (Our Lady of Happy Delivery and Plentiful Milk),[29] where thousands of women come each year to pray for the blessings of motherhood through Mary's intervention. And we occasionally find a modern artist who still portrays a Madonna as a powerful and empowering symbol of life-sustaining nourishment and sexual delight. Henry Moore's fascination with the figure of a woman and child in many of his more abstract sculptures may be read as a secular manifestation of the Madonna tradition, while the x-ray vision of the Canadian native artist Norval Morrisseaux in his *Virgin Mary with Jesus and John* (1973) exalts the God-Mother as a contemporary earth-mother.[30]

29. This shrine is the inspiration for the name of the international organization that promotes breastfeeding, La Leche League.

30. This essay is a revised, enlarged version of Part II of an illustrated lecture given at Redeemer College, on the occasion of Polman's inauguration as a full professor (October 16, 1992). That original lecture, "Mary: From Madonna to Magnificat, A Symphony in Four Movements," is available in print-form (but unfortunately without the illustrations) from the Redeemer College Bookstore.

# Prayers Made with Song:
# The Genevan Psalter, 1562-1994

## BARBARA JO DOUGLAS

When the Reformed Church in America celebrated its 350th anniversary, our church choir decided to mark the occasion by singing a psalm in Dutch. Most of us learned it laboriously by rote, knowing no Dutch, and we sang it, fairly slowly as I recall, to a tune as new to me as the sounds of the words. I found it lovely, though I wished it to go faster. The tune was from the Genevan Psalter.

Later, at the University of Iowa, I joined a Christian Reformed congregation. Worshipping there increased my familiarity with Genevan tunes — twenty-seven in all in the 1957 *Psalter Hymnal*.[1] They were staid and slow, with no rhythm to speak of.

My next contact with the Genevan tunes came when I moved to Toronto to study at the Institute for Christian Studies. There, in weekly chapel services, we sometimes sang Genevan tunes — but what a difference! Now they had new translations of the psalms or totally new words in modern language (usually by Calvin Seerveld), and when we sang them fairly fast, they revealed lively, almost jazzy rhythms. In *this* guise I found myself humming the Genevan tunes in preference to all the other, much newer music we sang. These tunes, these rhythms, caught the imagination.

---

1. *Psalter Hymnal* (Grand Rapids, Mich.: Board of Publications of the Christian Reformed Church, 1957, 1976). Psalm 42 with its altered Genevan tune can be found at number 74.

They illuminated the texts they matched. Some expressed a joy so great as to call for dancing; some a yearning for God and God's reign; and some a mourning, too often missing in contemporary Christian music, for all that is wrong and fallen in our world.

My excitement over these "new" hymns led to curiosity. I vaguely knew that they came from Calvin's Geneva, but I wanted to know why the psalms were set in just this way to just these tunes. Looking at the history of the Psalter has also led me to reflect on worship now, and the place that collection of tunes can have in it. This essay provides a brief history of the Genevan Psalter and a meditation on the relationship of music and liturgy.

## The History of the Psalter

### Liturgical Music before the Reformation

Before the Reformation, liturgical music had become a highly developed art which largely excluded the participation of the laity. Music written for the choirs of larger churches and cathedrals[2] reached amazing heights of exquisite artistry — or of tasteless excess, depending on the commentator. Andrew Wilson-Dickson sums up this ambivalence: "Music written for the well-endowed Roman monasteries and cathedral churches around this time is undoubtedly a high point in the history of Christian music. It deserves some attention not just because musicians today respect it so deeply but because . . . it was the very opposite of what Catholic reformers believed Christian music should be."[3]

---

2. The cathedral at Geneva, for instance, had a music master, eight choir clerks and six "enfants de choeur" — presumably boys — in the late fifteenth century. See Claude Tappolet, "Fragments d'une historie de la musique à Genève," *Revue Musicale de Suisse* 93 (1953): 15-16.

3. Andrew Wilson-Dickson, *The Story of Christian Music* (Oxford: Lion, 1992), p. 72. Polyphonic settings of the mass based throughout on a single, secular tune ("L'homme armé" was popular, with more than two dozen settings) and contrapuntal music that obscured the words came in for particular criticism. In 1549, Bishop Bernadino Cirillo wrote "They say, 'Oh, what a fine Mass was sung in chapel!' And what is it, if you please? It is L'Homme Armé, or Hercules Dux Ferrariae, or Philomena. What the devil has the Mass to do with the armed man, or with Philomena, or with the Duke of Ferrara? . . . [Composers] have put all their industry and effort into the writing of imitative passages, so that while one says 'Sanctus,' another says 'Sabaoth,' [and] still

Even outside the cathedrals "plainchant" had come to require trained singers,[4] and the Latin texts were unintelligible to most of the population.[5] In a formal festival mass of the fifteenth and early sixteenth centuries, the music obscured the words; but the music was glorious, and it combined with architecture, vestments, incense, and movement to form a total work of art such as Wagner only dreamed of. Imagine sight and sound and smell and (for the celebrant of the mass) taste and touch all caught up in a splendor dedicated to the glory of God. For the few faithful who understood what was going on, this must have been a wonderful experience of worship. Aesthetic contemplation can certainly be a way to come to prayer: for one who prays already, the experience of this richness of praise can serve to deepen prayer, and also to deepen the experience of God.

I say it can; there is no guarantee that aesthetic experience will enhance spiritual experience and knowledge. In the late medieval setting, there was no teaching except that done by the art itself, and the Reformers were quite right to insist that knowledge of Scripture and doctrine must be taught by words, as clearly as possible. While that does not mean that the artistic pre-Reformation liturgy taught nothing,[6] Protestant and Catholic reformers alike believed that church music needed to be reformed. They

---

another says 'Gloria tua,' with howling, bellowing and stammering" (quoted in Wilson-Dickson, p. 73).

4. "Both the unisonal plainsong and the contrapuntal figured-song were intended for priestly ministrants or trained choristers only." Waldo S. Pratt, *The Music of the French Psalter 1562* (New York: Columbia University Press, 1939, 1962), p. 33.

5. The leaders of the Reformation were highly educated men and fluent in Latin (Calvin's most serious work was written in Latin first, and later translated). They could understand the liturgy themselves. But they wanted everyone to understand. In 1536 Calvin wrote: "public prayers must be couched not in Greek among the Latins, nor in Latin among the French or English (as has heretofore been the custom) but in the language of the people, which can be generally understood by the whole assembly. For this ought to be done for the edification of the whole church, which receives no benefit whatever from a sound not understood." *Institution of the Christian Religion,* trans. and annotated by Ford Lewis Battles (Atlanta: John Knox Press, 1975), p. 101, cited on p. 27 in C. Garside, "The Origins of Calvin's Theology of Music, 1536-1543," in *Transactions of the American Philosophical Society,* vol. 69, pt. 4, 1979, pp. 1-36.

6. "Art is not vague because it is not analytically precise, and it is not confused because it is not articulated clearly in some language with dictionary references. Art is also neither ineffable nor mysterious nor more subjective a knowledge than analytic philosophical statements or straightforward English sentences about the weather." Calvin Seerveld, *Rainbows for the Fallen World* (Toronto: Tuppence Press, 1980), p. 79.

differed greatly, however, about the shape they thought reform should take. The Catholic Counter-Reformation asked only that the music be simpler and the words intelligible; the language was still to be Latin and the music the sole domain of the choir.[7] The Counter-Reformation continued to treat music as a decoration of the liturgy.

The Protestants, by contrast, wanted all the people to understand everything that happened in the worship service and to participate as fully as possible. This desire was worked out differently by various leaders. Luther sought to include as much of the Mass as could be brought in line with Reformation ideals, including some chanting at the altar and the option of using some Latin, where it was not a bar to understanding. He allowed choirs but encouraged people to sing, and he collected a large number of hymns (called "chorales") for that purpose. For the most part, Luther and his followers wedded newly written texts to familiar tunes. Luther (and later Calvin) made use of the fact that hymn singing had been a part of popular piety since the late Middle Ages,[8] and that the singing of psalms to common tunes had been a part of the Reformation from very early on.[9] Luther regarded congregational

7. Among the pronouncements of the Council of Trent was the following: "In the case of those Masses which are celebrated with singing and with organ, let nothing profane be intermingled, but only hymns and divine praises. The whole plan of singing . . . should be constituted not to give empty pleasure to the ear but in such a way that the words may be clearly understood by all . . . and thus the hearts of the listeners may be drawn to the desire of heavenly harmonies, in the contemplation of the joy of the blessed." Quoted by Wilson-Dickson, p. 74, from R. F. Hayburn, *Papal Legislation on Sacred Music* (Collegeville, Minn., 1979), pp. 25-31. Clearly the cardinals at Trent gave no serious consideration to the fact that not all understood enough Latin to follow the liturgy even when the words were plainly audible!

8. According to Erik Routley, *Hymns and Human Life* (London: John Murray, 1952), p. 31, hymn singing was a feature especially of ecstatic movements like that of the flagellants. Pratt adds: "The congregational singing of versified texts to appropriate melodies . . . had at times been a feature of Roman practice, but had become extremely rare, though decidedly common in secular life" (p. 5).

9. "The urge to sing psalms using known tunes seems to have been in the air on the eve of the Reformation." Walter Blankenburg, "Church Music in Reformed Europe," in Friedrich Blume, *Protestant Church Music: A History* (London: V. Gollancz, 1975), pp. 509-607; the quote is from p. 521. Blankenburg mentions evidence of sacred songs sung by Protestants at Meaux in 1524-25, and a collection including psalms published at Neuchatel in 1533. Garside quotes from a letter dated December 1525 from a visitor to Meaux to friends that "the singing of women together with the men was so wonderful that it was a delight to hear" (p. 13).

singing as a form of preaching. To that end he crammed great chunks of doctrine into the chorales.[10]

The English Reformation changed the language of worship from Latin to English and made some effort to encourage the laity to sing simplified chants. It proved possible to marry the vernacular to polyphony; the period following the Reformation is known as the golden age of English liturgical music. Although the most elaborate music was confined to the cathedrals and the chapels Royal, even ordinary parish churches tended more and more to exclude congregational participation and to return psalmody to the choirs, who chanted them in English. At no place in the liturgy were congregations explicitly encouraged to sing, and the matter was left up to the clergy of the individual parish.[11]

Zwingli represents the opposite extreme to Luther: he abolished music from services altogether.[12] Calvin seems to have been initially of Zwingli's mind, but through the influence of Bucer and from pastoral experience he came to view congregational singing as an invaluable aid to public prayer.[13]

## Calvin's Theology of Music

The Genevan Psalter sprang from Calvin's pastoral theology of music, developed between 1536 and 1543. To his thinking about music Calvin brought not only the medieval and classical theories about music that formed a normal part of Renaissance education but also an awareness of early Lutheran and Reformed efforts at congregational singing.[14] He turned

10. Luther wrote: "By the Grace of God I have brought about such a change that nowadays a girl or boy of fifteen knows more about Christian doctrine than all the theologians of the great universities used to know in the old days." Cited in Ivor H. Jones, *Music: A Joy For Ever* (London: Epworth Press, 1989), p. 79. On Luther's theology of music, see Jones, chapter 3.

11. In Scotland there was great enthusiasm for the Genevan model, as explored below, but due to the limitations of the meter of the psalm translations, almost none of the Genevan tunes were adopted.

12. Zwingli himself was an accomplished musician. Like many another musician, he may have felt that art music distracted from worship, and that anything less than art music, such as the singing of untrained masses, was intolerable and unworthy of God. This, however, is speculation born of the observation that for many musicians music is so engrossing in its own right that sincere worship is better accomplished in silence.

13. On the changes in Calvin's thinking, see Garside.

14. Garside, p. 9.

his attention to music when he had charge of his first congregation. Whereas in earlier writing he had noted that music is unnecessary to private prayer, in the *Articles* of 1537 he listed music as one of the three ingredients *necessary* to the right ordering of congregational life and public worship.

All of Calvin's considerations on music occur where he is discussing prayer. Congregational singing is, for him, congregational prayer. Calvin later saw private singing as prayer also; therefore he desired that all secular songs should be replaced by sung psalms, so that the people might sing continually and thus fulfill Paul's injunction to pray without ceasing.[15]

Calvin believed (following Plato and Augustine) that "song has great force and vigour to arouse and inflame [human] hearts" to either good or bad effect.[16] Music therefore needs to be moderated by a text, to which it must be subservient. Moreover, the text must be scriptural, since that is the only text good enough for the praise of God and wholly without taint of evil. Calvin wrote that what is joined to music "pierces the heart that much more strongly and enters into it; just as through a funnel wine is poured into a container, so also venom and corruption are distilled to the depth of the heart by the melody"[17] if the text is unholy. Hence, when the people's prayers are "so cold that we should be greatly ashamed and confused,"[18] they must sing the psalms, that they might be encouraged through them to pray more ardently. They must sing them in the vernacular, that they might pray with understanding.[19] And the music for the psalms must be appropriate to prayer: "There must always be concern that the song be neither light nor frivolous, but have gravity [*pois*] and majesty [*majesté*], as Saint Augustine says."[20] These songs must be sung

15. See Garside, pp. 24-25.

16. Calvin, *Epistle to the Reader*, 1542, trans. Garside, p. 32.

17. Calvin, *Epistle to the Reader*, 1542, trans. Garside, p. 32.

18. Calvin, *Articles*, 1537, trans. Garside, p. 10.

19. "The psalms can stimulate us to raise our hearts to God and arouse us to an ardor in invoking as well as in exalting with praises the glory of [God's] name. Moreover, by this one will recognize of what advantage and consolation the pope and his creatures have deprived the church, for he has distorted the psalms, which should be true spiritual songs, into a murmuring among themselves without any understanding." Calvin, *Articles*, trans. Garside, p. 10.

20. Calvin, *Epistle to the Reader*, 1542, trans. Garside, p. 18. Garside notes that the source of the reference to Augustine remains untraced, and he suggests that here Calvin's originality begins to assert itself, as this concern with musical style is not to be found in Bucer either. The concern is not out of line with that of Augustine and indeed of Plato, but it is not precisely taken from either.

One wonders why, with his concern for a specifically sacred style and for reclaiming

from the heart, with intelligence, and from memory.[21] In other words, musical prayer must be sincere, understood by the singer, and so familiar that the singer is free from distractions to concentrate on praying.

There are a few points here that the modern worshipper might wish to contest or to state differently. The first is that the music of worship should completely replace the music of everyday life. One could argue instead that, while prayer may be appropriate at all times, formal public prayers are not, and indeed these would constitute such a disruption as to make impossible the proper carrying out of daily tasks, which surely is also a Christian duty. Likewise, work and play have their own worth and their own music, music which should be conformed to the Gospel, perhaps, but not necessarily to the dictates of public worship.

Further, Calvin, like Plato and many others, held what I would call a "magical" understanding of music's effect — that music invariably has the same or a similar emotional and moral effect on everybody. Crudely put, marches make everybody want to go to war. Or, to bring the idea up to date, rock music saps moral fiber. This view treats music purely as a cause, like a drug to be administered, and is too simple an understanding of music's undeniable power and significance. This is not the place for a full exploration of music's capacity for meaning, expression, communication, and possible manipulation; but one's response to music depends on association and the desire to understand and respond. Unfamiliar music will

---

the practice of the early church, Calvin did not return to a simplified form of chanting the psalms by the congregation in prose translation, as Merbecke did in England. Perhaps the tradition of simple chants and congregational chanting was completely forgotten on the continent; or perhaps plainchant was too firmly wedded to Latin in his and other's minds. Blankenburg comments: "That, contrary to the Anglican liturgy, no form was ever considered other than versified psalms and canticles, all in the vernacular, is undoubtedly due to an accident of history: Calvin had already become acquainted with the singing of rhyming psalms, probably in France but mainly in Basel and Strasbourg, before he began his reformative work" (p. 517).

21. Calvin, *Epistle*, 1543: "As for the rest, it is necessary for us to remember what Saint Paul says, that spiritual songs can be sung truly only from the heart. Now the heart requires intelligence, and in that (says Saint Augustine) lies the difference between the singing of men and that of the birds. For a linnet, a nightingale, a parrot may sing well, but it will be without understanding. Now the peculiar gift of man is to sing knowing what he is saying. After the intelligence must follow the heart and the affection which is impossible unless we have the hymn imprinted on our memory in order never to cease from singing." Trans. Garside, p. 33.

elicit an inappropriate response, if any, and music cannot make you feel what you do not already feel at least a little. Music *can* be used to manipulate where the associations and feelings of a group are already appropriate, however, and to that extent Calvin's caution was justified.[22] And he under-stood rightly that liturgical music without sincere prayer in the heart is empty noise.

Within worship itself, Calvin's requirement that music have gravity *(pois or poids)* and majesty *(majesté or maiesté)* may alarm today's readers. We are more likely to demand that worship be lively. But Calvin's desire for music to have weight and majesty did not indicate that he wanted music to be dull: Calvin approved the music of the Genevan Psalter, which, while never "frivolous," is often lively. What he opposed was the artistic excess of the Roman church and the simple adoption of rowdy popular tunes. Neither was, in his view, appropriate to worship. Garside suggests that the text rather than tempo was to moderate the music, and that, although Calvin "does not explain further what he intends by the words *poids* and *maiesté*, . . . he has in mind some kind of ecclesiastical music the *unique* character of which is underscored in what follows: 'And thus there is a great difference between the music which one makes to entertain [people] at table and in their homes, and the psalms which are sung in the Church in the presence of God and [God's] angels.'"[23]

Singing psalms in meter ensured for Calvin the participation of all worshippers in public prayer without admitting the non-Scriptural texts allowed by Luther. Though Calvin does not mention it, psalm singing also provided a way to teach Scripture to the illiterate: since most psalms were assigned a proper tune,[24] the music could aid in the memorization and recall of the psalms.

## *Origins of the Psalter*

To be sung to folk or folk-like tunes, which are fairly short, psalms must be in verse, rather than prose translations.[25] The most important poet-translator of

22. For further reading in this area, an accessible place to start is William Edgar, *Taking Note of Music* (London: SPCK, 1986).

23. Garside, pp. 18-19, quoting from Calvin's *Epistle to the Reader* of 1542, in Garside's own translation.

24. There were 123 tunes for 150 psalms and several canticles.

25. Popular, as opposed to liturgical, psalm singing tended to be in verse transla-

the Genevan Psalter came, surprisingly, not from a hotbed of the Reformation, but from the French court. Clément Marot translated a few of the psalms into metrical French verse[26] and distributed them around the court, where they were sung to popular airs.[27] These travelled well beyond the court even before he could get them published. Calvin probably knew both Marot[28] and popular psalm singing before he went to Geneva. In 1537, just before his exile, Calvin proposed the addition of psalm singing to worship services in Geneva, where music in worship had been eliminated altogether when the Mass was abolished in Geneva in 1533. He became even more convinced of the desirability of psalm singing through his experience as a pastor in Strasbourg, where in 1539 he published his own collection of versified psalm translations with music,[29] including altered versions of some of Marot's translations, and possibly translations of his own. Two Strasbourg musicians, Matthäus Greiter and Wolfgang Dachstein, edited or wrote some and possibly all the tunes.[30] Here, already, Calvin turns to experts for help when he needs it.

---

tions from very early on. The earliest known verse translations date from the fourth century. See Nicholas Temperley et al., "Psalms, Metrical," article in *The New Grove Dictionary of Music and Musicians*, ed. Stanley Sadie, vol. 15 (London: Macmillan, 1980), pp. 347-82.

26. Marot's motives have received very diverse reports. Erik Routley refers to Marot as a "poetaster" and asserts that he "was by no means of the Reformed persuasion" (*Church Music and the Christian Faith* [London: Collins, 1980], pp. 27-28), while Pratt says "Marot's spiritual awakening was gradual, erratic and more mystical than logical" (p. 63), and Orentin Douen in his *Clement Marot et le psautier huguenot,* 2 vols. (Paris, 1878-1879), 1:373 describes Marot as "un protestant homme du monde, chose rare de tout temps et presque introuvable au xvi^e siècle. . . . Loin d'être un protestant tiède, il fut en France l'un des premiers propagateurs de l'Évangile." ("A Protestant man of the world, a rare thing at any time and nearly unknown in the sixteenth century. . . . Far from being a lukewarm Protestant, he was in France one of the foremost propagators of the Gospel.")

27. Precisely what sort of popular airs is unknown: "It is not clear what melodies were used — that is, whether they were folk song or chanson tunes — but the latter seems more likely, since Marot's artful verse forms, created out of the spirit of humanism, had a natural relationship to the contemporary French chanson." Blankenburg, p. 518.

28. François Wendel mentions that the two men had a joint friend in the Duchess of Ferrara, who "had attracted a number of Protestant refugees to her court, including the poet Clément Marot." *Calvin: The Origins and Development of His Religious Thought,* trans. Philip Mairet (London: Collins, 1963), p. 47.

29. Entitled *Aulcuns pseaulmes et cantiques mys en chant.*

30. For details, see Blankenburg, p. 519.

On his return to Geneva in 1541, Calvin went about getting all the psalms translated, versified, and set to music. It was a long process, involving two poet-translators and several musical editors. In 1542 *La forme des prieres des chants ecclésiastiques* was published, with thirty-nine psalms, canticles, and prayers, thirty-two of them by Marot (in corrected versions). Another edition was published in 1543 with fifty psalms, the Nunc Dimittis, and the Ten Commandments, all translated by Marot.[31] In 1550, after the death of Marot in 1544, Theodore Beza (later Calvin's successor) took up the translation work, publishing partial psalters in 1551,[32] 1559, and 1561. By 1562 the complete work was published.

Guillaume Franc, then cantor at St. Peter's Church in Geneva, was probably the musical editor of the 1542 and 1543 editions. Louis Bourgeois, who arrived in Geneva in 1541, probably worked on the Psalter under Franc from 1542 and took over Franc's position in 1545.[33] Bourgeois made four-part arrangements of the existing tunes that were published in Lyons in 1547,[34] and he edited (or arranged or possibly composed)[35] the thirty-four tunes added for the new texts by Beza in the 1551 edition. According to Blankenburg, the 1551 edition "set the standard for the musical character of the Genevan Psalter, to which later additions of still missing material were made to conform."[36] Thus, though neither the first nor the last of the musical editors, Bourgeois is considered the primary musical influence on

---

31. The 1551 edition has not survived, but it may also have contained a Credo, a Lord's Prayer, a Magnificat, and some graces. See Blankenburg, p. 518 and Millar Patrick, *Four Centuries of Scottish Psalmody* (London: Oxford University Press, 1949), p. 19. Patrick also notes that Marot left Geneva in 1543 because the council refused to pay him (he had arrived toward the end of 1542).

32. Entitled *Pseaumes octante trois de David, mis en rime francoise. A savoir quarante neuf par Clement Marot avec le Cantique de Simeon et les dix commandemens. Et trente quatre par Theodore de Beze.*

33. Pratt, p. 61.

34. Bourgeois' harmonized collection is an important source of information about earlier editions of the Psalter, many of which have not survived and are known only by contemporary references. For details of the various early editions of the Psalter, see the preface to Pierre Pidoux, *Le Psautier huguenot du XVIe. siècle. Melodies et documents . . .* (Bâle, 1962).

35. Blankenburg is of the opinion that "Melodic creation as reflected in the Genevan Psalter can, for the most part, mean no more than it generally does in the 16th century: arranging, modifying, or sometimes transforming existing materials" (p. 521).

36. Blankenburg, p. 520. Pratt, chapter 8 details just how the selection of 1551 differed from earlier editions.

the final, 1562 version of the Genevan Psalter, which included all eighty-five tunes of the 1551 edition.[37]

## Usage of the Psalter

The Psalms, the Apostle's Creed, the Ten Commandments, the Song of Mary ("Magnificat"), and the Song of Simeon ("Nunc Dimittis") were all sung at several points before and during services at Geneva. The entire Psalter would have been worked through gradually every six months or so.[38] For these psalms to be sung as Calvin wished, they had first to be learned by all, including those who did not read or have access to books and who were not conversant with the formal methods by which music was taught. Calvin's remedy for this educational problem was to teach the psalms to the children first.[39] To this end, the *Ecclesiastical Ordinances* of 1541 state: "It will be good to introduce ecclesiastical song, the better to incite the people to pray to and to praise God. For a beginning the little children are to be taught; then with time all the church will be able to follow."[40]

Bourgeois may have gone even farther and taught the adults to read music. In 1550 he published a book on how to read music which is extraordinary for its time both for simplifying the "solfier" system and for being aimed at amateurs rather than at other professional musicians. Astoundingly down to earth for its time, Bourgeois' text may well have arisen out of the practical experience of teaching adults in Geneva.[41] Hence children's

37. Pierre Dagues, cantor at St. Peter's Church from 1556, seems the most likely candidate to have completed the musical work for the final edition of 1562. The surviving documents refer only to a "maistre Pierre." Since at least three other Pierres were working as musicians in Geneva at the time, there is room for doubt.

38. Blankenburg, p. 531.

39. "The manner of beginning in this seemed to us well advised if some children who have previously practiced a modest church song sing in a loud and distinct voice, the people listening with complete attention and following with the heart what is sung with the mouth until little by little each one accustoms himself to singing communally." Calvin, *Articles*, 1537, trans. Garside, p. 10.

40. Calvin, *Ecclesiastical Ordinances*, trans. Garside, cited p. 16. Garside notes that "The proposal that 'little children are to be taught' is . . . one of far-reaching significance, for it marks the effective beginning of musical education in sixteenth-century Geneva" (p. 16).

41. Louis Bourgeois, *Le Droict Chemin de musique of 1550* (Facsimile and translation), trans. and introduced by Bernarr Rainbow (Kilkenney, Ireland: Boethius Press,

choirs were allowed as a temporary measure for instructional purposes, and the musical education of the entire congregation was sought.[42] Presumably choirs were to be replaced by the congregation when the people knew the psalms by heart.

Psalm singing at this time was quite enthusiastic. A young man who visited Strasbourg in 1545 wrote home as follows: "On Sundays . . . we sing a psalm of David or some other prayer taken from the New Testament. The psalm or prayer is sung by everyone together, men as well as women with a beautiful unanimity, which is something beautiful to behold. . . . Never did I think that it could be as pleasing and delightful as it is."[43] The enthusiasm of the singing suggests that the tempo of the psalms was less funereal than is sometimes supposed. The music itself supports this: melodies that seem formless at a very slow pace make musical sense, and even reveal syncopations, when sung a bit faster.[44]

Singing was in unison and unaccompanied.[45] Calvin, whose antipathy towards harmony in church music stemmed from his opposition to the complex polyphony of the Roman Catholic liturgy, also regarded instrumental accompaniment as unedifying and unnecessary. He wanted only "simple and pure singing of the divine praises, forasmuch as where there is no meaning there is no edification. Let them come from heart and mouth, and in the vulgar tongue. Instrumental music was only

---

1982). Rainbow sums it up thus: "At a time when music was still an arcane art, its terminology abstruse, and its study the task of a lifetime, Bourgeois humanized musical instruction, recognizing that music was not only for the specialist. He applied his experience as a successful teacher of children to bring simple musical instruction, couched in the vernacular, to the adult" (p. 23).

42. This attitude is a far cry from the comment so frequently encountered today, that "the congregation will never learn that!"

43. Alfred Erichson, *L'eglise française de Strasbourg au seizième siècle d'apres des documents inédits* (Strasbourg: Librarie C. F. Schmidt, 1886), pp. 21-22, cited in Garside, p. 18. See also the similar sentiments in the letter to Jean Du Bois, ibid., p. 15.

44. Walter Blankenburg suggests: "While it must be assumed that Calvin's demands for a melodic style with *poids* and *majesté*, but at the same time *modéré* and *modeste*, had to be fulfilled by his followers, they were undoubtedly concerned not with a solemn, slow tempo (though an inappropriate fast one was out of the question) but with melodic and particularly rhythmic simplicity" (p. 530).

45. Claude Tappolet notes that the cathedral organ was sold in 1543. "Fragments d'une Historie de la musique à Genève (VI)," *Revue Musicale Suisse*, 98 (1958): 191. Apparently the Genevoise were more thrifty-minded than iconoclastic.

tolerated in the time of the Law (that is, the Old Testament) because of the people's infancy."[46]

## The Music of the Psalter

### Melodic Characteristics

The Genevan tunes share the melodic characteristics of other sixteenth-century tunes, yet they have a style that is unique to them as a collection and that binds them together, regardless of their original sources.[47] This unanimity flows from the editors' compliance with Calvin's desire for a distinctive church style. According to Blankenburg, "The fact that most of the Genevan psalm tunes have their origin in various existing models did not . . . prevent the various melodists from following an editorial concept completely unified in its basic principles and obviously guided by Calvin himself. They developed an entirely original melody type, different from melody types of other Reform regions."[48]

The melodies are characterized by repetition or simple developments of melodic phrases, by bar form,[49] and by frequent use of common melodic formulas.[50] Their restricted range makes them easy for congregations to

46. John Calvin, *Sermons on Job*, 79-80, cited by Erik Routley in *The Church and Music: An Enquiry into the History, the Nature and Scope of Christian Judgement on Music* (London: Duckworth, 1950), p. 125.

47. Discovering the sources for the Genevan tunes is a vexing problem. Relatively few have been positively identified; likewise, relatively few are thought to be original tunes by one of the various editors. Genevan tunes are anonymous, and the musical editors have left no other melodies for comparison. It is thought that more of the tunes are adaptations of sacred than of secular tunes. Blankenburg, writing in 1962, lists five tunes for which secular models can be found, thirteen from Gregorian chant, and five (42, 47, 72, 91, and 136) that seem to be original (Blankenburg, p. 523). He cites Pidoux for the identification of those likely to be original. Subsequent research may have turned up other identifications.

48. Blankenburg, p. 523.

49. In "Bar form" the first phrase of a melody is repeated and then answered by new (sometimes related) material. It can be represented schematically as AAB. Many variations on this form are also common, as for instance "rounded bar form" AABA and "doubled bar form" AABBC.

50. See Routley, *Church Music*, pp. 197-205 for examples of motifs common to many Psalter tunes.

sing. All these characteristics lend themselves to easy learning, at least compared to the Lutheran chorales, which may have depended on the congregation's prior knowledge.

## Modality and Expressivity

I have said that the Genevan tunes are very expressive. Much of their expressivity arises from notes that are slightly higher or lower than we expect; that is to say, they are "modal." Modes are ways to arrange the distance, or intervals, between notes.[51] We commonly use two patterns today, the major and minor scales. Those are only two of twelve modes in common use during the sixteenth century, though they were gradually becoming the most common ones.[52] Music in the less familiar modes can be incredibly expressive of sorrow, suffering, guilt, or anger; it can hint at ranges of feeling beyond what can be expressed in so simple a tune in major. This intensity makes modal music wonderful for prayer and for psalms. A good example of a modal tune, because it is in one of the less common modes, is that to Psalm 51, used aptly for Seerveld's "A Congregational Lament" as well.[53]

51. The modes can be imagined as scales beginning on each note of the C major scale (except B), but using only the white keys of a piano. In plainchant, the modes determine the melody to a greater extent than do the scales in our major/minor system; small changes that can be accommodated by the modern major or minor change a mode altogether. This apparent lack of flexibility increases the individuality and identifiability of each mode, so that each mode has its own range of expression. See Blankenburg, p. 529, and Pratt, chapter 5, for more technical and detailed discussions of how modality affects the Genevan tunes.

52. Douen suggests that approximately fifty-two Genevan tunes are fully modal, thirty-five are closest to what we now call minor, and thirty-eight are closest to what we now call major. Precision is difficult for music of this transitional period; though the Psalter as a collection may be moving historically in the direction of modern tonality, enough of it is firmly modal to sound different to us! For a good summary, see Pratt, pp. 35-38.

53. See number 576 in the most recent edition of the *Psalter Hymnal* (Grand Rapids, Mich.: CRC Publications, 1987). Seerveld hints at the range of expression music or any art must achieve to match the psalms: ". . . art permeated by the biblical spirit of reconciliation will be painting and sculpture, song and literature, dance and architecture that is busy with all the nuances of our dedicated, sin-plagued lives. A reconciling Christian art will not be boxed in . . . but will range as wide as the Psalms — Psalm 8 and 90 *(la gloire et la misère de l'homme)*, 18 *(ein feste Burg)* and 51 *(Too late the*

## Meter and Rhythm

All commentators on the Genevan psalms mention rhythms. At first this is surprising, since the Psalter commonly used only two note values, where the Lutheran chorale tunes used many. But Routley notes: "The Genevan psalms are . . . distinguished by the subtlety of the rhythm which with these limited resources they . . . achieve. No Genevan tune is ever four-square; it can never be intelligibly divided into four-beat units — there is always the odd pair of beats that require the occasional six-beat bar. Even the Old Hundredth in its Genevan form has six long notes in its final line and four in all the others."[54]

The Genevan tunes and texts use an amazing number of different meters,[55] yet they have great discipline rhythmically. In modern notation, the tunes use only quarter and half notes, with a whole note to end each tune, yet the Genevan tunes bear an unusually subtle relation to their original texts. Rather than slavishly following speech rhythms, the tunes move in rhythmic counterpoint, producing a kind of "polymeter" within the apparent simplicity of the syllabic rhythmic scheme.[56]

There are two basic rhythmic models for the entire Psalter, with very few exceptions.[57] In one model, long notes occur at the beginning and ends of the lines, with short notes between (think of the first line of "All Creatures of our God and King" to the tune "Lasst uns Erfreuen"). The second model has short notes interrupted by one or more longs (see for example psalms 25 and 47). Within these two models, the greatest possible variety was

---

*Phalarope),* 139 ('The Hound of Heaven'), the litany of 119, *de profundis* pilgrim psalm 130 and the great Hallel 146-150" (Seerveld, *Rainbows,* p. 39).

54. Routley, *Church Music,* p. 55.

55. The meter is simply how many syllables there are in each line. A glance at the first half-dozen of the Genevan tunes used in the 1987 *Psalter Hymnal* revealed 6 different meters, of which 5 appear only once in the hymnal! Looking further through the unique meters in the index reveals that many of them are Genevan tunes.

56. See Blankenburg, pp. 523-28. He suggests that the rhythmic treatment of the Psalter tunes was influenced by the humanistic French experiments in strophic forms and fixed meters.

57. These two rhythmic models are sorted by Pratt into seventy-five common rhythmic patterns for individual lines; for details see Pratt, pp. 40-46. Blankenburg notes only three exceptions to these two models, 1, 103, and 155, which include "a short appoggiatura, in the Wittenburg style, at the beginnings of two lines" (p. 528). An appoggiatura is a short, unaccented note which precedes the first main stress of a phrase.

pursued, especially under Bourgeois' editorship. Blankenburg suggests the following reason for this variety within uniformity: "This rhythmic schematicism of the Genevan Psalter is unquestionably rooted in a certain rationalism derived from pedagogical considerations in an attempt to find melodies suitable for the congregation. The extraordinary success of the procedure speaks for itself."[58]

## Harmonic Settings and Part Writing

There have been many harmonized versions of the Psalter tunes, the first published even before the collection was finished. They were originally meant for private use, since Calvin opposed polyphony in church.[59] Bourgeois published four-part harmonizations for fifty of Marot's psalms in 1547, and in 1561 he published settings of eighty-three Psalms by Marot and Beza for four, five, or six voices. Claude Goudimel's 1565 collection of the whole Psalter remained popular until the nineteenth century, so popular, in fact, that Goudimel sometimes mistakenly receives credit for writing the tunes of the Genevan Psalter.[60] These early settings are all for multiple voices singing a cappella, rather than for unison singing with instrumental accompaniment as has become the rule since the nineteenth century. Space does not permit me to say more on the subject of part-singing in worship, other than that, when undertaken joyfully by the congregation, it is a wonderful experience of unity-in-diversity, for which some congregations lack musical preparation.[61]

58. Blankenburg, p. 529.

59. How long it was before those accustomed to singing parts at home sang them at church is unknown. In Scotland, which followed the Genevan model but with different tunes, there were eventually complaints about people singing parts from *different* harmonizations in church! "An abuse observed in all churches, where sundrie Trebles, Bases and Counters set by divers Authors, being sung upon one, and the same Tenor, do discordingly rub each upon another, offending both Musicall, and rude ears. . . ." From Edward Millar's preface to the 1635 Scottish Psalter, quoted in Routley, *Church Music,* p. 47.

60. See Pratt, chapter 9.

61. Perhaps Calvin's example should spur us to emulate his program of education!

## Aesthetic Analysis

The aesthetic analysis of music, under the guise of music criticism, usually restricts itself to great works of art that exhibit significant individuality and call for aesthetic contemplation. But artistic works which, like the Genevan psalm tunes, are not intended primarily for aesthetic contemplation, nevertheless have aesthetic properties which should be considered. What aesthetic criteria can be applied to music for congregational worship?

Whereas music made for aesthetic contemplation calls attention to itself and the relationships it reveals internally, music written for worship must point away from itself. It must be transparent rather than opaque. It is not there to be listened to, but to deepen the worshipper's relationship with God. This is the modesty asked of music by Calvin and many others. Yet to do its job of deepening worship and pointing beyond itself to God and God's Word, music must not be dull or banal; it must be musically good as well as modest. Therefore many of the same criteria apply to music for worship as to art music (with the possible exception of originality). We must talk about nuance, beauty, balance, variety, rhythmic invention, integration, and musical autonomy. Some of these have been discussed above; the others I will touch on below.

Calvin Seerveld has coined the word "allusivity" for what he understands to be the normative characteristic of all aesthetic objects, that is, the ability to suggest, to hint playfully, rather than to refer directly. Language seeks clarity of reference; art and music, however, allude to things (e.g., emotions) that are best grasped not with logic but with intuition. Music almost never refers directly; rather it points to things not easily put into words.

"Allusive" is a good description of the collection of Genevan tunes. While on the surface they impress with their austerity and discipline, on closer inspection the tunes possess a richness and variety to match that of the Psalms themselves. They have a wide range of expression despite their shared melodic and rhythmic idioms. They vary in meter, in length, in mode, in rhythm. One has a fairly regular (though never four-square) rhythm; the next is syncopated. One uses the most melancholy Phyrgian mode; the next, the jolliest major. This collection encompasses the grandeur of "Old Hundredth" (Ps. 134), the yearning of Psalm 42, the exultation of Psalm 47, the deep sorrow of Psalm 51. "Suggestion-rich" indeed, these tunes allude to a very wide range of human emotional experience.

Though many of the tunes are very beautiful, they do not conform to an academic notion of beauty. Their melodic proportions are not those of symmetry and the golden mean. Their rhythms are not balanced or regular. They have nothing to do with Neo-classical ideals. The tunes are untidy; sometimes lines end quite unexpectedly. (Consequently, many have been evened out and regularized over the years.) Though they use stock phrases that come up again and again, as does all folk-like music, they lack repetition for the sake of balance, and this makes them a better vehicle for seeing the unpredictability and wildness of God's creation and work in the world.

The formation and use of the Genevan Psalter provides an interesting example of the shifting dynamics of artistic integration and differentiation. Geneva appears to us as a community that was musically more integrated than our own. Music permeated the culture in the form of work songs, drinking songs, and so on. At the same time there was a degree of increasing differentiation, of music being developed by particularly gifted individuals. Before the Reformation, this process of differentiation had gone a very long way towards alienating most people: church music was entirely in the hands of professionals. Calvin's reforms changed that radically, but church music in Geneva did not thereby return to a state of folk art. Instead, Calvin asked the professionals to make music in which the community could participate. This stage of re-integration did not deny differentiation and musical development. Professionals served the community, especially within the church. Unfortunately, Calvin limited further development and differentiation, however: after the Psalter project and its extension to life outside of worship, the composer had nothing more to do. There should always be scope for those called to be artistically or musically active to serve their community.[62] By contrast, today's culture has total musical freedom and differentiation, but little opportunity for service and integration. Almost all the music in our culture is made by professionals for people to listen to; though we may be constantly surrounded by music, few of us sing or play during work or leisure.

62. Seerveld offers a compelling image of a community which integrates a fully developed and differentiated art: "Such a faith project in Christian artistry will never be healthy among us until there is a living sense of Christian community, and the misplaced emphasis on 'individual' has been corrected. God has set things up so that cultural endeavour is always a communal enterprise, done by trained men and women in concert, gripped by a spirit that is larger than each one individually and that pulls them together as they do their formative work" (*Rainbows*, p. 37).

One remarkable feature of the music of the Genevan Psalter is the way it embodies Calvin's theological ideas. The musical editors of the Psalter found a purely musical way to express Calvin's ideas: the rhythmic construction, in its independence from the text and in its varied simplicity, musically demonstrates Calvin's principles for congregational prayer. This is not music merely restricted by extra-musical demands (as for instance when confined to one word per note, a frequent requirement for church music); this is music shaped within its own norms to express an ideal. Though limited in its independence, the music displays a kind of autonomy nonetheless. And, far from being an "inhibition" of musical creativity, as Blankenburg thinks, it is a notable musical achievement.[63]

## The Liturgical Legacy of the Genevan Psalter

The music of the Genevan Psalter did what Calvin wanted it to do. He believed that music is a great gift of God for joy and pleasure but also a dangerous tool. Consequently, it must be moderated by a text from Scripture. Then the joining of music to psalm could inflame the zeal of the people and enhance their prayers. To that end, Calvin employed a succession of professional musicians who created a style combining aesthetic integrity with accessibility and ease of learning, to be learned by heart by all the people, and to be used for freely and sincerely worshipping God, without adornment or distraction.

Music for worship has, I believe, a duty to be comprehensible to the worshippers. No one can worship while feeling bewildered or alienated! Music intended for congregational singing has an added duty to be accessible; that is, it must not be too difficult for the people of a given time and

---

63. Blankenburg writes: "Of course, the rhythmic element, because of the possibilities of its special effect, gains here a significance unequaled elsewhere in that period. The intimate interweaving of text and melody, typical for other regions of Reform song, is replaced here by a goal of rhythmic construction, i.e. by a certain measure of musical autonomy. There is no other feature in church music as typically Calvinist as this one; it is an order for artistic creation to be put to use in the organization of the congregation. Despite the great musical achievement in the melodization of the Genevan Psalter, particularly if one takes into consideration the large number of melodies created, the directed rhythmic uniformity inhibited true artistic creativeness. And yet, this is balanced to a certain degree by the wealth of beautiful melodic lines" (p. 529).

place to learn and sing. We tend to regard the Psalter tunes as difficult (with the exception of "Old Hundredth"), but this was not necessarily the case when they were written. They are full of stock phrases, rooted in the common idioms of the day.[64] They probably seemed quite singable to sixteenth-century congregations, especially if most were sung at a reasonable pace, so the longer ones did not seem to last forever. (Longer tunes would have been a positive boon where the entire psalm, rather than a mere selection of verses, was to be sung. Four-line tunes pall after ten or more verses!) In fact, their popularity is often attributed to the ease with which contemporary congregations learned them.[65]

Later, in the age of strictly tonal, harmonically based, rhythmically regular, common meter psalm and hymn tunes, the Genevan tunes and Lutheran chorales became difficult to sing. The rhythm seemed capricious, the harmony alien, and the modality weird. Throughout the eighteenth and nineteenth centuries, the Genevan tunes survived[66] because they were seen as a sacred style, but a style that was increasingly alien. To suit the tastes of the times, those who retained the Genevan tunes regularized the rhythms, so that the tunes lost their vitality. When sung too slowly, they became the dirges they are popularly supposed to be.[67]

Where the Genevan tunes were not known, it would not have been liturgically responsible, or acceptable, to introduce them. They would have been musically meaningless to the great majority of people. But that is no longer the case. Since the beginning of the twentieth century, the slow revival of both "ancient" music and "folk" music and the gradual introduction of folk tunes into the stock of hymn tunes[68] have meant a return of modal sounds to modern ears. Jazz and rock have returned to us a rhythmic freedom unknown in European music before the turn of the century. Syncopation and modal melodies are once again part of our musical vernacular.

---

64. See Routley, *Church Music*, pp. 197-203, for examples of common melodic idioms.

65. Blankenburg notes that "it was early observed that they were simpler and easier to grasp [than German Chorale tunes]" (p. 530).

66. As for instance in Dutch, French, and middle-European Reformed churches, and those founded by their missionaries.

67. See for example the Genevan tunes in the *Psalter Hymnal* (1957). Number 74 is psalm 42 regularized.

68. As for example Vaughan Williams' arrangements of English folk music for *The English Hymnal*.

The Genevan tunes, properly introduced, no longer exceed the reach of the average congregation.

Liturgically, the Psalter accomplished a number of positive things. It returned the psalms to the people, giving positive, corporate shape to their congregational and private prayer. It created a music that supported but did not obscure the psalms. This music is all of a piece with the rest of Genevan worship: word- and prayer-oriented, modest, universal in application, accessible. In its reserve, it does not manipulate the emotions, yet it is expressive enough to enhance and deepen the meaning of the psalms. It is of the time of its creation while remaining rooted in its past, at once new and old. In being confined to scriptural material, the Psalter avoids the danger of popularizing shoddy thinking by association with "catchy" music, as happens today with some contemporary choruses. The Psalter as a whole has balance and variety. Its musical idiom was relevant at the time and can be relevant again.

The liturgical gains of the Reformed service with congregational singing are, I think, great enough to offset the loss of elaborate liturgy, with this one proviso: the time has come, I hope, when Protestants can recognize that ritual and ceremony are also true worship; that worship need not always be the same; and that special times and places may call for all the resources of the arts to contribute to our praise. Not every week, not every congregation, but in some times and places austerity should give way to splendor. All this testifies in favor of the experiment at Geneva. It has stood the test of time remarkably well (though that in itself is no proof of excellence), and indeed, having become stylistically foreign for a time, seems to be making a comeback now, if the number of Genevan tunes turning up in new hymnals and being used by writers of new hymns is anything to go by.

There are a few points on which I think Calvin was liturgically mistaken. One is the elimination of instrumental music from worship.[69] Singing,

---

69. Calvin's supposed biblical argument does not hold water: there is no evidence in the Bible that instrumental music was only allowed in the Old Testament because of the "infancy of the people." Instrumental music was confined to the temple, and, after the fall of the second temple in Jerusalem, disappeared from Jewish worship; but that was because instruments were considered especially festive, and therefore inappropriate to the synagogues. The church fathers distrusted instruments because of their associations with immorality and paganism. But we are called, surely, to redeem, rather than reject, all cultural areas.

indeed, does not need the support of accompaniment; in my experience congregations sing with more joy and fervor when accustomed to singing unaccompanied. But instrumental music can add aesthetic dimensions to worship that Calvin needlessly excluded. Similarly, as I have said, Calvin was mistaken to restrict all music to that of the Psalter.

Despite the amazing variety of musical material available, churches constantly run the risk of being too narrow and culturally dated to reach out to others. Christians tend to adopt a style and to stick with it through thick and thin. In fact, during the Genevan Psalter's earlier history, the Reformed churches did just that. But the church's needs today are different. We are part of a culturally much more diverse situation than was the case in Geneva (or even Europe) in the sixteenth century. We must be open to points of view that differ culturally from our own. The music of the Psalter can help widen our horizons.

If we are to further reclaim the riches of our heritage, what is required? Firstly, the tunes should be made accessible in their original rhythms and be sung quickly enough to make rhythmic sense. Secondly, the tunes should be paired with modern words, whether psalms or new hymns, that have relevance and meaning for contemporary worshippers. These two things have occurred to a certain extent. My reacquaintance with some of the music of the Genevan Psalter was made possible by the work of Emily Brink, Calvin Seerveld, and others in revising the *Psalter Hymnal.* They put 40 Genevan tunes into the hymnal, almost all restored to their original rhythms, and they matched these renewed tunes with new (or at least modern) versifications of the psalms or with new hymns, creating composite works that are both profoundly traditional and entirely contemporary. Although the 1987 *Psalter Hymnal* has done more of this than any other hymnal I know of, the trend occurs in many of the latest hymnals. *Rejoice in the Lord,* for instance, has a dozen or so Genevan tunes, some altered, but most in their Genevan form, and again often paired to contemporary translations or new hymn texts.[70]

I believe that in this postmodern era, of all times, music for worship, especially hymns, ought to come from a wider repertoire than hitherto:

---

70. *Rejoice in the Lord: A Hymn Companion to the Scriptures* (Grand Rapids, Mich.: Eerdmans, 1985) is the newest hymnal of the Reformed Church in America, and the last hymnal edited by Erik Routley, who himself wrote some new hymns for Genevan tunes.

from our own tradition and from others, from the distant past through the present, from all the styles that are comprehensible to actual and potential congregations. With so much from which to draw, there is no excuse for aesthetically poor selections, even though the primary consideration in liturgical music should be worship rather than art. The music and especially the ideals of the Genevan Psalter provide an invaluable resource, and the latest translations and versifications by Seerveld and others make this resource new and usable again. Therefore let us explore this legacy!

# In Praise of Proverbs[1]

## RAYMOND C. VAN LEEUWEN

Pervasive among Calvin Seerveld's diverse intellectual loves is an underlying passion for biblical Wisdom. Inevitably this entails a love of proverbs, those verbal jewels wherein Wisdom's treasure lies scattered and hidden.[2] To profess a passion for proverbs may mark a man as one untimely born into the wrong century. It is ages since folk both high and low, learned and unlearned, revered proverbs as keys to unlock the common doors of life.[3]

1. An earlier version of parts of this essay in honor of Cal Seerveld was presented as the presidential address at the 1994 Annual Meeting of the Midwest Region of the Society of Biblical Literature (Evanston, Illinois). I have generally retained the oral style of these sections, as befits the subject of proverbs, but have added references.

2. Seerveld's love for and learning in the biblical book of Proverbs appeared most notably during the 1970s in a long series of articles on Proverbs in the now defunct Canadian journal *Vanguard*. In that period he also preached on Proverbs, and notably, a sermon on the love of Lady Wisdom. He dealt with Proverbs again in *Rainbows for the Fallen World* (pp. 95-102). Rare among Christian scholars, he took the trouble to master the biblical languages (as in his translation of *The Greatest Song*). His early interest in the literary and spiritual unity of Proverbs has become a major topic in recent Proverbs research. See R. C. Van Leeuwen, *Context and Meaning in Proverbs 25–27* (Atlanta, 1988); R. N. Whybray, *The Composition of the Book of Proverbs* (Sheffield, 1994); and S. Weeks, *Early Israelite Wisdom* (Oxford, 1994). Seerveld stands in the long Augustinian tradition, mediated through Calvin and Kuyper, which sees the Scriptures, among other things, as a book of divine wisdom for life on earth. See the Seerveld Bibliography in this volume.

3. See N. Z. Davis, "Proverbial Wisdom and Popular Errors," *Society and Culture in Early Modern France* (Stanford, 1975), pp. 227-67, 336-46. Davis points out, as do others, that learned disdain of common proverbs reached its peak in the eighteenth-

Half a millennium ago, Erasmus of Rotterdam could produce a bestseller of *Adages*. And Martin Luther's immense historical power — for good and ill alike — lay largely in his verbal craft, including his mastery of the telling proverb. Shakespeare's proverb lore once entertained the masses and her majesty's court.[4] Less known is that the great George Herbert produced, besides his poetry, a collection called *Outlandish Proverbs*, a title which reflected not xenophobia but the international character of its sayings. And only a century ago, Lord Randall Churchill could bring down the House of Lords by quoting a biblical saying. "Once," writes biographer William Manchester, "the Liberals thought he was napping. They introduced a specious motion, concealing a trap. [Suddenly alert,] Churchill said: 'Surely in vain is the net spread in the sight of any bird.'"[5] Manchester seems to think that the witticism was original; Hebraicists and biblically literate folk know it came from Proverbs 1:17.

Today, however, the wealth of proverb lore serves mainly to keep an occasional paremiologist from the worse option of "publish or perish." Ironically, this academic proverb takes only three words to sum up an entire world of academic anxiety about jobs, salary, status, and which frogs are big enough for our pond. And yet scholars are little inclined to give honor where honor is due. Usually the humble proverb, workhorse of the language, escapes scholarly notice. Of course, you can't footnote a proverb. But we do use them, they do for us their incredibly efficient verbal work, while our debt to them remains largely unacknowledged. Once, long ago, when I told a psychologist friend my dissertation was on Proverbs, she said

---

century world of the *philosophes* (p. 253). Interest in proverbs revived in the romantic and nationalist movements of the nineteenth century.

4. Shakespeare, like Chaucer before him, was a master of the vernacular English proverb. See F. P. Wilson, *The Proverbial Wisdom of Shakespeare* (London, 1961) and Charles George Smith, *Shakespeare's Proverb Lore* (Cambridge, 1963). Shakespeare also delved into the biblical Proverb book to set the background for his tale of the moral education of Prince Hal in *Henry IV, Part 1* (I.ii; II.ii; cf. Prov 1:10-33). For Chaucer's use of biblical wisdom, see the article "Wisdom" in David Lyle Jeffrey's masterful *A Dictionary of Biblical Tradition in English Literature* (Grand Rapids, 1992) with its valuable bibliographies. Further bibliography may be found in Wolfgang Mieder, *Proverbs in Literature: An International Bibliography* (Bern, 1978) and in the yearly bibliographies in the valuable but little known journal *Proverbium*, produced by the University of Vermont.

5. *The Last Lion: Winston Spencer Churchill*, 2 vols. (Boston, 1983). Vol. 1: *Visions of Glory, 1874-1932*, p. 141.

with a nuance of pity, "Well, whatever turns you on. . . ." Ironically, she dismissed proverbs with a proverb whose origin was in her own turned-on sixties generation.

Stephen Toulmin's book *Cosmopolis: The Hidden Agenda of Modernity* may help us understand the intellectual demise of the proverb. Why is it so hard for modern folk to enter the world of proverbs with sympathy and insight? Toulmin argues that the modern era generally followed the paradigm of Descartes rather than Montaigne. In the face of the wars of religion, modernity began a "quest for certainty" (John Dewey's phrase) that would bind all religions and peoples together in a peaceable kingdom of abstract, scientific reason.[6] According to Toulmin, this entailed a series of shifts in cultural currency, all of them, I believe, significant for the demise of the status of proverbs. Toulmin's cultural shifts are as follows: "From the Oral to the Written . . . From the Particular to the Universal . . . From the Local to the General . . . [and] From the Timely to the Timeless." Toulmin's summary of the significance of these shifts is worth quoting.

> These four changes of mind — from oral to written, local to general, particular to universal, timely to timeless — were distinct; but, taken in an historical context, they had much in common, and their joint outcome exceeded what any of them would have produced by itself. All of them reflected a historical shift from *practical* philosophy, whose issues arose out of clinical medicine, juridical procedure, moral case analysis, or the rhetorical force of oral reasoning, to a *theoretical* conception of philosophy: the effects of this shift were so deep and long-lasting that the revival of practical philosophy in our own day has taken many people by surprise.[7]

The modern concern for the scientific, the theoretical, the abstract, and for the universally valid has rendered proverbs of ill repute among the intellectual and, finally, the popular heirs of the Enlightenment. This ill repute affected not only vernacular proverbs, which appear so often patently false and contradictory, but also biblical proverbs, which are subject to the same objections.[8]

6. Leibniz, to give an example not noted by Toulmin, actually devised a moral system based on geometry.

7. S. Toulmin, *Cosmopolis: The Hidden Agenda of Modernity* (New York, 1990), p. 34.

8. See my "Wealth and Poverty: System and Contradiction in Proverbs," *Hebrew Studies* 33 (1992): 25-36. It may be noted that the revival of scholarly interest in the

Like one from another century, I have always loved proverbs. Lest this claim seem too extreme or merely trivial, let me explain. As far back as I can remember, I have loved words, especially when they were compacted into memorable lines that "said it all," while never saying more than tact required. For this love, I thank my father, whose mind was a treasure-store of poetry, stories, Dutch psalms, and proverbs. My father had mastered basic English before he left his native Holland, but most of the stories and sayings I remember are in Dutch.

With an appeal to Clifford Geertz's principle of "local knowledge," adapting it to the personal as that which is most local,[9] allow me to recount just one of these parental stories, for it documents my claim always to have loved proverbs. But it may also reveal some important truths about the proverb genre, whether in or out of the Bible.

My father told this story sometime in the late fifties as we drove through the Southern California landscape, amid the orange groves and palm trees and dairy farms. The story itself is of the contest genre, a macho battle of words and the egos behind them. The great poet Vondel, Holland's answer to Shakespeare, is sitting with another, unknown bard in a seventeenth-century tavern drinking, not Heineken, but Grolsch, the beer with the little porcelain cap. By candle light, in their cups, they argue about who is the greater poet. One challenges the other to a duel, right there on the spot. Only this duel will be fought with words not swords: Who can make the shortest poem?

Mr. Anonymous picks up the hot candle like a sword, and with a flick of his wrist flings a glob of hot tallow on Vondel's embroidered shirt, and says with a smirk, "Vet smet!" (Something like, "Fat splat" or more literally and prosaically, "Fat stains.") Mr. X's thrust was designed, of course, to stain

---

biblical book of Proverbs in the twentieth century began, *not* with a consideration of its intrinsic worth and significance, but with the discovery of the literary dependence of part of Proverbs (22:17–24:22) on the Egyptian Wisdom work, Amenemope. Here, as often, Ancient Near Eastern and biblical scholarship confused knowledge of literary genesis with insight. See A. Erman, "Eine ägyptische Quelle der 'Sprüche Salomos,'" *Sitzungsberichte der Preussischen Akademie der Wissenschaften* 15 (1924): 86-93 and Table VI-VII; D. Römheld, *Wege der Weisheit: Die Lehren Amenemopes und Proverbien 22,17–24,22* (BZAW 184; Berlin, 1989).

9. C. Geertz, *Local Knowledge: Further Essays in Interpretive Anthropology* (New York, 1983). See especially the essay, "Common Sense as a Cultural System," with its discussion (and use of) proverbs.

both Vondel's shirt and reputation. Thereupon Vondel rises, smacks Mr. Anonymous on the side of the head, and roars, "Ik tik!" ("I knock!" or "I box!"). So Vondel won the context by simultaneously "knocking" Anonymous's poetry and "boxing his ears."

I admit the subtleties of this funny exchange were lost on me as a boy. Yet some three decades latter, I remember the story and its punch lines with their hard hitting onomatopoeia. Of course, "Ik tik" is not a real proverb. But "Vet smet" is, like the English saying of comparable shape, "Money talks." "Vet Smet" has entered the store of Dutch sayings, and is found in several proverb collections.

The great Dutch *Woordenboek,* the multivolumed equivalent of England's *Oxford English Dictionary,* informs us that the tale about Vondel and his anonymous companion is a literary legend. Thus, while our combat myth is apocryphal, it is also an etiology, purporting to explain the origin of the proverb "Vet smet." Before we leave this greasy saying behind, we must briefly discuss its biblical significance. We are helped here by a twentieth century proverb collection, *Nederlandse spreekwoorden, spreuken en zegswijzen.*[10] This fine work explains the meaning of "Vet smet." It does this simply by quoting the Greek saying from Menander which the Apostle uses in 1 Corinthians 15:33. In short, "Vet smet" is how the Dutch say "Bad company ruins good morals."

This detour on a Dutch proverb story may remind us of much that is significant also for biblical and Ancient Near Eastern proverbs. First, such sayings and stories are traditional, handed down from parent to child in settings where there is room to talk and time to experience life together. Stories like the one above arise in the comfortable silence that generates speech. They exist in the absence of TV. They are told to entertain and to reveal human nature and the ways of the world.

Second, proverbs usually solve problems. It takes a concrete problem to generate a "proverb performance." Old folk, who may be storehouses of proverbs, often have little to say when asked, "Tell me some proverbs." But ask an old farm wife for wisdom on a human problem, and proverbs will be the spice that seasons her solution. "Well, dear," she might say, "What goes around comes around," or perhaps, "Different strokes for different

10. K. Ter Laan, *Nederlandse spreekwoorden en zegswijzen* (The Hague, 1977), p. 366.

folks," or even the biblical, "A soft answer turns away wrath" (Prov. 15:1). In real life, then, proverbs are "a social use of metaphor."[11]

Third, proverbs are usually short, to the point, and poetically powerful. Proverbs contain no fat, no frills. Every word counts and does its job. When my friend Frank Flynn once referred to proverbs as "the tin-can-opener of language," he meant that their insights opened up the problems of life, but also that they were the key to whatever nourishment we find in words. A proverb sounds good in the ear and sticks in the mind like a burr to the pants. It goes with you, a fellow traveler, until it drops into some other human soil, there to sprout meaning, to bear fruit in another plot.

Proverbs have a rhythmic snap, they often rhyme, their vowels harmonize, and their consonants dance together in happy alliteration. Not every proverb does all these things, but of this sonic stuff, of these vocal moves, proverbs, like poems, are made. Let us just say it. Proverbs *are* the shortest poems. "Vet smet." And sometimes, though not always, they are the best. "Ik tik."

At its best, this shortest of genres exhibits a wonderful collaboration of form and function. This point is worth illustrating with a close investigation of several biblical sayings.[12] These two-line proverbs are a virtual compendium of Hebrew poetic artistry. Most of what will be said applies also to the sayings' near generic kin, the admonition.[13]

---

11. P. Seitel, "Proverbs: A Social Use of Metaphor," *Genre* 2 (1969): 143-61; reprinted in W. Mieder and A. Dundes, eds., *The Wisdom of Many: Essays on the Proverb* (New York, 1981), pp. 122-39.

12. In Proverbs, the primary locus of sayings are the "Solomonic collections," namely, Prov. 10:1–22:16 and 25:1–29:27. A "saying" consists of one or more short indicative statements; in Proverbs there are usually two. An "admonition" gives persuasive or disuasive direction, usually followed by a motive or reason for the precept. Admonitions predominate in chapters 22:17–24:34. Chapters 1–9 are a worldview and hermeneutic introduction to the short sayings and admonitions which follow; they provide the godly parameters within which all the sayings are to be understood: "The fear of the Lord is the beginning of knowledge, fools despise wisdom and instruction" (1:7; cf. 9:10; 31:30). G. von Rad's magisterial treatment of this epistemological life-principle remains indispensable: *Wisdom in Israel* (Nashville, 1972), pp. 53-73. See the next note for further references.

13. My focus here is on the artistry of individual sayings. For a treatment of the Proverb book as a composite, aesthetic whole, see R. C. Van Leeuwen, "Proverbs," in Leland Ryken and Tremper Longman III, eds., *A Complete Literary Guide to the Bible* (Grand Rapids, 1993), pp. 256-67. The artistry of individual sayings is studied by J. G. Williams,

When reading the sayings of Proverbs in English, it is easy to forget that we are reading two-line poems. But the Hebrew words are arranged like jewels in an exquisitely crafted setting, artful gems whose every verbal facet has been carefully chosen, matched, and polished to form a splendid whole. Though sayings in Proverbs have their roots in oral culture, the two-part sayings actually found in Proverbs, in their symmetry and polish, and in their purposeful juxtapositions, appear to be literary in character.[14]

---

"Proverbs and Ecclesiastes," in R. Alter and F. Kermode, *The Literary Guide to the Bible* (Cambridge, Mass., 1987), pp. 263-82. Among recent commentators, L. Alonso Schokel is perhaps the most consistently engaged with the literary artistry of the Proverb book, both on the micro and macro levels. See his *Proverbios* (Madrid, 1984) in the series *Nueva Biblia Española: Comentario teológico y literario.* For an introduction to the workings of biblical Hebrew poetry, see A. Berlin, "Parallelism," in D. N. Freedman, ed., *The Anchor Bible Dictionary V* (New York, 1993), pp. 155-62. More comprehensive treatments are her *The Dynamics of Biblical Parallelism* (Bloomington, Ind., 1985), J. Kugel, *The Idea of Biblical Poetry: Parallelism and Its History* (New Haven, 1981), and R. Alter, *The Art of Biblical Poetry* (New York, 1985), which includes a chapter on Proverbs.

14. H.-J. Hermisson, *Studien zur israelitischen Spruchweisheit* (Neukirchen-Vluyn, 1968). By contrast, C. Westermann, *Wurzeln der Weisheit: Die ältesten Spruche Israels und anderer Völker* (Göttingen, 1990) follows the old form-critical agenda of seeking shorter (in this case, one-line) sayings which purportedly lie behind the less original two-line sayings presently found in the book. Westermann's approach suffers from two main problems. It cannot account for the many two-line sayings in which neither line can be understood or exist independently. Nor does it take into account the transformation which occurs even when strictly oral sayings are incorporated in a literary work. See J. Goody, *The Domestication of the Savage Mind* (Cambridge and New York, 1977); *The Logic of Writing and the Organization of Society* (Cambridge and New York, 1986); and W. J. Ong, *Orality and Literacy: The Technologizing of the Word* (London, 1982). On the significance of Goody's work for understanding the development of literary culture in the Ancient Near East, and for a magisterial treatment of the same, see J. Bottero, *Mesopotamia: Writing, Reasoning, and the Gods* (Chicago, 1992), pp. 4, 67-137. Bottero's analysis of divination texts shows that two apparently unrelated phenomena are juxtaposed, but nonetheless possess an inner relationship which has an underlying logic to be discerned by the reader. This is not unlike the subtle juxtaposition of two lines which sometimes appear in biblical proverbs. Proverbs (and biblical poetry in general) generate meaning by immediate juxtaposition; the reader must "read between the lines" to get the point or possible points. The most fruitful readings are thus a matter of wisdom and insight, for "as the legs of a lame person hang useless, so is a proverb in the mouth of fools" (Prov. 26:7). A good reading of a biblical proverb requires one to make sense of the juxtaposition of the two lines, of the proverb's relation to other sayings or narratives, and finally of its relation to a life-situation in which the saying may usefully function. A wise person knows which proverb fits which situation, person, time, etc. On juxtaposition in Hebrew poetry, see N. Ridderbos, *Die Psalmen: Stilistische Verfahren*

Their artistry and richness of suggestion are all the more dazzling in view of their brevity.

In Hebrew the sayings are incredibly compact. This is partly due to the ellipsis which parallelism and non-verbal clauses make possible. But it is also due to the synthetic nature of Hebrew words.[15] By using affixes, a Hebrew verb can contain prepositional subjects and objects as well as indicate verbal tense, aspect, and modality. Thus, in a Hebrew proverb six to eight tightly bound Hebrew words do the work of a dozen or more in English translation. Proverbs 28:11 contains seven Hebrew words, four in the first line and three in the second. But in English the verse stretches to a prose-like eighteen words in the Authorized Version (KJV) and twenty in the New International Version (which renders literally the masculine forms of the original):

> A rich man may be wise in his own eyes,
> but a poor man who has discernment will see through him.

Dashes between the awkward English words suggest the combinatory power of Hebrew:

| Ḥākām | be'ênâw | 'îš | 'ašîr |
|-------|---------|-----|-------|
| Wise | in-his-own-eyes | a man | rich |

| Wĕdal | mēbîn | yaḥqĕrennû.[16] |
|-------|-------|----------------|
| but-a-poor-man | understanding | will-find-him-out. |

This saying revels in ironic reversal. In Solomon, the archetypal wise man, wisdom and wealth went hand in hand. But here wealth robs the wealthy

---

*und Aufbau, mit besonderer Berücksichtigung von Ps. 1–41* (BZAW 117; Berlin, 1972). Ridderbos calls this the "aphoristic style" that characterizes Hebrew poetry. This phenomenon occurs on the levels of clause, line, and poetic section.

15. Hebrew words are generally made up of a skeleton or "root" of three consonants, which carries a word's semantic freight. This root is varied through vowel changes and the addition of prefixes and suffixes. For example, the consonants *MLK* convey kingship and words based on this skeleton include terms for king *(MeLeK)*, queen *(MaLKâ)*, kingdom *(MaLKût)*, and all the verbs expressing kingly rule *(MāLaK, yi MLōK,* and so forth). For present purposes, certain niceties of linguistic and semantic theory are not relevant.

16. "B" following a vowel is pronounced as "v." "Ḥ" is pronounced as "ch" as in German "Bach." The "š" is like English "sh."

of self-knowledge (cf. 26:12) as they confuse their wealth and status with what might produce them (8:18-19). Complacent expectations which connect wealth with wisdom and poverty with ignorance are here undone in the space of seven words. The last is made first, and the poor comes out on top (cf. 1 Sam. 2:3-8; Luke 1:51-55).

It should be noted that sayings appear not only in Proverbs but in a variety of literary settings in the Old Testament.[17] In fact, one of the most perfect weddings of form and sense appears in Genesis 9:6, a legal proverb which sanctions imperfect human judgments of death for murder:[18]

> Whoever sheds the blood of man,
> by man shall his blood be shed;
> for in the image of God
> has God made man (NIV; 12 words in Hebrew).

The first two lines read,

| ŠōPēK | DaM | hā'aDāM | bā'āDāM | DāMô | yiŠŠaPēK[19] |
|---|---|---|---|---|---|
| He-shedding | blood | of-man | by-man | his-blood | will-be-shed. |
| A | B | C | C' | B' | A' |

Here the punishment perfectly fits the crime. The inverted sequence of three words embodies the murderer's own reversal of fortune. What one has done is done to one; the tables are turned (cf. Lev. 24:17-22; Matt. 26:52). The graphic image of shed blood represents the loss of life and selfhood (*nepeš*, often translated "soul," cf. Lev. 17:11-14). This symbolic identity of blood and life/self is reinforced by the rhyme of *dam* (blood) and *'adam* (man/humankind). Indeed, the center of this tiny poem is haunted by the fourfold echo of

---

17. C. Fontaine, *Traditional Sayings in the Old Testament: A Contextual Study* (Sheffield, 1982), provides an exemplary study of the function of proverbs in biblical narratives.

18. "Society's justice will never be true justice, but always justice and guilt intertwined in a self-renewing cycle of injury and restitution. Offended society cries out for satisfaction, and is covered with guilt when it takes it." Thus O. O'Donovan in his profound analysis of Cain, Abel, and the Cross of Christ in *Resurrection and Moral Order: An Outline for Evangelical Ethics* (Grand Rapids, 1986), pp. 74-75.

19. In the original Hebrew only the consonants were written; the root consonants of each word have been capitalized. "Š" is pronounced "Sh" and, in this context, "P" is pronounced "f," and "K" is "Ch" as in German "Bach." The word for "shed" has an onomatopoetic flowing, hissing sound.

blood. (As a legal proverb, this six-word saying can function independently of the theological motive clause in verse 6b.)

The pithy, poetic character of proverbs makes a proverb nearly impossible to translate adequately. Erasmus put the matter with scholarly restraint: "Some proverbs have this peculiarity, that they need to be quoted in their native tongue, otherwise they lose much of their charm; just as some wines refuse to be exported."[20] So much of the sparkle and shine of a proverb's wit and wisdom gets lost in translation. Its verbal craft is battered and swamped by a disorderly sea of foreign sounds, which seem not to fit the thought or one another. It is true, of course, that proverbs often cross language boundaries, especially between closely cognate languages. English, "Many hands make light work," is Dutch, "Veel handen maken licht werk." And Chaucer, of course, would have understood its Dutch form. But the shining facets of many proverbial gems fit only the language in which they were originally set.

We return from our detour on the poetry of sayings to the matter of their life functions. Here a look at contemporary use of proverbs may be suggestive. M. Scott Peck, whose modern wisdom book *The Road Less Traveled*[21] has been on the *New York Times* bestseller list for over ten years, recently pointed out the important role of proverbs in the amazing success of Alcoholics Anonymous.[22] In comparison to AA, he notes, psychiatrists like himself are relative failures in treating alcoholism. (Indeed, rates of alcoholism among doctors remind us how difficult it is for physicians to heal themselves.) AA'ers succeed, says Peck, because they take it "One day at a time." They tell each other, "I'm not OK, you're not OK, but that's OK." When they do not feel like whole, competent persons, they remind themselves to "Act as if" they were, to "Fake it to make it," and so they become more whole through the things they do. This insight, by the way, goes back to Aristotle's understanding of the relation of act, habit, and character. Aristotle put it in near proverb form:

We are what we repeatedly do.
Excellence, then, is not an act, but a habit.[23]

20. Quoted by Davis, "Proverbial Wisdom," p. 235.
21. New York, 1978.
22. *Further Along the Road Less Travelled* (New York, 1993), pp. 141-44. Peck includes an account of his grandfather teaching him proverbs as a boy. I owe this reference to John Vriend.
23. As cited by another modern wisdom teacher, S. R. Covey, *The Seven Habits of*

Modernity has objected most to the unscientific, contradictory character of proverbs. But it is precisely the ability of proverbs to contradict one another that lends them their versatility and power. Rather than being a defect, this is essential to the genre. A proverb, even when couched in a universal form, is not a universal absolute, like the law of gravity or the speed of light. Proverbs are diverse and contradictory because human life is contradictory and diverse.

The principle of propriety or "fittingness" applies here.[24] Or, in proverbial terms, "If the shoe fits, wear it." A fit proverb always "hits the nail on the head." A hesitant daughter may to be told, "She who hesitates is lost," while an impetuous son needs, "Look before you leap." Wise parents do not treat their children equally but fittingly. Again, some marriages are "Opposites attract," but more often they are "Birds of a feather flock together." And yet, from another angle, without the attraction of opposites, marriage would not exist.[25]

---

*Highly Effective People* (New York, 1990), p. 46. I have not been able to find the formulation used by Covey, but the thought is fundamentally Aristotelian and central to Aristotle's ethics and politics. See, for example, *The Nichomachean Ethics* II.ii.8-9 (1104a-b); II.vi.3 (1106a); III.v.10-12 (1114a); X.ix.5-10 (1179b-1180a).

24. The notion of "fittingness" is developed in aesthetic terms by N. Wolterstorff in his *Art in Action* (Grand Rapids, 1980), pp. 96-121. But — as Wolterstorff himself notes — it is a fundamental factor in our experience of and action in the world. Thus it is at home in ethical and wisdom reflection, both ancient and modern. See Aristotle, *Nich. Eth.* II.ix.2 (1109a) and III.i.16 (1111a) for lists of factors with respect to which acts may be judged as fitting or unfitting. In the biblical wisdom literature, the problem of fittingness is explicitly elaborated in Proverbs 26:1-12. See R. N. Whybray, *Proverbs* (Grand Rapids, 1994), pp. 371-75. In contemporary Christian ethical theory, O'Donovan's *Resurrection and Moral Order* is in many respects an ethics of "fittingness." See especially his second chapter, "Created Order."

Fitting behavior presupposes a created order in terms of which actions are right or wrong, fitting or unfitting, and so forth. Apparently the created order, in biblical terms, permits humans a great deal of freedom to act both individually and collectively, to build lives and to develop cultures. This is the point of freedom to eat from all of the trees of the garden, but one (i.e., much more freedom than restriction) and of the free cultural, linguistic activity implicit in naming the animals (Genesis 2). Yet such freedom appears to have created limits or boundaries, which ought not to be crossed. This is true even of human cultural products.

25. Popular culture (including advertising) is one arena in which the power of proverbs is still valued and exploited. Paula Abdul's witty song and music video, "Opposites Attract," exploits the present saying and others in creative fashion. See W. Mieder, *Proverbs Are Never out of Season: Popular Wisdom in the Modern Age* (New York and Oxford, 1993).

To use proverbs fittingly requires wisdom, a sort of virtuous hermeneutic circle. Proverbs 26:4-5 presents this dilemma well: Verse 4 says,
"Answer not a fool according to his folly, lest you be like him yourself." But
verse 5, "Answer a fool according to his folly, lest he be wise in his own
eyes." So, as Proverbs 26:7 has it, "as lame legs hang useless, so is a proverb
in the mouth of fools." The quoting of proverbs, like the quoting of Scripture, can be the habit of fools. The wise person knows which is which.

The contradictory character of proverbs is essential to their local wisdom, their wisdom for this particular time and place. North Americans say,
"Money talks." And yet, "Money isn't everything." These proverbs are implicitly contradictory, and of diverse application, as Barbara Kirschenblatt-
Gimblet has pointed out.[26] But certain proverbs tend to be culturally dominant, revealing the heart and soul of a people.[27] In North America "Money
talks" is a dominant saying, for we are culturally obsessed with the bottom
line, with the almighty dollar. And, in the USA, if sex is our other national
pastime (more than ever since the greed-based collapse of baseball), Madi-
son Avenue knows that "Sex sells." We reveal our cultural idols when we
insist against all objections that "business is business."

In the United States today, despite pervasive biblical religiosity (the
situation is somewhat different in Canada), mammon too frequently
silences the voices of justice and righteousness. Jesus knew you cannot serve
God and mammon, but Americans do their damndest to do both. And so,
it is every one for themselves and the devil take the hindmost. We "look
out for Number One" because "We owe it to ourselves." ("Number One"
is not a reference to God.) I was astonished to discover that Wolfgang
Mieder's recent *Dictionary of American Proverbs* did not have among its
15,000 proverbs the saying, "The sky's the limit." To me this is a quintes-
sential American proverb, meaning that for us there are no limits.[28] Our
western frontiers had no limits, our aspirations no bounds. That is why
European Americans of an earlier generation used to say, "The only good

---

26. "Toward a Theory of Proverb Meaning," *Proverbium* 22 (1973): 821-27. Reprinted in Dundes and Mieder, *The Wisdom of Many,* pp. 111-21.

27. See Alan Dundes, "Folk Ideas as Units of Worldview," *American Journal of
Folklore* 84 (1971): 93-103.

28. In recent memory, it has appeared in the title of an editorial by Bert Witvoet
in *Calvinist Contact,* in an advertisement for "Safari" men's cologne in *Rolling Stone*
magazine, and in an after-the-service discussion at a local church concerning business
opportunities.

Indian is a dead Indian." This evil proverb was still playing in the myth-making, black and white TV Westerns of my youth.

You don't have to see *Schindler's List* or visit the Holocaust Museum to observe cultural evil. You can start closer to home. Canadian anthropologist Stanley Barrett has argued that contradictory proverbs reflect the fundamental confusions and tensions within a culture.[29] But proverbs also express a people's profoundest ideals, whether for good or ill. Generally it takes some wisdom to see which ideals are culturally dominant, which proverbs speak the loudest and sway human hearts the most. On the other hand, as the sixties saying has it, you don't need to be a weatherman to see which way the wind is blowing. Especially when the wind is a hurricane.

It is perhaps on this issue of limits, of moral and cultural restraint, that the *functional* worldview of modern North America most radically conflicts with the biblical book of Proverbs.[30] The song writer Leonard Cohen portrays the cultural loss of functional limits in his chilling, prophetic song, "The Future":

> Things are going to slide in all directions
> Won't be nothing
> Nothing you can measure anymore
> The blizzard of the world
> has crossed the threshold
> and it has overturned
> the order of the soul.
> When they said REPENT
> I wonder what they meant. . . .

29. "Contradictions in Everyday Life," in *The Rebirth of Anthropological Theory* (Toronto, 1984), pp. 145-76.

30. But no matter how corrupt and chaotic a society or subculture may be, the reality of limits and norms continues to make itself felt. A healthy respect for limits seems to distinguish Quentin Tarantino's recent film *Pulp Fiction* from Oliver Stone's *Natural Born Killers*. The former film, with dazzling aesthetic control, insists on the persistent claims of goodness and moral order in the face of brutal realities which seem to deny them. This is conveyed by the debate on the ethical significance of a foot massage, by Travolta's debate with himself in the bathroom, by the peace made between the boss and the boxer, by the need to clean up Bonnie's house before she gets home, and by the conversion of a sinner. In contrast, Stone's film lacks all conviction because it purports to condemn the media for reveling in violence. But this is a case of the pot calling the kettle black because *Natural Born Killers* itself lacks aesthetic and moral restraint. It becomes what it condemns.

There'll be the breaking of the ancient western code. . . .
I've seen the future, baby:
it is murder.[31]

Proverbs, and the Bible generally, presents a cosmic-cultural world that insists upon freedom within form, love within limits, and life within law. In Proverbs things, like fire, are good when kept within their proper bounds. According to Proverbs 1–9, your neighbor's wife may be a very good woman indeed, a biblical "delight to the eyes." But the point is, she is not good for you. For you she is off limits, and out of bounds. For you, she is not fitting, and you might get burnt (Prov. 6:27-29). This principle is of much wider application than to our sexuality. It applies to money, to the environment, to politics, to art, to existence as a whole. It entails a creation theology, the essence of which Irenaeus articulated long ago. He wrote: "[God] . . . has created the whole world . . . and to the whole world [God] has given laws, that each [creature] keep to [its] place and overstep not the bound laid down by God, each accomplishing the work marked out for [it]."[32] In Proverbs 1–9, and elsewhere, such bounds for human activity are most powerfully symbolized by Yahweh's limiting command to the sea: "thus far shall you come, and no farther, and here shall your proud waves be stayed" (Job 38:11; Prov. 8:29; Ps. 104:9; Jer. 5:22-23). Such cosmo-social limits are not the death of freedom, but its possibility.[33]

Modernity has too often mistakenly taken humanity's immense cultural and technological freedom to mean that there are no limits. The view of Proverbs is that we find our freedom within limits, and outside those reality limits, we encounter damage, as when a hurricane sends the sea roaring over the Carolina shore, or a marriage is destroyed for lack of zipper control, or when the pianist hits F Sharp instead of G Sharp.

When we defy the limits of reality, culturally or individually, we die a little or a lot, like the proverbial fish out of water. Limits are the condition of our freedom, the constraints that make life possible. The blues player

31. Leonard Cohen, *The Future* (compact disc with published text; New York: Columbia/Sony, 1992).
32. *The Demonstration of the Apostolic Preaching*, paragraph 10. This is one of the earliest descriptions known to me of what Abraham Kuyper centuries later elaborated as "sphere sovereignty."
33. See more extensively, R. C. Van Leeuwen, "Liminality and Worldview in Proverbs 1–9," *Semeia* 50 (1990): 111-44.

knows this well. She is bound by a rigid twelve-bar pattern of chord progressions, and if she strays outside their bounds, it just ain't the blues. But within those twelve bars there is a freedom whose scope seems almost infinite to those who know how good, how "bad" the blues can be. This teaching of and, even more, the active observance of cosmic, social, and personal limits as articulated in Proverbs and throughout the Bible is a wisdom our world sorely needs.[34]

There is another aspect to the wisdom of Proverbs that should be mentioned. It is the so-called "act-consequence sequence," or as some have put it, the "character-consequence sequence." Though this idea has received conflicting theoretical formulations,[35] in essence the wisdom principle at stake is that humans reap what they sow. This idea can be formulated with a variety of images. People and nations fall into the pit which they themselves have dug for others, and in this "natural" sequence of events, the judgment of God is operative in all its mystery (Ps. 7:15-16; 9:15-16; Prov. 26:27; 28:10). In response to the wicked, this is a sort of *lex talionis* thinking, a matter of "just deserts," where "the punishment fits the crime." Underlying this mode of thinking is a belief in the integrity of creation, and in the Creator who rewards people (positively or negatively) according to their deeds. This theme pervades Scripture. It is even basic to the New Testament, Protestant misreadings of Paul and appeals to "cheap grace" notwithstanding (Ruth 2:12; Job 34:11; Pss. 28:4 and 62:12; Prov. 24:12; Isa. 59:18; Jer.

---

34. The necessity of a "horizon" which limits but also enables self-definition and cultural character-formation is a theme developed by Charles Taylor in his important work, *Sources of the Self: The Making of the Modern Identity* (Cambridge, 1989). Western culture as a whole seems to have lost (or radically transmuted) the Augustinian view, which Taylor articulates as follows: "My existence as a moral agent may seem to me dependent on the existence of an order of things, in human society and perhaps also in nature, and this in two ways: I am aware of having learnt what it is to be a spiritual being from my society or church; and the order itself in its goodness calls forth a sense of awe and gratitude which empowers me. The order is a moral source for me. But the goodness of the order in turn is inseparable from a notion of providence; I can only see it as rooted in God. And so by this route as well, I find God to be as undeniable as the spiritual dimension of my existence" (p. 311).

35. The formulations differ, for example, concerning the degree of divine involvement or "intervention" in the nexus of act and consequence, and concerning the degree to which the nexus is an "automatic" or "mechanical," "inner-worldly" phenomenon. See K. Koch, ed., *Um das Prinzip der Vergeltung in Religion und Recht des Alten Testaments* (Darmstadt, 1972). K. Koch, "Is There a Doctrine of Retribution in the Old Testament?" in J. L. Crenshaw, ed., *Theodicy in the Old Testament* (Philadelphia, 1983), pp. 57-87.

25:14; 50:29; Lam. 3:64; Amos 8:7; Matt. 6:4,6,18 and 16:27; Rom. 2:6-11; 1 Cor. 3:5-15; 2 Cor. 11:15; 1 Tim. 5:24-25; 2 Tim. 4:14; Heb. 6:10-12; Jas. 2:21,25; 1 Pet. 1:17; Rev. 2:23; 14:13; 18:6; 20:12-13; 22:12).[36]

The metaphor that humans reap what they sow is quite flexible, however, in keeping with the absurdities and irrationalities that disturb human experience. One should not reduce the metaphor to a simplistic, dogmatic schema of rewards and punishments, as Job's "friends" did (Job 4:8).[37] Even the divine Sower of the parable has mixed results in his sowing. Not every seed that falls bears fruit, far from it. Nonetheless, and this is the point, God's harvest is ultimately certain (Mark 4 and parallels). In Proverbs, the act/character consequence schema is most rigorously presented in chapters 10–15. It is as if young people, whom Proverbs addresses, need to learn first that success requires hard work in season (Prov. 10:4-5). There is plenty of time later to learn the hard lesson that sometimes even the best efforts of good "mice and men go oft awry" (Prov. 16:1-9; 19:21; 20:24; 21:30-31; 27:1)[38]

In its concern for limits and for consequences, biblical wisdom teaches humans the basic patterns of reality which they need to know in order to live well and righteously. And in its concern for fittingness, wisdom also requires of us the knowledge of individual differences, the knowledge of particular persons, places, cultures, and circumstances. In Levi-Strauss's terms, wisdom requires the "science of the concrete."[39] This knowledge, too, technological culture and mass communication seem to erode.

---

36. This is only a sampling of passages. It is left standing in the text, rather than placed in this note, to call attention to the righteousness and justice of God in a time when these are largely ignored, also by Christians. The "wrath" and "pathos" of God is the measured corollary of God's love and compassion for the good creation and creatures that God holds precious, and which God will not forever yield hostage to agents of evil. The great text here, with echoes throughout Scripture, is Exodus 34:6-7. See A. Heschel, *The Prophets* II (New York, 1962). For further bibliography, see R. C. Van Leeuwen, "Scribal Wisdom and Theodicy in the Book of the Twelve," in L. G. Perdue, et al., eds., *In Search of Wisdom: Essays in Memory of John G. Gammie* (Louisville, Ky., 1993), pp. 31-49.

37. In addition to the normal pattern, there are many cases of disruptions and deflections in the sequence sowing and reaping. See Job 31:8; Ps. 126:5-6; Prov. 11:18; 22:8; Jer. 12:13; Hos. 8:7; 10:12; Mic. 6:15; Hag. 1:6; Zech. 8:12; Matt. 6:26 and 25:24,26; John 4:37; 1 Cor. 9:11; 15:36-44; 2 Cor. 9:6; Gal. 6:7-8; Jas. 3:18.

38. This is the burden especially of Ecclesiastes and Job. But it is already implicit in the *later* sections of Proverbs. See G. Von Rad, "Limits of Wisdom," *Wisdom in Israel*, pp. 97-110; Van Leeuwen, "Wealth and Poverty."

39. C. Levi-Strauss, "The Science of the Concrete," *The Savage Mind* (London, 1966), pp. 1-33.

I would like to conclude with an exploration of just one biblical proverb, for it adds to our discussion what is really its *sine qua non.* Scholars universally agree that Proverbs 1:7 is the book's motto. This verse is the fundamental cultural ideal and the all-inclusive context for the diverse sayings, admonitions, and instructions which follow. The saying is well known:

> The fear of the Lord is the beginning of knowledge;
> fools despise wisdom and instruction.

Here God and humans, wisdom and folly, knowledge and sweat born of parental urging (cf. 1:8; 10:1, 4-5) are all related in the tight space of eight Hebrew words. As will appear in the subsequent chapters of Proverbs, humans are caught in a quasi-erotic pull between Lady Wisdom and Dame Folly. In the male-oriented imagery of Proverbs 1–9, life is not just a matter of structures and limits, but of ultimate loves for one inviting "Lady" or another (9:1-6, 13-18). What you love determines where you are headed, and at which "house" you will arrive. More, the word "beginning" in Proverbs 1:7 contains the hint, to be elaborated throughout the first nine chapters, that life is not static, but a journey whose end is found in its beginning. T. S. Eliot said it surpassingly well in *Four Quartets:*

> What we call the beginning is often the end
> And to make an end is to make a beginning.
> The end is where we start from. . . .
>     We shall not cease from exploration
> And the end of all our exploring
> Will be to arrive where we started
> And know the place for the first time. ("Little Gidding" V)

Proverbs 1:7, and the introductory verses which precede it, provide a series of key concepts that set forth the book's fundamental principles. These great principles, justice, righteousness, and discipline among them, give order and unity to the overwhelming diversity of insights and admonitions in the sprawling collections of Proverbs as a whole. They set the hermeneutical parameters; they determine the destinies. As Oliver O'Donovan has written, "We will read the Bible seriously only when we use it to guide our thought towards a comprehensive moral viewpoint, and not merely to articulate disconnected moral claims. We must look within it not only for moral bricks, but for indications of the order in which the bricks belong together."[40] It is the function of Proverbs 1:7 and its context in chapters 1–9 to point the reader to the order which encompasses Wisdom's bricks and holds her house together.

But if Proverbs 1:7 is correct —

The fear of the Lord is the beginning of knowledge,
but fools despise wisdom and discipline —

if this is correct, then many of the foundational presuppositions of modernity and postmodernity need reexamination. And the church too needs to recapture the wisdom of Proverbs in these matters.

For Proverbs 1:7, faith is not opposed to reason, but constitutes its possibility, its connection to reality.[41] Proverbs 1:7 and its elaboration throughout the book are a fundamental assault upon an assumption basic to most current worldviews: namely, that knowledge of the real world has nothing to do with the "fear" or "knowledge" of the one God Yahweh. This modern assumption is elaborated, even in works of biblical scholarship, by various separations of "sacred" and "secular" realms: public vs. private, facts vs. values, science vs. religion, reason vs. faith, "objective" vs. (merely) "subjective." But the critique of Proverbs 1:7 on modernity concerns not just ideas and opinions, for the problematic patterns, structures, and institutions of our communal life have been largely shaped by "autonomous" reason, science, and technique. Early modernity's "rational" solution to the wars of religion created problems of a different sort.

For Proverbs, all of reality is God's reality (cf. 8:22-31). Though we may legitimately distinguish worship and "secular" activities, in Proverbs "all of life is religion."[42] That is, the ordinary affairs of daily life as well as cult and worship are to be lived in service of Yahweh and according to the norms, limits, and constraints Yahweh has placed in reality.[43] Thus, for example, the various "worldly" activities of the "valiant woman" in Proverbs

---

40. *Resurrection and Moral Order*, p. 200.
41. See G. von Rad, *Wisdom in Israel*, pp. 53-73.
42. I learned this saying from my teacher, H. Evan Runner, as did many others. See H. Vander Goot, ed., *Life is Religion: Essays in Honor of H. Evan Runner* (St. Catherines, Ont.: Paideia Press, 1981).
43. The mention of worship in the sayings of Proverbs is very rare. See 15:29; 17:1; 21:3, 27; 28:9, 13.

31 (31:10-33; cf. Ruth 3:11) are not opposed to or separate from her "fear of the Lord," but its living manifestation.[44] On the other hand, one does not have to be a Yahwist to know that theft, lying, and adultery are wrong.

The great Old Testament scholar G. von Rad put it well: "Humans are always entirely in the world, yet are always entirely involved with Yahweh" (my translation). Again, "experiences of the world were for [Israel] always divine experiences as well, and the experiences of God were for her experiences of the world."[45] (This, of course, without confusing God and world.) Conversely, says von Rad, "Folly is practical atheism." Israel was "of the opinion that effective knowledge about God is the only thing that puts a man [sic] in a right relationship with the objects of his perception, that it enables him to ask questions more pertinently, to take stock of relationships more effectively and generally to have a better awareness of circumstances."[46]

In sum, Proverbs 1:7 is the ultimate context within which all the sayings and admonitions find their place, no matter how "worldly" the latter may seem. This world and all within it are God's, and without cognizance of God the details of life do not harmonize. Indeed, the unbridled love of the goods of this world bid fair to usurp God as the ultimate good, and to destroy God's reign as the realm within which all created goods find their proper, but limited place.

In the Sermon on the Mount, Jesus tells his followers to consider the lilies of the field and the birds of the air, for whom God provides. He puts all the cares and difficulties of life into perspective when he says, "seek first the kingdom of God and his righteousness" (6:33; cf. Eccl. 12:13-14).[47] This

---

44. Al Wolters, "Nature and Grace in the Interpretation of Proverbs 31:10-31," *Calvin Theological Journal* (1984), pp. 153-66.

45. *Wisdom in Israel*, pp. 95 and 62.

46. *Wisdom in Israel*, pp. 65, 67-68.

47. The pervasive and crucial place of "righteousness" or "righteousness and justice" in Scripture, both Old and New Testaments, is a matter that requires urgent attention by Evangelical and Reformed folk who would seek biblical guidance for their mode of life in the world. In the present context it is important to point out that righteousness is not only a social-cultural concept (Gen. 18:19; Isa. 5:1-7; Amos 5:21-24) but a cosmic one encompassing the social and cultural (Pss. 50:7; 72; 97:7; 2 Cor. 5:17-21; 2 Peter 3:13). On 2 Cor. 5:17-21 see the commentary of V. P. Furnish, *Second Corinthians* (Anchor Bible; Garden City, N.Y., 1984). The writings of the Swiss Reformed Old Testament scholar, H. H. Schmid are especially important for the cosmic scope of righteousness. See his *Gerechtigkeit als Weltordnung* (Tübingen, 1968) and *Altoriental-*

is nothing less than the "fear of the Lord and the beginning of wisdom." In such a blessed situation, the goods of this world are enjoyed but not idolized, and humans are content with the goodness of the Creator, even though sufficient to the day is the evil thereof. Christ here appears as a second Solomon, and more, as the very Wisdom of God. His words are the ultimate commentary on the wisdom of Proverbs, his life and death the final commentary on the fear of the Lord.

---

*ische Welt in der alttestamentlichen Theologie* (Zurich, 1974). Schmid's essay, "Creation, Righteousness, and Salvation: 'Creation Theology' as the Broad Horizon of Biblical Theology" (in B. W. Anderson, ed., *Creation in the Old Testament* [Philadelphia, 1984], pp. 102-117) does not translate the section in the German original which discusses "righteousness" in the New Testament. That essay may be found in *Altorientalische Welt.* For New Testament (Pauline) "righteousness," see also Schmid's essay, "Rechtfertigung als Schöpfungsgeschehen: Notizen zur alttestamentlichen Vorgeschichte eines neutestamentlichen Themas," in J. Friedrich et al., eds., *Rechtfertigung: Festschrift für E. Käsemann* (Tübingen, 1976), pp. 403-14. More recently, see the balanced overview of H. Graf Reventlow, "The World Horizon of Old Testament Theology," *Problems of Old Testament Theology in the Twentieth Century* (Philadelphia, 1985), pp. 134-86.

The work of R. Knierim is also of the utmost significance in regard to biblical thinking regarding righteousness and the cosmos. See his "Cosmos and History in Israel's Theology," *Horizons in Biblical Theology* 3 (1981): 59-123; and "The Task of Old Testament Theology," *HBT* 6 (1984): 25-57. The responses to the latter essay (printed with it in *HBT*) reflect the general historicism and aversion to systematic analysis which typifies the Enlightenment legacy of biblical scholarship. On historicism in the guild, see the incisive critique by Jon D. Levenson, "Historical Criticism and the Fate of the Enlightenment Project," *The Hebrew Bible, The Old Testament, and Historical Criticism: Jews and Christians in Biblical Studies* (Louisville, Ky., 1993), pp. 106-26, 177-79.

# Writings and Speeches by Calvin G. Seerveld, 1957-1994

## COMPILED BY PERRY RECKER

1957     "A Note on a School of Thought and Disciples." *Reformed Journal* 7 (June 1957): 27-28.

1958     *Benedetto Croce's Earlier Aesthetic Theories and Literary Criticism.* Kampen: J. H. Kok, 1958.

"Gone With the Resurrection." *Christianity Today* 2 (31 March 1958): 11-13.

1960     "A Christian Perspective for Cosmetology." Address. Convention of State Boards of Cosmetology, July 1960. Printed in shortened form in *National-Interstate Council Bulletin* 15 (no. 1, September-October 1960): 3-5.

"Philosophical Historiography." *Journal of the American Scientific Affiliation* 12 (no. 3, September 1960): 87-89.

*Skeleton to Philosophy 101 at Trinity Christian College.* Mimeograph. [Palos Heights, Ill., n.d.]

1962     "A Christian Critique of Art." Lectures. Study Conference of the Association for Reformed Scientific Studies, Unionville, Ontario, August 1962.

1963     *A Christian Critique of Art.* Hamilton: Association for Reformed Scientific Studies, 1963.

"A Christian Critique of Literature." Lectures. Study Conference of the Association for Reformed Scientific Studies, Unionville, Ontario, August 1963.

"Perspective for Our Christian Colleges." *Christianity Today* 7 (no. 24, 13 September 1963): 1169-71

"What Makes a College Christian?" *Christianity Today* 7 (no. 23, 30 August 1963): 1103-5.

1964 *A Christian Critique of Literature.* Hamilton: Association for Reformed Scientific Studies, 1964.

"The Christian School in American Democracy." In *Convention Addresses: 44th Annual Christian School Convention,* 2-19. Grand Rapids, Mich.: National Union of Christian Schools, 1964.

*Christian Workers, Unite!* Convention Address. Christian Labour Association of Canada, 1964.

Review of *Religious Art in the Twentieth Century,* by P.-R. Regamey. *Christianity Today* 8 (28 August 1964): 1063.

1965 "The Artistic Imperative of Psalm 150." *The Banner* 100 (no. 22, 28 May 1965): 4-5.

Commencement address. Illiana Christian High School, Lansing, Illinois, June 1965.

"Dooyeweerd's Contribution to the Historiography of Philosophy." In *Philosophy and Christianity: Philosophical Essays Dedicated to Professor Dr. Herman Dooyeweerd,* 193-202. Kampen: J. H. Kok, 1965.

*Labour: A Burning Bush.* Convention Address. Rexdale, Ontario: Christian Labour Association of Canada, 1965.

*The Rub to Christian Organization or . . . Christian Camel Drivers Unite?* Address. Groen van Prinsterer Society, Calvin College, March 1965. *Torch and Trumpet* 15 (no. 7, September 1965): 8-13.

"So That the Enemies See." [Meditation on Psalm 86.] *The Guide* 13 (no. 1, January 1965): 1. [Publication of the Christian Labour Association of Canada/CLAC.]

*The Song of Moses and the Lamb: The Joke of A.R.S.S. Education.* Hamilton: Association for Reformed Scientific Studies, 1965. [Keynote Address, A.R.S.S. Study Conference, Unionville, August 1965.]

"The Temptation of Art." *Christianity Today* 10 (no. 5, 3 December 1965): 239-41.

1966 *Cultural Objectives for the Christian Teacher.* Seattle: Pacific Northwest Christian Teachers Association, 1966.

*Take Hold of God and Pull: Moments in a College Chapel.* Palos Heights, Ill.: Trinity Pennyasheet Press, 1966.

**1967**   *For a Sick Man and Woman: The Christian Touch.* Chicago: Rest Haven, 1967.

*The Greatest Song: In Critique of Solomon.* Palos Heights, Ill.: Trinity Pennyasheet Press, 1967; Amsterdam: ten Have, 1966.

"The Meaning of Silence for Daily Life and Sunday Worship." International Reformed Bulletin 10 (no. 3, July 1967): 6-19.

"The Umbrella over Trinity Christian College." Retreat address. Camp Lake Geneva, Wisconsin, September 1967.

**1968**   "A Case Study: Reading Numbers 22–24." In *Understanding the Scriptures: How to Read and Not to Read the Bible* (with Arnold DeGraaff). Toronto: Association for the Advancement of Christian Scholarship, 1968.

*A Christian Critique of Art and Literature.* Toronto: Association for the Advancement of Christian Scholarship, 1968.

"Comic Relief to Christian Art." *Christianity Today* 12 (no. 11, 1 March 1968): 10-12.

*Skeleton to Philosophy 101 at Trinity Christian College.* Mimeograph. [Palos Heights, Ill., n.d.]

Review of *Censorship, Obscenity and Sex,* by Alfred P. Klausler. *Gordon Review* 11 (Fall 1968): 169-71.

**1969**   "Christian Art." *The Banner* 104 (no. 39, 10 October 1969): 4-5.

"A Christian Case For Free Love." Lecture. Montana State University, Bozeman, February 1969.

Education theory and art history lectures. Potchefstroom University for Christian Higher Education, South Africa, September-October 1969.

"How a Christian Cosmology and Christian Anthropology Orient Christian Curriculum." Faculty Summer Seminar, Wheaton College, Illinois, June 1969.

"The Most Fundamental Philosophical Question and Its Relevance For Communication." Lecture. Montana State University, Bozeman, February 1969.

"Transcendental Method at Work in the Humanities." Seminar in Philosophy of the Sciences, American Scientific Affiliation, December 1969.

**1970**   Answer to "voices" responding to "Christian Art" article. *The Banner* 105 (no. 1, 2 January 1970): 24-25.

"Bastards or Sons of God." *The Guide* 15 (no. 5, May 1970): 8-10.

"How a Christian Cosmology and Christian Anthropology Orient

Christian Curriculum." Faculty Summer Seminar, Wheaton College, Illinois, June 1970.

"A Modest Proposal for Reforming the Christian Reformed Church in North America." In *Out of Concern for the Church,* by John A. Olthuis, et al., 46-73. Toronto: Wedge Publishing Foundation, 1970.

"On the Nature of Christian Critique of Literature." *Bulletin van die Suid-Afrikaanse Vereniging vir die Bevordering van Christelike Wetenskap* 20 (January 1970): 21-57.

"The Problems and Spirit of American Painting." Lecture. Dordt College, Iowa, March 1970.

Review of *Somewhat Less Than God: The Biblical View of Man,* by L. Verduin. *Christian Scholar's Review* 1 (no. 1, Fall 1970): 78-80.

1971    "Is the Christian Faith Relevant Today?" Public debate with Michael Scriven of Berkeley University. Oregon State University, Corvallis, February 1971.

"Not Peace, but Faith, Shalom . . . and a Sword." *The Guide* 19 (no. 12, December 1971): 1-3, 10.

"The Relation of the Arts to the Presentation of Truth." In *Truth and Reality: Philosophical Perspectives on Reality Dedicated to Dr. H. G. Stoker,* 161-75. Braamfontein: De Jong's Bookshop, 1971.

1972    "Christian Faith for Today." *Vanguard* (January/February 1972): 7-11.

*For God's Sake Run With Joy: Moments in a College Chapel.* Toronto: Wedge Publishing Foundation, 1972.

"Proverbs 25." [Under Column title "Take Hold of God and Pull."] *Vanguard* (March/April 1972): 5, 34.

"Proverbs 25 Again." *Vanguard* (May/June 1972): 5.

"To Be Led into Fresh Obedience." In *Will All the King's Men,* edited by Robert Lee Carvill, 115-49. Toronto: Wedge Publishing Foundation, 1972.

1973    "Biblical Wisdom underneath Vollenhoven's Categories for Philosophical Historiography." In *The Idea of a Christian Philosophy: Essays in Honour of D. H. Th. Vollenhoven,* 127-43. Published as a special edition of *Philosophia Reformata* 38, by J. H. Kok, Kampen, and as a separate volume by Wedge Publishing Foundation, Toronto, 1973.

"Courtesy," " Innocence," " Kiss, Kissing," "Modesty," and "Nudism." In *Baker's Dictionary of Christian Ethics,* edited by Carl F. H. Henry. Grand Rapids: Baker Book House, 1973.

"Historical Origins of Aesthetic Theory." Lecture. Free University, Amsterdam, May 1973.

"A Kiss Smack on the Lips." [Meditation on Proverbs 24:26, 28-29 and 26:17-28.] *Vanguard* (April/May 1973): 24-25, 31.

"Proverbs 6:1-5, 11:15, 17:18, 22:26-27, and 27:12-13." [Under Column title "Take Hold of God and Pull."] *Vanguard* (December 1973): 30-31.

"Tomorrow is a Gift of the Lord." [Meditation on Proverbs 27:1-11.] *Vanguard* (August 1973): 24-26.

"Will You Be a Joke to God?" [Meditation on Proverbs 24:30-34, 26:13-16.] *Vanguard* (January/February 1973): 15, 30-31; also appeared in *The Guide* 21 (no. 4, April 1973): 10-11.

1974    "Art, Christian," "Botticelli," "Cranach," "Dürer," "Giotto," "William Holman Hunt," "Fra Filippo Lippi," "Rembrandt," "Rouault," "Rubens," and "Rogier van der Weyden." In *The New International Dictionary of the Christian Church,* general editor J. D. Douglas. Grand Rapids: Zondervan, 1974.

"The Biblical Charter for Artistic Activity in the Christian Community." Lecture. [Cassette sound recording.] St. Paul: Bethel College, 1974.

"Exercise in Bible Reading During Inflation." [Meditation on Proverbs 24:27.] *The Guide* 22 (no. 11, November 1974): 6.

"Iconographic Themes and Artistic Idiom at the Time of the Reformation." *Patmos Quarterly Bulletin* 2 (Summer 1974). [Patmos Art Gallery.]

"Proverbs 27 Again." *Vanguard* (March/April 1974): 24-25.

*A Turnabout in Aesthetics to Understanding.* Inaugural address. Toronto: Institute for Christian Studies, 1974.

"Uncover Wrong to Heal Things Straight." [Meditation on Proverbs 24:23b-25, 25:2-10.] *Vanguard* (May/June 1974): 27.

"A Wink of Mercy." [On Psalm 123.] *Vanguard* (November/December 1974): 6-7.

Review of *Bunk Among Dragons,* by F. Tamminga. In *Vanguard* (May/June 1974): 27.

1975    "The Christian and the Arts." *For the Time Being* 3 (no. 3, Spring 1975): 14-17.

Colloquium on *A Turnabout in Aesthetics to Understanding,* with J. Bywater. Allegheny College, Meadville, Pennsylvania, October 1975.

"The Evil of Authoritarianism: An Exploration in Proverbs 29." *Van-guard* (September/October 1975): 8-9, 24-25.

"He Hodos." Poem. *Vanguard* (May/June 1975): 7.

"How God's Word of Proverbs Communicates." [Proverbs 28:15-18.] *Vanguard* (May-June 1975): 10-11.

"Nexus of Aesthetic Theory, Art and Literary Studies." Lecture. Car-negie-Mellon University, Pittsburgh, February 1975.

"The Pedagogical Strength of a Christian Methodology in Philo-sophical Historiography." In *Crosscuts and Perspectives: Philo-sophical Essays in Honour of J. A. L. Taljaard*, 269-313. Published as a special issue of *Koers* 40 (nos. 4-6, 1975).

"The Topsy-Turvy World of Faith, or God's Word for Those 'In Authority.' " [On Proverbs 28:1-14.] *Vanguard* (January/Febru-ary 1975): 12-14, 31.

Response to address on "Creation" by J. Houston. Regent College/In-stitute for Christian Studies Colloquium. York University, On-tario, May 1975.

Review of *Kants Kunsttheorie und die Einheit der Kritik der Ur-teilskraft*, by Karl Kuypers. *Journal of Aesthetics and Art Criticism* 34 (no. 2, Winter 1975): 210-12.

**1976**   "Agur and Christ on False Witness and Sin Against the Holy Spirit." [On Proverbs 30:10-14, Matthew 12:31-37.] *Vanguard* (June 1976): 6-7.

"Agur's Prayer for Daily Bread." *The Guide* 24 (no. 7, July-August 1976): 4-5.

"The Christian and the Arts." *Vanguard* (March 1976): 8-12.

"Early Kant and a Rococo Spirit: Setting for the *Critique of Judg-ment*." Annual meeting of the Canadian Society for Eighteenth-Century Studies. Halifax, April 1976.

"Equus: Two Views." *Vanguard* (May 1976): 21-22.

"Gallantry as a Recreative Moment in Life." *Vanguard* (October 1976): 19-21.

"Give the Helpless Justice or Be Damned." [On Proverbs 29:1-14.] *Vanguard* (January/February 1976): 4-5, 22.

"Magi from the East: A Warning and a Signpost." [On Matthew 2:1-2, 10-11 and Isaiah 60:1-6.] *Vanguard* (November/December 1976): 4-5.

"A Psalm for Autumn." [On Psalm 2.] *Vanguard* (October 1976): 4-5.

"A Way To Go in the Definition of 'Aesthetic.'" Eighth International Congress on Aesthetics, Darmstadt, August 1976.

"A Wisdom Hymn and Agur's Parable." [On Proverbs 3 and 30.] *Vanguard* (March 1976): 4-5.

**1977**     Aesthetics and historiography of art. Lecture series. Loma Linda University, California, April 1977.

"An Allusive Touch: 'Glory to God in the Kitchen.'" *Vanguard* (January/February 1977): 22-24.

"Biblical Character of Artistic Activity within the Christian Community." Lecture. [Cassette sound recording.] Loma Linda University, California, 1977.

"The Call to Aesthetic Obedience." Lecture. [Cassette sound recording.] Loma Linda University, California, 1977.

*A Christian Critique of Art and Literature.* 2d ed. Toronto: Association for the Advancement of Christian Scholarship, 1977.

"Dumb Animals and Christian Leadership." [On Proverbs 30:24-33.] *Vanguard* (March/April 1977): 32-33.

"Import of a Distinction Between 'Aesthetic' and 'Artistic' for Christian Aesthetic Theory." Lecture. Wheaton College Annual Philosophy Conference, Illinois, October 1977.

"Telltale Statues in Watteau's Painting." Annual meeting of the Canadian Society for Eighteenth-Century Studies, Hamilton, October 1977.

"Things Mother Taught Me." [On Proverbs 31:2-9.] *Vanguard* (June/July 1977): 9-10.

Review of *Marxism and Literary Criticism,* by Terry Eagleton. *Vanguard* (July/August 1977): 26-27.

**1978**     "A Christian Approach to Art and Aesthetics." [Cassette sound recording.] New York: Chautauqua Institution, 1978.

"A Christian Case for Free Love." Lecture. [Cassette sound recording.] New York: Chautauqua Institution (Department of Religion), 1978.

"A Cloud of Witnesses and a New Generation." Address. [Twentieth AACS Conference, Niagara, Ontario.] *Vanguard supplement* (November/December 1978): 16.

"The Cross of Scholarly Cultural Power." Vanguard (August/September 1978): 19-22.

"Early Kant and a Rococo Spirit: Setting for the *Critique of Judgment.*" *Philosophia Reformata* 43 (nos. 3-4, 1978): 145-67.

"The Meaning of Our Nakedness." Frostburg State College, Maryland, March 1978. Also for Department of Religion, Chautauqua Institution, New York, 1978.

"Modern Art and the Birth of a Culture." Lecture. University of Michigan, Ann Arbor, March 1978.

"Modern Art in Christian Culture." Lecture. [Cassette sound recording.] New York: Chautauqua Institution (Department of Religion), 1978.

"Normative Aesthetic in a Secular Age." Lecture. [Cassette sound recording.] New York: Chautauqua Institution, 1978.

"The Only True Direction." [On Proverbs 4:20-26.] *Vanguard* (August/September 1978): 11-12.

"Proverbs 23:19-35 and Holiday Spirits." *Vanguard* (November/December 1978): 14-15.

"Reading the Bible at Home as a Family." *Calvinist Contact* 34 (no. 1636, 17 March 1978): 8-9.

"Watteau — Disguised Critique of Fashionable Society." Lecture. University of Michigan, Ann Arbor, March 1978.

Review of *In Praise of Shadows,* by J. Tanizaki. *Patmos Quarterly Bulletin* 17 (Spring 1978): 2.

Review of *Truth and Method,* by H. G. Gadamer. *Journal of Aesthetics and Art Criticism* 36 (no. 4, Summer 1978): 487-90.

1979     "Free Labour." *The Guide* 27 (no. 7, September 1979): 11.

"The Influence of Periodisation Upon Art Historiography of the Enlightenment." Fifth International Congress on the Enlightenment, Pisa, Italy, August 1979.

"Modal Aesthetics: Preliminary Questions with an Opening Hypothesis." In *Hearing and Doing: Philosophical Essays Dedicated to H. Evan Runner,* edited by John Kraay and Anthony Tol, 263-94. Toronto: Wedge Publishing Foundation, 1979.

"Proverbs 1:10-19 vs. the Lure of Respectable Sin." *Vanguard* 9 (no. 3, May/June 1979): 6-7.

"Reading the Bible at Home as a Family." *Calvinist Contact* 35, Fall book issue (no. 1715, 19 October 1979): 17. [Reprint of 1978 article.]

"Telltale Statues in Watteau's Paintings." Lecture. Fine Arts Department and Philosophy Club, University of Alberta, Edmonton, January 1979.

Review of *Recovering Biblical Sensuousness,* by William E. Phipps. *Christian Scholar's Review* 8 (no. 4, 1979): 347-48.

1980     *Balaam's Apocalyptic Prophecies: A Study in Reading Numbers 22–24.* 2d ed. Toronto: Wedge Publishing Foundation, 1980.

"Characteristics of Christian Culture." *Anakainosis* 3 (no. 1, September 1980): 14-16.

"Christmas Means Lord of the Angels and Kids Playing in the Streets." *Perspective* 14 (no. 6, November-December 1980): 1-3. Reprinted in *Calvinist Contact* 36 (no. 1770, 5 December 1980): 10.

"Committed Art, Propaganda, and Advertising." *Proceedings of the Ninth International Congress on Aesthetics* 3 (1980): 317-20. [Held in Dubrovnik, Croatia, published in Belgrade, Serbia.]

*Rainbows for the Fallen World: Aesthetic Life and Artistic Task.* Toronto: Tuppence Press; Beaver Falls: Radix Books, 1980.

"Relating Christianity to the Arts." *Christianity Today* 24 (no. 19, 7 November 1980): 1349-50.

"Telltale Statues in Watteau's Paintings." *Eighteenth-Century Studies* 14 (no. 2, Winter 1980-81): 151-80. [Awarded the James L. Clifford prize for 1980-81 by the American Society for Eighteenth-Century Studies in the Spring of 1982.]

"Toward a Cartographic Methodology for Art Historiography." *Journal of Aesthetics and Art Criticism* 39 (no. 2, Winter, 1980): 143-54.

Review of *Art in Action,* by N. Wolterstorff. *Vanguard* 10 (no. 6, November/December 1980): 5, 18-19. [Under the title "Cal Looks at Nick."]

**1981**    "Art: Luxury or Necessary." Lecture. New York Arts Group Festival 1981, New York City, September 1981.

"Artist: Freedom vs. Responsibility." Lecture. New York Arts Group Festival 1981, New York City, September 1981.

"Can Art Survive the Secular Onslaught?" *Christianity Today* 25 (17 July 1981): 968-69, 971-72.

"Christian Art." In *The Christian Imagination: Essays on Literature and the Arts,* ed. L. Ryken, 383-90. Grand Rapids: Baker Book House, 1981. Revised and expanded version of article published in *The Banner* (10 October 1969).

"A Christian Tin-Can Theory Of Man." *Journal of the American Scientific Affiliation* 33 (June 1981): 74-81.

Colloquia (on left brain/right brain) with Paul Vitz of New York University. Dordt College, Iowa, November 1981.

"Human Responses to Art: Good, Bad, and Indifferent." Lecture. Dordt College, Iowa, November 1981.

"The Influence of Periodisation Upon Art Historiography of the

Enlightenment." *Studies on Voltaire and the Eighteenth-Century* 190 (1981): 183-89.

"Literary Norms for Hymns." *The Banner* 116 (no. 12, 23 March 1981): 23.

"Old Favourites." *The Banner* 116 (no. 5, 2 February 1981): 23.

"The Problem of Committed Art in Society." Lecture. Cornell University, Ithaca, October 1981.

"La Ricerca Filosofica Christiana. Alcune Tesi Aggiuntive." *Certezze, Rivista dei Gruppi Biblici Universitari* 30 (March 1981): 14-19.

"A Worship Service Where Two People Walked Out." *The Banner* 116 (no. 3, 19 January 1981): 8-10.

**1982**  "Canonic Art: Pregnant Dilemmas in the Theory and Artwork of Anton Raphael Mengs (1728-79)." Annual meeting of the Canadian Society for Eighteenth-Century Studies, Edmonton, October 1982.

"The Contribution of Christian Aesthetic Theory toward Reading the Bible." Lecture. The King's College, Edmonton, October 1982,

"The Historical Milieu and Literary Structure of the Biblical Proverb Book." Lecture. Canadian Association for Reformed Faith and Action, Ontario, April 1982.

"Joined Tasks Within the Artworld." Lecture. Annual Festival of the Arts Center Group, London, England, September 1982.

"Joy and Laughter for People of God Minding Advent." *Perspective* 16 (no. 6, November/December 1982): 1-4.

"The Messiah Showed Up in Diapers." *Calvinist Contact* 38 (no. 1863, 10 December 1982): 3.

"Operation Bread and Fish for the Davis Government." *Calvinist Contact* 37 (no. 1844, 2 July 1982): 10.

"Philosophy as Schooled Memory." *Anakainosis* 5 (no. 1, September 1982): 1-6.

"Reform in Reading Biblical Wisdom Literature." Lecture. Canadian Association for Reformed Faith and Action, Ontario, April 1982.

"Singing Psalm 137." *The Banner* 117 (no. 10, 15 March 1982): 12.

"Songs to Sing Standing Up." *The Banner* 117 (no. 12, 29 March 1982): 23.

"The Spirit and Contribution of Modern Art." Greenbelt Festival, Knebworth Park, England, August 1982.

"What Are the Arts For?" Greenbelt Festival, Knebworth Park, England, August 1982.

"Why Humans Should Play" Greenbelt Festival, Knebworth Park, England, August 1982.

Review of *Signs of Our Times: Theological Essays on Art in the Twentieth Century,* by G. S. Heyer, Jr. *Christianity Today* 25 (19 February 1982): 54-55.

**1983**    "Art and Bible Reading." Presentations at the All-Ontario University Student Retreat organized by the CRC chaplains in Ontario, February 1983.

"An Exhortation on Ephesians 4 Celebrating Marriages." *Calvinist Contact* 39 (no. 1901, 28 October 1983): 10-12.

"A Haunted Mennonite." With Anya Seerveld. Review of *My Lovely Enemy,* by Rudy Wiebe. *Calvinist Contact* 39, Fall book issue (no. 1902, 4 November 1983): 14, 16.

"Human Responses to Art: Good, Bad, and Indifferent." In *Human Responses to Art,* with Paul C. Vitz, pp. 1-18. Sioux Center: Dordt College Press, 1983.

"Integrated or Patched-Together Christian Art?" Greenbelt Festival, Knebworth Park, England, August 1983.

"The Meaning of Clothes." Lecture. Greenbelt Festival, Knebworth Park, England, August 1983.

"Methodological Problems in Eighteenth-Century Studies." Interdisciplinary Seminar. Department of History, University of Western Ontario, London, November 1983.

"The Moment of Truth and Evidence of Sterility in Aesthetic Theory and Art of the Later Enlightenment." In *Transactions of the Sixth International Congress on the Enlightenment,* 149-51. Oxford: The Voltaire Foundation, 1983.

"Philosophy of Culture and Art History." [Lectures.] London Institute for Contemporary Christianity, England, August 1983.

"The Vexing Problem of Canonic Art: A. R. Mengs and Sir Joshua Reynolds." English and Philosophy and Art Department, University of Ottawa, Ontario, October 1983.

"What Christians Can Learn From Trotsky About Literature." Greenbelt Festival, Knebworth Park, England, August 1983.

Review of *Ah, But Your Land is Beautiful,* by Alan Paton. *Third Way* 6 (no. 10, November 1983): 27.

**1984**    "Aesthetics, Christian View of," and "Art, Christian." In *Evangelical Dictionary of Theology,* 16-18, 82-85. Edited by Walter A. Elwell. Grand Rapids: Baker Book House, 1984.

"Canonic Art: Pregnant Dilemmas in the Theory and Practice of

Anton Raphael Mengs." In *Man and Nature/L'Homme et la Nature: Proceedings of the Canadian Society for Eighteenth-Century Studies*, vol. 3, pp. 113-30. Edited by Robert J. Merrett. 1984.

"The Christian Rationale for Artistic Activity." [Lectures.] Mennonite Brethren and the Christian Mennonite Bible Colleges, Manitoba, January 1984.

"Christianity and the Arts — Christianity for the Whole Person." An interview with contributing editor Nancy Pearcey. *Bible Science Newsletter* 22 (no. 6, June 1984): 7-10. Reprinted in *Perspective* 18 (no. 3, June 1984) insert.

"Essential Foci of Aesthetic Theory." Lecture. Redeemer College, Ontario, November 1984.

"Imaginativity." Canadian Society for Aesthetics/Société canadienne d'esthétique. Tenth International Congress on Aesthetics, Montreal, August 1984.

"Introduction to an Oratorio Performance of the Old Testament Song of Songs." Performance by the Toronto Trinity Players, directed by Alan Richardson. Annual Convention of the Popular Culture Association of America, Toronto, March 1984.

"Kurelek Art: Preaching in the Footnotes." *Calvinist Contact* 40 (no. 1946, 5 October 1984): 8; (no. 1950, 2 November 1984): 9; (no. 1952, 16 November 1984): 12, 18.

"Learning at Trotsky's Shoulder." *Third Way* 7 (no. 7, December 1983/January 1984): 20-23.

"Looking at Paintings." Lecture. Redeemer College, Ontario, November 1984.

"The Meaning of Clothes and Games in the Christian Life." Lecture. Mennonite Brethren and the Christian Mennonite Bible Colleges, Manitoba, January 1984.

"An Ontological Framework for a Hermeneutics of Leadership." Department of Religion and the Doktorklub, McGill University, Montreal, March 1984.

*Opuscula Aesthetica Nostra: A Volume of Essays on Aesthetics and the Arts in Canada.* Co-editor with C. Cloutier Wojciechowska. Edmonton: Academic Printing and Publication, 1984.

"Patched-Together, or Integrated Christian Art, Kurelek and Krijger — a Contrast." Lecture. Regent College, Vancouver, October 1984.

"Reformation Perspective in Art." Lecture. St. Michael's College, University of Toronto, November 1984.

"Renaissance Humanist, Roman Catholic Christian, and Reformation Christian Paradigms in Painting and Sculpture." Trinity College, University of Toronto, November 1984.

"Say Amen, Somebody." *Calvinist Contact* 39 (no. 1937, 6 July 1984): 12; (no. 1938, 20 July 1984): 8; (no. 1939, 3 August 1984): 10; (no. 1940, 24 August 1984): 10-11.

"The Spirit and Contribution of Modern Art, with Marxist and Christian Alternatives." Department of Religion and the Doktorklub, McGill University, Montreal, March 1984.

"The Status of Aesthetic Theory in English-Speaking Canada." *Anakainosis* 7 (nos. 1-2, September/December 1984): 22-24.

"The Suicide of 'Art for Art's Sake Alone.'" Jubilee Conference, Coalition for Christian Outreach, Pittsburgh, February 1984.

"A Way to Go in the Problem of Defining 'Aesthetic.'" In *Die Ästhetik, das Tägliche Leben und die Künste,* 44-49. Edited selection of the VIIIth International Congress on Aesthetics, ed. Gerd Wolandt. Bonn: Bouvier Verlag Herbert Grundmann, 1984.

1985    "Art History and Problems of Method." Graduate Visual Arts Program, York University, Ontario, March 1985.

"Artists in Society: Toward an Understanding of Their Role." Department of Religion, Syracuse University, March 1985; Calvin College, Michigan, April 1985.

"Dooyeweerd's Legacy for Aesthetics: Modal Law Theory." In *The Legacy of Herman Dooyeweerd,* 41-79. New York: University Press of America, 1985.

"A Good Church Organist." *The Banner* 120 (no. 5, 11 February 1985): 10.

"Herder's Revolutionary Hermeneutic and Aesthetic Theory." Annual meeting of the Canadian Society for Eighteenth-Century Studies, Guelph, October 1985.

"Moorings." [Meditation on Ephesians 6:1-10.] *Perspective* 19 (no. 2, 1 April 1985): 5.

"No Prayer in the Grave." [Meditation on Psalm 6.] *The Banner* 120 (no. 6, 18 February 1985): 6.

"The Only Thing That Counts." [Meditation on Philippians 1:27-29.] *The Banner* 120 (no. 4, 4 February 1985): 6.

"A Rubric for Normative Art Critique." Lecture. Calvin College, April 1985.

"Set Free." [Meditation on Psalm 130.] *The Banner* 120 (no. 7, 25 February 1985): 5.

"Temptation, Education and Wisdom." Commencement Address. Dordt College, Iowa, May 1985.

"Turning Points in the History of Aesthetics." Conceived, refereed, and edited by Calvin Seerveld. Part III of *The Reasons of Art/L'Art a ses Raisons: Artworks and the Transformations of Philosophy,* general editor Peter McCormick, 185-284. Ottawa: University of Ottawa Press, 1985. From the Tenth International Congress on Aesthetics, Montreal, 1984.

"Wisdom and Rigged Scales." [Meditation on Proverbs 10:31–11:2]. *The Banner* 120 (no. 5, 11 February 1985): 5.

**1986**   "The ABC's of Christian Aesthetic Theory." Seminar. New York Cooperative Academy for Reformed Theology, Brooklyn, May 1986.

"Background and Examples of Black American Art." Staley Lecture. Trinity Christian College, Illinois, March 1986.

"Bernard Zylstra (1934-1986)." *Calvinist Contact* 41 (no. 2016, 21 March 1986): 12.

"Changing Images of the Crucifixion." Staley lecture. Sterling College, Kansas, February 1986.

"Christian Responsibility in the Arts." *FOCUS* 8 (no. 2, Fall 1986): 8-13. [Publication of Regent University, Virginia Beach.]

"A Comparative Critique of Kurelek and Krijger." Lecture, illustrated with slides. Ukrainian Cultural and Educational Centre, Winnipeg, June 1986.

"Diego Rivera's Art: Worth Respectful Attention." *Calvinist Contact* 41 (no. 2020, 18 April 1986): 8.

"The Difference Between Roman Catholic Christian and Reformed Christian Art." Lecture. Faculté Reformé in Aix-en-Provence, France, November 1986.

"How the Biblical Christian Faith Gives Wisdom for our Redemptive Engagement in the Arts." Series of seminars and lectures. Regent University, Virginia Beach, February 1986.

"How to Read the Bible." Staley lecture. Sterling College, Kansas, February 1986.

"The Meaning of our Nakedness." Staley lecture. Trinity Christian College, Illinois, March 1986.

"Method of Art Historiography." Lecture. Redeemer College, Ontario, April 1986.

"O Christ Our Lord, Dear Son of God." Lenten hymn text. Selected and sung at a festival of contemporary Canadian hymns, for the Annual Meeting of the Hymn Society of America, Toronto, July 1986.

"On Being Human." Third International Symposium of the Association for Calvinian Philosophy, Zeist, The Netherlands, August 1986.

"The Place of the Christian Artist in Society." Seminar. New York Cooperative Academy for Reformed Theology, Brooklyn, May 1986.

"Promise for Art Historiography." Annual meeting of the Canadian Society for Aesthetics/Société canadienne d'esthétique, University of Manitoba, Winnipeg, May 1986.

"The Promise of Joy in Hard Times." Bible Study and Art lectures. Christian Reformed World Relief and Mission Workers' Retreat, Sierra Leone, Africa, October 1986.

Psalm 121, Genevan Versification. In *A Psalm Sampler*. Philadelphia: The Westminster Press, 1986.

"Reading Literary Texts with Christian Antennae." Lecture. Calvin College, Michigan, May 1986.

"Scripturally Led Writing of History." Lecture. Redeemer College, Ontario, April 1986.

"What Good is Art for the Christian Life." Staley lecture. Sterling College, Kansas, February 1986.

Review of "Born of a Glorious Thunder." *Calvinist Contact* 42 (10 October 1986): 20.

1987    "Aftermath of the Enlightenment: Idealistic Philosophy in Checkmate." Seventh International Congress on the Enlightenment, Budapest, Hungary, July 1987.

"A Best Way to Read the Bible." Scripture Union headquarters. Sponsored by the Association for Christian Scholarship, Australia, June 1987.

A Biblical orientation for understanding the nature, meaning, and task of the arts today. Staley lectures. Colorado Christian University, Lakewood, February 1987.

"Both More and Less than a Matter of Taste." Annual meeting of the American Society for Aesthetics, Kansas City, Missouri, October 1987.

"A Cartographic Theory of Art Historiography Amid the Current Options." Graduate Department of Art History, Monash University, Melbourne, Australia, June 1987.

"Imaginativity." *Faith and Philosophy* 4 (no. 1, 1987): 43-58.

"The Import of Herder's Hermeneutics for Text Performance." Lecture. Herder Today: An Interdisciplinary International Conference, organized by Stanford University, California, November 1987.

Introduction for a performance of *The Greatest Song*. Truth and

Liberation Concern. Sponsored by the Association for Christian Scholarship, Australia, June 1987.

Lectures and discussions with 60 young professional artists. Sponsored by the Association for Christian Scholarship, Australia, June 1987.

Lectures for faculties and students of Christian schools in the Melbourne and Sydney areas. Sponsored by the Association for Christian Scholarship, Australia, June 1987.

"Long-Range Mercy for Africa." *Calvinist Contact* 42 (no. 2057, 6 February 1987): 13-14; (no. 2058, 13 February 1987): 13-14; (no. 2059, 20 February 1987): 11-12; (no. 2060, 27 February 1987): 11-12; (no. 2061, 6 March 1987): 11; (no. 2062, 13 March 1987): 11; (no. 2063, 20 March 1987): 11.

"The Nature of Christian Aesthetics: Interview with Jacques Fauquex." *Christianisme au XXe Siecle*, no. 100 (26 January 1987): 11.

"The Place of Art and Aesthetics in Our Lives." Interview and lecture. Taped and produced for Ronald Nichols' program "Insight" by the National Australian Broadcasting Corporation, July 1987.

"The Place of Philosophy and Cultural Theory in the Modern University." Lecture Series. For faculty in the General Studies and Language Departments, Satya Wacana University, Salatiga, Indonesia, July 1987.

*Psalter Hymnal.* Grand Rapids: Christian Reformed Publications, 1987. [Member of committee that worked for ten years to produce a complete, versified psalmody (in current English) and a hymnody representative of the church at large throughout the ages and at present. Seerveld's contributions include versifications of the psalms, new translations of ancient hymns, new hymn texts, and a couple of melodies.]

Discussion of *Rainbows for the Fallen World* and problems of art critique and art historiography. CARA (Professional Artists), Sydney. Sponsored by the Association for Christian Scholarship, Australia, June 1987.

"Reading Old Testament Wisdom Literature." Geelong Theological College. Sponsored by the Association for Christian Scholarship, Australia, June 1987.

"Real Faith Is Living the Resurrection." *Calvinist Contact* 42 (no. 2067, April 1987): 13.

"Temptation, Education, and Wisdom." *Pro Rege* 15 (no. 3, March 1987): 16-21.

"Theory and Praxis of Writing Art History." Lecture. Art History and Art Studio Departments, Chisholm Institute, Melbourne, Australia, June 1987.

"Trends in Modern Painting." Zadok Institute for Christianity and Society, Canberra. Sponsored by the Association for Christian Scholarship, Australia, June 1987.

"A Way to Go in Writing Art History, With Contributions from Bryson and Badt." Annual meeting of the Universities Art Association of Canada/Association d'art des universites du Canada, November 1987.

Review of *De Eerste en Tweede Geschiedenis: Nagelaten Geschriften van Meyer C. Smit,* edited by J. Klapwijk. *Calvinist Contact* 42 (no. 2068, 24 April 1987): 24.

Review of *The New Art History,* edited by A. L. Rees and Frances Borzello. *Journal of Aesthetics and Art Criticism* 45 (no. 3, Spring 1987): 30.

Review of *The New Art History,* edited by A. L. Rees and Frances Borzello. *Third Way* 10 (no. 5, May 1987): 30.

**1988**  "Aesthetic Theory Relevant for Artistry in the Modern World." Lecture. Arts Centre Group, London, England, July 1988.

"Aesthetics and Art as they Impinge on the Christian Life." Staley Lecture. Ontario Bible College, March 1988.

"Affairs of the Art." *Third Way* 11 (no. 1, January 1988): 16-17.

"After College: Visionary Scholarship, Leadership and Relevance." Convocation Address. The King's College, Edmonton, April 1988. [Printed by the Institute for Christian Studies, Toronto.]

"Art, Icons, and Imaginativity." Seminar. Redeemer College, Ontario, April 1988.

"Bearing Fresh Olive Leaves: Redemptive Artistry in the Modern World." Wheaton College, Illinois, March 1988.

"A Case for Christian Art." Review of *Art in Question,* edited by Tim Dean and David Porter. *Calvinist Contact* 43 (no. 2104, 5 February 1988): 23.

"Cultural Dynamics of Philosophical Aesthetics: Part I, the First 100 Years." Eleventh International Congress of Aesthetics, Nottingham, England, August-September 1988. [Presented in conjunction with Heinz Paetzold of Hamburg, who did Part II, the last 150 years.]

"An Integrative Perspective for Understanding, Interpreting, and

Teaching the Meaning of Artworks and Literary Texts." Institute for Christian College Teaching, Lincoln, Nebraska, June 1988.

"The Joys Are Simply Told." Lecture. Jubilee Conference, Coalition for Christian Outreach, Pittsburgh, February 1988.

"The Meaning of Clothes and Games in the Christian Life." Lecture. Logos, Yorkminster Park Baptist Church, February 1988.

"Methodological Notes for Assessing What Happened 1764-1831 in Philosophical Aesthetics." Combined annual meeting of the American Society for Aesthetics and Canadian Society for Aesthetics/Société canadienne d'esthétique, Vancouver, British Columbia, October 1988.

"Methods of Art History." Lecture. Redeemer College, Ontario, April 1988.

*On Being Human: Imaging God in the Modern World.* Burlington: Welch, 1988.

"The Poetry and Passion of the Psalms." Conference on Liturgy and Music, Calvin College, Michigan, July 1988. Sponsored by Christian Reformed Church Publications and Calvin College.

"Rainbows for the Fallen World." Conference on problems of style, play and games, clothes, and artists in society. College House, Cambridge University, England, July 1988.

**1989**  "Art Historical Imagination in the Period of Renaissance and Reformation Art." Seminar. Art Department, Redeemer College, Ontario, September 1989.

"Developing Taste in Children, Youth and Parents." Sectional workshop. Christian Educators Convention, Calgary, October 1989.

"The Failure of Neoclassical and Romantic Artistic Policies as Judgment on Enlightenment Aesthetics." Combined meeting of the Canadian Philosophical Association and Canadian Society for Aesthetics/Société canadienne d'esthétique, Quebec City, May 1989.

"Idealistic Philosophy in Checkmate: Neoclassical and Romantic Artistic Policy." *Studies in Voltaire and the Eighteenth Century* 263 (1989): 467-72.

"The Mind of Christ." Interview with Joel Nederhood. Faith 20 TV (USA)/Vision TV (Canada), May 1989.

"The Necessity of a Christian Philosophy for Integrating the Humanities." Jubilee Conference, Coalition for Christian Outreach, Pittsburgh, February 1989.

"Peace with Tears in the Christian School." Christian Educators Convention, Calgary, October 1989.

"Problems in Art History: Current Options and a Christian Look." With Graham Birtwistle [Free University, Amsterdam], John Walford [Wheaton College], and Charles Young [Calvin College.] Team-taught interim at the Institute for Christian Studies, Toronto, January 1989.

"Proverbs and the Song of Songs — Biblical Wisdom Literature." Ontario Theological Seminary, November 1989.

"Redemptive Art and the Problem of Propaganda." Jubilee Conference, Coalition for Christian Outreach, Pittsburgh, February, 1989.

"A Retrospective of Henk Krijger in North America." In *Hommage à Senggih: A Retrospective of Henk Krijger in North America*, edited by Jan de Bree. Toronto: Patmos Gallery, 1989. [Opening address on the occasion of an exhibition at the Redeemer College Art Gallery, Ontario, January 1989.]

"Teaching the Arts and Literature from a Christian Perspective." European Seminar of Adventist College and Secondary School Teachers and Leaders, 17-19 July 1989, Collonges-sous-Saleve, France.

"Using the Bible." Interview with Joel Nederhood. Faith 20 TV (USA)/Vision TV (Canada), May 1989.

Versifications of Psalm 103 (Genevan), 130 (Luther), 146 (Genevan), Bible song for Zechariah 8:2-8 (M. Apelles von Lowestern, 1644), hymn text, "When Eve with Adam Disobeyed" (Matthaus Greiter, 1552). In *Songs of Rejoicing: Hymns for Worship, Meditation and Praise*. New Brunswick, N.J.: Selah Publishing, 1989.

Review of essays on art and the Christian imagination. *Redeemer Reflections* 8 (no. 4, June 1989): 5. [Redeemer College, Ontario.]

**1990** "CBC Radio and the Canadian Nation." *Calvinist Contact* 45 (no. 2218, 22 June 1990): 12; (no. 2219, 29 June 1990): 12; (no. 2220, 6 July 1990): 13.

"Concluding Theses." In *Philosophy in the Reformed Undergraduate Curriculum*, edited by J. Roose and G. Pierson, 79-89. Palos Heights: Trinity Christian College, 1990.

"God's Tongue-Talking." *The Banner* 125 (no. 40, 12 November 1990): 12-13.

"Living Out the Faith in Poetry." *Calvinist Contact* 45 (no. 2206, 30 March 1990): 10.

"Mennonite Art: The Insider as Outsider." Calvinist Contact 46 (no. 2227, 14 September 1990): 11.

"The Nature of Aesthetics and Christian Interpretation of Painting and Poetry." Senior Interdisciplinary Seminar. Redeemer College, Ontario, March 1990.

"The Pain of the Cross Like a Psalm of Love: On Poetry of Paul Celan." *Calvinist Contact* 45 (no. 2207, 6 April 1990): 10.

"Satin Bedsheets in a Real World." *Globe and Mail* (Tuesday, 6 June 1990): A7.

Invited presenter as "arts specialist." Three year Planning Conference of CBC Radio Public Affairs Division, Toronto, May 1990.

1991    Critique of local poet contributions. British Columbia Arts Conference, November 1991.

"The Distinctive Nature of Christian Schooling." Lecture. Annual dinner of the Thunder Bay Christian School Society, Ontario, 15 February 1991.

"Footprints in the Snow." *Philosophia Reformata* 56 (no. 1, 1991): 1-34.

"The Halo of Human Imagination." Lecture. Oxford Conference '91, Keble College, Oxford, 30 June-12 July 1991. Sponsored by the C. S. Lewis Foundation. Also delivered at the London Institute for Contemporary Christianity, London, England, 23 July 1991; and at the British Columbia Arts Conference, Langley, November 1991.

"How to Deal with Art and Literature Redemptively, with Ideas for Developing 'Aesthetic Taste.'" Workshop. Thunderbay Christian School Teacher's Professional Development Day, Ontario, 15 February 1991.

"Imagination and the Fall into Sin: Icarus, Lot's Wife, Kitsch, Dachau, and Hiroshima." Lecture. Oxford Conference '91, Keble College, Oxford, 30 June–12 July 1991. Sponsored by the C. S. Lewis Foundation.

"Kitsch." Workshop. British Columbia Arts Conference, Langley, November 1991.

1992    "Aesthetic Taste." Lecture. Philosophy Department, University of Stellenbosch, South Africa, May 1992.

"Art Censorship." Public discussion leader. Greenbelt Festival '92, Northampton, England, August 1992.

"Art Historical Problems." Art History Department, University of Stellenbosch, South Africa, May 1992.

"Artistry as Vitamins in Human Life." Keynote address. ICS Family Conference, Alberta, July 1992.

"Cartographic Methodology for Art History." Lecture. Art History Department, Potchefstroom University for Christian Higher Education, South Africa, April 1992.

"A Christian Philosophical Method for Understanding Painting, Sculpture, Literature and Song." International Faith and Learning Seminar, Union College, Lincoln, Nebraska, June 1992.

"Coming to Know God in the Psalms." Lecture. All Angels' Episcopal Church Community Retreat, New York, September 1992.

"Creation Order and Artistic Disorder." Dordt College, Iowa, October 1992.

"The Difference the Christian Faith Makes in Studying the Arts and in Doing Sports." Staley Lecture. Northwestern College, Iowa, October 1992.

"Examining the Arts and Popular Culture from a Biblically Christian Perspective." Lecture series. Greenbelt Festival '92, Northampton, England, August 1992.

"Examining the Arts with Christian Antennae." Summer Course. Institute for Contemporary Christianity, London, England, August 1992.

"Imagination." Colloquium. Arts faculty and senior students, Redeemer College, Ontario, March 1992.

"Imagination." Lecture. Art History Department, Potchefstroom University for Christian Higher Education, South Africa, April 1992.

"Kitsch Kills People." ICS Family Conference, Alberta, July 1992.

"Kitsch Kills People, God's People Too." Lecture. Northwestern College, Iowa, October 1992.

"Lenten Emblems." *Calvinist Contact* 47 (no. 2284, 29 November 1992): 12.

"Modern and Postmodern Art's Critique of Traditional Art." Whitworth College, Spokane, Washington, March 1992.

"Mythologizing Philosophy: From Hesiod to George Steiner." Colloquium seminar. Philosophy faculty and staff, Free University, Amsterdam, November 1992.

"The Nature of Aesthetic Taste." Rand Afrikaans University, Johannesburg, April 1992.

"Necessary Art in Africa: A Christian Perspective." Plenary address. Pan-African Conference on Africa Beyond Liberation: Reconciliation, Reformation and Development, Potchefstroom, 27 April–1 May 1992. [Plus participation in the presentation of "A Christian Manifesto on the Arts," to combat gutting of theatre and art programs in the universities under current cutbacks.]

"Reform in Traditioning Aesthetics." Colloquium. With faculty of The University of the Orange Free State, Bloemfontein, May 1992.

"Vollenhoven's Legacy for Art Historiography." Vollenhoven Herdenking, Free University, Amsterdam, November 1992. Organized by the Historisch Documentatiecentrum voor het Nederlandse Protestantisme.

1993    "Approaching the Holy God." Response to Cornelius Plantinga at the Sixth Annual Calvin College Symposium on Worship and Church Music, Grand Rapids, January 1993. [Printed in *Christian Courier* 48 (no. 2344, 15 March 1993): 11-12.

"Mythologizing Philosophy as Historiographic Category." In *Myth and Interdisciplinary Studies*, 28-48. Edited by M. Clasquin et al. Pretoria: University of South Africa, 1993.

"Necessary Art in Africa: A Christian Perspective." In *Art in Africa*, 1-15. Study Pamphlet No. 312, December 1993. Potchefstroom: PU for CHE, 1993. [Text of address delivered at the Pan-African Conference on Africa Beyond Liberation, hosted by the Institute for Reformational Studies at the Potchefstroom University for Christian Higher Education (PU for CHE).]

"Vollenhoven's Legacy for Art Historiography." *Philosophia Reformata* 58, (no. 1, 1993): 49-79.

1994    "God's Compassionate Aesthetic Order as 'Wanton Chance.'" Presented as a seminar at the Twenty-fifth Anniversary Conference of the Institute for Christian Studies, June 1992; forthcoming.

"Insights and Problems with Dooyeweerd's Conception of (Historical) Unfolding Process and Differentiation." Workshop. Fifth International Symposium of the Association for Calvinist Philosophy, The Netherlands, August 1994.

"Which Antiquity is Transumed, How and Why: Art Historical Methods in Question." In *Antiquity and Antiquity Transumed: An Interdisciplinary Conference Exploring the Transference of Culture in the Visual Arts of the Renaissance*. Graduate Department of History of Art and the Centre for Reformation and Renaissance Studies, University of Toronto, March 1994.

# Biographies of Contributors

For **Barbara Douglas,** a B.A. in music performance (trumpet) and education (University of Iowa) and an interest in philosophy could only lead to study in aesthetics with Calvin Seerveld. She wrote her M.Phil.F. thesis at the Institute for Christian Studies on the work of musicologist and aesthetician Carl Dahlhaus. She presently lives in Westminster College, Cambridge, England, where her husband Nigel is studying for the ministry, and looks after their two small children. She hopes to continue her studies in musicology and musical aesthetics. In the meantime, she directs chapel music rehearsals each week, works for the college library (which includes the notable Elias library of hymnology), and speaks occasionally on music in worship.

**Peter Enneson,** B.A. (philosophy/math; art history/chemistry, Trinity Christian College, Palos Heights, Illinois), M.Phil. (Aesthetics, Institute for Christian Studies, Toronto), co-operates a design studio in Toronto with James Ireland and is art director for *Rotunda* (the magazine of the Royal Ontario Museum). He has taught magazine design and production at Ryerson Polytechnical University, has art-directed the *Globe and Mail's Report on Business Magazine,* and was Design Director at King West Communications 1987-89. Enneson recently designed the first edition of John Terpstra's award-winning poem *Captain Kintail* (Netherlandic Press, 1992). He has pursued a biographical interest in Henk Krijger and his work since 1978.

**Carroll Guen Hart** began studying with Calvin Seerveld at the Institute for Christian Studies in 1980, receiving her M.Phil. in 1983. Since completing her

350

Ph.D. at the Free University of Amsterdam with a dissertation on Richard Rorty and John Dewey, titled *Grounding without Foundations,* she has been teaching a course in Women's Studies at the Institute for Christian Studies. Previous publications include "Gadamer, Objectivity, and the Ontology of Belonging" in *Dialogue* (1989) and "'Power in the Service of Love': John Dewey's *Logic* and the Dream of a Common Language" in *Hypatia* (1993). Work in progress includes an essay on ecology and ethics in Dewey and Kosuke Koyama.

**Donald L. Knudsen** has been working in ministry to the poor and needy in the city of Philadelphia for the past several years. Since entering a project sponsored by Westminster Theological Seminary in 1989, he has assisted in fund-raising, food distribution (especially at Thanksgiving time), counselling, editing of texts, and communications management. As a doctorandus candidate at the Free University of Amsterdam, he pursues his studies as time permits. Fruitful research with Calvin Seerveld resulted in an M.Phil.F. in philosophical aesthetics from the Institute for Christian Studies in 1987.

**Gudrun Kuschke** studied under the direction of Calvin Seerveld at the Institute for Christian Studies in 1978, with the aid of a research grant from the University of Potchefstroom. She completed her Ph.D. at the University of the Witwatersrand with a dissertation on Christian poetry during the Third Reich. She taught German literature at the University of Potchefstroom until the department was rationalized in 1994. At present she is teaching courses in literary studies at the University of Natal in Durban, South Africa.

Professionally speaking, **James Frederick Leach,** who is also a husband, father of two, playwright, and fiction writer, is perhaps less an aesthetic philosopher than a philosophical aesthete. Leach defended his master's thesis on the *Lehrstücke* of Bertolt Brecht and Heiner Müller under Seerveld's able tutelage, and he is currently working on a doctorate with the same wise guidance. If listed on a continuum from the academic to the recreational, Jim's interests include: German theater, German theorists, interactive performances, cyberspace happenings, easy-to-use computers, and difficult music.

**Henry Luttikhuizen,** Assistant Professor of Art History at Calvin College, studied under the direction of Calvin Seerveld at the Institute for Christian Studies from 1986-89. After receiving his master's degree from the Institute in the field of philosophical aesthetics, Luttikhuizen pursued an M.A. in art history at the University of Virginia. He is currently completing a doctorate at Virginia, writing his dissertation on the relationship between late medieval piety and an early Netherlandish painting, Geertgen tot Sint Jans's altarpiece for the Haarlem Jansheren. Luttikhuizen has also curated exhibitions at the Grand Rapids Art Museum and the Muskegon Museum of Art.

**Mary Leigh Morbey,** Associate Professor of Art at Redeemer College in Ancaster, Ontario, appreciates the years of support and the good influence of her friend Calvin Seerveld, to whom she was introduced by her professor at the Free University of Amsterdam, Hans Rookmaaker. Morbey's research focuses on electronic technologies, the visual arts, and gender. She received her Ph.D. from The Ohio State University, working with its Advanced Computing Center for the Arts and Design. Her articles on computer-based visual arts have appeared in various journals, including *Revue d'art canadienne/Canadian Art Review* and *Arts and Learning Research.*

**Bert Polman** received his B.A. from Dordt College, Sioux Center, Iowa, and his M.A. and Ph.D. in Musicology from the University of Minnesota, Minneapolis. He studied with Calvin Seerveld at the Institute for Christian Studies in 1972-73 and served together with Seerveld on the *Psalter Hymnal* Revision Committee of the Christian Reformed Church, 1977-87. Polman has taught music at Ontario Bible College, Toronto, 1975-85, and since then at Redeemer College in Ancaster, Ontario. He is a primary author of the *Psalter Hymnal Companion,* an editor of three other hymnals, a regular contributor to journals such as *Reformed Worship* and *The Hymn,* and has served on the Executive Committee of the Hymn Society in the United States and Canada. His interdisciplinary interests encompass popular culture, gender studies, and North American native studies.

**Perry Recker,** while a high school student, heard Calvin Seerveld speak several times. He can't recall what Seerveld said, but he remembers being impressed and moved. As a student at Trinity Christian College, 1966-71, Recker enjoyed Seerveld's chapel talks and his lectures in aesthetics and ethics, and he began collecting Seerveldana in print. After receiving an M.Phil. degree from the Institute for Christian Studies in 1977, Perry worked for Christian Educational Services with Peter Steen in western Pennsylvania and continued to collect and record Reformational literature. He is currently the Special Collections Assistant in charge of the Elizabeth Nesbitt Room at the University of Pittsburgh, where he received his M.L.S. degree in 1986.

**William D. Romanowski** received B.A. and M.A. degrees in English and a Ph.D. in American Culture Studies from Bowling Green State University. As Associate

Professor of Communication Arts and Sciences at Calvin College, he teaches courses in film, communication, and culture studies and lectures widely on various aspects of American culture. Romanowski has co-authored *Dancing in the Dark: Youth, Popular Culture and the Electronic Media* (Eerdmans, 1991) and *Risky Business: Rock in Film* (Transaction, 1991), has written numerous book chapters, journal essays, and popular articles, and has worked as a musical and dramatic performer. Having met Calvin Seerveld as an undergraduate, Romanowski became Seerveld's "informal" student. Since then, the two have conducted seminars together, conversed in hotel rooms and subway trains, and visited one another at home. Cal says Bill is like "good tonic."

**Johan Snyman** is a graduate of Potchefstroom University for Christian Higher Education and Rand Afrikaans University. After learning Dooyeweerd's philosophy and co-editing a popular journal of cultural critique (emulating Seerveld's style, to the chagrin of Afrikaner stalwarts), he decided to learn the "real stuff" in Frankfurt am Main, Germany. He and Lambert Zuidervaart embarked on their study of Adorno's aesthetics in Germany at the same time, with Lambert clearing all the hurdles in 1981 and Johan profiteering from this to achieve *Doktor-Wuerde* in 1986. Johan is chairperson of the Department of Philosophy at the Rand Afrikaans University in Johannesburg, South Africa, where he teaches social philosophy and aesthetics. He is editor and co-author of *Conceptions of Social Inquiry* (Human Sciences Research Council, 1993) and review editor of the *South African Journal of Philosophy*. Currently he is writing a book on cultural manifestations of the Holocaust and of apartheid.

**Raymond C. Van Leeuwen** learned a great deal about Seerveldian aesthetics while playing racquetball with Cal during graduate school at the University of St. Michaels College, Toronto (Ph.D. 1984). Thereafter, Ray taught Old Testament for thirteen years at Calvin College and Calvin Theological Seminary before becoming Professor of Bible at Eastern College in St. Davids, Pennsylvania and the first Carl Morgan Visiting Professor at Eastern Baptist Seminary. The author of *Context and Meaning in Proverbs 25–27* (Scholars Press, 1988), he is currently writing *Proverbs* for the *New Interpreter's Bible*.

**Merold Westphal** is Professor of Philosophy at Fordham University. A quondam church choir director, his artistic interests focus on classical music, theater, and painting. He is the author of *History and Truth in Hegel's Phenomenology; God, Guilt, and Death: An Existential Phenomenology of Religion; Kierkegaard's Critique of Reason and Society; Hegel, Freedom, and Modernity;* and *Suspicion and Faith: The Religious Uses of Modern Atheism*. He has recently been devoting considerable attention to the theological implications of the critique(s) of metaphysics developed by Heidegger, Levinas, Derrida, and Marion.

**Fran Wong,** Seerveld's first student in film theory at ICS, received her M.Phil.F. degree in 1992 with a thesis on George Lucas's *Star Wars* trilogy. Recently Cineaction magazine published her article on Satyajit Ray's *Managar*. As facilitator for a film group in the Academy for Lifelong Learning at the University of Toronto, Wong enjoys and discusses many contemporary films. She believes Christians need to respond insightfully to film, a powerful artistic medium, and she plans to write about film indefinitely. Fran currently earns her living teaching piano and shares her home with a son, a daughter, and a dog.

**Lambert Zuidervaart** is Professor of Philosophy and Chairperson of the Philosophy Department at Calvin College. He also serves as the President of the Board of Directors for the Urban Institute for Contemporary Arts in Grand Rapids, Michigan. The first student to complete graduate degree programs under Calvin Seerveld's direction, Zuidervaart received an M.Phil. from the Institute for Christian Studies in 1975 and a Ph.D. from the Free University of Amsterdam in 1981. He is the author of *Adorno's Aesthetic Theory: The Redemption of Illusion* (MIT Press, 1991) and a co-author of *Dancing in the Dark: Youth, Popular Culture and the Electronic Media* (Eerdmans, 1991). He is currently completing a book on *Cultural Politics and Artistic Truth* and co-editing a collection of new essays on Adorno's aesthetics.